WHAT'S THE GOOD OF COUNSELLING & PSYCHOTHERAPY?

WHAT'S THE GOOD OF COUNSELLING & PSYCHOTHERAPY?
THE BENEFITS EXPLAINED

EDITED BY COLIN FELTHAM

SAGE Publications
London • Thousand Oaks • New Delhi

First published 2002

SAGE Publications Ltd
6 Bonhill Street
London EC2A 4PU

SAGE Publications Inc
2455 Teller Road
Thousand Oaks, California 91320

SAGE Publications India Pvt Ltd
32, M-Block Market
Greater Kailash - I
New Delhi 110 048

British Library Cataloguing in Publication data

A catalogue record for this book
is available from the British Library

ISBN 0 7619 6954 3
ISBN 0 7619 6955 1 (pbk)

Library of Congress control number: 2002102785

Typeset by C&M Digitals (P) Ltd., Chennai, India
Printed and bound in Great Britain by Athenaeum Press, Gateshead

CONTENTS

NOTES ON CONTRIBUTORS

Janis Abernathy works as a psychologist/therapist at the Royal Edinburgh Hospital and teaches in the Department of Psychological Medicine at the University of Edinburgh. She is also currently working towards a PhD in the Department of Psychiatry, exploring stress, emotional expression and health.

Juliana Brown is, together with Richard Mowbray, a co-director of the Primal Integration Programme in London and member of the Open Centre, one of the UK's longest established growth centres. She has been practising Primal Integration, a form of deep personal growth work, since 1979.

Eva Burns-Lundgren is a Cognitive Analytic (CAT) Psychotherapist at Warneford Hospital, Oxford. Previously, she worked at Kingston University. She has been a CAT supervisor/tutor at Guy's and St Thomas Hospitals, London. She qualified in Social Work in Sweden in 1974. She has extensive experience in psychiatric social work in the UK, including work in therapeutic communities. She has trained in family and individual therapy and is accredited by the UKCP as well as in Sweden.

Cary L Cooper is BUPA Professor of Organizational Psychology and Health in the Manchester School of Management Institute of Science and Technology (UMIST). Among his many roles and achievements, he has authored over 80 books, founded and edits several journals and has several fellowships of professional bodies. He is President of the British Academy of Management and is Editor, with Professor Chris Argyris of Harvard Business School, of the Blackwell Encyclopedia of Management (12 volume set). In 2001 Cary was awarded a CBE in the Queen's Birthday Honours List for his contribution to health.

Helen Cowie is Research Professor of Psychology and Counselling at Roehampton University of Surrey. She has published widely in the field of children's relationships, child development and counselling psychology, and is the co-author (with Patti Wallace) of *Peer Support in Action* (Sage, 2000) and (with Peter K Smith and Mark Blades) of *Understanding Children's Development* (Blackwell's, 4th edn., 2002). She is currently researching the promotion of emotional health and well-being among children and adolescents.

Graham Curtis Jenkins was a general practitioner paediatrician for 28 years. He trained as a psychotherapist and in 1991 was appointed the first Director of the Counselling in Primary Care Trust. He has written about child health, counselling and psychotherapy research and practice. He is a past president of the Section of General Practice of the Royal Society of Medicine, London.

Peter Dale is the author of *Adults Abused as Children: Experiences of Counselling and Psychotherapy* (Sage, 1999). Working for the NSPCC, he established the counselling service for adults abused as children described in his chapter. He maintains a counselling, supervisory and child protection consultancy practice in Hastings, East Sussex.

Judith Dawkins is a consultant child and adolescent psychiatrist based in an independent practice in Surrey. Prior to this she was a Senior Lecturer in Child and Adolescent Psychiatry at St Georges Hospital Medical School where she developed a research and clinical interest in bullying in schools. Since then she has continued her interest in children experiencing difficulties in school and has recently contributed to a report from the DfES on emotional health and well being.

Colin Feltham is Reader in Counselling at Sheffield Hallam University and Course Leader for the MA Counselling & Psychotherapy and Postgraduate Certificate in Counselling Supervision. He is Co-Editor of the *British Journal of Guidance and Counselling*. He edits three book series for Sage Publications. His most recent publications include *Controversies in Psychotherapy and Counselling* (Sage, 1999) and (with Ian Horton) the *Handbook of Counselling and Psychotherapy* (Sage, 2000).

Lisa Firestone, PhD, is Program and Education Director of the Glendon Association, and adjunct faculty at the University of California, Santa Barbara Graduate School of Education. She received her PhD in Clinical Psychology from California School of Professional Psychology, Los Angeles. She has conducted nationwide research with over 1300 subjects, in the assessment of suicidal risk, which resulted in the development of The Firestone Assessment of Self-destructive Thoughts (FAST) (Psychological Corporation, 1996). Dr Firestone's other publications include: 'Voices in Suicide: The Relationship Between Self-destructive Thoughts and Self-destructive Lifestyles' (*Death Studies*, 1998); co-author with Joyce Catlett of 'The Treatment of Sylvia Plath'; *The Good Life: Sustaining Feeling, Passion and Meaning in a High-Tech Age* (APA, in press); and *Conquer Your Critical Inner Voice: A Revolutionary Program to Counter Negative Thoughts and Live Free from Imagined Limitations* (New Harbinger Publications, 2002).

Robert W Firestone, PhD, is a consultant and the principal theoretician for the Glendon Association. He summarized his conceptualizations about schizophrenia in a theoretical dissertation entitled *A Concept of the Schizophrenic Process*, and expanded these ideas into a systematic theory of neurosis that addresses the psychodynamics in couple and family relationships, child abuse, suicide, and self-destructive behavior. Dr Firestone's major works include: *The Fantasy Bond* (Glendon Association, 1985); *Combating Destructive Thought*

Processes (Sage, 1997); *Fear of Intimacy* (APA, 1999) (with Joyce Catlett), and most recently, *The Good Life: Sustaining Feeling, Passion, and Meaning in a High-Tech Age* (APA, in press). His studies of negative thought processes led to the development of an innovative therapeutic methodology, which was described in *Suicide and the Inner Voice: Risk Assessment, Treatment, and Case Management* (Sage, 1997). In collaboration with Dr Lisa Firestone, he developed the Firestone Assessment of Self-destructive Thoughts (FAST) (Psychological Corporation, 1996), a scale that assesses suicide potential.

Helena Hargaden is a registered Integrative Psychotherapist and a Teaching and Supervising Transactional Analyst. She lives and works in South London where she has a private psychotherapy and supervision practice, and teaches on the MSc programme in transactional analysis at the Metanoia Institute in West London. She is the co-author of a new book, *TA – A Relational Perspective* (Routledge, 2002) and has a keen interest in politics and psychotherapy.

Douglas Hooper is a Consultant Clinical and Counselling Psychologist and a Fellow of the British Psychological Society. Past President of the British Association for Counselling and Psychotherapy, he has taught, practised and researched in psychological treatment methods over many years, with a particular interest in disturbed relationships. He edited (with Windy Dryden) *Couple Therapy: A Handbook* (Open University, 1991). He is also Emeritus Professor, University of Hull.

Carolyn Marchington-Yeoman is an independent consultant in the area of work stress, workplace counselling and audit and evaluation services. She was previously a Research Fellow at the Manchester School of Management, UMIST, where she conducted the first nationwide independent assessment and evaluation of British workplace counselling programmes for the Health and Safety Executive.

Richard Mowbray is, together with Juliana Brown, a co-director of the Primal Integration Programme in London and member of the Open Centre, one of the UK's longest established growth centres. He has been practising Primal Integration, a form of deep personal growth work, since 1979.

Shahid Najeeb is a psychiatrist and a training psychoanalyst of the Australian Psychoanalytical Society. He works full time in private psychotherapy and psychoanalytical clinical practice in Sydney, and has an interest in the applied aspects of psychoanalysis, especially the inter-relationship of psychoanalysis with Buddhism.

Ian Palmer has worked in both the army and the NHS for over 20 years. Prior to studying psychiatry he was a GP. His interests are in helping individuals to adjust and change to new realities following difficult events; communication between doctor and patient; the neglected lessons of history and psychotherapy in general. During 1992-3 he was the first military psychiatrist in the Balkans and travelled extensively, examining both UN troops' situations and those of local ex-combatants as well as the humanitarian work undertaken by the UN. In 1994 he was the UN psychiatrist in Rwanda, carrying out much the same work but also delivering over a dozen babies – including his first set of twins! He was made Professor of Military Psychiatry in 1999.

Mick Power is Professor of Clinical Psychology at the University of Edinburgh and a practising clinical psychologist at the Royal Edinburgh Hospital. He has published widely in the areas of emotion, depression, therapy and quality of life and is one of the founding editors of the journal *Clinical Psychology and Psychotherapy*.

Hilde Rapp is an independent psychotherapist, supervisor, lecturer and researcher. Among her many roles are: Mental Health National Service Framework implementation adviser in the UK; Chair of the British Initiative for Integrative Practice (BIIP); Chair of the Qualifications and Curriculum Authority (QCA) approved Counselling & Psychotherapy Central Awarding Body (CPCAB); Chair of the Training Standards Committee of the Universities Psychotherapy and Counselling Association (UPCA).

Stephen M Saunders obtained his doctorate in Clinical Psychology at Northwestern University, where he studied with Dr Ken Howard. He is currently Associate Professor in the Department of Psychology at Marquette University. He is the Director of Clinical Training at the Clinical Psychology Program and is the Director of the Center for Psychological Services. He has published extensively on help-seeking behaviour, the therapeutic alliance and the effectiveness of psychotherapy.

Digby Tantam is Clinical Professor of Psychotherapy at the University of Sheffield (1995–present) and was previously Professor of Psychotherapy at the University of Warwick (1990–95). He is a practising psychotherapist, psychiatrist and psychologist. Digby is co-Director of the Centre for the Study of Conflict and Reconciliation in the University of Sheffield, and a partner in Dilemma Consultancy in Human Relations (www.dilemmas.org). Digby has been Registrar of the European Association of Psychotherapy (1999–2001) and Chair of the United Kingdom Council for Psychotherapy (1995–98). His book, *Psychotherapy and Counselling in Practice: A Narrative Approach* was published by Cambridge University Press in 2002.

Keith Tudor is registered with the UKCP both as a Humanistic and a Group Psychotherapist and Facilitator. In addition to his small private practice, he is a Director of Temenos in Sheffield and works as a trainer and consultant. He is a widely published author, most recently, with Tony Merry, of the *Dictionary of Person-Centred Psychology* (Whurr, 2002) and is the editor of a series of books on *Advancing Theory in Therapy* (published by Brunner-Routledge). With a background in community politics, he is interested in the contribution that therapy, in its practice and theory, can make to the social and political world.

THE BENEFITS OF COUNSELLING AND PSYCHOTHERAPY: AN INTRODUCTION

Colin Feltham

The aim of this book is to present a responsibly positive case for psychotherapy and counselling as beneficial. Obviously, this field is regarded positively by its practitioners but, arguably, its benefits have not been as clearly promoted to a wider audience as they might or should have been. As a practitioner who is also a critic of the field, I am acutely aware of such tensions. On the one hand, like all practitioners, I sincerely believe I have seen beneficial changes – however modest – occurring before my very eyes in clients' altered feelings, thoughts and behaviour. I am in constant contact with other practitioners and I admire their dedication and genuineness in their work – especially in a profession where jobs are scarce, pay is moderate and media criticisms are plentiful – in a world that seems to stockpile pain, hatred and stupidity and to be moving in frighteningly inhuman directions. On the other hand, I also see the internecine wars between therapists and therapeutic professions and I cannot help but be bemused by and critical of these phenomena (Dryden and Feltham, 1992; Feltham, 1999a, 1999b).

While remaining discriminatingly critical of certain *aspects* of this field, I think it has arrived at a point where its proponents must begin to clarify and integrate the values, aims and scope of the field. The critics are not going to disappear and therapists will not help their cause by attempting to ignore them. The problems of proliferation in the field – dozens of competing models and several competing professions – and the tensions between the concepts of vocational artistry and aspirations towards professionalisation – do little to advance public understanding of or confidence in psychotherapy and counselling. In traditional theology, it has long been recognised that the different functions of internal explication (dogmatics) and external explication (apologetics) are both crucial. Arguably, debates internal to the field of counselling and psychotherapy have received detrimentally disproportionate attention. If counselling and psychotherapy are to survive, develop and thrive, considerably more attention must be given to articulate, transparent descriptions of psychological therapy and to an even-handed defence of its benefits and scope.

Of what would such a defence consist? Probably, in simplified form, questions such as:

- What questions and problems do psychotherapy and counselling claim to address?
- What are the components of effective therapy and how do we know?
- How do we go about evaluating whether therapists' claims have reliable evidence to support them?
- Which endeavours compete with therapy (e.g. religion, philosophy, medicine, education) and how can comparative effectiveness be assessed?
- Who are the 'stakeholders' and how can we address their respective voices and needs equitably?
- What problems exist in the conceptualisation and delivery of therapy?
- What exactly are the complaints of the critics and how are they to be addressed?
- Do therapists have something distinctive and useful to say about the kind of society that produces the levels of distress they have witnessed?

We are still not clear about the scope of counselling and psychotherapy, there being some tendency – in common with other disciplines – to want to expand so as to colonise all problems in living. More work needs to be undertaken to clarify what can and cannot be realistically addressed by psychological therapists. A great deal of work has already been done to identify effective components and to provide evidence of therapeutic gains. While this is not universally accepted as methodologically precise, the evidence base for therapy is growing and deserves greater acknowledgement as well as wider dissemination in accessible form. Very little has been done to compare the work and effects of therapy with endeavours in other fields and disciplines. Does therapy provide more (and more effective) succour and help than religion, for example? In the context of finite resources, are some people better served by educational opportunities or improved housing or health care than by psychological therapy? Should we not look at the different relevant issues of stakeholders – the competing clinical professions, professional bodies, training institutions, funders, researchers, consumers/users – in order to improve communication, rationalise services and understand conflicts?

Paradoxically, it is the critics of therapy who must be thanked for pinpointing its weaknesses and preventing complacency. It is no mere artful manoeuvre to say this. Much of the spur for improved empirical research, clearer conceptualisation, less proliferation of conflicting schools and more concern for consumers' and complainants' voices can be traced back to the critics of counselling and psychotherapy. However, an apologetics of psychological therapy also needs to address the misunderstandings and unhelpfully motivated aspects of critics' attacks. A brief summary of kinds of critique can be found in Feltham (1999b). Critics themselves may be well informed about, involved in and responsive to consumers' views about the field (Pilgrim, 1997) but nevertheless dissatisfied; or be highly critical of the field yet still prepared to concede that therapy is better than nothing (Erwin, 1997).

One front on which the public relations representatives of the professional bodies in this field seem to have to continue to fight is against overly negative journalists. It has been suggested that the profession of journalism may be as dogged by stress, cynicism and assorted unsuccessful self-remedies such as alcohol abuse (Phillip Hodson, personal communication, 2000) as the profession of psychotherapy and counselling has been by the Pollyannaish 'navel-gazing' and evidence-indifferent tendencies of some of its practitioners. Perhaps more moderation on both sides of this war is called for. Alternatively, it is an option for therapists to go on the offensive and analyse the motives of journalists, in particular, who are engaged in what Hodson calls an 'anti-counselling rage', a rage that may mask a need for and fearful denial of help and of emotional reality generally.

The purpose of this book is to offer something of an apologetics for therapy, or a case for its benefits, that is sober, evenly considered and reasonably accessible. A number of representative topics have been chosen rather than attempting to produce an exhaustive coverage of the many areas in which therapy is applied. An attempt has been made to ensure that some of the wide range of therapeutic schools, professions and settings has been represented. This book is structured in the following way. Chapter 1 sets the scene by outlining the scope of mental health problems or mental distress in order to demonstrate (a) that there are indeed huge problems to be appropriately addressed by some form of psychological therapy, (b) that there is some manageable shape to this problem, however huge it may be and (c) that there is an evidence base for having confidence in the ability of psychological therapy to help relieve these problems. Continuing in Part One, Chapter 2 looks at some of the ways in which psychotherapeutic thinking and practice is improving the daily experiences of children and adolescents. Chapter 3 examines evidence of the helpfulness of therapy in cases where adults' functioning is compromised by experiences of childhood sexual abuse. The case for the significance of therapy for helping to reduce the incidence of suicide and suicidal behaviours is made in Chapter 4. The well-publicised problem of relationship breakdown is the focus of Chapter 5, which also shows the part played by therapy in understanding this phenomenon and its amelioration. Finally, Chapter 6 tackles the vexed question of how effective therapy can be with people diagnosed with borderline personality disorders. Linking all these subject areas is the reality of individual human suffering and its damaging social effects. These chapters should go some way towards answering critics who claim that therapy is merely a self-indulgence for the worried well.

In Part Two an attempt is made to demonstrate some of the ways in which the psychological therapies have important applications beyond the short-term, individual, introspective and remedial. Consumers' own voices in Chapter 7 tell some of the story of the significant gains in functioning reported by those receiving therapy. In Chapter 8 an argument is made for respect to be accorded to people who reach critical choice/growth points in their lives and where deep personal growth work might be much better understood, valued and supported. The interplay between therapy and certain forms of spirituality, and the problems inherent in distorted or immature concepts of spirituality, are examined in Chapter 9. Topical attention is paid in Chapter 10 to connections being made between the private work of therapists and the public, political world that we all live in as citizens. Finally, in Chapter 11, the topic of emotional intelligence and its current and potential applications is expounded.

Part Three looks at two of the settings where therapy is growing most rapidly in the UK and at one relatively under-publicised application, in military settings. Chapter 12 examines the expansion of counselling in primary health care in the UK and some of the problems and politics associated with evaluating its effectiveness. Chapter 13 focuses on the setting of the workplace and the counselling services provided there, again with an examination of problems of evaluation and causes for being pleased with beneficial results. The contribution of certain psychotherapeutic principles and practices to traumatised army personnel is the subject of Chapter 14, which is included expressly to help demonstrate at least one 'tough' application of therapy in a domain in which its critics might not expect to see it entertained. Chapter 15 examines some of the growing body of evidence for the clinical effectiveness of psychotherapy; contrary to the powerful arguments put forward by Hans Eysenck from the 1950s, there is now a vast research literature demonstrating the positive benefits of psychological therapy. Finally, Chapter 16 puts forward philosophical arguments concerning the concept of benefit, particularly as it applies to the field of counselling and psychotherapy.

I would like to emphasise the intention behind this book to present a sober argument, or set of arguments, for the benefits of therapy, including mild to moderate benefits and also little realised benefits, *but without dismissing critics' concerns*. My own belief is that no uncritical account of therapeutic benefits is credible; counselling and psychotherapy are probably not 'the best thing since sliced bread', a panacea, an unmixed blessing or the meaning of life and we do ourselves a disservice when we fall into such hyperbolic traps.

To some extent the material here may be seen as combining a new triumph of the therapeutic (Rieff, 1966) with the gradual construction of an apologetics of the field and its philosophical underpinnings (Holmes and Lindley, 1989; Levin, 1989; Roth and Fonagy, 1996; Smith et al., 1980). Celebration of the marks of progress of the psychological therapies is now quite in order, yet we still have some way to go before we are able to witness the kinds of visible marks of substantial progress evident in medicine, for example (Porter, 1997). For all that, we may modestly claim that counselling and psychotherapy are, at the very least, certainly rather better than 'better than nothing'. In a world currently in grave danger of elevating the values of competitiveness and profit far above human welfare, a powerful moral case exists for bringing together human psychological welfare needs with the expanding group of skilled, ethically sensitive people ready to listen and respond in the most deeply human and needed way: the counsellors and psychotherapists.

References

Dryden, W. and Feltham, C. (eds) (1992) *Psychotherapy and its Discontents*. Buckingham: Open University Press.

Erwin, E. (1997) *Philosophy and Psychotherapy*. London: Sage.

Feltham, C. (ed.) (1999a) *Controversies in Psychotherapy and Counselling*. London: Sage.

Feltham, C. (1999b) Facing, understanding and learning from critiques of psychotherapy and counselling. *British Journal of Guidance and Counselling,* 27 (3), 301–11.

Holmes, J. and Lindley, R. (1989) *The Values of Psychotherapy.* Oxford: Oxford University Press.

Levin, D. (1989) *The Listening Self: Personal Growth, Social Change and the Closure of Metaphysics.* London: Routledge.

Pilgrim, D. (1997) *Psychotherapy and Society.* London: Sage.

Porter, R. (1997) *The Greatest Benefit to Mankind: A Medical History of Humanity From Antiquity to the Present.* London: Harper Collins.

Rieff, P. (1966) *The Triumph of the Therapeutic: Use of Faith After Freud.* Harmondsworth: Penguin.

Roth, A. and Fonagy, P. (1996) *What Works For Whom? A Critical Review of Psychotherapy Research.* New York: Guilford Press.

Smith, D.L., Glass, G.V. and Miller, T.I. (1980) *The Benefits of Psychotherapy.* Baltimore, MD: Johns Hopkins University Press.

PART ONE

ADDRESSING HUMAN SUFFERING

1
THE EPIDEMIOLOGY OF MENTAL DISTRESS
Janis Abernathy & Mick Power

The field of psychiatric epidemiology[1] has undergone dramatic developments over the past six decades, particularly during the 1990s. The present chapter describes some of the milestones in this developmental history, including the evolution of increasingly sophisticated interview schedules used to assess prevalence and correlates of psychiatric morbidity[2] in worldwide populations. Some of the key findings from recent studies utilising these new measures are given, whilst a survey focused primarily on neurotic disorders in Great Britain is described in some greater detail, to illustrate the breadth of information that is now possible to be derived through comprehensive epidemiologic studies. In addition, recent conceptual advances in the field have served to pivot our attention beyond the assessment of prevalence of psychiatric morbidity, and to explore the integration of effects of given disorders, or 'burden' of psychiatric disorders, upon studied populations. Finally, we look at worldwide rates of treatment for disorders, and at some of the implications arising for further research. We would like to point out that the chapter does not, in any way, address the suitability of various mental health professionals to treat specific categories of mental distress or disorder. Nor do we imply that 'talking therapies' are *only* recommended for those conditions or needs mentioned within the context of the present chapter.

The international context

Prior to the Second World War, very few studies were conducted to identify prevalence of mental disorders in specific populations, and these relied upon what are now regarded as unreliable methodologies, such as key informants or hospital records (see Weissman et al., 1986, for a review). With the advent of the Second World War, it became practicable to identify recruits to the US military who were likely to break down under the stress of combat, and considerable resources were mobilised to develop short screening scales which would identify those at risk. However, amongst other criticisms, these early studies focused only on impairment or symptoms of disorder, and researchers lacked a standardised framework for description of psychopathology or clinical diagnoses.

Over the years, critics of the low level of reliability in psychiatric epidemiological interviews pointed to several considerations for further research (Spitzer and Fleiss; 1974; Spitzer et al., 1975). These included the need to recognise that patients have different conditions at different times, or that the patient may be in different stages of the same condition at different times; that clinicians often have access to different sources of information or differ in what they might observe; and that the criteria used to formulate data into different diagnoses often differ. Costs incurred by psychiatric interviews conducted by professionals were also a formidable concern. In following years, there were increased and sustained efforts to develop interview and research methodology which would address these criticisms and identify prevalence and correlates of mental disorders in populations with a greater degree of reliability.

The National Institute of Mental Health (NIMH) Diagnostic Interview Schedule (DIS) was developed specifically to overcome some of the criticisms and inadequacies of earlier epidemiological studies (Robins et al., 1981). The DIS was designed as a highly structured research diagnostic interview so that it could be administered either by lay interviewers or clinicians, with questions and probes specifically laid out, avoiding evaluation bias. Assessment using the DIS was based solely on interviews with respondents, without input from hospital records or key informants. The interview schedule distinguished everyday worries, symptoms of physical illness and side effects of medication, alcohol and non-prescribed drugs from standardised psychiatric diagnoses, which were primarily formally defined by the prevailing version of the Diagnostic and Statistical Manual, the DSM-III (American Psychiatric Association, 1980).

The Diagnostic Interview Schedule (DIS) was then utilised in the largest and most comprehensive study ever to have been conducted within the United States. The Epidemiological Catchment Area Program was designed by the Division of Biometry and Epidemiology of the NIMH to collect data on both the prevalence and incidence of mental disorders, and of the use of, and need for, services by the mentally ill (Regier et al., 1988; Robins and Regier, 1991). Conducted in the early 1980s, the study sampled over 3,000 community residents and 500 institutional residents in each of five sites in the United States, which produced data from 18,571 respondents, aged 18 or over. Disorders covered by the survey included substance use disorders (alcohol or drug use/dependence), schizophrenia and schizophreniform disorder, affective disorders (manic episode, major depressive episode and dysthymia), anxiety disorders (phobia, panic disorder and obsessive–compulsive disorder), somatization disorder, antisocial personality disorder and severe cognitive impairment. The survey design overcame some of the methodological weaknesses from earlier surveys by conducting two interviews with each respondent, one year apart, with a brief telephone interview in between, which allowed for more precise reports of incidence and prevalence of mental disorders at one-month, six-month and lifetime rates.

The Epidemiological Catchment Area study, based on data combined from the five testing sites, found that 15.4% of the US population aged 18 years or older met criteria for at least one mental, alcohol or drug use disorder during the period including one month prior to the interview (Regier et al., 1988;

Robins and Regier, 1991). The most common disorders, at one-month prevalence rates, were phobia (6.2%), dysthymia (3.3%), alcohol use or dependence (2.8%) and major depressive episode (2.2%). All of the other assessed disorders had one-month prevalence rates at less than 2% of the population. Men were found to have higher rates of substance use and of antisocial personality disorder, whilst women were found to have higher rates of affective, anxiety and somatization disorders. Rates of schizophrenic disorders were the same for men and women at 0.7%. Higher prevalence rates of most of the mental disorders were found to occur in younger age groups, aged 45 or less. Overall rates for any of the disorders covered by the DIS increased significantly with the time period assessed, that is, whilst the one-month prevalence rate was 15.4%, this increased to 19.1% when the six months prior to interview were taken into consideration, and increased to 32.2% for lifetime prevalence.

During the early 1980s, the World Health Organization, Division of Mental Health, began a collaboration with the US Alcohol, Drug Abuse, and Mental Health Administration to develop a new measure to be used in cross-cultural epidemiologic studies of psychopathology to estimate prevalence of specific disorders and patterns of comorbidity across countries and regions (Robins et al., 1988). This new instrument, called the Composite International Diagnostic Interview (CIDI), was designed to retain characteristics of the Diagnostic Interview Schedule to cover DSM-III diagnoses, but also to incorporate criteria from the International Classification of Diseases (World Health Organization, 1993) and from the Present State Examination (PSE), which had been widely used in European surveys (Wing et al., 1974). There was also provision in the design of the CIDI for the possibility of posing additional questions investigating psychiatric morbidity, specific to areas of special enquiry by local regions that were utilising the measure.

Since the original preparation of the Composite International Diagnostic Interview and its subsequent release in 1990 (World Health Organization, 1990), several revised versions of the measure have been developed by various researchers throughout the world. In the United States, the National Comorbidity Survey (NCS) was considered to be a natural step beyond the earlier Epidemiologic Catchment Area (ECA) study, which had been the major source of information for American psychiatric epidemiologists for nearly a decade (Kessler et al., 1994). First of all, NCS diagnoses were based on the DSM III-R (American Psychiatric Association, 1987), rather than the DSM-III, and also included questions which allowed for some comparisons with the newly emerging DSM-IV (American Psychiatric Association, 1994). Whilst the ECA study was primarily concerned with incidence and prevalence of disorders, the National Comorbidity Survey was additionally concerned with risk factors for these disorders. In the NCS study, it was also possible to study regional variations in specific disorders, due to the fact that the respondents were elicited from almost the entirety of the United States, rather than confined to five elected sites. The NCS survey consisted of 8,098 respondents, aged 15 to 54 years, in private households, throughout 48 of the 50 United States. A sub-sample of students living in campus housing were also interviewed. Whilst most previous surveys had included only those respondents at or over the age of 18, the NCS included individuals aged 15 or over in an attempt to reduce bias as a result of individuals trying to remember events experienced from much earlier years. The 14 DSM III-R diagnoses included in the core NCS were major depression, mania, dysthymia, panic disorder, agoraphobia, social phobia, simple phobia, generalised anxiety disorder, alcohol abuse, alcohol dependence, drug abuse, drug dependence, antisocial personality disorder and non-affective psychosis (a summary category composing schizophrenia, schizophreniform disorder, schizoaffective disorder, delusional disorder and atypical psychosis).

A major finding of the US National Comorbidity Survey (Kessler et al., 1994) was that the prevalence of psychiatric disorders was greater than had been assumed from earlier studies. Forty-eight per cent of the sample reported having experienced at least one of the NCS disorders over a lifetime course, and 29% reported one or more of the disorders in the 12 months prior to interview. The most common psychiatric disorders in the sample were depression and alcohol dependence. In their lifetimes, more than 17% of respondents had a history of major depressive episode, with more than 10% having had an episode in the past 12 months. With regard to alcohol dependence, more than 14% had a lifetime history of this disorder, with more than 7% continuing to be dependent within the 12 months prior to interview. The next most common disorders were social and simple phobias, which had lifetime prevalence of 13% and 11%, respectively, and prevalence in the 12 months prior to interview at 8% and 9%, respectively. Substance use disorders and anxiety disorders were more prevalent than affective disorders, with approximately one in four informants reporting a lifetime history of substance use disorder and a similar number reporting lifetime history of at least one anxiety disorder. At the same time, only one in five respondents reported having experienced at least one affective disorder. For yearly prevalence rates in this American sample, anxiety disorders, as a group, were found to be much more likely to occur at 17%, than either substance use disorders at 11%, or affective disorders at 11%. The prevalence of all other NCS disorders was quite low, noticeably with antisocial personality disorder having a lifetime prevalence of no more than 3%. Schizophrenia and the non-affective psychoses sampled were found only in 0.7% of all respondents. Whilst overall prevalence of disorder showed no significant differences between men and women, there were sex differences in the prevalence of individual disorders. Women were much more likely to have affective disorders, with men much more likely to experience substance use disorders or antisocial personality disorder. Most of the disorders declined with age and with higher socioeconomic status.

As its title suggests, the National Comorbidity Study (Kessler et al., 1994) had a primary focus on the distribution or comorbidity of disorders in individuals, that is, those experiencing more than one lifetime disorder. Findings showed that whilst 48% of the respondents reported having had any disorder, 52% never had any of the NCS disorders, 21% of the sample had experienced only one of the disorders, 13% had two, and 14% had three or more disorders. Overall, 79% of the NCS disorders were comorbid, which means that the majority of disorders were concentrated in one group of highly comorbid individuals making up approximately only one-sixth of the population.

Apart from the NCS study carried out in the United States in the early 1990s, a number of large-scale community surveys utilising revised versions of the CIDI have been carried out in the last decade, worldwide. These include surveys in Brazil (Andrade et al., 1996), Canada (Offord et al., 1994), Germany (Wittchen, 1998), Mexico (Caraveo et al., 1998), the Netherlands (Bijl et al., 1998) and Turkey (Kýlýç, 1998). In 1998, a World Health Organization research consortium was set up to coordinate the results of these surveys and the findings have recently become available in an issue of the WHO Bulletin (International Consortium of Psychiatric Epidemiology, 2000). Cautions were issued by the consortium regarding the interpretation of results, first of all, because of the limited evidence of validity and reliability of CIDI versions in the various countries in which the surveys were carried out. There was also concern that actual prevalence rates reported were affected by bias due to variability in disclosure by the respondents, a factor that could have strong cultural differences between the countries involved. However, findings do suggest that mental disorders are highly prevalent in most countries throughout the world, and that these disorders persist throughout the life course. The highest prevalence of the mental disorders studied was found to occur amongst the youngest age groups. There were also findings consistent with previous research, that prevalence of anxiety and mood disorders is greater in women than in men, whilst there are higher rates of substance use disorders amongst men. Higher rates of most of the disorders were found in people with lower socio-economic status, as well as unmarried individuals, compared with those who were married.

A report on mental health was recently issued by the United States Surgeon General, and was the first ever comprehensive treatise by a Surgeon General dedicated to the identification of mental disorder in the US population (US Department of Health and Human Services, 1999). The report indicated that, during a one-year period, some 19% of the US population have a diagnosable mental disorder. An additional 3% of the population have both mental and addictive disorders, and 6% of the population have *either* a mental or an addictive disorder. Therefore, with regard to prevalence, about 28% per cent of the US population have either a mental or an addictive disorder. Around 9% of individuals were diagnosed with one of the disorders studied, and had significant functional impairment as a result of the disorder. Seven per cent of adults had disorders following a more chronic course for at least one year. In fact, about 2.6% of all adults in America were identified as having a severe and persistent mental illness, which included severe forms of depression, schizophrenia, bipolar disorder, panic disorder and obsessive–compulsive disorder.

Great Britain

The first ever national survey of psychiatric morbidity in Great Britain was carried out in the early 1990s. Following a report identifying mental illness as one of the five key areas for action by the Department of Health (Department of Health, 1992), the Office of Population Censuses and Surveys was commissioned to carry out a survey on behalf of the Department of Health, the Scottish Office and the Welsh Office. This broad-based survey had several aims: (1) to estimate the prevalence of psychiatric morbidity in adults aged 16–64 years in Great Britain; (2) to identify social disabilities associated with mental illness, which would look at functional limitations and restrictions of individuals within their homes, workplace and social relationships; (3) to examine use of services *vis-à-vis* diagnosis, symptoms and social disabilities; (4) to investigate recent stressful events which might be correlated with mental illness; and finally (5), to study comorbidity of mental illness with lifestyle indicators such as drinking, smoking and drug use.

The British Office of Population Censuses and Surveys study (conducted by Meltzer, et al., 1995a) was divided into eight separate reports, including coverage of prevalence of psychiatric morbidity in individuals in private households, institutions and in homeless persons, socio-demographic characteristics of all individuals included in the survey, and profiles of those respondents with a diagnosis of psychosis. However, the main focus of the survey was on neurotic psychopathology prevalent in private households, which involved over 10,000 respondents in England, Wales and Scotland completing an interview in their homes by trained lay interviewers. Children, defined as those under the age of 16, as well as adults aged 65 and over, were excluded from the survey because of the need for specialised sampling, interviewing and assessment procedures with these groups.

The interview utilised for the OPCS survey was based on the Clinical Interview Schedule (CIS) developed in 1970 by Goldberg and his associates for use in general practice and community settings (Goldberg et al., 1970). The CIS had previously been used widely to assess minor psychiatric disorder in hospital, occupational and primary care research studies. However, due to the need for increased standardisation, and to increase the efficacy of 'lay interviewers' in assessment of minor psychiatric disorders in the community, a revised version of the CIS was developed in the early 1990s (Lewis et al., 1992). The Revised Clinical Interview Schedule (CIS-R) is comprised of 14 sections covering various neurotic symptoms, including fatigue, sleep problems, irritability, worry, depression, depressive ideas, anxiety, obsessions, concentration and forgetfulness, somatic symptoms, compulsions, phobias, worry about physical health, and panic (Lewis and Pelosi, 1990). Each section of the interview begins with filter questions regarding the existence of a specific neurotic symptom within the past month and leads on to more detailed assessment of the symptom concerning frequency, duration, severity and time since onset, subsequent to positive responses. An advantage of the CIS-R in broad-scale use is that it has been standardised, requiring little or no judgement by the interviewer, and could therefore be administered by non-clinically trained lay interviewers to assess minor psychiatric disorder in the community. Another advantage of the CIS-R is that it is relatively brief in the length of time required to administer – about 30 minutes on average.

All of the informants in the OPCS survey were also screened for psychotic illness using the Psychosis Screening Questionnaire (PSQ), developed specifically for the project (Bebbington and Nayani, 1995). The PSQ covered aspects of mania, thought disorder, paranoia, delusions and auditory hallucinations that each respondent may have experienced in the past year. In addition, respondents were asked about any use of anti-psychotic drugs/injections, and contact with any health professional regarding a mental or emotional problem that had been labelled as a psychotic illness. All respondents were also asked to describe alcohol and drug dependence levels with two self-report measures.

In the event that a respondent in the OPCS survey appeared to meet criteria for a psychotic disorder, as evaluated by the lay interviewer finding a score at or above the threshold of 12 on the CIS-R, a psychiatrist then contacted the respondent within a few weeks to administer a clinical interview. This consisted of the use of the Schedules for Clinical Assessment in Neuropsychiatry (SCAN), a set of scales used to assess, measure and classify behaviour and psychopathology associated with major psychiatric disorders (Wing et al., 1990). Specifically, the PSE10 scale was used to cover anxiety, depressive disorder, bipolar disorder, schizophrenia and other delusional disorders, amongst other disorders.

From an initial sample of 18,000 addresses in England, Wales and Scotland, a group of 10,108 'co-operating adults', or 56%, agreed to be assessed for the OPCS survey. Findings from the study were discussed within the rubric of one of three main areas of interest: (1) the relationship between overall score on the CIS-R with characteristics of informants, specifically socio-demographic characteristics of those individuals with a score of 12 or above on the CIS-R; (2) the prevalence of the 14 neurotic symptoms covered by the CIS-R in the sample; and (3) the prevalence of psychiatric disorders, including neurotic disorders, functional psychosis, and alcohol and drug dependence.

Fourteen per cent of the OPCS sample had a CIS-R threshold score of 12 or above, indicating significant neurotic psychopathology. Of those scoring below this threshold, the majority of respondents scored 6 or less, which accounted for two-thirds of the total sample. Women, as a group, were more likely to have on or above threshold scores than men. Marital status was strongly associated with higher scores, as 30% of individuals comprising the three groups of divorced women, separated women and separated men had scores of 12 or more. At or above threshold scores on the CIS-R were twice as likely for the unemployed as for the employed sample. Higher scores were also reported for people living alone, individuals living in rented properties (compared with having individual ownership), and urban occupiers (compared with rural inhabitants). Age provided little variance in scores for respondents between the ages of 20 and 54, with the smallest proportion at or above threshold scores shown for men aged 16–19 at 6%, and for women aged 60–64, at 10%. Highest educational qualifications attained, or age of leaving full-time education, were both unrelated to overall scores.

Individual respondents were each rated on all 14 of the original symptoms covered by the CIS-R. Four symptoms were prominent in both men and women during the week prior to the interview. Fatigue affected 27% of all respondents, male or female. Three other symptoms also affected both males and females, with 25% reporting sleep problems, 22% with irritability, and

20% experiencing worry (not including worry about physical health). The next most common symptoms were depression, depressive ideas, anxiety and obsessions, affecting around 10% of all respondents. Panic was the lowest occurring symptom, at 2%. Women were found to be considerably more likely than men to experience every symptom except for worry about physical health, and were twice as likely to have experienced somatic symptoms and phobias.

In the establishment of prevalence of neurotic disorders in the survey, six were identified: depressive episode (including mild, moderate and severe depression); phobias, which included agoraphobia, social phobia and specific isolated phobias; obsessive–compulsive disorder; panic disorder; generalised anxiety disorder; and mixed anxiety and depressive disorder. Prevalence rates were established in cases per thousand where the respondent had experienced symptoms of the disorder in the past week. In accordance with this criterion, about one in six adults in Great Britain, aged 16–64, suffered from a neurotic disorder in the week prior to interview. Mixed anxiety and depressive disorder was the most prevalent neurotic disorder observed, with 77 cases per thousand. Of those individuals with this diagnosis, 66% of respondents reported symptoms of depression, depressive ideas or anxiety. The other respondents diagnosed with mixed anxiety and depressive disorder had symptoms of fatigue, sleep difficulty, irritability or worry. Following on from this, per 1,000 persons, 31 individuals had experienced generalised anxiety disorder, 21 had depressive episode, 12 had obsessive–compulsive disorder, 11 had phobia and 8 had panic disorder.

Overall, the prevalence of any neurotic disorder sampled was 160 individuals per 1,000. The prevalence of all six neurotic disorders was higher amongst women than in men. Mixed anxiety and depressive disorder had the highest difference in gender rates, with 99 per thousand for women and 54 per thousand for men. With regard to the prevalence of any neurotic disorder by age, rates did not reach any statistical significance, although there was some variation. Rates of neurotic disorders appeared to be lowest in the two extremes of the distribution, with 126 per thousand in individuals aged 16–19, and 133 per thousand in those aged 60–64.

Regardless of age group, prevalence of neurotic disorder was highest amongst women. However, the rates of individual disorders did vary in the sample. For example, mixed anxiety and depressive disorder tended to increase with age, peaking in the group aged 30–34, with a subsequent decline in older persons. Generalised anxiety disorder increased for both men and women with regard to age, but amongst men the prevalence reached highest rates in the 40–44 years age group and then fell. For women, generalised anxiety disorder peaked in the highest age group, of individuals aged over 50. Rates of obsessive–compulsive disorder were highest in both males and females amongst the 20–24 year age group, and phobias were most common in the youngest age group. There was not any obvious trend in prevalence rates of depressive episode or of panic disorder by age.

Functional psychosis, which included schizophrenia, manic depressive psychosis and schizo-affective disorder, had the same prevalence rates for both men and women at a yearly rate of four per thousand individuals. There were only small differences amongst age groups; however, the highest prevalence was found in women aged 30–34 years and men 55–64 years. In contrast, the survey found that men were three times as likely as women to experience alcohol dependence, and were twice as likely as women to be drug dependent. The highest prevalence of dependence, on either alcohol or drugs, was found in young adults aged 16–24, particularly younger men aged 20–24.

Aims for future assessment and treatment

Whilst we have learned a great deal about psychiatric morbidity of specific disorders from studies conducted over the past 20 years, the landmark Global Burden of Disease project provided us with a new model for assessment of various diseases or disorders worldwide (Murray and Lopez, 1996). The major contribution of this study, which was a collaborative effort between the World Health Organization, the World Bank and the Harvard School of Public Health, was the introduction of a new concept in psychiatric epidemiology, the Disability Adjusted Life Year (DALY). The DALY is a measure of burden associated with a specific disorder that allows for quantification of the number of deaths due to the disorder to be combined with the impact of years lived with the disorder on the population. The study explored the effects of major depression, bipolar disorder, schizophrenia, alcohol and drug use, panic disorder, obsessive–compulsive disorder, post-traumatic stress disorder and dementia, in addition to a number of primarily physical disorders. A significant finding of this study was that five out of the ten major causes of disability worldwide were mental problems, in both developed and developing countries. These included major depression, schizophrenia, bipolar disorder, alcohol use and obsessive–compulsive disorder. Mental disorders accounted for more than 10% of the global burden of disease (Murray and Lopez, 1997). Perhaps most importantly, study projections for the future suggest that, if present trends continue, depression will be the second leading cause of disease burden in the year 2020.

Recent attention has also focused on individuals with mild forms of serious disorders or 'subclinical conditions'. As the authors of the book *Shadow Syndromes* point out, the problems of many clients/patients do not fit neatly within the diagnostic categories of the DSM or ICD classification systems (Ratey and Johnson, 1997). Some individuals may have parts of several different syndromes, yet not present with all of the symptoms of any one syndrome. Others may be so very mildly affected by all of the aspects of any one syndrome that even the most skilful of therapists would overlook a potential diagnosis. Still others may have only one or two of the symptoms forming part of the diagnosis for any specific syndrome. Whilst none of these individuals would meet criteria for any classified disorder, each may none the less experience a great amount of distress and discomfort. Research has strongly supported the view that those with subclinical conditions have definite impairments in personal and interpersonal functioning, and an overall decrease in quality of life. This includes studies of anxiety, depression and somatization symptoms in primary care attenders with no formal mental disorder (Piccinelli et al., 1999), of impairments associated with subclinical obsessive–compulsive disorder compared with diagnosed obsessive–compulsive disorder (Grabe et al., 2000), of depression, anxiety and eating disorders associated with a diabetes disorder (Rubin and Peyrot, 2001), and of subthreshold depression in the elderly (Geiselmann and Bauer, 2000). These, and many other studies, have recognised a need to direct care and attention towards those individuals describing problems and symptoms outwith what have come to be seen as conventional diagnostic categories, yet continue to be in need of some therapeutic intervention.

Given findings that both diagnosable and subclinical mental disorders are increasingly a focus for concern worldwide, it is alarming then that concurrent research exists showing that, of those individuals experiencing problems, few ever actually receive treatment (see Andrews and Henderson, 2000). The National Comorbidity Survey (Kessler et al., 1994) was the first ever national survey to go beyond an inquiry into utilisation of professional services for emotional problems and to administer a diagnostic assessment used to define unmet need. In this comprehensive survey, only four in every ten individuals with a lifetime history of one of the survey disorders ever obtained any kind of professional help for the disorder, and only one in four obtained special help from the mental health sector. These findings were consistent with those from the Epidemiologic Catchment Area Study that showed the majority of individuals with recent disorders had not received any recent treatment (Shapiro et al., 1984).

The recent report from the United States Surgeon General, discussed earlier in this chapter, also addressed the issue that such a low minority of individuals with mental disorders actually present for some kind of treatment (US Department of Health and Human Services, 1999). Having established that some 28% of the US population have a diagnosable mental or substance use disorder, it was reported that less than one-third of these individuals had received treatment in one year. Only 8% of the respondents having a diagnosable disorder had also sought treatment for the disorder. This means that some 20% of those with a diagnosable disorder had not sought treatment or received care in a given year. Around 30–40% of the individuals with specific disorders saw some need for some kind of care. However, the majority of those respondents with disorders who declined to seek care stated as the primary reasons for not seeking help that they believed their problems would go away by themselves, or that problems could be handled without help (Kessler et al., 1997). Further to this, a recent telephone survey in the United States found that whilst 11% of respondents perceived a need for some kind of mental or addictive problem services, 25% of these individuals reported problems in obtaining needed care. Worry about costs was the prime reason cited for not seeking mental health care, expressed by 83% of uninsured individuals and by 55% of the privately insured (Sturm and Sherbourne, 1999).

One might reasonably assume that rates of seeking help for a mental disorder would be higher in countries where consultations with a general practitioner, psychiatric consultant or other mental health professional are available at no cost through a universal or national health service. However, this has been found repeatedly not to be the case. A study comparing rates of help-seeking in America and Canada found similar rates of seeking help for treatment of disorders, despite the fact that Canadians have access to mental health treatment without charge, whilst Americans do not (Kessler et al., 1997). In Australia, where universal health coverage is available, a study found that 50% of individuals with generalised anxiety disorder and 35% of individuals with depression had not sought help for their problems within the past 12 months, despite the fact that they were significantly disabled by the disorders (Andrews et al., 2000). The national survey of psychiatric morbidity in Great Britain, discussed earlier in the chapter, found that whilst 1,557 respondents (16% of the total survey sample) had a neurotic disorder, only 1 in 8 of these individuals were receiving any kind of treatment (Meltzer et al., 1995b). In fact, 25% of respondents with neurotic disorders said that they had not consulted a GP or other professional regarding a mental, nervous or emotional problem even when those around them thought that they should. The two most common reasons for not seeking help were that the respondent did not think anyone else could help, or that he or she felt they should be able to cope with the problem on their own. And in a World Health Organization report on worldwide rates of help-seeking, delays in obtaining treatment or non-treatment were commonly found in both single episodes of disorders and in 12-month cases, even where there was strong impairment associated with the disorder (International Consortium in Psychiatric Epidemiology, 2000).

Whilst it has been demonstrated that the majority of individuals decline to consult any source for help with mental problems, evidence suggests that people with neurotic disorders are much more likely than those without disorders to seek help from a general practitioner for physical complaints. In the OPCS survey carried out in Great Britain (Meltzer et al., 1995b), almost one in four women, and one in seven men, had presented to their GP with a physical complaint, without mention of a mental health problem, in the two weeks prior to the survey interview. Those survey respondents with a neurotic disorder were also more likely than those without a neurotic disorder to have consulted their GP within the 12 months prior to interview, a finding which was consistent amongst all age groups and between males and females. Fifteen per cent of women and 12% of men with a neurotic disorder had been an inpatient of a hospital during the past year, with the majority of inpatient stays for a physical health problem. Half of the individuals with neurotic disorders had also received treatment as an outpatient to a hospital or day clinic in the past year for a physical complaint. In other studies, it has been shown that presence of a psychiatric illness doubles the probability that a patient will consult his or her general practitioner, even though physical problems are the main reason given for the consultation (Vázquez-Barquero et al., 1999).

The role of the general practitioner as 'gatekeeper' to further mental health services, or as a vital part of the 'filter process' to help for a mental disorder, has been researched extensively since the early 1980s (e.g. Goldberg and Huxley, 1980). A recent study estimates that even in a small-sized general practice surgery of 2,000 patients, 4–12 patients will have schizophrenia, 6–7 will have an affective disorder, 4–5 will have organic dementia, 60–100 will have depression, 70–80 will have anxiety or other neuroses, 50–60 will have situational problems and 5–6 patients will have drug or alcohol problems (Strathdee and Jenkins, 1996). Clearly, the identification and treatment of psychological disorders by general practitioners, even in a small-sized practice surgery, could go a long way to alleviate mental distress experienced by many individuals, including those who present only with physical symptoms. However, the recent international study of psychological problems in primary care conducted by the World Health Organization, in 15 sites in 14 countries, found that the majority of individuals with mental disorders are not identified or treated in primary care (Sartorius et al., 1993; Üstün and Sartorius, 1995).This study of 26,422 individuals visiting general practitioners found that some 20% of primary care attenders had a well-defined mental disorder, increasing to 40% if subthreshold disorders were taken into account. The majority of mental disorders diagnosed were mood, anxiety or somatoform disorders, and neurasthenia (symptoms of fatigue, weakness, multiple aches and pains, and insomnia, as a form of neurotic depressive disorder), and were associated with significant levels of disability, in both developing and developed countries. Despite the fact that individuals with mental disorders suffered from disabilities of a chronic nature, with an increased utilisation of health care resources, general practitioners had failed to recognise the psychological bases of disorders in over 50% of presented cases. In recent years, considerable efforts have been directed at research related to factors that would increase general practitioners' identification and treatment of mental disorders in primary care (Tansella and Thornicroft, 1999).

Final comments

Methodological improvements have provided enormous strengths in the increased validity and reliability of psychiatric epidemiologic studies to identify prevalence of mental disorders in worldwide populations over the past 20 years. However, barriers to seeking and receiving help for mental health problems continue to exist, in both developing and developed countries. Elimination of an historically well-established stigma surrounding mental and emotional problems has been recognised by both the World Health Organization and the United States Surgeon General as a major target for work to address barriers to effective treatment for individuals in coming years (Garfinkel and Goldbloom, 2000; US Department of Health and Human Services, 1999). Certainly, it can be argued that worldwide we have taken enormous strides forward in attitudes since a 1931 British report titled 'Colonies for Mental Defectives' (Hadley, 1931), which, by its very use of language, served in some way to isolate individuals with mental or emotional problems into an unwelcome us/them dichotomy. Having said this, no one today would dispute the fact that much work can be done to assure individuals that effective treatments are available to eliminate mental distress, and to confront attitudes serving as barriers to treatment. Moreover, the call has been raised in recent research to improve conditions that would allow more scope for the provision of services to address the perceived needs of people with mental disorders. Primarily, these have been expressed by survey respondents as the opportunity to obtain more information regarding specific disorders, and in the perceived need for individual counselling or 'talking therapies'. It is worth noting that prescribed medicines have been shown to be the least favoured category of perceived need amongst survey respondents (Kessler, 2000; Andrews et al., 2000). These, and many other important issues in mental health care, will be discussed in much greater detail in the following chapters.

Notes

1 The study of the frequency and distribution of mental disorders and psychological distress in a population, or the study of the distribution and determinants of psychological health-related states or events in specified populations.
2 Broadly defined within this context, may be considered to be any departure from a state of psychological well-being.

References

American Psychiatric Association (1980) *Diagnostic and Statistical Manual of Mental Disorders,* 3rd edn. Washington, DC: APA.
American Psychiatric Association (1987) *Diagnostic and Statistical Manual of Mental Disorders*, 3rd edn, revised. Washington, DC: APA.
American Psychiatric Association (1994) *Diagnostic and Statistical Manual of Mental Disorders*, 4th edn. Washington, DC: APA.
Andrade, L. et al. (1996) Lifetime prevalence of mental disorders in a catchment area in Saõ Paulo, Brazil. Paper presented at VII Congress of the International Federation of Psychiatric Epidemiology, Santiago, Chile. (Cited in International Consortium of Psychiatric Epidemiology, 2000).
Andrews, G. and Henderson, S. (eds) (2000) *The Unmet Need in Psychiatry*. Cambridge: Cambridge University Press.
Andrews, G., Sanderson, K., Slade, T. and Issakidis, C. (2000) Why does the burden of disease exist? Relating the burden of anxiety and depression to effectiveness of treatment. *Bulletin of the World Health Organization*, 78, 446–54.
Bebbington, P.E. and Nayani, T. (1995) The Psychosis Screening Questionnaire. *International Journal of Methods in Psychiatric Research*, 5, 11–19.
Bijl, R.V. et al. (1998) The Netherlands Mental Health Survey and Incidence Study (NEMESIS): objectives and design. *Social Psychiatry and Psychiatric Epidemiology*, 33, 581–6.
Caraveo, J., Martinez, J. and Rivera, B. (1998) A model for epidemiological studies on mental health and psychiatric morbidity. *Salud Mental*, 21, 48–57.
Department of Health (1992) *The Health of the Nation: A Strategy for Health in England*. London: HMSO.
Garfinkel, P.E. and Goldbloom, D.S. (2000) Mental health–getting beyond stigma and categories. *Bulletin of the World Health Organization*, 78, 503–5.
Geiselmann, B. and Bauer, M. (2000) Subthreshold depression in the elderly: qualitative or quantitative distinction? *Comprehensive Psychiatry*, 41 (2), Suppl. 1 (March/April).
Goldberg D. and Huxley, P (1980) *Mental Illness in the Community. The Pathway to Psychiatric Care*. London and New York: Tavistock Publications.

Goldberg, D.P., Cooper, B., Eastwood, M.R., Kedward, H.B. and Shepherd, M. (1970) A standardized psychiatric interview for use in community surveys. *British Journal of Preventive and Social Medicine*, 24, 18–23.

Grabe, H.J., Meyer, Ch., Hapke, U., Rumpf, H.J., Freyberger, H.J., Dilling, H. and John, U. (2000) Prevalence, quality of life and psychosocial function in obsessive–compulsive disorder and subclinical obsessive–compulsive disorder in northern Germany. *European Archives of Psychiatry and Clinical Neurosciences*, 250, 262–8.

Hadley, W. (1931). *Colonies for Mental Defectives*. Great Britain Board of Control, Departmental Committee. London: HMSO.

International Consortium of Psychiatric Epidemiology (2000) Cross-national comparisons of the prevalences and correlates of mental disorders: results from the WHO International Consortium of Psychiatric Epidemiology. *Bulletin of the World Health Organization*, 78, 413–26.

Kessler, R.C. (2000) Psychiatric epidemiology: selected recent advances and future directions. *World Health Organization Bulletin*, 78, 464–74.

Kessler, R.C., McGonagle, K.A., Zhao, S., Nelson, C.B., Hughes, M., Eshleman, S., Wittchen, H-U. and Kendler, K.S. (1994). Lifetime and 12-month prevalence of DSM-III-R psychiatric disorders in the United States. *Archives of General Psychiatry*, 51, 8–19.

Kessler, R.C., Frank, R.G., Edlund, M., Katz, S.J., Lin, E. and Leaf, P. (1997) Differences in the use of psychiatric outpatient services between the United States and Ontario. *New England Journal of Medicine*, 336, 551–7.

Kýlýç, C. (1998) *Mental Health Profile of Turkey: Main Report*. Ankara: Ministry of Health Publications.

Lewis, G. and Pelosi, A.J. (1990) *Manual of the Revised Clinical Interview Schedule (CIS-R)*. London: Institute of Psychiatry.

Lewis, G., Pelosi, A.J., Araya, R. and Dunn, G. (1992) Measuring psychiatric disorder in the community: a standardized assessment for use by lay interviewers. *Psychological Medicine*, 22, 465–86.

Meltzer, H., Gill, B., Petticrew, M. and Hinds, K. (1995a) *The Prevalence of Psychiatric Morbidity Among Adults Living in Private Households*. Office of Population Censuses and Surveys (OPCS), Report 1. London: HMSO.

Meltzer, H., Gill, B., Petticrew, M. and Hinds, K. (1995b) *Physical Complaints, Service Use and Treatment of Adults with Psychiatric Disorders*. Office of Population Censuses and Surveys (OPCS) Report 2. London: HMSO.

Murray, C.J.L. and Lopez, A.D. (eds) (1996) *The Global Burden of Disease: A Comprehensive Assessment of Mortality and Disability for Diseases, Injuries, and Risk Factors in 1990 and Projected to 2020*. Cambridge, MA: Harvard University School of Public Health on behalf of the World Health Organization and the World Bank.

Murray, C.J.L. and Lopez, A.D. (1997) Alternative projections of mortality and disability by cause 1990–2020: global burden of disease study. *Lancet*, 349, 1498–504.

Offord, D.R. et al. (1994) *Mental Health in Ontario: Selected Findings from the Mental Health Supplement to the Ontario Health Survey*. Toronto: Queen's Printer for Ontario.

Piccinelli, M., Rucci, P., Üstün, B. and Simon, G. (1999) Typologies of anxiety, depression and somatization symptoms among primary care attenders with no formal mental disorder. *Psychological Medicine*, 29, 677–88.

Ratey, J. and Johnson, C. (1997) *Shadow Syndromes*. London: Bantam Press–Transworld Publishers, Ltd.

Regier, D.A., Boyd, J.H., Burke, J.D., Rae, D.S., Myers, J.K., Kramer, M., Robins, L.N., George, L.K., Karno, M. and Locke, B.Z. (1988) One-month prevalence of mental disorders in the United States. *Archives of General Psychiatry*, 45, 977–86.

Robins, L.N. and Regier, D.A. (eds) (1991) *Psychiatric Disorders in America: The Epidemiologic Catchment Area Study*. New York: The Free Press.

Robins, L.N., Helzer, J.E., Croughan, J. and Ratcliffe, K.S. (1981) National Institute of Mental Health diagnostic interview schedule. *Archives of General Psychiatry*, 38, 381–9.

Robins, L.N., Wing, J., Wittchen, H-U., Helzer, J.E., Babor, T.F., Burke, J., Farmer, A., Jablenski, A., Pickens, R., Regier, D.A., Sartorius, N. and Towle, L.H. (1988) The composite international diagnostic interview: an epidemiologic instrument suitable for use in conjunction with different diagnostic systems and in different cultures. *Archives of General Psychiatry*, 45, 1069–77.

Rubin, R. and Peyrot, M. (2001) Psychological issues and treatments for people with diabetes. *Journal of Clinical Psychology*, 57 (4), 457–78.

Sartorius, N., Üstün, T.B., Costa e Silva, J-A, Goldberg, D., Lecrubier, Y., Ormel, J., von Korff, M. and Wittchen, H-U. (1993) An international study of psychological problems in primary care. Preliminary report from the World Health Organization Collaborative Project on 'Psychological Problems in General Health Care'. *Archives of General Psychiatry*, 50, 819–24.

Shapiro, S., Skinner, E.A., Kessler, L.G., von Korff, M., German, P.S., Tischler, G.L., Leaf, P.J., Benham, L., Cottler, L. and Regier, D.A. (1984) Utilization of health and mental health services: three Epidemiological Catchment Area sites. *Archives of General Psychiatry*, 41, 971–8.

Spitzer, R.L. and Fleiss, J.L. (1974) A re-analysis of the reliability of psychiatric diagnosis. *British Journal of Psychiatry*, 125, 341–7

Spitzer, R.L., Endicott, J. and Robins, E. (1975) Clinical criteria for psychiatric diagnosis and the DSM-III. *American Journal of Psychiatry*, 132, 1187–92.

Strathdee, G. and Jenkins, R. (1996) Purchasing mental health for primary care. In G. Thornicroft and G. Strathdee (eds), *Commissioning Mental Health Services*. London: HMSO.

Sturm, R. and Sherbourne, C.D. (1999) Are barriers to mental health and substance abuse care still rising? Manuscript submitted for publication, cited in US Department of Health and Human Services, A Report of the Surgeon General (1999).

Tansella, M. and Thornicroft, G. (eds) (1999) *Common Mental Disorders in Primary Care. Essays in Honour of Professor Sir David Goldberg*. London and New York: Routledge.

US Department of Health and Human Services (1999) *Mental Health: A Report of the Surgeon General*. Rockville, MD: US Department of Health and Human Services, Substance Abuse and Mental Health Services Administration, Center for Mental Health Services, National Institute of Health, National Institute of Mental Health.

Üstün, T.B. and Sartorius, N. (1995) *Mental Illness in General Health Care. An International Study*. Chichester: Wiley.

Vázquez-Barquero, J.L., Herran, A. and Simon, J.A. (1999) Epidemiology of mental disorders in the community and primary care. In: A. Tansella and G. Thornicroft (eds), *Common Mental Disorders in Primary Care*. London and New York: Routledge.

Weissman, M.M., Myers, J.K., and Ross, C.E. (eds) (1986) *Community Surveys of Psychiatric Disorders*. New Brunswick: Rutgers University Press.

Wing, J.K., Babor, T., Brugha, T., Burke, J., Cooper, J.E., Giel, R., Jablensky, A., Regier, D. and Sartorius, N. (1990) SCAN: schedules for clinical assessment in neuropsychiatry. *Archives of General Psychiatry*, 47, 586–93.

Wing J.K., Cooper, J.E. and Sartorius, N. (1974) *The Description and Classification of Psychiatric Symptoms: An Instruction Manual for the PSE and CATEGO System*. London: Cambridge University Press

Wittchen, H-U. (1998) Early developmental stages of psychopathology study (EDSP): objectives and design. *European Addiction Research*, 4, 18–27.

World Health Organization (1990) *Composite International Diagnostic Interview* (CIDI, Version 1.0). Geneva: World Health Organization.

World Health Organization (1993) *The ICD-10 Classification of Mental and Behavioural Disorders: Diagnostic Criteria for Research*. Geneva: World Health Organization.

2
PROVEN BENEFITS OF PSYCHOTHERAPEUTIC INTERVENTIONS WITH CHILDREN AND ADOLESCENTS

Helen Cowie & Judith Dawkins

> While walking along a riverbank, a counsellor suddenly sees a child drowning. Immediately he dives in and saves a life. Once safely on dry land, the counsellor turns to see two more children in the same predicament and bravely dives in and saves two more lives. Exhausted but relieved, the counsellor sits down on the riverbank when a passer-by approaches and comments: 'I've just watched you save three children's lives. That's fantastic, but could I make a suggestion? Have you ever considered going round the bend in the river upstream to see who might be pushing them in?' (adapted from Mackay, 2000)

This story illustrates the dilemma facing professionals who would like to alleviate the social and emotional distress of young people. Children and adolescents today face an unprecedented number of developmental and social challenges at home, in school and in society. It is hard to be absolutely accurate about the incidence of mental health problems in the young. Estimates vary according to the definition and research methods used. A recent ONS survey (Meltzer, 1999) showed that 10% of 5–15-year-old children in the UK experience clinically defined mental health problems: 5% have conduct disorders, 4% an emotional disorder (anxiety or depression) and 1% hyperkinetic disorder (hyperactivity). A further 0.5% have less common disorders such as autism or psychosis. Eating disorders affect approximately 1% of 15–19-year-olds. Mild but none the less distressing mental health problems are more common and include sleep problems, feeding difficulties, misery, bedwetting, soiling, overactivity, tantrums and oppositional disorders. Psychosocial disorders amongst the young have increased in recent years (Rutter, 1999).

Most young people appear to cope with the difficulties that they encounter. They may be sad, angry, upset or disappointed, but they are not overwhelmed by the ups and downs of life. In fact, as Wilson (1996: 19) argues, 'children in "good enough" mental health are able to learn from their difficulties and make the most of their abilities'. Some children appear to cope well in the face of considerable adversity and recent psychosocial research has looked at resilience and protective factors (Rutter, 1999). At the same time, there is a substantial minority of children and adolescents who need help and support if they are to avoid the pain and stigma of mental health difficulties. Other more vulnerable children may be overwhelmed by a seemingly minor stressor, so research has also attempted to identify vulnerability factors.

Mental health problems have been defined in the following ways:

> A mental health problem can be seen as a 'disturbance in functioning' in one area of relationship, mood, behaviour or development. When a problem is particularly severe or persistent over time, or when a number of these difficulties are experienced at the same time, children are often described as having mental health disorders. (Mental Health Foundation, 1999: 6)

They can take the following forms:

- *emotional disorders*, such as anxiety, depression or phobias;
- *conduct disorders*, such as stealing, defiance, fire-setting, aggression and anti-social behaviour;
- *hyperkinetic disorders*, such as attention deficit disorder;
- *developmental disorders*, such as delays in acquiring certain skills;
- *eating disorders*, such as bulimia and anorexia nervosa;
- *somatic disorders*, such as sleeping problems;
- *psychotic disorders*, such as schizophrenia, manic depressive disorder, drug induced psychosis. (Mental Health Foundation, 1999: 6)

Children with externalising disorders or obvious behavioural problems (usually associated with conduct disorders or attention deficit hyperactivity disorder) are much more likely to come to the attention of professionals within health, education or social services, while children with internalising disorders, or problems experienced inwardly (usually anxiety and depression) may not. Young people's mental health difficulties are too often unrecognised or undiagnosed, and may be associated with stigma. There are times when interventions by a specialist psychiatrist, counsellor or psychologist are essential, but there are many ways in which adults in the child's immediate circle – for example, family members, teachers, youth workers and neighbours – can play an active part in helping young people by listening carefully to them and by attending to their particular emotional needs. Government policies also play a crucial part in creating supportive contexts that facilitate mental health in young people and their families, and that offer opportunities for young people to realise their potential.

In this chapter, we consider interventions to alleviate emotional distress at different levels. First we look at the role of the immediate family and the wider social context in which young people may experience distress. Second, we explore recent government policies to address the issue of mental health in young people, and third, ways in which the resources of the community can be mobilised, including interventions in school. Finally, we look at specialist therapeutic interventions by psychiatrists, counsellors and psychologists.

The role of the family

A large body of research confirms the fundamental part played by families in influencing the child's capacity to form close, trusting relationships with others and to have firmly established strategies for interacting socially in the wider community (Bretherton, 1990; Dunn, 1996; Fonagy et al., 1997). The early years lay a strong foundation for later emotional development and many difficulties experienced by children and adolescents can be traced back to the first relationships with primary caregivers.

Research by Dunn (1996) gives important insights into the quality and nature of the young child's interactions with caregivers and the impact that these relationships have on the child's understanding of the emotions. It appears that family discussions of emotional issues attune children to the different ways in which individuals deal with their feelings and express them. These discussions are especially helpful when they take place in a humorous or comforting atmosphere. In these kinds of context, children find it easier to talk about emotional issues and to deal with them in an open and free way. Interestingly, Dunn's research shows that siblings play a key role here with pre-schoolers spending more time discussing feelings with their brothers and sisters than with their mothers.

Fonagy et al. (1997) report that children who are securely attached in infancy have significantly lower antisocial scores on a narrative task involving completion of conflict-arousing stories. Securely attached children were less likely than insecurely attached children to express themes of jealousy, aggression, nonsharing, taunting and lack of empathy, and more likely to mention themes associated with discipline and boundary-setting, such as compliance, shame at wrong-doing, verbal (but not physical) punishment and limit-setting. Thus, securely attached children seemed to be more able to express empathy for others, the capacity for sharing and affiliation, and, in the case of wrong-doing, a willingness to make amends and experience shame or guilt. The implications for policy and practice are clear:

> systematic facilitation of the development of the children's awareness of mental states of those around them is an important target for preventive intervention in social and behavioural disorders in children as well as personality disturbance and antisocial behaviour in adolescence and adult life. (Fonagy et al., 1997: 37)

Evidence from these studies supports the view that secure attachment facilitates the development of feelings of self-worth, autonomy and trust – attributes that help young people to cope with the vicissitudes of life that they will inevitably encounter. Much of this security is built up through myriad everyday interactions in the family context in the course of mutual activity and play, story-telling, shared reminiscences and experiences.

There is much that adults in the child's immediate circle can do to alleviate distress (Sharp and Cowie, 1998). The single most important response is to listen to the young person, to give them time and to be aware of the non-verbal ways in which children and adolescents may express their unhappiness. Parents play an important part in helping children to face common fears and anxieties through active listening, fantasy play and drawing. They can also develop the child's inner world of imagination through shared reading of fiction and non-fiction, or mutual discussion of themes portrayed in the media that typically deal with issues like relationship difficulties, conflict, love, betrayal, death and danger. This can be a significant way of entering into the inner world of the child and so responding to common worries or fears as they arise and before they become acute.

In the case of bereavement or prolonged separation from an attachment figure, the child may regress to an earlier developmental stage. Some children may become incontinent, or have nightmares, or find it hard to sleep. When such symptoms appear, adults can be most helpful by ensuring that the child feels secure and loved. It is essential not to be punitive when faced with atypical tantrums, angry outbursts or regressive behaviour. The adult can demonstrate care and concern through practical help by being tolerant, expressing love and by praising the child for strength and resilience when this appears. Lendrum and Syme (1992) identify a range of practical ways in which adults can support a child through the grieving process and, while they recognise that counselling may be necessary in some cases, they point out that most young people can come through a period of separation or loss with the help of supportive interventions by trusted adults and peers in their immediate family and neighbourhood.

Aggressive behaviour is another very common behavioural problem during childhood and adolescence. Again, it is important to intervene early since research indicates that aggression in childhood predicts later delinquency, violence and anti-social acts (Farrington, 1992). We ignore childhood aggression at our peril since it is one of the most costly mental health disorders in society:

> A large proportion of these children remain involved throughout their lives, either in mental health agencies or within the criminal justice system. In other words, we all pay in the long run – personally, financially or both – when these children are left uncared for and their behaviour problems untreated. (Webster-Stratton, 1999: 27)

Parenting education can have an important influence and can act positively against the cycle of deprivation in which too many families are trapped. Support for parenting usually focuses on the emotional and psychological processes involved in the practice of parenting. There are times when parents are most likely to seek advice and guidance, including the period around the birth of the first child, the transition to school at around 4–5 years, the transition to secondary school at around 11 years, and the transition from school. At these times, it is possible to offer parenting education in ways that are supportive rather than critical or stigmatising since it is offered to all parents. At the same time, this can be an opportunity to provide more specialist services for those families most in need. Interventions that complement parent and child training in social skills, anger management and conflict resolution with support from schools produce the most sustained reduction in conduct disorders, not only in the family but also in the context of peer relationships (Webster-Stratton, 1999). Another example of successful intervention of this type comes from the High Scope Perry Project in the USA, a pre-school intervention project with children and families that fostered children's independence, self-esteem, effective problem-solving and a greater integration between home and school. The benefits were substantial and long term, and one important outcome was a reduction in anti-social behaviour on the part of young people. The project worked because it used a multimodal range of methods, including a partnership between parents and schools, a belief in the potential of parents to work effectively with their own children, and a willingness to work directly with the children and their teachers.

From this perspective, it is particularly important to identify high-risk children early and to offer the right sort of support, training and guidance to the families concerned. In addition, the family needs to be given protection and assistance so that it can fulfil its responsibilities within the community (Bronfenbrenner and Ceci, 1994; Children's Rights Development Unit (CRDU), 1994). In the absence of effective support systems, parents can be put under such external stresses that they are unable to provide for their children the emotional support that they need. Conger et al. (1994) found that financial hardship within a family led to more arguments and conflicts between the parents that in turn contributed to higher levels of stress among the children. There are some families in which caregivers are unable to provide a secure base. As Byng-Hall (1997) indicates, there are a number of factors that can undermine the security of the family. The most common of these is the loss, or threatened loss, of an attachment figure, whether because of divorce, separation, prolonged absences, illness or death. Where there are intense conflicts between parents, taking care of the child may lose its priority, or the child may become involved in taking sides. When faced with overwhelming difficulties of their own, some parents may turn to their children for care, and such role reversal can lead to attachment disorders in later childhood since the 'parentified child' may not consider that he or she has the right to be cared for.

This kind of dysfunction within the family can undermine the child's security and cause acute emotional distress. Furthermore, some families face on-going stresses and disadvantages that make it extremely difficult to cope. Research suggests that certain family characteristics put some children at higher risk of developing mental health difficulties. These include family poverty, single parenthood, teenage parenthood, parental psychotic illness and a family history of drug abuse or criminality (Farrington, 1992; Webster-Stratton, 1999). There are also biological factors such as learning disabilities, language and reading delay, attention deficit disorder and hyperactivity. As Webster-Stratton points out, children who have two or more of these risk factors are four times more likely to develop a mental health problem; those with four risk factors are ten times more likely to have a mental health problem. In the light of these findings, we need to turn to the wider social context and to the policies that can alleviate the conditions that undermine the capacity of families to cope with adversity. We look first at the role of government policies on mental health issues.

Government policies

Much government attention, policy and guidance has focused on action to tackle the cycle of disadvantage that can trap too many families in breakdown and emotional difficulties. Increasingly, attention has been focused on the best ways of giving families opportunities to give their children a 'good enough' start. This has been coupled with a realisation that limited public resources are most effectively used when different services work together in multi-agency programmes, and when problems are addressed at an early stage. These interventions should encompass both psychological and social factors and should not be constrained by traditional professional barriers. Issues of inequality in society must also be taken into account. The poorest families in the UK today face a lack of employment and training opportunities and bad housing; they are also more likely to fall ill and to experience mental health problems. A child growing up in a deprived environment or an environment where crime rates are high is less likely to do well at school, and is more vulnerable to becoming involved in juvenile crime. Furthermore, the ways in which young people engage with or disengage from formal systems of education and training are crucial to their later experiences in early adulthood. The multifactorial aetiology of child and adolescent mental health problems means that specialist and complementary skills of different descriptions are required to address them. An increasing emphasis has been placed on the need for the many professionals involved in the provision of child care to work together. A tiered model of Child and Adolescent Mental Health Services (CAMHS) has been developed consisting of a range of primary and specialised services purchased by the health/social services and the educational sector. The providers consist of a range of services and levels of expertise delivered by primary and secondary health care, education, social services, the voluntary sector and private sector organisations (Audit Commission, 1999; NHS, 1995).

Little (1999) argues that a range of interventions, some early and some later, coupled with an improvement in diagnosis, holds the answer to many social and psychological problems and can change the pattern and prevalence of a disorder. Rutter (1999) argues that the chances for intervening to reduce or prevent antisocial behaviour in young people begin in early childhood but that they also continue into adult life. So, although the presence of risk factors, such as a poor environment or unsupportive relationships with primary caregivers, increases the likelihood of a negative outcome for the individual, studies of competence and resilience have shown that, regardless of background, children are generally resourceful. Competence has been shown to be a mediating variable that predicts positive or negative outcomes in mental health (Garmezy and Masten, 1991); so too is the belief that others are available to offer support when it is needed (Wetherington and Kessler, 1991). Some young people appear to thrive and gain from their experience of the most adverse circumstances while others in the same or similar situations can be devastated and suffer emotional setbacks. Protective factors include the personal attributes of the individual (including health, temperament, a positive sense of self-esteem, a belief in one's own competence) and also environmental resources (including family income, religious affiliation, good educational facilities).

Working in school settings

Effective interventions in school include the development of social skills and a problem-solving stance towards interpersonal relationships within the peer group. The example of Circle Time (Mosley, 1996) indicates how a policy of inclusion can greatly enhance the ethos of a school and also mobilise the actions of staff and fellow pupils to help vulnerable pupils. Circle Time aims to enhance effective communication amongst members of a class group; to affirm the strengths of each member of the group; to create a safe space in which to explore issues of concern and difficulty experienced by members of that group. Circle Time is a time set aside each week in which teachers and pupils sit in a circle and take part in activities, games and discussion. It usually lasts for about 20–30 minutes, and provides a useful forum for the discussion of important issues including peer relationships, democratic principles, friendship, justice and individual freedom. The positive atmosphere that is generated in the well-managed circle usually spreads into other areas of class activity. Circle Time gives children the opportunity to discuss matters of personal concern, including friendship problems and bullying; to explore relationships with adults and peers; to develop a sense of being members of a community; to learn about the experience of reflection and silence. The method has been evaluated and the outcomes are generally very successful, as was indicated by a survey in Wiltshire primary schools (Dawson and McNess, 1998), where it was found that a key factor was that, at every stage, the children 'own the problem' and are treated as responsible citizens in their school community.

Circle Time is a therapeutic intervention that aims to enhance the self-esteem of participants and improve the quality of interpersonal relationships within the group. It is based on humanistic principles of respect for children, and the focus is on the group process. This person-centred approach forms the basis of the creation of a therapeutic environment, symbolised by the circle itself, a safe space where participants have an opportunity to gain greater self-awareness and to practise social skills. As Bliss, Robinson and Maines (1998: 10) point out, through Circle Time:

> there is a process that the group has to go through to move from being a collection of individuals, which sadly many classes remain, to a cohesive group able to work in a truly co-operative collaboration.

Many interpersonal difficulties experienced by children and adolescents can be alleviated by the therapeutic use of group work within the school setting (Berdondini and Cowie, in press). For such groups to work most effectively, it is important that there are clear boundaries between the group and the participants' social environment, as one would expect in a therapeutic group. At the same time, it is also helpful if there are lines of communication between the group and people outside the group, as one would expect in a group whose purpose is educational (Brown and Palincsar, 1989). For example, it is essential that senior management in the school provides endorsement for the existence of a group and supports its goals. It helps greatly if other colleagues are sympathetic to the aims of staff who use group work as a therapeutic intervention:

> The availability and continuity of group work is influenced by the structure, functioning and resources of school and community systems, and the power of those persons who initiate services. Attitudes towards group work with children and adolescents also have an effect on the support and development of such programs. (Rose, 1998: 17)

Another example is Circle of Friends (Newton and Wilson, 1999), a method that involves the participation of a selected group of peers who meet regularly, facilitated by a trained practitioner, such as an educational psychologist or counsellor, to give feedback and support to a young person whose behaviour is a cause for concern. Experienced facilitators comment frequently on the depth and richness of the support offered by Circle members. This method, with appropriate adjustments for the particular individual, is effective for focus children who show aggressive or isolated behaviour, who are about to start as a new member of the class after, for example, having been excluded from their previous school, or who have been experiencing learning difficulties. Children are also ingenious in devising practical strategies for defusing potentially difficult situations involving the target child. Case study evaluations (Newton and Wilson, 1999) confirm that Circle of Friends is a flexible method for the supportive role that young people can take in helping peers with relationship difficulties and re-integrating them into social circles. This is a creative and innovative approach for using the resource of peer support to offer help to troubled and troubling children and to form a peer network for individuals who experience difficulties in their relationships and behaviour.

Specialist therapeutic interventions

Attention has recently focused on preventative and early intervention strategies, for example to help identify and manage young people with eating disorders, depression, substance misuse or at risk of exclusion. Schools are being asked to address some of these issues as part of the Personal, Social and Health Education (PSHE) curriculum. Health professionals, for example nurses and psychologists, may go into schools and offer advice and counselling to young people experiencing these difficulties. 'Care committees' with a broad membership are another approach to the early identification and management of mental health problems. When a young person's personal difficulties are too complex or too severe to be managed at this level, they may be referred on to their local CAMHS and seen by a member of the multidisciplinary team. The team consists of professionals from a variety of backgrounds, usually nurses, social workers, psychologists and psychiatrists. They are able to offer a range of therapies, including family therapy, behavioural methods, cognitive behavioural therapy, psychodynamic psychotherapy and play therapy. Treatment is usually tailored to the individual's needs and involves working closely with the parents/caregivers too.

Where possible, the CAMHS team will endeavour to liaise with the school about the young person on an outpatient basis. A minority of young people with severe and incapacitating problems will require admission to a specialised inpatient unit. Some may attend as day patients when well enough. When discharge from such a service is being considered, a planning meeting involving all the professionals as well as the young person and his/her parents is convened to aid the person's transition back home and into school.

Developing appropriate mental health services for children and adolescents can present a challenging task. Difficulties can include the actual location of services, the approach adopted by professionals working in multidisciplinary teams, and the attitudes of the young people towards mental health issues. It seems appropriate, therefore, to end with the perspectives of the 400 children aged under 10 years and the 180 adolescents who were consulted by the Mental Health Foundation inquiry into the emotional well-being of children and young people as reported in *Bright Futures* (Mental Health Foundation, 1999). Some respondents reported that it was very hard for them to access services when they experienced mental health difficulties, and said that when they finally did get help, the professionals could be intimidating or apparently uncaring. Some young people also found it embarrassing or awkward to be asked too quickly to disclose details about distressing incidents in their lives. However, many *were* satisfied with the quality of the care that they received, and in these cases the common factors included a sense of being listened to, a sense of being cared for and a willingness on the part of professionals to be flexible and informal. The inquiry concludes:

> The responsiveness of the professionals they came into contact with was a major factor in determining how young people and their parents felt about the service they received. Where professionals were felt to be patronising, to be unwilling to share information with the young people about their illnesses, or appeared not to have any time for the young person, they in turn felt let down by the treatments on offer. A number spoke of the need for psychiatrists in particular to be 'less bow-tie and more youth worker'. It was clear that a great deal could be done to transform young people's experience of services if professionals were trained in listening empathetically to young people and were able to have a more flexible response to meeting young people in more informal settings. (Mental Health Foundation, 1999: 95)

The evidence indicates that national strategy on the mental health needs of young people should address the issue of adequate location of mental health services to ensure appropriate access and speed of response. In addition, professionals in education, health, social services and the community need to develop flexible ways of working together, to cooperate across traditional boundaries and to communicate effectively with the young people themselves. Most importantly, there is an urgent need for us all to take responsibility for children's emotional well-being and mental health and not to turn our backs on those who are vulnerable and at risk of being excluded and rejected.

References

Audit Commission (1999) *With Children in Mind*. London: HMSO.

Berdondini, L. and Cowie, H. (in press) Therapeutic groupwork with children in everyday settings. In P. Clarkson and T. Ormay (eds), *The Therapeutic Relationship in Group Psychotherapy*. London: Whurr.

Bliss, T., Robinson, G. and Maines, B. (1998) *Developing Circle Time*. Bristol: Lucky Duck Publishing.

Bretherton, I. (1990) Open communication and internal working models: their role in the development of attachment relationships. In R.A. Thompson (ed.), *Socioemotional Development: Nebraska Symposium on Motivation, 1988*. Lincoln, NB: University of Nebraska Press. pp. 57–113.

Bronfenbrenner, U. and Ceci, S.J. (1994) Nature–nurture re-conceptualised in developmental perspective: a bio-ecological model. *Psychological Review*, 10, 568–86.

Brown, A. and Palincsar, A. (1989) Guided cooperative learning and individual knowledge acquisition. In L. Resnick (ed.), *Knowing, Learning and Instruction*. Hillsdale, NJ: Lawrence Erlbaum Associates.

Byng-Hall, J. (1997) The secure family base: some implications for family therapy. In G. Forrest (ed.), *Bonding and Attachment: Current Issues in Research and Practice*. Occasional Papers No. 14. London: Association for Child Psychology and Psychiatry. pp. 27–30.

Children's Rights Development Unit (CRDU) (1994) *United Nations Convention on the Rights of the Child*. London: UNICEF/Gulbenkian/UNA.

Conger, R.D., Xiaojia, G., Elder, G.H., Lorenz, F.O. and Simons, R.L. (1994) Economic stress, coercive family process and developmental problems of adolescents. *Child Development*, 65, 541–61.

Dawson, N. and McNess, M. (1998) The key themes from a survey of Circle Time in Wiltshire schools. In J. Mosley (ed.), *Research into the Jenny Mosley Whole School Quality Circle Time Approach*. Trowbridge: All Round Success Publishing.

Dunn, J. (1996) Children's relationships: bridging the divide between cognitive and social development. *Journal of Child Psychology and Psychiatry*, 37, 507–18.

Farrington, D.P. (1992) Explaining the beginning, progress and ending of anti-social behaviour problems: stability and factors accounting for change. *Journal of Child Psychology and Psychiatry*, 31, 891–909.

Fonagy, P., Steele, H., Steele, M. and Holder, J. (1997) Attachment and theory of mind: overlapping constructs? In G. Forrest (ed.), *Bonding and Attachment: Current Issues in Research and Practice*. Occasional Papers No. 14. London: Association for Child Psychology and Psychiatry. pp. 31–40.

Garmezy, N. and Masten, A. (1991) The protective role of competence indicators in children at risk. In E.M. Cummings, A.L. Greene and K.H. Karraker (eds), *Life Span Developmental Psychology: Perspectives on Stress and Coping*. Hillsdale, NJ: Lawrence Erlbaum Associates.

Lendrum, S. and Syme, G. (1992) *Gift of Tears*. London: Routledge.

Little, M. (1999) The experience of early intervention: a review of practice in the USA and UK. In R. Bayley (ed.), *Transforming Children's Lives: The Importance of Early Intervention*. Occasional Papers 25. London: Family Policy Studies Centre.

Mackay, M. (2000) From cure to prevention. *Counselling at Work*, 31, 1–2.

Meltzer, H. (1999) *Mental Health of Children and Adolescents in Great Britain*. Office of National Statistics. London: HMSO.

Mental Health Foundation (1999) *Bright Futures*. London: Mental Health Foundation.

Mosley, J. (1996) *Quality Circle Time in the Primary Classroom*. Wisbech: Learning Development Aids.

National Health Service (NHS) (1995) *Together We Stand. The Commissioning Role and Management of Child and Adolescent Mental Health Services*. London: HMSO.

Newton, C. and Wilson, D. (1999) *Circles of Friends*. Dunstable: Folens.

Rose, S. (1998) *Group Work with Children and Adolescents*. Thousand Oaks, CA: Sage.

Rutter, M. (1999) Preventing anti-social behaviour in young people: the contribution of early intervention. In R. Bayley (ed.), *Transforming Children's Lives: The Importance of Early Intervention*. Occasional Papers 25. London: Family Policy Studies Centre.

Sharp, S. and Cowie, H. (1998) *Counselling and Supporting Children in Distress*. London: Sage.

Webster-Stratton, C. (1999) Early intervention in family life: experiences from the United States. In R. Bayley (ed.), *Transforming Children's Lives: The Importance of Early Intervention*. Occasional Paper 25. London: Family Policy Studies Centre.

Wetherington, E. and Kessler, R.C. (1991) Situations and processes of coping. In J. Eckenrode (ed.), *The Social Context of Coping*. New York: Plenum.

Wilson, P. (1996) *Mental Health in Your School*. London: Jessica Kingsley.

3
BENEFITS OF THERAPY WITH ADULTS WHO WERE ABUSED AS CHILDREN: SOME ISSUES FROM EVALUATION OF COUNSELLING SERVICES

Peter Dale

Adults abused as children have been a focus of my professional interest since the early 1970s, and a significant part of my career has been involved in the assessment of families where serious child abuse has taken place (Dale et al., 1986; Dale et al., 2002). Recognising the role that parents' own childhood abuse appears to play in serious child abuse, in 1987 I was involved in the establishment of a specific counselling service for adults who were abused as children. Over 14 years, the NSPCC East Sussex Counselling Centre has become a large provider of counselling for over 450 adults abused as children. The rationale for this service is two-fold. First, is to promote individual, family and community benefits in relation to the wide range of emotional, relational and behavioural difficulties that can be associated with childhood abuse. Second, is to help those clients who may be susceptible to abusing their own children.

At the beginning of the 1990s controversies about therapeutic interventions with adults abused as children were beginning to emerge that would become socially prominent in the decade to follow. In particular, a publishing industry promoting 'how to' counselling and 'self help' books for incest survivors grew at rapid pace. Reading many of these often superficially persuasive texts I began to feel uneasy that some of the suggested approaches did not appear to be based on any credible form of research or evaluation. A review of the literature confirmed that there was surprisingly little research in relation to effective counselling with adults abused as children.

Recognition of this gap provoked a part-time PhD study (sponsored by the NSPCC) entitled: 'Clients' and therapists' perceptions of the psychotherapeutic process: a study of adults abused as children' (Dale, 1996). In this research I undertook a total of 53 in-depth interviews across England with a sample comprised of adults abused as children who had received counselling, counsellors working with this client group, and counsellors who were themselves abused as children. One major conclusion was that the quality and effectiveness of counselling/ therapy varies considerably. While many people described life-changing/saving benefits, others reported that they had been significantly harmed by their 'therapeutic' experiences (Dale et al., 1998).

The finding in relation to people who had received forms of counselling that were quite inappropriate, and sometimes damaging, stimulated my current commitment to the development of evaluation systems for counselling services. Two separate evaluations of the Counselling Centre have been undertaken, focusing on the periods 1987–97 and 1998–99. Some issues arising from these evaluations will be discussed later in this chapter.

With this background as context, this chapter will focus on four themes:

- The impact and consequences of child abuse in adult life.
- Lessons from the few research and evaluation studies of counselling for adults abused as children.
- Whether 'special' counselling is needed for adults abused as children.
- The need for an evaluation culture to support effective counselling practice.

The impact and consequences of child abuse

Counselling takes place in a poignant atmosphere of remembered histories of cruelty to children that can have a powerful impact on the counsellor. The following verbatim descriptions, taken from the NSPCC East Sussex Counselling Centre Evaluation A in 1997, give some sense of the awful childhood experiences that some people have endured.

I was hit quite frequently and shouted at by both my parents. All this made me feel alone, unwanted, cold emotionally – I grew up too fast. My father would say sorry for hitting me – saying it was the tablets (he was dying which I had to deal with as well). I hated him. I hated home and hated school. (9707)

As a child I was beaten every day for wetting my bed. I was so terrified I used to wake up in the middle of the night to dry my bed by rubbing my head up and down the sheets to dry them with my hair. I was also left on the toilet for hours on end till I went, but I used to wet cardboard and put it down the toilet to fool the nuns that I had been. There was no toilet seat and it was very cold – I used to cry. (9708)

I remember having my head ducked under water several times. I remember having to wash my sick sheets early in the morning, I remember always my foster mother getting me out of my bed, to go to the toilet and having to stay there until I had been, sometimes I would be on the toilet a long time, that's because I kept wetting myself, at night and day time. (9712)

Father – violent outbursts: Hitting – fists, sticks, pokers, kicking and punching, hair pulling, banging head on floor. At age of 2–3 years hung by fingers from doors, with father sitting waiting for me to fall, to hit me if I did. Also stand on mantelpiece while there was an open fire on. Broken bones – arm and nose. Thrown across room. Put across chair, hit with belt, metal file or bamboo stick. Cigarette burns to arms and legs (unsure about who did these). These would/could be daily events, even more than once a day. No set rules really. (9715)

My father made me sit down and write all the swear words I knew: some of the words such as Fanny or Bloody – and the word Bugger that I didn't write – because the word frightened me, were used in a disgusting way. He told me – no taught me, what they meant. I had to write down the meanings but he then showed me what bugger meant. That was the worst thing of all, that was when me ceased to exist, the child was no more. This was the only time I remember him saying yes, well done, but you are forgetting one – bugger. That's when I learnt the meaning of the word. (9732)

My father, once or twice a week, sexual intercourse, anal intercourse, sometimes oral sex. My grandmother on my father's side, she'd put her hand into my knickers, touching my bottom, about 1 a week. Foster father, oral sex, 1 a week. Older boy, oral sex, putting fingers into my vagina, he'd urinate on me, about 6 times. (9702)

I was fondled by my foster dad who at the time was ill with rheumatoid arthritis, he was tied to crutches and had a wheelchair to sit in. My experience was one day he was sitting in his wheelchair and asked me to sit on his lap which I did. He then brought my mouth on to his and was kissing me open-mouth. I kept my lips shut, he then was touching my breasts and my legs up to my vagina which he fondled as well. After a few times he then put my hand to where his penis was. (9712)

I'm uncertain to how many abusers there was. There was at least 10 (of which two of them a husband and wife) brought different men and women in for sex. This happened most weeks. But details to my different abusers I'm unsure. But what I'm sure about I was made to have sexual intercourse, anal intercourse, oral sex, masturbation. (9728)

A major new prevalence study by the NSPCC has indicated levels of child abuse in the United Kingdom. Figures reveal that 7% of children suffer serious physical abuse, 6% serious neglect, 6% serious emotional abuse and 4% serious sexual abuse by a parent or relative (Cawson et al., 2000). Although these figures are lower than many previous estimates, they still extrapolate to large actual numbers of adults who grow up in the sorts of family environments illustrated above.

Counsellors working with adults abused as children listen to people who believe that their difficulties are connected, at least to some extent, with abusive childhoods. Problems are described that vary in severity, intensity and chronicity. It is from accounts and observations of such problems and their impact on people seeking help that counsellors develop their impressions of the consequences of childhood abuse. It is important, however, to note that counselling clients are members of *clinical populations* (i.e. people who experience problems and who have sought help). As such they should not be confused with the *general population* of adults who were abused as children. The general group is wider and, for example, includes those who do not experience problems, and those who experience problems but who do not seek therapeutic help. The point of this distinction is to clarify that not all adults abused as children require or request therapeutic help. Consequently counsellors tend to know less about the characteristics and qualities of people who were abused in childhood who appear to lead satisfying lives without enduring damage from their child-hood experiences.

It is no disrespect to people who were abused as children to recognise that a question arises as to whether childhood abuse *necessarily* causes lasting harm. Sanford (1991) referred to research on concentration camp victims, which showed that it is by no means automatic that lifelong emotional disability follows from severe early trauma. Sanford (1991) and Feinauer (1989) also noted that some people subjected to childhood abuse do lead very fulfilling lives without the need for therapy.

How does this happen? What are the characteristics of people who appear not to suffer long-lasting harm from childhood abuse? Were the circumstances and severity of their abuse different? Do they have particular qualities of resilience? These questions are very important for counsellors. The literature on successful adjustment in life following childhood abuse is limited. If we can learn more about resiliency then a focus to promote this can be incorporated into counselling with the clinical population. Solution-focused approaches can be particularly helpful in this respect with their resilience-oriented focus on learned coping skills and a future orientation. This emphasises the development of resilience factors – including the promotion of cognitions that abuse is not related to innate worthlessness. A focus on resilience also and specifically avoids some counselling activities (such as continual ruminating on memories of abuse and promoting repeated emotional catharsis) which can have harmful conse-quences through reinforcing negative characteristics, attitudes and responses.

Notwithstanding factors relating to resilience in the general population, therapeutic services to help overcome the effects of childhood abuse are greatly needed. In a major review Browne and Finklehor (1986) concluded that approxi-mately 40% of sexually abused children suffer consequences serious enough for them to need therapy in adulthood. Over the past quarter century there has been a mass of research focusing on the enduring adult consequences of child abuse. This research demonstrates that significant lasting problems are most likely for people who experienced chronic multiple abuse, beginning at an early age in the context of a significantly dysfunctional family. While no symptoms or clusters of adult problems are specific to childhood abuse, extensive empiri-cal and clinical material highlights clear categories of difficulties that are likely to be experienced by people who were seriously abused as children. These include psychiatric symptoms (especially depression) and a range of physical, emotional, cognitive, existential, relational, sexual and social problems.

Evaluation of abuse-focused counselling services

Considering the significant numbers of people who seek therapeutic help for the enduring psychological and emotional consequences of child abuse, it is surprising that little systematic evaluation has been undertaken of the range of services and types of therapy that are provided. Exceptions are:

- In Canada, Jehu (1988) reported a detailed analysis of measured outcomes from a cognitive-behavioural treatment programme with 41 female clients. Eighty-four per cent of clients who participated in the evaluation reported that the service had helped them 'a great deal' and 71% reported that they were 'very satisfied' with the help received. Whilst this sets a high standard, it does need to be borne in mind that certain categories of clients who might present particular therapeutic challenges were excluded from the programme.
- In the USA, Armsworth (1989, 1990) explored the self-reports of 30 female incest survivors respectively in relation to various therapies they had received. Armsworth presented the 'dismaying' finding that 46% of clients reported that they had been victimised or exploited by helping professionals.
- Also in the USA, Feinauer (1989) reported that from a sample of 36 users of therapy, 28% and 37% reported that the experience had been 'very' and 'quite' helpful respectively.
- In Holland, Frenken and Van Stolk (1990) explored the experiences of 50 incest survivors (49 female) regarding their therapeutic experiences. Satisfaction rates with the help received were poor and 58% reported that they felt let down by the professionals they had consulted.
- In the UK my own research involved in-depth interviews with 53 clients and therapists (Dale, 1999a). The 40 participants who had received therapy had a total of 130 episodes of therapy. Of these, 37% had helped 'a great deal' and 32% 'to some extent' (a 'some benefit' total of 69%). Thirteen per cent had not helped at all – and 10% had 'made things worse' (a 'no benefit' total of 23%).
- Also in the UK, two evaluations have been undertaken of the service provided by the NSPCC East Sussex Counselling Centre. In Evaluation A (covering the period 1987–96), 84% of service users reported that the counselling had 'some benefit' and in Evaluation B (covering the period 1997–99) the figure was 90%. These evaluations will be discussed in more detail below.

Because of small sample sizes and methodological variations, caution must be exercised in generalising findings from any of the approaches reflected in the above studies with confidence to general counselling practice with adults abused as children. Space precludes further discussion here of each study (see review in Dale, 1999a). However, it is clear that the picture is a very mixed one: some programmes report very high levels of satisfaction (e.g. Jehu in Canada, NSPCC in East Sussex), while other research suggests that poor – and even damaging – counselling outcomes are commonplace.

NSPCC East Sussex Counselling Centre

The Counselling Centre was established in 1987 and has provided free counselling by qualified staff and sessional counsellors for over 450 adults abused as children up to the year 2000. The majority of referrals are received on a contractual basis from local GPs, and others come from psychiatric services, social services and self-referrals. Initially, for several years, counselling was open-ended based around popular abuse-focused models (e.g. Briere, 1989; Courtois, 1988; Dale, 1993; Jehu, 1988). By the mid 1990s the waiting list had reached nine months and this prompted a fundamental review. One outcome was that the structure and ethos of the service became predominantly short-term. This major change in style was a consequence of the waiting list, the expectations within health-commissioned contracts that services will be brief, and also practitioners inclining further towards solution-focused approaches (de Shazer, 1985).

Two evaluations (A and B) of the Counselling Centre have taken place, involving separate groups of service users. Evaluation A took place in 1997 and involved a detailed research questionnaire sent to all past service users (1987–96, N = 270) whose current addresses we were able to confirm with some confidence (N = 133). The number of returned Evaluation A questionnaires was 47. Evaluation A clients received counselling when the service was predominantly open-ended and abuse-focused. Evaluation B took place in 1999 and involved a much briefer service evaluation questionnaire given to all service users between 1997 and 1999 (N = 105) at the conclusion of counselling. Forty-one of these were returned. Evaluation B clients received counselling that was predominantly short-term and goal-focused.

As noted earlier, and illustrated in Table 3.1, in Evaluation A, 84% of service users reported that the counselling had been helpful, and in Evaluation B this figure was 90%.

For counselling service providers it is rewarding via evaluations to receive high ratings of client satisfaction. However, it must be borne in mind that 'satisfied customers' are more likely to complete and return 'in house' evaluation forms (although highly dissatisfied clients can also be highly motivated to respond).

TABLE 3.1   *Has the counselling/therapy you have received at the NSPCC helped you to deal more effectively with the problems that led you to seek counselling/therapy? (N = 43 answered this question) (Evaluation A)*

To what extent has the counselling helped you to deal with the problems for which you sought help? (N = 41 answered this question) (Evaluation B)

	Evaluation A (N = 43)		Evaluation B (N = 41)	
Completely	N/A		3 (7.5%)	61%
A great deal	24 (56%)	84%	22 (53.5%)	
To some extent	12 (28%)		12 (29%)	90%
Uncertain/unsure	2 (4.5%)		1 (2.5%)	
Did not help	4 (9.25%)	11.5%	3 (7.5%)	7.5%
Made things worse	1 (2.25%)		0 (0%)	

Impact of counselling on parenting

Approximately 70% of clients who use the Counselling Centre are already parents. Many of those who are not are likely to become so one day. Problematic relationships with children are often a trigger point for seeking help. Evaluation A enquired into the perceived benefits from counselling in relation to parenting. Just over three-quarters of parents reported that the counselling helped them improve their relationships with their children either very much, or to some degree. The areas of reported improvement are illustrated by the following quotes:

> I used to hit my children as a release of anger. I don't hit, smack or anything else now. I think more before saying something to them. When they have problems I try to help them deal with the problem. I have more skills now. [39-year-old single mother of three children]

> It's OK to hug them, be affectionate, tell them I love them – and not feel strange about it. [35-year-old mother of two]

> I listen to my children and watch for tell-tale signs of unhappiness – because of this I picked up on one of them being bullied at school. We all dealt with it very successfully. [41-year-old mother of four]

> I was afraid to be close to them, I thought I would abuse them ('all abuse victims abuse their children' – media message). I can now love and cuddle my children without fear. [33-year-old mother of two]

> You focus on what your child is doing, feeling and learning and needing rather than how depressed you might be [31-year-old single mother of one]

While childhood abuse experiences can be a contributory factor in parents harming their own children, many adults who were abused as children are very alert to this possibility and take determined steps to be caring parents. The provision of effective counselling prior to an abused person becoming a parent can help prevent difficulties occurring (and children being adversely affected) when they do become parents.

Resolution of problems

In my UK study of 40 people who had completed various therapies relating to their abuse as children (not these two evaluation samples) – not one considered that post therapy they had 'no problems' in their lives that were connected with abuse (Dale, 1999a). 'Major problems' were still experienced by 17% and 'some problems' by 75% – a total continuing problem proportion of 92%. While it is clear that the therapy that some of these people received was poor from both a

TABLE 3.2   *Before you started your counselling with the NSPCC to what*
extent did you have problems in your life that are connected with having been
abused? (N = 43 answered this question) (Evaluation A)

To what extent do you feel that you still have problems in your life that are
connected with having been abused? (N = 46 answered this question)

	Before counselling (N = 43)	After counselling (N = 46)
Major problems	30 (70%)	10 (22%)
Some problems	8 (18.5%)	20 (43.5%)
Hardly any problems	0	11 (24%)
Uncertain	3 (7%)	2 (4%)
No problems	2 (4.5%)	3 (6.5%)

theoretical and practice perspective, it also indicates that therapies that are perceived as having been beneficial do not result in all problems being resolved.

The concept of 'resolution' is itself problematic and begs questions whether counselling aims to remove acquired 'problems' (returning clients to a pre-problem state), or whether counselling promotes adjustment and personal development to ensure maximum learning and growth from adverse experiences. This is a complex debate beyond the scope of this chapter, but one point is significant in this context regarding evaluation methods. The 'medical model' of problem (symptom) removal is far more accessible to 'evidence-based practice' evaluation methods than is an adjustment/growth model. It is important to recognise that being more conducive to positivist evaluation models does not in itself make an approach more effective or clinically valuable.

The NSPCC East Sussex Evaluation A questionnaire examined perceptions of outcomes in relation to problem-resolution, as shown in Table 3.2. The self-reported level of 'major problems' decreased from 70% pre counselling to 22% post counselling. Significantly, the reduction in 'major problems' is reflected in a corresponding increase in the 'some problems' category from 18.5% pre counselling to 43.5% post counselling. The combined 'hardly any' and 'no' problems categories increased from 4.5% pre counselling to 30.5% post counselling.

In the same evaluation (A), while 84% of ex-clients reported that counselling helped them to some extent to deal more effectively with their problems, 30% also reported that the extent of these problems remained unchanged at the end of counselling. One implication of this is that it may be unrealistic to expect that counselling will be able to fully 'resolve' the range of problems experienced by many adults abused as children. This is especially so for the most damaged people, who often have chronic mental health problems, personality disorders and significant substance misuse. Expecting that a therapeutic focus on childhood abuse will result in a miraculous cure for these clients is unrealistic. I would go so far as to suggest that abuse-focused therapy is often contraindicated in these circumstances. On this basis, counsellors need to have realistic expectations as to what changes can be expected from their interventions. I say this not to encourage a pessimistic perspective on change, but to indicate the need to avoid protracted therapies where further change is unlikely – and indeed where change may be specifically inhibited by an extended over-dependent therapeutic relationship.

Length of counselling

It is interesting that the change in structure and orientation of the Counselling Centre to a largely short-term service resulted in little difference in reported outcomes (84% of Evaluation A, and 90% of Evaluation B reported 'some benefit' from the counselling received). Clients receiving the short-term service (usually six or ten sessions with the flexibility to be re-referred for further sessions), were asked via the Evaluation B questionnaire whether they felt sufficient sessions had been provided. Respondents were almost equally divided in their views: 40% felt that not enough sessions had been provided, while 37.5% felt that they had had enough. Most of the people who responded to the invitation in the questionnaire to indicate how many more sessions they would have liked only indicated a need for a very small additional number. It may be that the experience of being rationed (where the client does not have control) is an important factor as well as the actual number of sessions provided.

In managing a counselling service, there is a trade-off between providing the amount of counselling that each client feels is necessary, whilst maintaining a short waiting list as the volume of referrals continues to expand. Given levels of need and demand, in the context of resource constraints and commissioning contracts, it is inescapable that 'free' (to client) counselling has to be rationed. However, this pressure can often be relieved by the Counselling Centre structure that allows re-referral for further 'bursts' of short-term counselling – a model that has proved to be effective and popular. The view of the Counselling Centre is that it is preferable to be able to respond quickly to new clients in crisis (via a short-term service) – than it is to provide extensive long-term counselling for a much smaller group of clients. This is not to say that long-term counselling is not necessary in some circumstances for adults abused as children. However, counsellors in the Counselling Centre who were originally orientated toward long-term therapy have been surprised by the degree of benefit gained by clients when a brief-therapy model has been adopted (Johnson, 1995; Miller et al., 1996).

Is 'special' counselling needed for adults abused as children?

The development of abuse-focused counselling does beg the question whether there are any significant differences in effective counselling of abused clients compared to clients whose problems stem from a range of other negative life experiences. This was one of the research questions I explored in my research (Dale, 1996, 1999a). My conclusions were equivocal: the answer seems to be both 'No' and 'Yes'. 'No' relates to the conclusion that the differences in the process of effective therapy may be much less than has been claimed in much of the 'survivor' literature. Clients who were abused as children require the same respectful and facilitative environment as does the general client population for counselling to be effective.

On the other hand, counselling practice with adults abused as children may involve some particular challenges:

- Resistance to help-seeking based on previous poor experiences of professional contacts.
- Challenges in establishing an effective therapeutic relationship (working alliance) with clients who may have particular tendencies towards *lack of trust* or (equally importantly) *over-trusting* tendencies.
- Clients' inclinations towards inhibition of communication – especially regarding feelings of dissatisfaction with counselling and shameful inner experiencing.
- Uncertainty whether abuse experiences need to be discussed in detail.
- A search for understanding why the abuse occurred and dilemmas about responsibility.
- Existential issues regarding the impact of abuse on the client's sense of identity.
- Questions as to what can feasibly constitute 'resolution' of the effects of abuse.
- Dilemmas regarding current and future relationships with abusers and other family members.
- Fears that the abuse will adversely affect clients' abilities to parent their own children successfully.
- Interpreting the nature of different types of memories of abuse – including the veracity of 'recovered' memories.

In this complex context certain factors seem to be associated with a particular risk of provoking negative therapeutic outcomes. Many clients (especially first time clients) are naïve about counselling. They do not know what to expect, are inhibited in asking questions, and often defer to the 'authority' of the counsellor and comply with his or her suggestions. They remain silent about their inner feelings of misgivings about what is happening or not happening (e.g. lack of progress/feeling worse). Too often, inadequate information is provided by counsellors in relation to the proposed counselling. This absence of appropriate information can be disorientating for clients, and disadvantages their ability to monitor discrepancies between actual and expected experiences.

It is important that counsellors recognise the significant impact of client naïveté and inhibition in communicating confusion, frustration or dissatisfaction. To counter this it is helpful if counsellors facilitate the development of a relationship in which clients are encouraged regularly to give feedback about their experience of counselling. Not only is this helpful for the counsellor as a form of on-going audit of the perceived effectiveness of the counselling, it is also often therapeutic in enabling clients to practise communicating about difficult matters to a significant other.

Another aspect of information that is often lacking or unclear is in relation to termination of counselling. Clients (especially those seeing private-practice counsellors) would often benefit from the provision of clear information and reassurance that they are free to cease counselling at any time – without having to explain and justify the reasons for this. They should not – as I have described in detail elsewhere (Dale, 1999a) – remain dissatisfied and marooned in unproductive (and expensive) counselling for long periods of time without the knowledge or the confidence to 'get out'. This seems to be an experience that adults abused as children may be particularly susceptible to in longer-term counselling: that is, to remain passively silent and compliant whilst feeling increasingly 'stuck' in an unhelpful – or destructive – therapeutic relationship. This is much less likely to occur in the context of counselling that is goal- and outcome-oriented and where a monitoring and feedback mechanism is built into the approach.

Clients need information about the style of counselling that the counsellor offers. And, preferably, information also about alternative approaches so that consent to participate is derived from an informed choice. Many counsellors seem curiously reluctant to give clients information about their approaches. Is this because they believe that this will not be of interest to potential clients, or that it might in some way contaminate the counselling process? Could it be that some counsellors are not clear about their approach and might find it difficult to explain? Counselling needs to be tailored to clients' unique needs and personal styles. To achieve this, clients require information about the range of possible approaches to their problems so that they can be collaboratively involved in constructing the specific nature of their therapy. This reinforces the need for counsellors to facilitate regular feedback from clients to enable the counsellor continually to adjust the therapeutic style.

It follows that clients should not be passive subjects of formulaic applications of counsellors' favoured (or only) therapeutic model. Standards of care, informed consent and evidence-based practice require that popular models of work with abuse 'survivors' should not be adopted without careful consideration being given to the theoretical and outcomes evidence which validates such approaches (Briere, 1997; Courtois, 1997). Certain approaches outlined in high profile books (e.g. Bass and Davis, 1988; Frederickson, 1992), which have strongly influenced many abuse-focused therapists in the past, do not withstand careful theoretical and empirical scrutiny and should no longer be used as a rationale or model for abuse-focused counselling approaches. It is now clear that the potential risks of such approaches are too great to justify their general use. The disastrous effects of the absence of critical scrutiny of the abuse literature as a whole is now apparent from the negative impact of the 'ritualistic abuse', 'recovered memory' and 'multiple personality' therapeutic era of the mid 1980s to mid 1990s. These were fiascos that have seriously harmed untold numbers of clients and damaged the general public reputation of therapy/counselling practice (Dale, 1999b). One consequence of the increasing concern about therapy-induced iatrogenic harm is that urgent attention needs to be given by practitioners and counselling organisations to necessary ethical practices for obtaining appropriate 'informed consent' from clients to participate in counselling (Beahrs and Gutheil, 2001).

Development of an evaluation culture

Current developments towards the establishment of an evaluation culture (e.g. NHS National Service Frameworks and Best Value regimes) provide a significant impetus for the counselling field as a whole to improve the extent and quality of its evaluation activities. Given the potential vulnerability of adults abused as children, it is particularly important to reinforce the need for quality assurance and standards of care for this client group.

The major focus of such counselling to date has been with people who have reported abuse as children within their own families. Such needs will continue to require resources in the future. However, a new group of adults abused as children is currently being identified, many of whom will also require high quality counselling services. These are adults where there is increasing formal acknowledgement that they were abused as children in institutional settings such as residential schools and children's homes. In some countries (e.g. New Zealand, Australia, Canada and Ireland) specific counselling services have been sponsored by government or churches, to help make reparation for such abuse.

Notwithstanding these developments, research has highlighted that many adults abused as children who are experiencing difficulties often do not know how to access appropriate help. The National Commission of Inquiry into the Prevention of Child Abuse (1996) and the NSPCC have stressed the scarcity of appropriate services: 'in large parts of the UK there are no services at all. We have heard of many cases of adults being passed from one agency to another and still finding no help or support ... ' (Harding, 1999: vii).

When people do receive counselling the little research and evaluation that exists suggests that outcomes can vary enormously, from reports of great benefit to accounts of significant harm. That well-intentioned counselling can be counter-productive – and sometimes harmful – is a matter of serious concern. This highlights the importance of evaluation of services, including the challenges for accreditation and registration bodies in auditing the work of private practitioners. Whether the perspective for this should be evidence-based practice or practice-based evidence is currently a matter of debate. This involves technical evaluation issues. The 'medical model' aim of problem/symptom removal is associated with 'harder' measurable ('evidence-based practice') evaluation methods. This contrasts with 'softer' less quantifiable evaluation data ('practice-based evidence') that is more relevant to adjustment/growth counselling models. There are rivalries between these models, but both have value in the necessary drive towards a more prominent evaluation culture in counselling practice. In striving for this it is important to avoid the (methodologically convenient) pitfall of the evaluation tail wagging the counselling dog.

While there are real dangers from potential over-regulation and constriction of counselling practice (for example by deterring the development of potentially effective innovatory approaches), a balance has to be struck to minimise the incidence and effects of practice that is known (or could be reasonably predicted) to present high risks of detrimental outcomes. One factor that could make a major contribution in this respect would be to significantly increase the amount of research-based knowledge required by trainers and practitioners to successfully complete counselling training and accreditation/registration procedures.

This call for more consistent, visible and accountable standards of practice is made in the context of considerable practice experience and evaluation evidence that counselling services for adults who were abused as children are of vital importance. As we have discussed, bad practice with this client group can cause real harm. However, evaluations such as that conducted by NSPCC East Sussex described in this chapter, and by Jehu (1988), alongside detailed accounts from clients (Dale, 1999a), illustrate that good quality counselling can have profound positive outcomes in helping people overcome the negative impact of childhood abuse.

Acknowledgement

I would like to acknowledge the important contributions of my NSPCC colleagues Ron Fellows and Richard Green in the NSPCC counselling evaluation, and for their helpful comments on drafts of this chapter.

References

Armsworth, M. (1989) Therapy of incest survivors: abuse or support? *Child Abuse and Neglect*, 13 (4), 549–62.

Armsworth, M. (1990) A qualitative analysis of adult incest survivors' responses to sexual involvement with therapists. *Child Abuse and Neglect*, 14 (4), 541–54.

Bass, E. and Davis, L. (1988) *The Courage to Heal: A Guide for Women Survivors of Child Sexual Abuse*. New York: Harper and Row.

Beahrs, J.O. and Gutheil, T.G. (2001) Informed consent in psychotherapy. *American Journal of Psychiatry*, 158, 4–10.

Briere, J. (1989) *Therapy for Adults Molested as Children: Beyond Survival*. New York: Springer.

Briere, J. (1997) An integrated approach to treating adults abused as children with specific reference to self-reported recovered memories. In J.D. Read and D.S. Lindsay (eds), *Recollections of Trauma: Scientific Evidence and Clinical Practice*. New York: Plenum Press.

Browne, A. and Finklehor, D. (1986) Impact of child sexual abuse: a review of the research. *Psychological Bulletin*, 99, 66–77.

Cawson, P., Wattam, C., Brooker, S., and Kelly, G. (2000) *Child Maltreatment in the United Kingdom – A Study of the Prevalence of Child Abuse and Neglect*. London: NSPCC.

Courtois, C. (1988) *Healing the Incest Wound: Adult Survivors in Therapy*. New York: Norton.

Courtois, C. (1997) Informed clinical practice and the standard of care: proposed guidelines for the treatment of adults who report delayed memories of childhood trauma. In J.D. Read and D.S. Lindsay (eds), *Recollections of Trauma: Scientific Evidence and Clinical Practice*. New York: Plenum Press.

Dale, P. (1993) *Counselling Adults Who Were Abused as Children*. Rugby: British Association for Counselling.

Dale, P. (1996) Clients' and Therapists' Perceptions of the Psychotherapeutic Process: A Study of Adults Abused as Children. Unpublished PhD thesis, University of Brighton.

Dale, P. (1999a) *Adults Abused as Children: Experiences of Counselling and Psychotherapy*. London: Sage.

Dale, P. (1999b) Multiple personality disorder: a sceptical perspective. In M. Walker and A. Black (eds), *Hidden Selves: An Exploration of Multiple Personality*. Buckingham: Open University Press.

Dale, P., Davies, M., Morrison, T. and Waters, J. (1986) *Dangerous Families: Assessment and Treatment of Child Abuse*. London: Tavistock/Routledge.

Dale, P., Allen, J. and Measor, L. (1998) Counselling adults who were abused as children: clients' perceptions of efficacy, client-counsellor communication and dissatisfaction. *British Journal of Guidance and Counselling*, 26 (2), 141–57.

Dale, P. and Fellows, R. (1999) Independent child protection assessments: incorporating a therapeutic focus from an integrated service context. *Child Abuse Review*, 8, 4–14.

Dale, P., Green, R. and Fellows, R. (2002) *What Really Happened? Child Protection Case Management of Infants with Serious Injuries and Discrepant Parental Explanations*. London: NSPCC.

De Shazer, S. (1985) *Keys to Solution in Brief Therapy*. New York: Norton.

Feinauer, L.L. (1989) Relationship of treatment to adjustment in women sexually abused as children. *American Journal of Family Therapy*, 17 (4), 326–34.

Frederickson, R. (1992) *Repressed Memories: A Journey to Recovery from Sexual Abuse*. New York: Simon and Schuster.

Frenken, J. and Van Stolk, B. (1990) Incest victims: inadequate help by professionals. *Child Abuse and Neglect*, 14 (2), 253–63.

Harding, J. (1999) Foreword. In P. Dale, *Adults Abused as Children: Experiences of Counselling and Psychotherapy*. London: Sage.

Jehu, D. (1988) *Beyond Sexual Abuse: Therapy with Women Who Were Childhood Victims*. Chichester: John Wiley and Sons.

Johnson, L. (1995) *Psychotherapy in the Age of Accountability*. New York: W.W Norton.

Miller, S.D., Hubble, M.A. and Duncan, B.L. (1996) *Handbook of Solution-Focused Brief Therapy*. San Francisco: Jossey–Bass.

National Commission of Inquiry into the Prevention of Child Abuse (1996) London: NSPCC.

Sanford, L. (1991) *Strong at the Broken Places: Overcoming the Trauma of Childhood Abuse*. London: Virago Press.

4
SUICIDE REDUCTION AND PREVENTION
Robert W. Firestone & Lisa Firestone

> Their 'right' is not to commit suicide but to have their need for psychological assistance met so that they may enjoy a satisfying life among us.
>
> C.V. Leonard (1967: 223)

> Most living people who are seen in consultation in relation to their 'being suicidal' have the deepest ambivalences between wanting (needing) to be dead and yearning for possible intervention or rescue.
>
> Edwin Shneidman (1985: 227)

Suicide is a tragic ending to life that in most cases can be averted. In the United States, suicide is a problem of considerable magnitude, occurring at a 67% higher rate than homicide. In 1998, 30,575 individuals committed suicide, which translates to 11.3 of every 100,000 Americans, or one suicide every 17.2 minutes[1] (Murphy, 2000). In the United Kingdom, suicide occurs at the rate of 7.4 per 100,000 individuals (McIntosh, 2000), and in Japan, 1998 statistics show the total number of suicides rising by 35% from 1997, while the suicide rate increased from 16 per 100,000 in the late 1960s to 26 in 1998. The highest suicide rates in the world are recorded in Lithuania – reaching a rate of 79.3 suicides per 100,000 people in the population in 1996. Over the past decade, the suicide rates in Russia, Estonia and the Ukraine, especially among middle-aged men, have also shown a dramatic increase.[2]

Attempts to understand this seemingly perverse anti-life phenomenon are of immense concern to practitioners in the mental health field. It is also important to try to understand the 'contagion' effect of one person committing suicide on other vulnerable individuals. As Colt (1991: 450) noted in *The Enigma of Suicide*, 'To the survivor [a family member or friend of the suicide victim] there is no statistic more chilling than the research that shows survivors to be at eight times higher risk for suicide than the general population'.

Because suicide has a very low base rate, its prediction and prevention are challenging and extremely complex issues; however, they are not impossible goals to achieve. Suicidologists Silverman and Maris (1995: 12) declared that 'prevention holds the promise of providing more good to more people, more effectively and more efficiently', and Richman (1994: 391) has asserted that 'suicide in the elderly [the age group with the highest suicide rate] is treatable and preventable'.

In fact, studies (Fox, 1973; Varah, 1980) have 'demonstrated a drop in the suicide rate over the course of 20 years in the area of the United Kingdom that had Samaritan[3] services' (Wallace, 2001: 245). Despite the fact that studies regarding the effects of crisis hot lines and suicide prevention centres have been plagued by methodological problems and are not conclusive, 'some research has shown that telephone interventions have immediate or proximal effects that may be theoretically linked to decreased suicidality' (Mishara and Daigle, 2001: 162). According to Shneidman (1985), 'Suicide, although enormously complicated, is not totally random and it is amenable to a considerable amount of prediction' (p. 149). 'Prevention rests on assessment; assessment rests on definition' (p. vi).

Shneidman (1985: 203) defined suicide as 'a conscious act of self-induced annihilation, best understood as a multidimensional malaise in a needful [ambivalent] individual who defines an issue for which the suicide is perceived as the best solution'. More recently, Shneidman (1996: 5) expanded his earlier definition, stating that 'its [suicide's] essential nature is *psychological*. That is, each suicidal drama occurs in the *mind* of a unique individual'. The present authors conceptualise suicide as representing the extreme end of a continuum of destructive mental processes that result in the ultimate annihilation of self (R. Firestone, 1997b). It is important to recognise that clients who see suicide as 'the best solution' (as Shneidman put it) are not basing their perceptions on rational thinking, but on irrational, malevolent cognitive processes.

Cautious optimism with respect to prevention also comes from anecdotal accounts from survivors of potentially lethal suicide attempts who later reported feeling ambivalent, up to the last moment, about taking their own life. For example, Heckler (1994) documented intensely conflicted feelings about living or dying in most of the 50 individuals he interviewed after they had made a serious suicide attempt. The fact that most people who commit suicide are probably ambivalent about ending their lives offers an opportunity for interrupting the suicidal process at some point prior to actual completion. In addition, Shneidman (1985: 39) asserted that 'the vast majority (about 80%) of suicides have a recognisable presuicidal phase'.

One of the author's (R. Firestone) conceptual models suggests an incisive approach to understanding the precursors and warning signs of suicide and provides the basis for intervening in and preventing an ultimate act of self-destruction. His approach is based on investigations into negative thought processes that regulate maladaptive, self-destructive and suicidal behaviours (R. Firestone, 1988, 1997a, 1997b). Findings from other studies (Beck et al., 1993; Rose and Abramson, 1992) of cognitive processes known to be associated with presuicidal and suicidal states tend to support this conceptual framework.

The antiself system and self-destructive thought processes

I have a good self, that loves skies, hills, ideas, tasty meals, bright colors. My demon would murder this self by demanding that it be a paragon, and saying it should run away if it is anything less. From 'Letter to a Demon' by Sylvia Plath (in Hughes and McCullough, 1982: 177)

The theoretical approach delineated here focuses on internalised negative thought processes underlying suicidal manifestations and elucidates the ambivalence existing within individuals who are in a suicidal crisis. All people are faced with a basic existential conflict or dilemma. They want to live their lives, act on their wants and priorities, individuate and find personal satisfaction, yet these goals are compromised by a fundamental ambivalence toward self. As a result, people vacillate between motives to actualise and to destroy themselves (R. Firestone, 1997b).

Destructive attitudes toward self are incorporated early in life as part of a defence, first against interpersonal pain and later in relation to existential anxiety. During the developmental sequence, these attitudes and the associated affect of aggression and hostility eventually become part of the *antiself system*, a separate and discrete, alien part of the personality.[4] Under painful circumstances, children tend to depersonalise in an attempt to escape from disturbing emotions of anxiety, frustration and anger. Simultaneously, they internalise or incorporate the attitudes and feelings that are directed toward them. Their negative parental introjects or internalised 'voices' lead to an essential dualism within the personality. These are part of an integral system of negative thoughts and attitudes, antithetical to the self and cynical toward others, that is at the core of maladaptive, self-destructive behaviour. They reach their most dangerous and life-threatening expression in suicidal acting-out behaviour. Suicide can be conceptualised as a triumph of the antiself – the self-destructive aspect of the personality (R. Firestone, 1997b).

Negative reactions against the self are an integral part of each person's psyche, ranging from critical attitudes and mild self-attacks to severe assaults on the self. The latter includes feelings and attitudes that predispose physical injury to the self and eventually the complete obliteration of self. No one reaches maturity completely unharmed by their experiences during the developmental years, and no person is completely exempt from a suicidal process that leaves its mark on every life. In other words, each individual has within him or herself a potential for self-destruction. Clearly, a multitude of external factors will influence the probability that a given individual will attempt or complete suicide. While the majority of people will not go on to commit the ultimate act of self-annihilation, under certain conditions, such as a profound loss, public humiliation, financial setback, developing a psychiatric disorder or disorders, or excessive use of alcohol, a few individuals will do so. It is the authors' contention that understanding the nature of this destructive thought process, which exists to varying degrees in each individual, is fundamental to developing a psychotherapy and a preventative mental health programme relevant to suicide.

Our objectives in this chapter are: to provide a brief overview of empirical studies related to the outcome of current psychotherapeutic interventions used with suicidal patients; to discuss the risk factors for suicide; to describe the development of the FAST, an instrument for assessing suicide intent; to describe a psychodynamic/cognitive paradigm that can facilitate the planning of intervention and prevention strategies; to outline the elements of an effective crisis intervention; to delineate an intervention strategy for brief and long-term treatment of suicidal patients that addresses issues of case management, acceptable standards of care, and malpractice concerns; and to describe prevention measures that may help avert suicidal crises as well as improve the emotional health of many people.

Brief review of the literature

Outcome studies of interventions used with suicidal clients

In *The Enigma of Suicide*, journalist George Colt (1991) posed the question: 'How do clinicians treat suicidal people?'. In *Treating Suicidal Behavior*, Rudd, et al. (2001: 4) attempted to answer a related and even more important question: 'What treatments have been demonstrated effective for suicidality?'. These suicidologists found that surprisingly few interventions specifically used with suicidal clients have been subjected to a critical outcome analysis; however, several treatment modalities showed promise.

Thirteen of the 16 treatments studied demonstrated positive outcomes. Among these were ten short-term interventions that utilised cognitive-behaviour therapy (CBT), 'integrating problem solving as a core intervention' (Rudd, 2000a: 57). This form of CBT was found to be 'effective at reducing suicidal ideation, depression, and hopelessness over periods up to 1 year'. Several longer-term treatments were also reviewed and evaluated by Rudd et al. (2001), including: dialectical behavioural therapy (DBT) (Linehan et al., 1991), which was found to reduce 'subsequent attempts, hospital days, and improve treatment compliance over a year follow-up period' (Rudd et al., 2001: 11) and 'a more *intensive long-term* follow-up care cutting across multiple therapeutic approaches, rather than a specific therapy model' (Rudd et al., 2001: 10) reported by Allard et al. (1992). Another study, applying a problem-solving intervention to 264 young adult outpatients also demonstrated 'reductions ... in suicidal ideation and behavior' (Rudd et al., 1996: 179).

In concluding this meta-analysis of suicide interventions, Rudd (2000a) recommended longer-term treatments for chronically suicidal patients that focus on specific 'skill deficits, such as emotion regulation, poor distress tolerance (i.e., impulsivity), anger management, and interpersonal assertiveness, as well as other enduring problems such as interpersonal relationships and self-image disturbance (i.e., personality disorders)'. He also suggested that 'high-risk suicidal patients can be safely and effectively treated on an outpatient basis if acute hospitalization is available and accessible' (p. 57).

Other treatment approaches

Despite the fact that few studies have been conducted to evaluate the effectiveness of interventions used with suicidal clients, a number of therapeutic approaches based on diverse theoretical positions have been described in the literature. Indeed, Jacobs (1989: 329) has emphasised that 'because suicide cuts across the whole spectrum of psychiatric illness, a therapist should be familiar with several theories as part of developing a therapeutic strategy'. These approaches include: psychological (Shneidman, 1999); psychodynamic (Maltsberger, 1999); biological/evolutionary/neurobiological (Arana and Hyman, 1989; Bunney and Fawcett, 1965; Mann and Arango, 1999); existential and biomedical (Maris, 1989); empathic methods, integrating psychodynamic, existential and self psychology (Jacobs, 1989); cognitive-behavioural therapy (Beck, 1996; Beck et al., 1979; Beck et al., 1993; Beck et al., 1985; Ellis and Newman, 1996); dialectic behavioural therapy (Linehan, 1999); voice therapy (Firestone, 1997b); and family therapy (Richman, 1986).

Risk assessment

Summary of known risk factors for suicide

In crisis intervention as well as long-term treatment, therapists should first assess for the presence of psychiatric, psychological and social risk factors. There are numerous signs that can be used to evaluate[5] the level of risk in an individual client at a specific point in time. Therapists should determine if the client has a history of a psychiatric disorder, including major depression, bipolar disorder, alcohol dependence, drug addiction, schizophrenia, organic psychosis, borderline or compulsive personality disorder, a history of suicide or suicidal behaviour in the family, and a history of abuse.[6]

Recent research by Read et al. (2001) has demonstrated that child sexual abuse and neglect are important factors contributing to later suicidality. Their study found sexual abuse (which had taken place many years previously) was a better predictor of current suicidality than was depression. According to Read et al. (2001: 371), 'statistically speaking, it seems to be even more important to know whether clients have suffered child sexual abuse than whether they are depressed'.[7] They also noted that many researchers and clinicians recommend that the 'taking of abuse histories should be a routine part of assessment processes so as to ensure accurate formulation and appropriate treatment planning' (p. 370). However, 'Evidence that this still may not be the case' comes from a number of countries, including the United States, the United Kingdom and New Zealand. In addition, 'Some clinicians seem particularly unlikely to ask two groups with particularly high suicide rates: men and clients diagnosed as schizophrenic' (p. 370).

Clinicians should ask questions regarding current stressors: recent losses and how they relate to past losses (such as loss of a parent in childhood), loss of job, loss of an important relationship, lack of a social support system, and health problems. Suicide intent can be assessed by asking the client about suicidal ideation, plans, methods under consideration, availability of means, precautions against discovery, and past suicide attempts (see below, Conducting the Clinical Interview).

Rudd (2000b) has suggested that therapists focus on specific symptoms of 'psychache' in the client which have been described by Shneidman (1993), 'especially such distressing feelings as guilt, shame, fear, anger, thwarted ambition, unrequited love, hopelessness, helplessness, and loneliness' (Shneidman, 1993: 152). It is also important to enquire about the nature of the client's past suicidal thinking and self-destructive behaviours and the frequency and intensity of current suicidal ideation. Enquiries that elicit the client's attitudes of perfectionism are also important, because according to Hewitt (1994: 455), 'perfectionism [is] involved in suicide ideation even when other psychological factors, such as depression and hopelessness are considered' (see Blatt, 1995).

In other writing (R. Firestone, 1997a, 1997b; Firestone and Catlett, 1999), the authors have described a syndrome of specific personality traits and behaviour patterns that are particularly evident in suicidal individuals. The primary characteristics of this syndrome of 'inwardness'[8] are (a) a tendency toward isolation, (b) use of addictive substances or routines, (c) marked feelings of self-hatred and cynical attitudes toward others, (d) a lack of direction in life leading to a sense of hopelessness and despair, and (e) progressive denial of priorities and withdrawal from favoured activities and relationships.[9] It is significant that the traits and habit patterns of individuals who lead an inward, self-protective lifestyle correspond directly to a number of the precursors of suicide delineated by suicidologists including David Shaffer and Edwin Shneidman (see MacNeil–Lehrer, 1987). They indicated that when an individual moves toward increased isolation and becomes exceptionally quiet and withdrawn, one should be concerned. Signs of depression and hopelessness such as losing interest in special goals, dropping out of favoured activities, or retreating from an important relationship for no apparent reason are also a cause for concern. If the person increasingly relies on substances, showing signs of excessive drinking or drug usage, is preoccupied with fantasy, self-depreciating thoughts, or has a victimised orientation, he or she may be at risk for suicide (R. Firestone, 1997b).

Assessment instruments

After the clinician has assessed for risk factors, conducted a mental status examination, reflected on his or her clinical impressions of the client, especially any personal reactions of dislike or hostility and collected information regarding history and lethality of past attempts from family members and physicians, he or she should try to determine the degree of 'resolved plans and preparation', which includes availability of means, a sense of courage and competence to make an attempt (Joiner et al., 1999), and whether the client has a history of two or more suicide attempts, by asking direct questions regarding these issues. The clinician then attempts to reach a decision in considering whether or not the client is at risk for suicide. If uncertain about the possibility of any risk, the therapist should administer an objective assessment instrument or battery of instruments.

Research studies showing correlations between suicide and suicidal ideation (Bedrosian and Beck, 1979; Bonner and Rich, 1987; Linehan, 1981; Rich et al., 1986; Shafii et al., 1985) led to the development of self-report instruments to

Levels of increasing suicidal intention	Content of voice statements
Thoughts that lead to low self-esteem or inwardness (self-defeating thoughts):	
1. Self-depreciating thoughts of everyday life	*You're incompetent, stupid. You're not very attractive. You're going to make a fool of yourself.*
2. Thoughts rationalizing self-denial; thoughts discouraging the person from engaging in pleasurable activities	*You're too young/old and inexperienced to apply for this job. You're too shy to make any new friends, or Why go on this trip? It'll be such a hassle. You'll save money by staying home.*
3. Cynical attitudes towards others, leading to alienation and distancing	*Why go out with her/him? She's cold, unreliable; she'll reject you. She wouldn't go out with you anyway. You can't trust men/women.*
4. Thoughts influencing isolation; rationalizations for time alone, but using time to become more negative towards oneself	*Just be by yourself. You're miserable company anyway; who'd want to be with you? Just stay in the background, out of view.*
5. Self-contempt; vicious self-abusive thoughts and accusations (accompanied by intense angry affect)	*You idiot! You bitch! You creep! You stupid shit! You don't deserve anything; you're worthless.*
Thoughts that support the cycle of addiction (addictions):	
6. Thoughts urging use of substances or food followed by self-criticisms (weakens inhibitions against self-destructive actions, while increasing guilt and self-recrimination following acting out)	*It's okay to do drugs, you'll be more relaxed. Go ahead and have a drink, you deserve it. (Later) You weak-willed jerk! You're nothing but a drugged-out drunken freak.*
Thoughts that lead to suicide (self-annihilating thoughts):	
7. Thoughts contributing to a sense of hopelessness, urging withdrawal or removal of oneself completely from the lives of people closest	*See how bad you make your family/friends feel. They'd be better off without you. It's the only decent thing to do – just stay away and stop bothering them.*
8. Thoughts influencing a person to give up priorities and favored activities (points of identity)	*What's the use? Your work doesn't matter any more. Why bother even trying? Nothing matters anyway.*
9. Injunctions to inflict self-harm at an action level; intense rage against self	*Why don't you just drive across the center divider? Just shove your hand under that power saw!*
10. Thoughts planning details of suicide (calm, rational, often obsessive, indicating complete loss of feeling for the self)	*You have to get hold of some pills, then go to a hotel, etc.*
11. Injunctions to carry out suicide plans; thoughts baiting the person to commit suicide (extreme thought constriction)	*You've thought about this long enough. Just get it over with. It's the only way out!*

FIGURE 4.1   *Continuum of negative thought patterns*

assess aspects of the suicidal client's belief system and thinking. Beck developed several scales relevant to suicide: the Beck Depression Inventory (Beck, 1978a), the Beck Suicide Inventory (Beck, 1991), and the Beck Hopelessness Scale (Beck, 1978b). A follow-up study (of 5–10 years) by Beck et al. (1985) of 207 patients hospitalised for suicidal ideation showed that hopelessness was more important than depression as a risk factor for suicide. (Neither Beck's nor Firestone's suicide scale had been developed at the time of this study.) Pfeffer et al. (1980) developed a battery of scales that have been useful in studying suicidal behaviour in children. These scales are used in semi-structured interviews with the child and the family. Reynolds (1985) developed the Suicide Ideation Questionnaire in two forms to predict self-destructive trends: the SIQ for senior high school students and the SIQ-JR for junior high school students.

Development of the Firestone Assessment of Self-Destructive Thoughts

Recently, the Firestone Assessment of Self-Destructive Thoughts (FAST) (R. Firestone and L. Firestone, 1996) was added to the repertoire of instruments for assessing suicide. The FAST was derived from 20 years of investigations into destructive thoughts and attitudes that restrict or impair an individual's psychological development. The authors conjectured that it was logical to use these negative thought patterns, gathered from participants in the investigations, to predict increasingly aggressive cognition and affect toward self that are closely related to self-destructive behaviour and actual suicide (R. Firestone, 1986, 1988, 1997b).

The FAST is a self-report questionnaire consisting of 84 items drawn from 11 levels of progressively self-destructive thoughts. Clients endorse the frequency with which they experience these thoughts on a 5-point, Likert-type scale from 'Never' to 'Most of the time.' The scale includes items drawn from each level of the 'Continuum of Negative Thought Patterns' (see Figure 4.1 above). The scale is used to assess a client's suicide potential and to identify other forms of self-destructive behaviour he or she may be engaging in. It allows the clinician to target his or her interventions to areas where the client is experiencing the greatest degree of distress. Studies investigating the reliability and validity of the FAST demonstrated that it discriminated suicide attempters from non-attempters more accurately than a number of other scales used in clinical practice (R. Firestone, 1997a; R. Firestone and L. Firestone, 1998).[10] The FAST has also been translated into Urdu and found to discriminate between suicide attempters and non-attempters in a sample population in Pakistan (Farooqi and Hussain, 2000). Additional cross-cultural comparison studies are being planned.

The FAST was developed based on the following hypotheses regarding the relationship between destructive thought processes and self-destructive behaviour and suicide:

(a) A conflict exists within each individual between life-affirming propensities to actively pursue goals in the real world, and self-denying, self-protective, and self-destructive tendencies that are related to seeking gratification primarily through fantasy processes; (b) thoughts antithetical to the self vary along a continuum of intensity from mild self-reproach to strong self-attack and actual suicidal thoughts; (c) self-destructive behaviour exists on a continuum from self-denial and self-limitation to isolation, drug abuse, and other self-defeating behaviors, culminating in actual bodily harm; and (d) both processes, behavioral and cognitive, parallel each other, and suicide represents the acting out of the extreme end of the continuum. (R. Firestone, 1997b: 221)

Results from investigating the reliability as well as the construct and criterion validity of the FAST tended to validate these hypotheses, indicating that an individual's internalised voices are directly related to self-destructive behaviour in general and suicide in particular.

A number of writers have noted that self-destructive behaviours are interrelated, including Durkheim (1897/1951), Menninger (1938), Farberow (1980) and Shneidman (1966). In *The Many Faces of Suicide*, Farberow (1980) delineated a wide range of self-destructive behaviours which:

by their very familiarity and frequency of occurrence ... must merge into the normal, acceptable end of the continuum of behavior. On the other hand, if they can be so self-destructive or self-injurious, they must merge into the pathological end of the continuum represented by overt suicidal activity. (1980: 2)

'In this sense, we can say that all people have the potential for suicide; it is only the individual style and strength of the movement toward self-destruction that varies from one individual to the next' (Firestone, 2000: 68).

The FAST identifies the level on the continuum at which the client is experiencing the highest frequency (intensity) of self-destructive thoughts. Using this information, clinicians can direct their interventions toward the area where clients are experiencing psychological pain, thereby potentially averting the acting out of the corresponding self-destructive behaviour. In addition, scores on the FAST identify less extreme types of self-destructive thoughts so that they can be addressed by the clinician before they lead to or precipitate a suicidal crisis. The additional knowledge gained through accessing and identifying the partially unconscious thought processes driving a suicidal individual toward death can well be used to set into motion potentially life-saving interventions.

In assessing suicide risk, it is important for clinicians to recognise that any combination of thoughts and behaviours listed in Figure 4.1 and on the FAST can eventually culminate in serious suicidal action. Most particularly, thoughts promoting isolation, ideation about removing oneself from people's lives, beliefs that one has a destructive effect on others, voices urging one to give up favourite activities, malevolent, angry self-attacks and, of course, voices urging self-injury or actual suicide are all indications of high suicide risk.

A conceptual model for treating the suicidal client

> Suicide is a human malaise tied to what is 'on the mind,' including one's view
> of the value of life at that moment. (Edwin Shneidman, 1989: 9)

Psychodynamics

What therapists need, in addition to a sound risk assessment strategy, is a conceptual model that can further their understanding of the psychodynamics
involved in the suicidal process and provide a sound basis for treatment. In considering such a model, there appears to be a clear-cut relationship between
suicide, psychological pain and hopelessness. Depression and self-destructive,
suicidal behaviour, however, are always multidetermined; other factors, such as
biological and existential issues, must be considered in determining their aetiology. In the authors' investigations, the focus has been primarily on the
psychodynamic issues involved in suicide (R. Firestone and L. Firestone, 1998).

As noted, findings from studies related to the construction of the FAST
demonstrated a correlation between internalised voices or destructive thought
processes and self-destructive behaviour. Unconscious or partly conscious
aspects of this negative thought process can be brought into conscious awareness and identified through voice therapy procedures. Data obtained from
investigations that utilised these procedures led to the following hypotheses
regarding the aetiology of these internalised voices. The primary sources of
negative thought processes and their development within the personality are
related to: (a) parents' negative state of mind toward the child, age-inappropri-
ate expectations of children and projection of negative parental traits onto the
child; (b) the child's imitation of one or both parents' maladaptive defences;
and (c) the internalisation and incorporation of parental attitudes of covert and
overt aggression toward the child. As the degree of trauma experienced in childhood increases, the level of intensity of voice attacks parallels this progression,
and there are increasingly angry, vicious attacks on the self. These destructive
thoughts are manifested in an individual's retreat into inwardness, feelings of
extreme self-hate, and eventually impulses toward self-destructive action.

Destructive thought processes in depression
and suicidal states

> Every single instance of suicide is an action by the dictator or emperor of
> your mind. But in every case of suicide, the person is getting bad advice from
> a part of that mind, the inner chamber of councilors, who are temporarily in
> a panicked state and in no position to serve the person's best long-term inter-
> ests. (Edwin Shneidman, 1996: 165)

Cognitive-behavioural therapists, psychodynamic theorists and others have written extensively about irrational or dysfunctional beliefs (Arieti and Bemporad,
1980; Ellis, 1973), automatic thoughts (Beck et al., 1979), and specific cognitive
styles (Abramson et al., 1989; Hamilton and Abramson, 1983) in depression and

suicide and have discussed the aetiology of these inimical thought processes (Richman, 1986; Rosenbaum and Richman, 1970). More recently, conceptual models have been proposed, based on a review of relevant research, demonstrating the role that cognition plays in mediating between early life experience, psychopathology, physical illness, environmental stress, and interpersonal problems on the one hand, and suicidal behaviour on the other (Orbach, 1999; Orbach, et al., 1998; Yang and Clum, 2000).

A number of other clinicians have identified the origins of hostile cognitions and suicidal ideation in faulty parenting practices. Describing the influence of early life experience in the formation of negative thought processes, Maltsberger (1986) found that the suicidal patients he treated had parents who were unusually critical or hostile. He conjectured that what once was experienced as criticism from outside had become criticism from inside in the form of an aggressive, critical 'superego', which frequently took on 'ogre-like' proportions. Introjection of parental attitudes had resulted in a severe and markedly sadistic superego: 'The critical activities of the superego [are] experienced subjectively like an interior demon, revealing its origins in the parents from which it sprang' (p. 13). Commenting on the conceptual models described above, Ellis (2001: 136) asserted that 'it is reasonable to predict from this model that the effects of adverse life experiences can be ameliorated if cognitive factors can be modified'.

In the authors' view, the suicidal client has reached a stage where the balance shifts in such a way that the alien point of view represented by internalised voices actually becomes the client's own point of view. In other words, the depressed or hopeless client adopts the prohibitions, constrictions and directives of the voice process – as his or her own. For whatever reason, because of current stressors or losses, the client is now more *against* him or herself than *for* him or herself. He or she wholeheartedly believes the negative, hostile statements of the voice about him or herself and about other people. Consequently, to a great extent, the person no longer has contact with his or her real self and feels hopelessly estranged from others as well.

At this point, the client is at high risk for suicide. By now, his or her way of thinking is severely constricted, that is, almost completely 'possessed' by the voice process, and he or she finds the alternatives narrowed down to the two options described by Shneidman (1985: 140), that is, that of 'either having some magical resolution or being dead'. In describing *egotic* suicides, Shneidman stated:

> Such deaths can be seen as egocide or ego destruction; they are annihilations of the 'self', of the personality, of the ego. At the time it happens, the individual is primarily 'self-contained' and responds to the 'voices' (not in the sense of hallucinatory voices) within him. (1985: 25)

Heckler (1994) has depicted this stage in the progression toward ending one's life as the 'suicidal trance':

> At this point in the trance, the inner pull toward suicide dramatically intensifies. Often it comes in the form of a voice. In fact, mention of a voice is so common that

I've learned to inquire directly about this during interviews. This voice grows in volume with the stress of the suicidal ordeal. It demands increasingly to be heard above everything else, and it begins to occupy a greater part of the person's psyche until it smothers more reasonable voices altogether. Often people experience this voice as relentlessly driving them toward self-destruction. (1994: 74)

Crisis intervention

The immediate antidote for suicide lies in reduction of perturbation ... Reduce the person's anguish, tension, and pain and his level of lethality will concomitantly come down. (Edwin Shneidman, 1993: 153)

Prior to committing suicide, people usually indicate to one or more persons, in more or less overt ways, their intention to die. In crisis intervention, an understanding of the conceptual model described above can be valuable in ameliorating perturbation and lethality during the actual crisis and is conducive to quickly establishing the therapeutic relationship. The agitation and angry affect toward themselves experienced by suicidal individuals are directly associated with the voice attacks typical of the 'suicidal trance'. Thus, the therapist or crisis hotline worker who has a knowledge of internalized voices has tremendous leverage in establishing the rapport necessary to continue the dialogue and possibly save the caller's or the client's life.

The goal in crisis intervention is, obviously, a simple one – that is, as Leenaars (1994) put it, 'to keep the person alive' (1994: 46). Leenaars described a model of crisis intervention that included (a) establishing rapport, (b) exploring, (c) focusing and (d) developing options and a plan of action.

Clinicians or crisis workers need to establish rapport quickly to reduce the level of lethality (the probability of the person's killing him or herself). An empathic, non-evaluative and matter-of-fact tone is necessary; sometimes a more active or directive intervention is helpful. To elicit the negative thoughts that the caller or client may be experiencing, one might ask, 'What are the things you are telling yourself?' 'What kinds of thoughts are you having about yourself?' 'What are you telling yourself about that event (loss, rejection, public humiliation)?'

Secondly, the therapist can help the caller or client redefine the problem that he or she plans to solve by committing suicide with a further exploration of his or her thoughts, feelings and conceptualisation of the problem. Leenaars (1994) has pointed out that if therapists passively accept the patient's perspective – that is – 'I can't live with this' – they are 'tacitly colluding with the person's decision to die, and the patient cannot survive' (1994: 50). Clearly, naïve reassurances or judgemental statements about the patient's self-destructive thinking and behaviour should be avoided.

Thirdly, therapists can help patients who may be too anxious to concentrate on one topic for any length of time to focus their attention on reality considerations in their lives with questions such as 'What were you hoping to accomplish by calling?' or 'What would be most helpful to you right now?' These questions also help communicate the therapist's empathy and concern.

Last, therapists can help the caller or client begin to develop alternative options to suicide and plan constructive actions. The primary goal at this point is to assist clients in solving what to them seem to be insurmountable problems. Leenaars emphasised that 'the person wants prompt relief. To save the person's life, the therapist has to do something!' (1994: 52). Relief from intense perturbation comes when the patient can see alternatives for action other than suicide. Shneidman (1981) has described a crisis technique that involves listing options (often over the patient's objections) other than suicide and ranking them in order of the patient's preference. (See example in Leenaars, 1994: 54.) Therapists should provide alternatives to taking suicidal action that would put some time between the impulse and the behaviour. Enquiries such as 'Are you willing to wait 24 hours before taking action?', 'Can you commit to calling me before taking action if the suicidal impulse feels compelling?' can help accomplish this goal. Therapists should also take steps to remove the means for committing suicide from the client's immediate surroundings.

One of the most important considerations in dealing with a person in crisis is recognising the role that guilt plays in the suicidal process. Guilt reactions are regulated by the voice process, and the more crisis workers understand the various manifestations of guilt mediated by the voice the better equipped they will be to help people in a suicidal state. Given the ambivalence between the desire to live and the impulse to die that exists in the suicidal individual until the last moment of life, it is crucial to avoid any response that might play on the guilt of the patient. Such communication (evaluative or judgemental) strengthens the voice process and tends to push the patient closer to suicidal action. Therapists may inadvertently precipitate these guilt reactions in a misguided effort to restrict a patient's acting out of self-destructive behaviour (Firestone, 1997b).

Overall, therapists need to support any investment in life regardless of the form it may take for that particular moment. It is the sincere and personal expression of caring, without judgement, that is most likely to reach a person at risk. It is important to remember, however, that there are no foolproof procedures or responses to a person in a suicidal crisis. A great deal depends on the caseworker's or therapist's personality and authentic concern for the client's well-being.

Long-term treatment strategies

Conducting the clinical interview

Using the information about major risk factors in suicide discussed above, clinicians next attempt to estimate the level of suicidality of the client. It has been found that when clients are asked to rate how suicidal they are, and clinicians are asked to perform the same assessment, clients consistently rate themselves as more suicidal than do their therapists. Eddins and Jobes (1994: 172) found that 'clinicians consistently underrated the perturbation dimension in comparison to their patients' self-ratings'. There may be several reasons why this is so.

1 Clinicians experience considerable anxiety when faced with a life-or-death situation, which tends to interfere with their clinical judgement.
2 Clients often evoke 'countertransference hate' in therapists who pick up their clients' malevolent thoughts toward themselves. Experiencing feelings of dislike, aggression, discomfort and even malice toward a client should alert the therapist that the client may be at risk for suicide.
3 The level of despair and hopelessness the client is experiencing makes it difficult for the clinician to fully empathize with him or her. On the one hand, the therapist may never have experienced this level of psychological pain and despair, while on the other hand, the client's perturbation and despair may precipitate repressed pain in a therapist who has experienced episodes of depression and despair.
4 A taboo still exists in society against communicating about suicide, which may limit the therapist's ability to ask directly about suicide and hinder the client's ability to fully disclose his or her suicidal ideation.

One excellent resource, *The Practical Art of Suicide Assessment* (Shea, 1999), can be useful in expanding clinicians' knowledge of how best to conduct the clinical interview and establish rapport. Shea outlined ways of phrasing questions that would 'help ensure that the large database regarding suicidal ideation is comprehensively covered (e.g., errors of omission are decreased)' and that would 'increase the validity of the information elicited from the patient' (1999: 150). Shea's Chronological Assessment of Suicide Events (CASE Approach) simplifies the enormous task of dealing with a large amount of information by dividing the database into smaller areas for questioning. The goal is to 'create an atmosphere that enhances the likelihood that the client will want to share suicidal planning' (p. 145).

First, the clinician tries to uncover the full extent of the client's concrete planning for suicide. If the client has made a recent suicide attempt, efforts should be made to enter 'the client's world at the time of the suicide attempt and ... [understand] how the client feels about the fact that he or she did not die' (p. 154). Next, the clinician attempts to 'elicit the types of suicidal thoughts and actions that the patient has had during the previous two months' (p. 162). In gathering information about past suicide attempts (an area where Shea claims therapists spend too much time), clinicians are advised to limit questions to only those that 'could potentially change the decision on the safe disposition of a patient' (p. 177). Enquiries about events immediately preceding the suicidal crisis and their impact on the client should focus on trying to determine the strength of the client's current suicidal intent, and might include questions such as: 'What would you do later tonight or tomorrow if you begin to have suicidal thoughts again?' (p. 180).

Read et al. (2001: 371) recommended that clinicians attempt to develop a 'shared understanding of the cause of feeling suicidal' with the client and to discuss 'ways to address those causes [which] may be, for some clients, a prerequisite for a therapeutic relationship'. These researchers called attention to findings from a survey of users of mental health services conducted by Lothian (1998) which showed '67% had been abused but that only 20% had been asked about abuse during their assessment ... Perhaps, then, it is important to ask, "Why do you think you are feeling so bad that you want to kill yourself?"' (1998: 371). Read et al. (2001: 371) concluded:

> Knowing that a client was abused as a child may sometimes also enhance the effectiveness of the longer term treatment of suicidal clients through (a) the improved therapeutic relationship that can result from a shared understanding of the cause of feeling suicidal and (b) the instillation of hope that those issues can be addressed.

Psychotherapeutic interventions

Suicidal individuals are a heterogeneous group in most respects and can benefit from a variety of treatments. It is important that therapists develop a treatment plan that is consistent with their personal values, beliefs and theoretical approach. For clinicians planning interventions from a family therapy perspective, Joseph Richman's (1986) *Family Therapy for Suicidal People* is recommended; for cognitive therapists, Aaron Beck's (Beck et al., 1979) *Cognitive Therapy of Depression* (especially the chapter on 'Specific Techniques for the Suicidal Patient'), Ellis and Newman's (1996) *Choosing to Live*, and Linehan's (1993) dialectic behaviour therapy (described in *Cognitive-Behavioral Treatment of Borderline Personality Disorder*); for practitioners with a psychodynamic perspective, Maltsberger's (1986) *Suicide Risk*; and for voice therapy, the first author's *Suicide and the Inner Voice* (R. Firestone, 1997b) are recommended.

The first author (R. Firestone) has developed a therapeutic methodology that brings introjected, hostile thoughts, with the accompanying negative affect, to consciousness, rendering them accessible for treatment. Voice therapy is a cognitive/affective/behavioural methodology that is used to identify the negative cognitions driving suicidal actions, which in turn helps clients gain a measure of control over all aspects of their self-destructive or suicidal tendencies. Clients become cognisant that the way they negatively perceive or distort stressful events, not the events themselves, is the principal cause of their depression, dysphoria, perturbation and hopelessness. They are able to generalise the understanding they develop in voice therapy sessions to their everyday lives.

The techniques of voice therapy consist of three components:

1   Eliciting and identifying negative thought patterns and releasing the associated affect, a process that makes the negative thoughts more accessible and susceptible to control. Clients learn to verbalise their self-critical, self-destructive thoughts in the second person as though another person were addressing them, that is, in the form of statements toward themselves rather than as statements about themselves; for example, 'You're worthless. You don't matter to anybody,' rather than 'I feel like I'm a worthless person. I really don't matter to anybody.' Expressing internalised voices in this format facilitates the process of separating the suicidal client's own point of view from alien, hostile thought patterns assimilated during childhood.
2   Discussing insights and reactions to verbalising the voice. In this step, clients attempt to understand the relationship between their voice attacks and their

self-destructive behaviour patterns and often attain insight into the sources of their destructive thinking.

3 Counteracting self-destructive behaviours regulated by the voice through the collaborative planning and application of appropriate corrective experiences. Corrective suggestions for behavioural change are directed toward reducing self-defeating, self-destructive behaviours and increasing behaviours that correspond to a client's interests, goals and priorities.

The identification of the specific content of negative thinking and suicidal ideation and the release of associated feeling provides suicidal clients with tools to counter serious injunctions to injure themselves. Uncovering elements of negative thinking that have previously existed only on an unconscious level can interfere with further self-destructive acting out. This awareness is vital for clients who act out self-destructive behaviour with little or no insight; it provides them with a sense of mastery over behaviours they previously perceived as being beyond their control. This understanding is particularly valuable for suicidal clients who are subject to panic attacks and impulsivity, that is, those clients who studies have shown are the most likely to commit suicide.

Voice therapy techniques are also fundamental to identifying and supporting the special wants, priorities and interests of clients that give meaning to their lives. These unique predilections are factors that keep the client's spirit alive; thus understanding these factors can help in crisis intervention as well as in long-term treatment. An understanding of voice therapy theory, the self and antiself systems, focuses the therapist's attention on specific needs in the client that were being frustrated and that may have precipitated the suicidal crisis.

Clinicians treating suicidal individuals must help them understand that abuse of oneself reflects anger turned inward and is never an acceptable alternative. They need to learn that it is not appropriate to attack themselves even when the self-criticism has some basis in reality. In our work, we attempt to show patients that it is maladaptive to punish or hate themselves for self-destructive actions or for possessing negative traits or personal limitations. In addition, learning to deal with anger is a central issue in the treatment of suicidal patients because of their strong propensity to turn their aggression against themselves.

An understanding of voice therapy theory is more important than the specific techniques used in the treatment of high-risk clients. In voice therapy, an important factor in outcome has been found to lie in the personality of the therapist and his or her degree of maturity and capacity for feeling. Therapists need to have a strong conviction that if individuals address the issues involved in their self-destructive thinking and show courage in accepting corrective suggestions, they can alter patterns of self-destructive and suicidal behaviour.

Acceptable standards of care in managing the suicidal client

Nowhere in the range of professional activities of the clinician is he or she under more intense and significant stress than when treating a potentially suicidal patient. The stress and anxiety that this clinical situation provokes in the therapist is a two-edged sword, however. It can mobilize the clinician to greater clinical alertness and therapeutic vigilance. Thus, lives can be saved. (Bongar, 1998; citing Kahn, 1982)

Although it is clear that a client's suicide is not always preventable, there are certain principles that define an acceptable standard of care for high-risk clients, both legally and ethically. According to Berman and Cohen-Sandler (1982), it is the duty of a clinician or institution to prevent suicide 'through the use of reasonable care and skill. "Reasonable" is considered by [US] law to be "the average standard of the profession" – "the degree of learning, skill, and experience which ordinarily is possessed by others of the same profession"' (American Jurisprudence, 1981).

Because past behaviour is a good predictor of future behaviour, it is important that clinicians make a concerted effort, with the client's permission, to locate past psychiatric and psychotherapy records and also to obtain information on current medical status. They should carefully document in their progress notes the client's diagnosis, the specifics regarding all treatment plans, actions taken, reasons for their decisions, and their effects on the patient's responses. The case records should also include a formal informed consent for treatment, assessment of competence and explanation regarding the limitations of confidentiality conveyed to the client at the onset of treatment.

Consultation is essential in treating suicidal individuals. Bongar (1991) has emphasised that 'Psychologists should routinely obtain consultation and/or supervision (or make referrals) on all cases where suicide risk is determined to be even moderate, and after a patient suicide or serious suicide attempt' (1991: 203). Therapists should understand the therapeutic use and side effects of drugs in current use for psychiatric conditions (schizophrenia, alcoholism, depression, bipolar disorders). If medication could be helpful or if the client has a condition of a known medical nature, psychotherapists should make a referral to a psychiatrist.

Clinicians should also warn the client's family, friends, or persons who are in daily contact with the client, regarding his or her potential for suicide, and enlist their involvement in management and treatment, unless such involvement is clinically contraindicated due to toxic family interactions. Read et al. (2001: 371) stressed the importance of ascertaining whether the client has been abused by family members when considering family involvement. They argued that 'Not all child abuse takes place within families, but knowing the client's abuse history enables the psychologist (in consultation with the client) to assess whether and, if so, how to involve family members'.

If the clinician determines that the client is in imminent danger, he or she should evaluate whether the client can be maintained in intensive outpatient treatment or requires hospitalisation. The client's permission regarding hospitalisation should be sought through collaborative discussion with the client. If permission is not obtained, and the therapist has assessed the client's level of dangerousness to self to be extremely elevated and imminent, involuntary hospitalisation may need to be instituted. Following hospitalisation, whether voluntary or involuntary, it is essential that the clinician take the necessary steps to remain an integral part of the client's ongoing treatment programme. According to Friedman (1989), one of the highest risk periods for suicidal clients is upon release from the hospital. Thus intensive outpatient treatment should begin immediately upon release, and the risk element must be closely monitored. (See Figure 4.2, which provides a structure for the evaluation process and includes the essential steps in case management, modelled on the flow chart developed by Fremouw et al., 1990.)

Clinicians should make judicious use of antisuicide contracts. These are written or verbal agreements in which the client agrees not to kill him or herself during the next period of time (decided upon by clinician and client). The client commits to contact the therapist at any time he or she feels unsure of his or her ability to resist suicidal impulses. Although antisuicide contracts can be conducive to establishing a therapeutic alliance, clinicians should not be lulled into a state of security that fails to appraise the ongoing risk situation.

A knowledge of community resources, preparations for a crisis, made well in advance, and contact with referral sources other than medical groups, should be part of the clinician's repertoire. He or she should become familiar with these resources and institutions, including day treatment, 24-hour emergency backup and crisis hotline (that doesn't put a caller on hold) and use them when necessary.

Lastly, clinicians should be aware of all of these standards and obtain the knowledge, training and experience, as well as become familiar with clinical resources before accepting high-risk patients (Bongar, 1991). It is clear that no clinician should burden him or herself with more of the serious cases than he or she can reasonably handle, given the amount of personal attention required by suicidal clients and the resulting stress.

Case study

K. was a 22-year-old, attractive, well-groomed mother of three, who was referred to one of the authors (L. Firestone) by a home visiting nurse shortly after the birth of her last child. Although she was able to take care of her new baby, she was incapable of caring for her other children or carrying out simple household tasks. In the initial session, she appeared extremely depressed and teary-eyed, made very little eye contact, and was very anxious, fidgeting with her hands and expressing numerous worries and fears. K. had difficulty concentrating and was confused about what day it was.

History
K.'s childhood history included physical and sexual abuse, abandonment, and profound neglect in relation to highly dysfunctional family members. Her maternal grandmother was diagnosed with schizophrenia, while

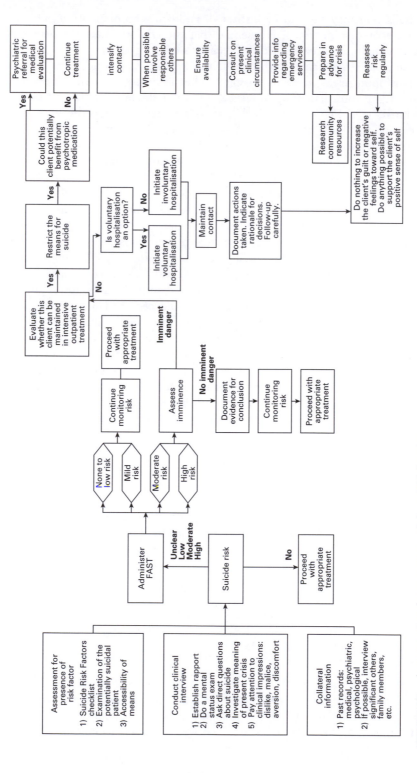

FIGURE 4.2   *Assessment and management of the suicidal patient*

her mother appeared to manifest two distinct personalities, a rebellious drugged-out teenager or a judgemental, punitive 'church lady' as K. referred to her. K.'s parents were divorced when she was 2 years old, and her mother had a succession of boyfriends, some of whom molested K. When K. was 11 and her brother was 9, they lived alone, on their own, in a house separate from their mother and her new wealthy boyfriend because he refused to allow the children to live with them. As K. matured and began having relationships with boys, her mother attempted to seduce them and often succeeded. K.'s mother introduced her to drugs, including cocaine, at age 14.

At 15 K. began living with the man who would become the father of her four children. Throughout the relationship, he repeatedly abused both her and the children. When K. was 16, her first child was born. The child had been born with a heart defect that had required many surgeries, the last of which culminated in the child's death. K. broke down, angrily attacked her daughter's doctors, and cried uncontrollably for several days. However, after one week she went back to work full time as a highly paid computer programmer and acted as if the event had never happened. At present, her third daughter was approaching 2 years of age and bore an uncanny resemblance to her deceased sister. Off and on during this same period, K.'s mother came to live with her. Invariably, K. would end up having to take care of her mother.

Diagnosis and risk factors

K. was diagnosed with major depressive disorder, panic disorder without agoraphobia, bulimia nervosa, post-traumatic stress disorder, delayed onset, and borderline personality disorder. Symptoms of depression began approximately two months prior to the birth of her newest baby. Her lack of energy, insomnia and forgetfulness appeared to result from unresolved grief regarding her oldest daughter's death. Another factor contributing to K.'s depression was the deterioration of the long-term relationship with the father of her four children. She reported feeling 'like I'm losing it. I used to be able to get so much done, keep my house organised, and take care of everything. Now, I can't even get to the store.' Her current behaviours stood in contrast to her usually active approach to life and focus on accomplishing tasks.

Assessment

K.'s scores on the Firestone Assessment of Self-Destructive Thoughts (FAST) indicated an extremely elevated risk of suicidality, especially scores on Levels 7 and 8 (hopelessness and giving up) and the suicide intent subscale. Her score on the Beck Hopelessness Scale was 18, the Beck Anxiety Inventory 54, and the Beck Depression Inventory 44, all indicating extremely high levels for concern.

Intervention

The treatment strategy began with helping K. deal with the unresolved mourning about her daughter. Prior to therapy, she had not allowed a headstone to be placed on the grave and never visited the cemetery. During the course of therapy, she experienced deep feelings of sadness about her daughter and actually visited her daughter's grave.

Another focus of treatment was K.'s irrational, negative thinking, or vows. She was helped to understand that her reactions to events in her current life were based on feelings from the past and negative thoughts she told herself about these events: 'You only hurt people. You don't have anything to give. You're just like your mother. Your children would be better off if you were dead.' Exploring these negative thoughts about the ongoing situations in her life helped her to understand her feelings and gave her more control over her impulsive acting out.

In the past, she had tried to compensate for her self-depreciating attitudes by convincing herself that she was the brightest, smartest, prettiest one in the family. She also expressed feelings of victimisation, wondering why she didn't have what other people had. She came to recognise that the source of these malicious thoughts was her mother's judgemental attitude toward her. Together she and the therapist (L.F.) planned behaviours that built on the strengths that she already possessed. The therapist took a non-judgemental, compassionate stance toward K. and offered her a feeling response in relation to her pain. The therapist also tried to provide a supportive, nurturing relationship for K. to which she gradually responded, and a strong therapeutic alliance was formed.

Methods were explored for helping her to regulate her affect and not respond to strong feelings with self-destructive outbursts. Time was spent developing her skills for tolerating negative emotions without dissociating. K. and the therapist talked about K.'s difficult past and how it had impacted her. K. demonstrated the ability to form important insights about herself, and began to have a greater understanding for herself and compassion for her current difficulties. She evidenced this more empathic view toward others by being less reactive, which led to improvement in her friendships and romantic relationship. K. also began dating a man who, in contrast to her ex-boyfriend, was kind and demonstrated significant warmth for both her and her children. She began to enjoy this man's company and increasingly sought out his friendship.

After three months, K.'s symptoms of depression dissipated and she significantly reduced her purging behaviour. She obtained a good position at a large company and, most important, she succeeded in finally breaking off the relationship with her ex-boyfriend. She also informed her mother that she would have to find somewhere else to live.

Breaking this destructive tie with her mother proved the most difficult challenge. Her feelings of guilt and responsibility for her mother often got the best of her. In addition, she had to face the fact that she would never get the love and care she wanted from her mother. Ultimately, she realised that as an adult, she no longer needed that kind of love.

Regression and suicide attempt

At this point, K.'s new boyfriend asked her to marry him. In the weeks that followed, K. regressed and began to engage in self-defeating, self-destructive behaviours. First, she seduced a man at her office, which led to the break-up of the most stable relationship she had ever had. Also during this period of time, her abusive ex-boyfriend broke into the house and raped her. She began to experience persistent thoughts of suicide in the form of a soothing, melancholy voice that told her: 'Look, it would be so peaceful [to kill yourself]. You wouldn't have to worry any more, because you wouldn't be here. You've had a short, but intense life, and this is enough. Besides, your children would be better off without you.'

Initially, she tried, in a sense, to run away from the voices and her problems by travelling to San Diego. However, she took with her a large number of pills, including a supply of painkillers, enough pills for an overdose. She was able to resist the voices urging her to overdose until she returned to Los Angeles. At this point, she took the pills and was found unconscious at home by her mother, and was taken to the hospital. She was released only 24 hours later by hospital personnel who neglected to obtain a follow-up psychiatric appointment for her. She resumed treatment with the therapist two days later, who arranged child care and other resources to offer her relief during the remainder of the crisis.

Outcome

Throughout the treatment, with K's cooperation, the therapist helped her build a support network made up of her friends and other family members so that the therapist could involve them in helping safeguard her when necessary. Following her suicide attempt, K.'s aunt in Seattle invited her to come to live with her, and the therapist attempted to facilitate her making use of this unique offer. The one condition of her aunt's offer was that K. would break all contact with her mother. However, K. was unable to bear the guilt of leaving her mother behind.

Several weeks later, after coming out of her suicidal crisis, K. made a permanent move to San Diego. Follow-up indicates that she obtained a well-paying job and her suicidal ideation was reduced; however, she reunited with her mother who continues to live with her, ostensibly to help her take care of the children. Referrals were made to clinicians in her new area who have an expertise in treating clients similar to K., particularly those trained in dialectic behavioural therapy. These therapists were contacted and are available for K.

These interventions, and most importantly the relationship that K. formed with the therapist (L.F.), did help avert suicide during this period of crisis. However, to progress further and avoid future suicide crises or a pattern of chronic suicidality, she would have to work through aspects of her borderline personality disorder, control her addictive behaviours, learn to tolerate strong affect, and develop her interpersonal skills. In order for K. to emancipate herself from her traumatic past, she needs to break the destructive tie to her mother, a connection that is based on guilt and her longing to have a real mother.

Suicide prevention

An overview

In 1987, the Committee on Prevention of Mental Disorders recast the concepts of primary, secondary and tertiary prevention as *universal, selective* and *indicated* preventative interventions (Dorwart and Ostacher, 1999).[11] Universal prevention procedures would include 'gun control and easy access to mental health facilities (community mental health centers, crisis centers, hotline, etc.)' (Silverman and Maris, 1995: 13).

The prevention programmes most studied in relation to suicide are school-based suicide prevention programmes (universal), suicide prevention centres (selective) and the effects of the Samaritans (indicated), as well as the reduction of specific means of suicide. The effectiveness of each of these efforts has been difficult to assess. However, Lester (1997: 304) conducted a meta-analysis of 14 studies of suicide prevention centres and Samaritans, and found that 'the evidence provides support for a preventive effect from suicide prevention centres, albeit small and inconsistently found'.

In addressing reduction of the means for committing suicide, it is interesting to note that the suicide rate was reduced in Great Britain and other countries when the chemical content of domestic gas was detoxified (Kreitman, 1976; Lester, 1990). Similarly, Alan Berman (1997), in a Consensus Statement on Youth Suicide by Firearms, declared:

> There is clear evidence that intervening in or preventing the immediate accessibility of a lethal weapon can save lives. We have identified the safe storage of guns as one preventive intervention approach that would result in a decrease in the number of youth suicides.

Primary or universal preventative interventions

Silverman and Felner (1995: 72) defined primary (universal) prevention as those measures that seek 'to reduce the incidence of new cases of disorder ... [They are] targeted to entire populations, not to particular individuals'. To effectively employ these preventative measures in our most vulnerable population groups, children and adolescents, we need to consider early environmental factors that predispose the formation of self-destructive thought processes. Early on in an illness, we can also make use of known medical treatments that could prevent the danger of repeated episodes.

In most cases, the authors believe that psychological factors are predominant in the causation of depression, self-destructive behaviour and alienation from the self. In exploring these psychological factors, we have found that destructive thought processes underlying suicidal behaviour are closely related to parental attitudes and communications that have been incorporated into the personality (R. Firestone, 1990, 1997a). Therefore, it is logical that prevention efforts should be directed toward improving the environment in which children grow and develop.[12] The following guidelines include several basic principles regarding child-rearing practices that could help parents provide the basis for the healthy development of children: (1) a secure and loving parental climate, (2) teaching children to avoid developing inward, self-nurturing (addictive) habit patterns, and (3) avoiding disciplinary measures that inculcate the image of the child as 'bad'.[13]

1 Parents need to be positive role models in setting the emotional climate for their children's development of self-esteem and sense of well-being. Their integrity, openness and honesty are as necessary for the child's emotional development as food and drink are for their physical survival. In addition to the benefit of having parents who serve as good role models, children need adults who will relate to them openly and directly in terms of their real thoughts and feelings. The parents' state of emotional health will to a large degree impact their ability to parent. Parents need to be able to regulate and tolerate feelings themselves in order to help their children learn this skill and to serve as role models for their children.

2 Disciplinary techniques that foster isolation and an inward, self-protective posture in children should be strenuously avoided. Children should be discouraged from developing self-nurturing, addictive habit patterns, including excessive eating, television watching, video game playing and other such compulsive activities. Parents who abuse alcohol or drugs set an example of unhealthy self-indulgence and promote the use of soothing mechanisms to avoid psychological pain. When children manifest these patterns, parents could interrupt these actions and explore why the child is engaging in those behaviours. In addition, they could seek help for their children early on instead of allowing these patterns to become deep-seated personality traits and coping strategies.

3 Most children grow up feeling that they are bad or unlovable. Parents must try to avoid labelling their child as bad, evil, or essentially hostile, for example, as 'the angry one,' 'the troublemaker', 'the difficult one', and so on. These characterisations stigmatise the child and induce the very behaviours for which the child will later hate him or herself. Parents should strive to 'let their child be', that is, to avoid constant evaluations and comments, either positive or negative, on their child's posture, mannerisms, way of speaking and other personality characteristics. They should support children in expressing their opinions, stating their perceptions and asking questions about so-called forbidden subjects such as sex, death and 'family secrets'. Lastly, it is extremely important that parents never shake, hit, or physically abuse their child. Harsh, sadistic punishment creates strong tendencies in children to provoke mistreatment from others and causes them to turn the incorporated parental hostility against themselves. In the context of harsh or inappropriate child-rearing practices, it is important to mention that sexual abuse has been found to be linked to suicidal behaviour much later in the victim's life. For example, in a survey of 200 outpatients, Read et al. (2001: 367) found that 'current suicidality was predicted better by child sexual abuse (experienced on average 20 years previously) than by a current diagnosis of depression'.

Selective and indicated preventative interventions

> We need to be reminded that to work in suicide prevention is risky and dangerous and there are casualties and that is to be expected. (Robert E. Litman, personal communication cited in Shneidman, 1993: 157)

'*Selective interventions* are directed at individuals who are at greater risk for diseases or disorders than the general population', whereas indicated interventions are directed at small groups who have been found to 'manifest a risk factor, condition, or abnormality that identifies them, individually, as being at sufficiently high risk to require the prevention intervention' (Silverman and Maris, 1995: 13). Selective measures include interventions directed at groups of individuals who display behaviours or symptoms associated with suicide, such as substance abuse, mood disorders, anxiety disorders and schizophrenia. Silverman and Maris recommended 'increasing the number and availability of support networks for those individuals most at risk or who have already entered into self-destructive behaviour ... [and] providing easily accessible treatment for depression and hospitalizing serious suicide attempters' (p. 13).

Recognising that there is considerable overlap between the three modes of prevention discussed here, a number of suicidologists have adopted a perspective wherein 'tertiary [indicated] prevention becomes *treatment*, secondary [selective] prevention becomes *early intervention*, and primary [universal] prevention assumes the sole mantle of *prevention*' (Silverman and Felner, 1995: 73). In any classification system, however, the major goal of preventative interventions remains that of modifying 'those *processes that lead to or maintain suicidal actions*, *thoughts, and tendencies*' (Silverman and Felner, 1995: 72). Each preventative procedure should be designed to interrupt the 'pathways' from health to disorder that have been identified through research and theory development with respect to the suicidal process.

Preventative measures derived from R. Firestone's conceptual model focus on altering the psychological factors known to increase the risk for suicidal actions, especially those behaviours and tendencies that make up an inward, self-protective lifestyle. For example, therapists can discourage substance abuse or any other addictive pattern in their clients, whether suicidal or non-suicidal, while encouraging them to substitute activities and relationships that are real and constructive. For clients who are socially isolated, self-protective and inward, it is important to help them schedule time with others and work through the initially painful anxiety states involved in making interpersonal contact. Other suggestions for preventing suicide prior to a suicidal crisis are described in chapter 3 of *Suicide and the Inner Voice* (R. Firestone, 1997b).

Lastly, preventative procedures should be directed to those people most affected when a family member, close friend, or fellow student commits suicide. Shneidman (1969) conjectured that there are at least six 'survivors' following a suicide. During the past 40 years, it is estimated that more than 1 million children have lost a parent or parents to suicide. In these cases, the normal feelings of grief are complicated by guilt, anger and an intensified tendency to give up one's individuality and adopt the deceased parent's identity and point of view. The process of negative identification is powerful in that children and adolescents tend to follow the destiny or developmental pathway of their parents, especially that of the parent of the same sex. When a parent commits suicide, the identification can develop into a powerful compulsion to imitate the self-destructive act.

The 'contagion' effect or future incidents of 'copy-cat' suicides in other people, not only the immediate survivors, must be addressed. For example, Phillips (1985) documented a 12% increase in suicides in the United States, particularly among young females, in the month following Marilyn Monroe's suicide (Berman and Jobes, 1991: 103). The phenomenon of teenage cluster suicides and the influence of the media on imitative behaviour should be taken seriously. Berman and Jobes (1991) also noted that the well-publicised suicides of four adolescents in New Jersey in 1987 was followed by a dozen 'copycat suicides' over the next several months.

Conclusion

> There are thousands of people who have been helped, their lives saved, by the intervention of therapy by psychologists, psychiatrists, physicians, suicide prevention workers and others ... Suicide is prevented by changing our perception of the situation, and redefining what is unbearable. (Edwin Shneidman, 1996: 164–5)

Suicidologists expect that, in the near future, therapists will be treating patients in suicidal crises or chronically suicidal patients 'with fewer resources, and under more severe time constraints' (Rudd et al., 2001, p. viii). Surveys have shown that one in five psychologists lose a patient to suicide sometime during their professional career, and with psychiatrists, the odds increase to one out of every two. Yet in the United States, only 40% of clinicians receive any formal training in suicidology – the study of suicide. Clearly, one of the most important preventative measures lies in educating mental health professionals and physicians about the risk factors for suicide. These people, in particular, need to be familiar with research findings and information regarding signs of potential suicide in the people they treat.

For example, Fawcett (1999) conducted a comprehensive prospective study with a large sample (954) of patients with major affective disorders. After 10 years, 34 of these patients had committed suicide.

A major new finding of the NIMH collaborative study was the association of severe anxiety symptoms (severe psychic anxiety, such as worry and fear, and panic attacks) that statistically significantly differentiated patients who committed suicide within one year of assessment from the majority of depressed patients who survived the one-year follow-up period. (1999: 116)

Translated into clinical practice, the results stress the importance of assessing and treating a patient's high levels of anxiety and panic attacks, which are symptoms that fortunately can be readily modified with medication and psychotherapy.

It is well to remember that 'there is no universal formulation regarding how to respond to a highly lethal person', as Anton Leenaars (1994: 58) succinctly put it. Even in an effective treatment programme with a competent, compassionate therapist who understands the suicidal process, who does not treat his or her patient in isolation but consults with colleagues, and who follows the other guidelines for case management described above, the patient may ultimately choose to end his or her life. At this point, it is important for us to recognize that, as psychotherapists, we are 'neither omniscient or omnipotent ... When our best efforts fail, we share with other survivors, a "despair born of death too soon"' (Slawson et al., 1974: 63).

Finally, the way that human beings function and the way they are damaged are closely linked to negative internalised thoughts. The knowledge gained through accessing and identifying the partially unconscious thought processes driving a suicidal person towards death can well be used to set into motion potentially life-saving interventions. The authors believe that the conceptual model described here is an important tool for psychotherapy with high-risk individuals, in that it has both predictive capability and therapeutic value as well as having merit for a preventative mental health programme (Firestone, 1997b).

Notes

1 Homicide claimed 18,272 lives in 1998 in the United States.

2 Students of the demographics of suicide noted that economic conditions in Japan, as well as in Russia and certain countries in Eastern Europe, correlate with the increase in suicide rates in the male population. However, it is interesting to note that male suicide rates decreased slightly in other Eastern European countries, Hungary, Slovenia and Czechoslovakia.

In Japan in 1997, males between the ages of 55 and 64 had a suicide rate of 45.3 per 100,000, which was exceeded only by the rates for males over 75 (52.6 per 100,000). Takahashi, Hirasawa, Koyama, Senzaki and Senzaki (1998: 275) conjecture that 'there was a tendency for more males to commit suicide because of financial and work-related problems'.

3 The Samaritans is a voluntary organisation started by Chad Varah in 1953, originally to offer psychotherapy at no cost for suicidal individuals in London. Mishara and Daigle (2001: 154) reported that 'The Samaritan movement has grown to such an extent that the parent organisation, Befrienders International, has 350 centers in over 40 countries with 31,000 volunteers, of which the Samaritans of the United Kingdom has over 19,000 volunteers'.

4 The unique characteristics of the individual, including his or her biological, temperamental and genetic traits, the synchronistic identification with parents' affirmative qualities and strivings, and the ongoing effects of experience and education make up the *self system*. Parents' lively attitudes, positive values, and active pursuit of life are easily assimilated into the self system through the process of identification and imitation and become part of the child's developing personality, whereas internalised, parental hostility and rejecting attitudes together with other forms of negative internalised self-attitudes, remain alien.

5 A distinction should be made between prediction and assessment. 'Given the current state of the art, suicide prediction is not very precise or useful. This is one reason why many suicidologists may prefer to speak of assessment' (Maris, 1991: 2).

6 Psychiatric risk factors include presence of a diagnosable Axis I or Axis II disorder, including affective disorder, which carries a 15% lifetime risk of suicide; schizophrenia, a 10% lifetime risk; and alcoholism and substance abuse, a 2–3% lifetime risk. Clients diagnosed with a borderline personality disorder have shown a 9.5% suicide rate. There is 'a 45 percent rate for suicide in patients with borderline personality disorder and comorbidity for two disorders: major depression and substance abuse' (Jacobs et al., 1999: 15). More recently, attention has been focused on studies showing that severe anxiety symptoms are acute risk factors for suicide (Fawcett, 1999).

7 Read et al. (2001) also cited studies of the effects of childhood neglect on adult (van der Kolk et al., 1991) and adolescent (Lipschitz et al., 1999) suicidality which found neglect to be 'at least as predictive as child sexual abuse'. According to van der Kolk (1991: 1669), 'This implies that although childhood trauma contributes heavily to the initiation of self-destructive behavior, lack of secure attachments maintains it'.

8 The inward syndrome needs to be distinguished from self-reflection, introspection, time spent alone for creative work or planning, contemplation of nature, meditation and other forms of spiritual or intellectual pursuits.

9 These behaviours and personality characteristics are strongly influenced or controlled by the negative thought patterns listed on the Continuum of Negative Thought Patterns (see Figure 4.1).

10 The FAST (Total Score and Suicide Intent Composite) was found to have higher correlations with respect to the criterion variables (previous suicide attempts and current suicide ideation) than any of the other measures included in the study (Suicide Probability Scale and Beck Hopelessness Scale) (Firestone and Firestone, 1998).

11 Universal interventions are directed toward 'an entire population thought to be at risk for developing mental disorders in the future. For example, public education campaigns to inform the general public about the dangers of substance abuse or the early signs of depression would be classified as universal' (Dorwart and Ostacher, 1999, 53).

12 Suicidologist Pamela Cantor (1989) listed the factors most frequently cited as related to feelings of hopelessness and the rising suicide rate in adolescents and young adults: the violence that children and adolescents are exposed to, that is, real violence and created violence in the media; the disappearance of the extended family; the pressures put on children to grow up quickly; the special sensitivity of many children to social isolation; the lack of socially acceptable ways for youngsters to express anger; and a high level of social and academic competition and pressure.

13 These guidelines refer more to parental qualities that predispose action rather than rigid, how-to-do-it, practical techniques. These suggestions were derived from a series of parenting seminars in which parents discussed pragmatic approaches to child-rearing based on sound mental health principles; they are described in depth in chapters 10 and 11 in *Compassionate Child-Rearing* (R. Firestone, 1990).

References

Abramson, L.Y., Metalsky, G.I. and Alloy, L.B. (1989) Hopelessness depression: a theory-based subtype of depression. *Psychological Review*, 96, 358–71.

Allard, R., Marshall, M. and Plante, M. (1992) Intensive follow-up does not decrease the risk of repeat suicide attempts. *Suicide and Life-Threatening Behavior*, 22, 303–14.

American Jurisprudence (1981) *Second volume 61 Review*. New York: Lawyer's Cooperative Publishing.

Arana, G.W. and Hyman, S. (1989) Biological contributions to suicide. In D. Jacobs and H. Brown (eds), *Suicide: Understanding and Responding: Harvard Medical School Perspectives*. Madison, CT: International Universities Press. pp. 73–86.

Arieti, S. and Bemporad, J.R. (1980) The psychological organization of depression. *American Journal of Psychiatry*, 137, 1360–65.

Beck, A.T. (1978a) *Beck Depression Inventory*. San Antonio, TX: Psychological Corporation.

Beck, A.T. (1978b) *Beck Hopelessness Scale*. San Antonio, TX: Psychological Corporation.

Beck, A.T. (1991) *Beck Suicide Inventory*. San Antonio, TX: Psychological Corporation.

Beck, A.T. (1996) Beyond belief: a theory of modes, personality, and psychopathology. In P. Salkovkis (ed.), *Frontiers of Cognitive Therapy*. New York: Guilford Press. pp. 1–25.

Beck, A.T., Rush, A.J., Shaw, B.F. and Emery, G. (1979) *Cognitive Therapy of Depression*. New York: Guilford Press.

Beck, A.T., Steer, R.A. and Brown, G. (1993) Dysfunctional attitudes and suicidal ideation in psychiatric outpatients. *Suicide and Life-Threatening Behavior*, 23, 11–20.

Beck, A.T., Steer, R.A., Kovacs, M. and Garrison, B. (1985) Hopelessness and eventual suicide: a 10-year prospective study of patients hospitalized with suicidal ideation. *American Journal of Psychiatry*, 142, 559–63.

Bedrosian, R.C. and Beck, A.T. (1979) Cognitive aspects of suicidal behaviors. *Suicide and Life-Threatening Behavior*, 9, 87–96.

Berman, A.L. (1997) *Consensus Statement on Youth Suicide by Firearms*. Washington, DC: American Association of Suicidology.

Berman, A.L. and Cohen-Sandler, R. (1982) Suicide and the standard of care: optimal vs. acceptable. *Suicide and Life-Threatening Behavior*, 12, 114–22.

Berman, A.L. and Jobes, D.A. (1991) *Adolescent Suicide: Assessment and Intervention*. Washington, DC: American Psychological Association.

Blatt, S.J. (1995) The destructiveness of perfectionism: implications for the treatment of depression. *American Psychologist*, 50, 1003–20.

Bongar, B. (1991) *The Suicidal Patient: Clinical and Legal Standards of Care*. Washington, DC: American Psychological Association.

Bongar, B. (1998). Introduction. In B. Bongar, A.L. Berman, R.W. Maris, M.M. Silverman, E. A. Harris. and W. L. Packman (eds), *Risk Management with Suicidal Patients*. New York: Guilford Press. pp. 1–3.

Bonner, R.L. and Rich, A.R. (1987) Toward a predictive model of suicidal ideation and behavior: some preliminary data in college students. *Suicide and Life-Threatening Behavior*, 17, 50–63.

Bunney, W.E., Jr. and Fawcett, J.A. (1965) Possibility of a biochemical test for suicidal potential: an analysis of endocrine findings prior to three suicides. *Archives of General Psychiatry*, 13, 232–9.

Cantor, P.C. (1989) Intervention strategies: environmental risk reduction for youth suicide. In M.R. Feinleib (ed.), *Report of the Secretary's Task Force on Youth Suicide*, Vol. 3, *Prevention and Interventions on Youth Suicide*. Washington, DC: US Department of Health and Human Services. pp. 285–93.

Colt, G.H. (1991) *The Enigma of Suicide*. New York: Simon and Schuster.

Dorwart, R.A. and Ostacher, M.J. (1999) A community psychiatry approach to preventing suicide. In D.G. Jacobs (ed.), *The Harvard Medical School Guide to Suicide Assessment and Intervention*. San Francisco: Jossey–Bass. pp. 52–71.

Durkheim, E. (1951) *Suicide: A Study in Sociology* (trans. J.A. Spaulding and G. Simpson). New York: Free Press. (Original work published 1897)

Eddins, C.L. and Jobes, D.A. (1994) Do you see what I see? Underlying dimensions of suicidality. *Suicide and Life-Threatening Behavior*, 24, 170–3.

Ellis, A. (1973) *Humanistic Psychotherapy: The Rational-Emotive Approach*. New York: Julian.

Ellis, T.E. (2001) Psychotherapy with suicidal patients. In D. Lester (ed.), *Suicide Prevention: Resources for the Millennium*. Philadelphia, PA: Brunner–Routledge. pp. 129–51.

Ellis, T.E. and Newman, C.F. (1996). *Choosing to Live: How to Defeat Suicide through Cognitive Therapy*. Oakland, CA: New Harbinger Publications.

Farberow, N.L. (1980) Introduction. In N.L. Farberow (ed.), *The Many Faces of Suicide: Indirect Self-destructive Behavior*. New York: McGraw-Hill. pp. 1–12.

Farooqi, Y.N. and Hussain, S. (2000) Suicidal potential among Pakistani psychiatric patients and non-clinical adults. Unpublished paper.

Fawcett, J. (1999) Profiles of completed suicides. In D.G. Jacobs (ed.), *The Harvard Medical School Guide to Suicide Assessment and Intervention*. San Francisco: Jossey–Bass. pp. 115–24.

Firestone, R.W. (1986) The 'inner voice' and suicide. *Psychotherapy*, 23, 439–47.

Firestone, R.W. (1988) *Voice Therapy: A Psychotherapeutic Approach to Self-destructive Behavior*. Santa Barbara, CA: Glendon Association.

Firestone, R.W. (1990) *Compassionate Child-rearing: An In-depth Approach to Optimal Parenting*. Santa Barbara, CA: Glendon Association.

Firestone, R.W. (1997a) *Combating Destructive Thought Processes: Voice Therapy and Separation Theory*. Thousand Oaks, CA: Sage.

Firestone, R.W. (1997b) *Suicide and the Inner Voice: Risk Assessment, Treatment, and Case Management*. Thousand Oaks, CA: Sage.

Firestone, R.W. (2000) Microsuicide and the elderly: a basic defense against death anxiety. In A. Tomer (ed.), *Death Attitudes and the Older Adult: Theories, Concepts, and Applications*. Philadelphia, PA: Brunner–Routledge. pp. 65–84.

Firestone, R.W., and Catlett, J. (1999) *Fear of Intimacy*. Washington, DC: American Psychological Association.

Firestone, R.W., and Firestone, L. (1996) *Firestone Assessment of Self-Destructive Thoughts*. San Antonio, TX: Psychological Corporation.

Firestone, R.W. and Firestone, L. (1998) Voices in suicide: the relationship between self-destructive thought processes, maladaptive behavior, and self-destructive manifestations. *Death Studies*, 22, 411–43.

Fox, R. (1973) The Samaritan contribution to suicide prevention. In C. Varah (ed.), *The Samaritans in the '70s*. London: Constable. pp. 136–45.

Fremouw, W.J., dePerczel, M. and Ellis, T.E. (1990) *Suicide Risk: Assessment and Response Guidelines*. New York: Pergamon Press.

Friedman, R.S. (1989) Hospital treatment of the suicidal patient. In D. Jacobs and H.N. Brown (eds), *Suicide: Understanding and Responding: Harvard Medical School Perspectives*. Madison, CT: International Universities Press. pp. 379–402.

Hamilton, E.W. and Abramson, L.Y. (1983) Cognitive patterns and major depressive disorder: a longitudinal study in a hospital setting. *Journal of Abnormal Psychology*, 92, 173–84.

Heckler, R.A. (1994) *Waking Up, Alive: The Descent, the Suicide Attempt, and the Return to Life*. New York: Ballantine Books.

Hewitt, P.L., Flett, G.L. and Weber, C. (1994) Dimensions of perfectionism and suicide ideation. *Cognitive Therapy and Research*, 18, 439–60.

Hughes, T. and McCullough, F. (eds) (1982) *The Journals of Sylvia Plath*. New York: Ballantine Books.

Jacobs, D. (1989) Psychotherapy with suicidal patients: The empathic method. In D. Jacobs and H.N. Brown (eds), *Suicide: Understanding and Responding: Harvard Medical School Perspectives*. Madison, CT: International Universities Press. pp. 329–42.

Jacobs, D.G., Brewer, M. and Klein-Benheim, M. (1999) Suicide assessment: an overview and recommended protocol. In D.G. Jacobs (ed.), *The Harvard Medical School Guide to Suicide Assessment and Intervention*. San Francisco: Jossey-Bass. pp. 3–39.

Joiner, T.E., Jr, Walker, R.L., Rudd, M.D. and Jobes, D.A. (1999) Scientizing and routinizing the assessment of suicidality in outpatient practice. *Professional Psychology: Research and Practice*, 30, 447–53.

Kahn, A. (1982) The moment of truth: psychotherapy with the suicidal patient. In E.L. Bassuk, S.C. Schoonover and A.D. Gill (eds), *Lifelines: Clinical Perspectives on Suicide*. New York: Plenum Press. pp. 83–92.

Kreitman, N. (1976) The coal gas story: United Kingdom suicide rates, 1960–61. *British Journal of Preventive and Social Medicine*, 30, 86–93.

Leenaars, A.A. (1994) Crisis intervention with highly lethal suicidal people. In A.A. Leenaars, J.T. Maltsberger and R.A. Neimeyer (eds), *Treatment of Suicidal People*. Washington, DC: Taylor and Francis. pp.45–59.

Leonard, C.V. (1967) *Understanding and Preventing Suicide*. Springfield, IL: Charles C. Thomas.

Lester, D. (1990) The effect of detoxification of domestic gas in Switzerland on the suicide rate. *Acta Psychiatrica Scandinavia*, 82, 383–4.

Lester, D. (1997) The effectiveness of suicide prevention centers: a review. *Suicide and Life-Threatening Behavior*, 27, 304–10.

Linehan, M.M. (1981) A social-behavioral analysis of suicide and parasuicide: implications for clinical assessment and treatment. In J.F. Clarkin and H.I. Glazer (eds), *Depression: Behavioral and Directive Intervention Strategies*. New York: Garland. pp. 229–94.

Linehan, M.M. (1993) *Cognitive-Behavioral Treatment of Borderline Personality Disorder*. New York: Guilford Press.

Linehan, M.M. (1999) Standard protocol for assessing and treating suicidal behaviors for patients in treatment. In D.G. Jacobs (ed.), *The Harvard Medical School Guide to Suicide Assessment and Intervention*. San Francisco: Jossey–Bass. pp. 146–87.

Linehan, M.M., Armstrong, H.E., Suarez, A., Allmon, D. and Heard, H.L. (1991) Cognitive-behavioral treatment of chronically parasuicidal borderline patients. *Archives of General Psychiatry*, 48, 1060–4.

Lipschitz, D.S., Winekar, R.K., Nicolaou, A.L., Hartnick, E., Wolfson, M. and Southwick, S.M. (1999) Perceived abuse and neglect as risk factors for suicidal behavior in adolescent inpatients. *Journal of Nervous and Mental Disease*, 187, 32–9.

Lothian, J. (1998) From Paternalism to Participation: Consumers' Views and Experiences of the Initial Assessment Process in Mental Health. Unpublished master's thesis, University of Auckland, New Zealand.

MacNeil–Lehrer (1987) Open door policy? Teen suicide: Fall from grace (Transcript 2989 of the MacNeil/Lehrer NewsHour, 12 March). New York: MacNeil–Lehrer Productions, WNET, WETA.

Maltsberger, J.T. (1986). *Suicide Risk: The Formulation of Clinical Judgment*. New York: New York University Press.

Maltsberger, J.T. (1999) The psychodynamic understanding of suicide. In D.G. Jacobs (ed.), *The Harvard Medical School Guide to Suicide Assessment and Intervention*. San Francisco: Jossey–Bass. pp. 72–82.

Mann, J.J. and Arango, V. (1999) The neurobiology of suicidal behavior. In D.G. Jacobs (ed.), *The Harvard Medical School Guide to Suicide Assessment and Intervention*. San Francisco: Jossey–Bass. pp. 98–114.

Maris, R.W. (1989) Suicide intervention: the existential and biomedical perspectives. In D. Jacobs and H.N. Brown (eds), *Suicide: Understanding and Responding: The Harvard Medical School Perspectives*. Madison, CT: International Universities Press. pp. 449–58.

Maris, R.W. (1991) Assessment and prediction of suicide: introduction. *Suicide and Life-Threatening Behavior*, 21, 1–17.

McIntosh, J.L. (2000) International comparisons. In *American Association of Suicidology 1998 Official USA Statistics Overhead Set*. South Bend, IN: American Association of Suicidology. p. 41.

Menninger, K. (1938) *Man against Himself*. New York: Harcourt, Brace and World.

Mishara, B.L. and Daigle, M. (2001) Helplines and crisis intervention services: challenges for the future. In D. Lester (ed.), *Suicide Prevention: Resources for the Millennium*. Philadelphia, PA: Brunner–Routledge. pp. 153–71.

Murphy, S.L. (2000) Deaths: final data for 1998. *National Vital Statistics Report*, 48 (11). Hyattsville, MD: National Center for Health Statistics. DHHS Publication No. (PHS) 2000-1120.

Orbach, I. (1999) Brief cognitive therapy for depressed and suicidal adolescents: a critical comment. *Clinical Child Psychology and Psychiatry*, 4, 593–6.

Orbach, I., Mikulincer, M., Stein, D. and Cohen, O. (1998) Self-representation of suicidal adolescents. *Journal of Abnormal Psychology*, 107, 435–9.

Pfeffer, C.R., Conte, H.R., Plutchik, R. and Jerrett, I. (1980) Suicidal behavior in latency-age children: an outpatient population. *Journal of the American Academy of Child Psychiatry*, 19, 703–10.

Phillips, D.P. (1985) The Werther effect. *The Sciences*, 25, 33–9.

Read, J., Agar, K., Barker-Collo, S., Davies, E. and Moskowitz, A. (2001) Assessing suicidality in adults: integrating childhood trauma as a major risk factor. *Professional Psychology, Research and Practice* 32, 367–72.

Reynolds, W.M. (1985) *Suicide Ideation Questionnaire*. Unpublished manuscript: University of Wisconsin, Madison.

Rich, A.R., Bonner, R.L. and Reimold, A. (1986) *Suicidal Ideation in College Students: Support for a Vulnerability Model*. Paper presented at the Annual Meeting of the American Psychological Association, Washington, DC.

Richman, J. (1986) *Family Therapy for Suicidal People*. New York: Springer.

Richman, J. (1994) Psychotherapy with suicidal older adults. *Death Studies*, 18, 391–407.

Rose, D.T. and Abramson, L.Y. (1992) Developmental predictors of depressive cognitive style: research and theory. In D. Cicchetti and S.L. Toth (eds), *Rochester Symposium on Developmental Psychopathology, Vol. 4: Developmental Perspectives on Depression*. Rochester, NY: University of Rochester Press. pp. 325–49.

Rosenbaum, M. and Richman, J. (1970) Suicide: the role of hostility and death wishes from the family and significant others. *American Journal of Psychiatry*, 126, 1652–5.

Rudd, M.D. (2000a) Integrating science into the practice of clinical suicidology: a review of the psychotherapy literature and a research agenda for the future. In R.W. Maris, S.S. Canetto, J.L. McIntosh and M.M. Silverman (eds), *Review of Suicidology, 2000.* New York: Guilford Press. pp. 47–83.

Rudd, M.D. (2000b) The suicidal mode: a cognitive-behavioral model of suicidality. *Suicide and Life-Threatening Behavior*, 30, 18–33.

Rudd, M.D., Joiner, T. and Rajab, M.H. (2001) *Treating Suicidal Behavior: An Effective, Time-limited Approach.* New York: Guilford Press.

Rudd, M.D., Rajab, M.H., Orman, D.T., Stulman, D.A., Joiner, T. and Dixon, W. (1996) Effectiveness of an outpatient intervention targeting suicidal young adults: preliminary results. *Journal of Consulting and Clinical Psychology*, 64, 179–90.

Shafii, M., Carrigan, S., Whittinghill, J.R. and Derrick, A. (1985) Psychological autopsy of completed suicide in children and adolescents. *American Journal of Psychiatry*, 142, 1061–4.

Shea, S.C. (1999) *The Practical Art of Suicide Assessment: A Guide for Mental Health Professionals and Substance Abuse Counselors.* New York: John Wiley.

Shneidman, E.S. (1966) Orientations toward death: a vital aspect of the study of lives. *International Journal of Psychiatry*, 2, 167–200.

Shneidman, E.S. (1969) Prologue: Fifty-eight years. In E.S. Shneidman (ed.), *On the Nature of Suicide.* San Francisco: Jossey–Bass. pp. 1–30.

Shneidman, E.S. (1981) Psychotherapy with suicidal patients. *Suicide and Life-Threatening Behavior*, 11, 341–8.

Shneidman, E.S. (1985) *Definition of Suicide.* New York: John Wiley.

Shneidman, E.S. (1989) Overview: a multidimensional approach to suicide. In D. Jacobs and H.N. Brown (eds), *Suicide: Understanding and Responding.* Madison, CT: International Universities Press. pp. 1–30.

Shneidman, E.S. (1993) *Suicide as Psychache: A Clinical Approach to Self-destructive Behavior.* Northvale, NJ: Jason Aronson.

Shneidman, E.S. (1996) *The Suicidal Mind.* New York: Oxford University Press.

Shneidman, E. (1999) Perturbation and lethality: a psychological approach to assessment and intervention. In D.G. Jacobs (ed.), *The Harvard Medical School Guide to Suicide Assessment and Intervention.* San Francisco: Jossey-Bass. pp. 83–97.

Silverman, M.M. and Felner, R.D. (1995) The place of suicide prevention in the spectrum of intervention: definitions of critical terms and constructs. In M.M. Silverman and R.W. Maris (eds), *Suicide Prevention: Toward the Year 2000.* New York: Guilford Press. pp. 70–81.

Silverman, M.M. and Maris, R.W. (1995) The prevention of suicidal behaviors: an overview. In M.M. Silverman and R.W. Maris (eds), *Suicide Prevention: Toward the Year 2000.* New York: Guilford Press. pp. 10–21.

Slawson, P.F., Flinn, D.E., and Schwartz, D.A. (1974) Legal responsibility for suicide. *Psychiatric Quarterly*, 48, 50–64.

Takahashi, Y., Hirasawa, H., Koyama, K., Senzaki, A. and Senzaki, K. (1998) Suicide in Japan: present state and future directions for prevention. *Transcultural Psychiatry*, 35, 271–89.

Van der Kolk, B.A., Perry, J.C. and Herman, J.L. (1991) Childhood origins of self-destructive behavior. *American Journal of Psychiatry*, 148, 1665–71.

Varah, C. (1980) Introduction. In C. Varah (ed.), *The Samaritans in the '80s.* London: Constable. pp. 17–76.

Wallace, M.D. (2001) The origin of suicide prevention in the United States. In D. Lester (ed.), *Suicide Prevention: Resources for the Millennium.* Philadelphia, PA: Brunner–Routledge. pp. 239–54.

Yang, B. and Clum, G.A. (2000) Childhood stress leads to later suicidality via its effect on cognitive functioning. *Suicide and Life-Threatening Behavior*, 30, 183–98.

5
RELATIONSHIP DIFFICULTIES: CAUSES AND CURES
Douglas Hooper

The capacity of one human being to establish a relationship with another human being lies at the very roots of being human. From the early days following birth, human infants' prime goals are to secure adequate physiological comfort through relief of hunger, thirst, pain and the establishment of comfortable ambient conditions. But these are all mediated by the infant's capacity for communicating both distress and pleasure to his or her caregivers. This facility for communicating interpersonally soon becomes a goal in itself. The infant seeks out a parent by voice or gaze in order to initiate interaction with the adult because this process gives pleasure to the child over and above the more physical rewards we have already listed. Generally this initiation and response by the child stimulates a parent to continue to provide the child with the physical and psychological requirements for growth and development. Clearly there are ancient genetic programmes here which will ensure that the 'helpless' infant can call out these resources over the extended period during which the growing child must rely utterly on an adult caregiver.

These powerful genetically based activities by child and parent provide some of the templates for subsequent behaviour in close relationships which we shall discuss more fully later. The process is often known as bonding – a word that resonates with similar processes observed in the natural world both in simpler animals and, more importantly, in our genetic cousins the primates. In some ways, though, the bonding concept seems more attuned to the psychophysiological part of the process than the psychosocial processes that come to dominate the experience in human behaviour. Attachment theory, developed first by Bowlby (1969,1973,1980) in the context of child/adult disturbance, is a more useful set of hypotheses because it can deal with the subtle intrapsychic activity as well as the interpsychic ones. Attachment theory as it has been applied to adult relationship breakdown will also be considered later in this chapter.

But what is the point of emphasising these early psychogenetic influences if we shall be largely concerned with the progression and breakdown of adult relationships? The answer is that subsequent relationship difficulties can and often do lead to a wide range of physical, psychological and social problems which are far-reaching in effect because of the fundamental importance of healthy relationships to stability and growth, probably throughout the life cycle.

The common way in which people suffering from the effects of relationship difficulties seek help is at their local GP surgery, and increasingly general practitioners are employing counsellors and therapists to deal with these issues. Recent studies therefore are helpful because they catalogue the reasons for counselling referral. One such study conducted on 385 sequential referrals for counselling in 13 GP practices has some interesting data which illuminate these issues (Baker et al., 1998). The commonest reasons for referral were help with presenting symptoms of stress, anxiety and depression. The research then examined the underlying factors from which the symptoms arose and this revealed that the most significant issues were relationship with partner (18%) and bereavement (8%), followed by work (4%) and physical illness (3%). In a similar smaller study of 60 people referred to the counsellor in a single general practice surgery, 32% reported that their major problem was either with their partner or with the consequences of separation through bereavement, divorce etc. (Corney and Jenkins, 1993).

These and a number of similar studies demonstrate that the consequences of problematic or failing and broken relationships are widespread and that there is a considerable cost in terms of personal health and social life. Often the G.P and/or the counsellor may choose to refer the person to one of the agencies that offer a more specific service for relationship difficulties.

In the UK the marriage support agencies offer counselling and other services for those with marital and other couple problems. Of these, Relate is the major service, which aims to provide couple counselling on a nationwide basis in England, Wales and Northern Ireland, with a similar service in Scotland. In addition there are the so-called 'faith' agencies which are oriented towards the Roman Catholic and Jewish communities, and very much smaller organisations offer a similar service to the Asian and Afro-Caribbean cultural minorities. The data from the GP studies also show that bereavement is a significant cause of distress and ill-health and Cruse Bereavement Care offers a counselling service nationwide for widows, widowers and bereaved children. A similar service is also often available to bereaved family members with a dying relative in a hospice.

One of the reasons why these services have developed is that when the relationship between two adult family members is disturbed or entirely broken, then there are wider deleterious effects on other close family members. Children, especially, are particularly affected by parental divorce. In practice, the 165,000 children under 16 years of age who experience a family split get little or no help with problems arising as a result of the broken parental relationship. There has been substantial research on the problems experienced by these children yet few services have developed as a result, and those that there are tend to be available to very few children. This is despite the fact that the deleterious and often long-term effects on children's development are now well recognised.

In a recent meta-analysis of this research Rogers and Pryor (1998) conclude that as a rule of thumb adverse outcomes are roughly twice as prevalent amongst children who experience parental divorce as compared with those of similar backgrounds whose parents stay together. In particular, the children have lower socio-economic success in later adult life; increased rates of behaviour problems as children; lower achievement; more reported health problems; more depressive symptoms and greater use of drugs (both social and otherwise) than their peers in adolescence and adulthood; and finally they are sexually active earlier than their peers, with consequent early pregnancy and cohabitation. We are not concerned here with the provision or efficacy of services for children. But it is clear that the prevention or amelioration of the parents' poor relationship is likely to have a direct effect on the children's well-being in terms of these characteristics.

Finally in this section we should consider some of the economics of relationship breakdown. The available material is largely to do with marital and couple relationships and the cost to society and government of the legal fees and then the financial support required by the broken family. Hart carried out a review of these and other matters for the Lord Chancellor's Department (Hart, 1999), in which he reviewed the public expenditure involved. Using a variety of evidence, he concludes that 'marital breakdown' incurs public costs in the UK of £3.7–4.4 billion per year. Of this expenditure, Legal Aid accounts for £470 million and the remainder is largely spent on Social Security benefits with some National Health Service costs in addition.

Our conclusion must be that there are many grounds for being vigorous in the provision of effective methods for ameliorating or (hopefully) preventing the disruption of close relationships, particularly those between adult intimate couples. The next issue then is to look more closely at the theories about the nature of these close intimate relationships.

Theories about relationships

We perhaps need first to define the relationships with which we are dealing. A useful set of definitions is provided by Henderson and his colleagues (1979). Using the concept of social interaction as the key idea, they suggest these interactions are of three types, namely:

Type 1: Affectively intense with one and only one person. The person may be within or without the individual's primary group. (The primary group comprises kin, nominated friends, close work associates and neighbours.)

Type 2: Affectively intense interaction with more than one person: or affectively superficial interaction with one or more others from within the primary group.

Type 3: Affectively superficial interaction with one or more others outside the primary group.

Henderson suggests that these types of relationship form an individual's primary group and the concern here is therefore with Type 1 relationships. The emphasis is upon interaction and the importance of the interactive processes is fundamental to most theories of relationship. This is elaborated in an important recent paper by Reis and his colleagues which identifies those aspects of individual behaviour and experience which are part of the capacity to form and maintain relationships.

These writers say that the essence of a relationship is in the interaction and that the hallmark of the interaction is influence (Reis et al., 2000). They define 'close relationships' as those where strong mutual influence exists between partners for extended time and for which the mental representations of the relationship are idiosyncratic to the relationship and are very affect-laden. These approaches highlight the differences that occur in the theories underlying the provision of counselling and psychotherapy – certainly for adult intimate couple relationships – and which we shall see focus on certain aspects of the internal and external worlds of a couple.

Hinde (1981) has appraised the essence of the relationship experience over a number of publications. His view is that the interaction has to be examined for its content, diversity and quality, together with the relative frequency and patterning of the events. Reciprocity and complementarity are two further important characteristics, as is the degree of intimacy. Lastly, Hinde says the perception by the individual of the other, together with the degree of commitment *to* the other will complete the descriptive patterning of the relationship. Curiously, these theoretical concepts have not been put to much use by those trying to explain the breakdown of relationships. They rely more often on more general psychological theories, although attachment theory, whilst partially rooted in overarching psychoanalytic theory, does have a more general theory of relationships, which we shall examine in detail later in the chapter.

Generally, the fundamental approaches to human relationships assume that there are both antecedent and current aspects to a healthy interaction which involve the external world of behaviour as well as the internal representational and symbolic world. In addition, intimate (Type 1) relationships engage major cognitive and emotional experiences which intertwine with each other in complex ways. This conceptual framework could be applied to same sex couples as well as heterosexual couples, and also does not assume that the heterosexual couples are married. However, the vast majority of the studies we shall discuss concern heterosexual couples and very often married couples.

Theories and therapies

How then do these ideas get translated into therapeutic action? We now take a sharper focus to discuss the marital and non-marital couple relationship alone, since this is where most of the work has been done. A significant review in this area which partially overlaps with the broader review of Reis et al. (2000) is that presented by Karney and Bradbury (1995). The review is entitled 'The longitudinal course of marital quality and stability' and the authors say that they have evaluated over 100 studies for their meta-analysis. Much of the research on which

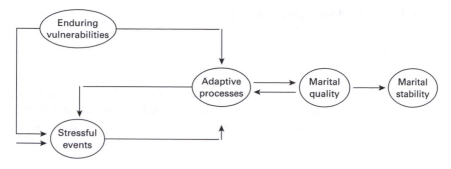

FIGURE 5.1   *A life-course model of stress/adaptation and marital outcome (from Karney and Bradbury, 1995).*

they base their meta-analysis originates from the USA but it has reasonable face-validity for the marital situation in the UK. They summarise the material in Figure 5.1, which is based both on the empirical data and the four major theories that have been advanced to account for marriage life-courses and subsequent breakdown. The theories underlying the empirical work upon which the meta-analysis is based are :

1 Social exchange – emphasising the reciprocity or otherwise of the relationship.
2 Attachment theory – emphasising the historical models of early attachment which have formed the matrix for marital relationships.
3 Crisis theory – seeking to explain both development and breakdown of a marriage in critical events occurring during the marriage.
4 Cognitive-behavioural theory – which focuses attention on the acts of interaction together with the associated expressive statements.

The model emphasises the interactional effects of the 'architectural' properties of the couple members (like personality, social class, attachment style); the inter-current events which a couple must adapt to at various points in their marriage (like the birth of children, economic hardship/affluence, sexual behaviour changes etc.) and adaptive processes (e.g. enhanced affection, withdrawal, blame), all of which then form the subsequent and continuing marital quality (often referred to as satisfaction) and stability.

They conclude that none of the theories is solely able to explain adequately the issue of marital breakdown or stability, mostly because the concepts do not incorporate one or other part of the diagram in Figure 5.1. For instance, the behavioural approaches do not handle developmental processes adequately and attachment theory does not handle the modification of attachment style. But the main approaches to couple counselling and therapy arise from a particular theoretical approach. This may mean that for some difficulties the specific therapy may not facilitate the changes that are required. Either this area of problem goes unresolved or the couple will need further assistance elsewhere.

Couple breakdown and stability

Longitudinal studies of actual couples are unusual, but there are some significant studies completed in the USA, in particular those by Gottman (in conjunction with his colleagues) (1994). The studies are significant because Gottman observed the interaction of couples at the outset of their marriage and then at intervals over some years using psychological, interactional and physiological measures. He characterised stable couples as having one of the three patterns in their joint lives:

1   Conflict avoiding couples with low levels of expressed emotion.
2   Volatile couples with high emotionality but which was both positive and negative.
3   Validating couples who do not avoid conflict but who strive to 'validate' each other as well as acknowledge difference.

Of considerable importance was that these characteristic styles, together with their negative counterparts, enabled the researchers to predict with 80% accuracy the *happiness/unhappiness* and *divorcing/remaining married* status of the couples after a number of years. In particular, the stable styles were based on both experimental observation and self-report measures so that the measures support each other.

By studying the same couples over a number of years, these researchers found there were some characteristic interpersonal processes which were involved in poor relationships. Within the psychological patterns, the ratio of positive to negative statements was critical. For good relationships this was observed to be 5:1 but in poor relationships the ratio was sharply reduced to 1:1. In addition, the characteristics of the development of poor and incompetent interactive patterns have been worked out.

Gottman and his colleagues observed that the process (often started with wives) moves from comment and argument to complaining and criticising. This then leads over time to contempt of one – or both – for each other. This then moves into a negative defensiveness in which neither is now able to interact constructively. The final stage is withdrawal, when poor communication moves to being non-communication. But this work is also marked by the attention which the researchers paid to physiological variables which were measured in their laboratory at the same time as the psychological characteristics.

These measures demonstrated different response modes for wives and husbands. Broadly speaking, the men were experiencing unpleasant negative emotional responses more rapidly than the women: and following this arousal, the unpleasant emotion took longer to subside than in the women. It follows then that, in accordance with learning theory, men will avoid these situations, by using a behavioural response which Gottman calls 'stonewalling'. He reports that this was an observation across a series of subjects. This then may lead a wife to intensify her efforts to gain a response by enhancing the emotional tone of her communication. Because this is physiologically aversive, this may well lead her partner to further withdrawal.

The critique of this series of studies is that it does not deal with the enduring personal characteristics which the couple bring to the marriage and which will enhance or alternatively modify their responses in the situations observed by Gottman and some others. These researchers' partial reply is to point to their success in predicting the breakdown of the relationship through divorce by these observations rather than relying on measures of personality characteristics. In addition, some critics have suggested that external stressors, too, will play a part in enhancing the breakdown pattern described by Gottman, but this is not strongly supported by other evidence, such as that from unemployment and similar adverse events.

Other studies have looked at a variety of factors influencing couple stability but these are often architectural, for example, educational level, parental stability, age at marriage, reasonable income, and so on rather than the dynamic characteristics of the couple. Where these have been considered, the data support the notion that it is the appraisal *by* the partner *of* the other person which is as important as the intrinsic personality characteristics of each partner. A good example of these findings is Hill and Peplau's 15-year follow-up study of couples in Boston, USA (in Bradbury, 1998).

Therapeutic approaches

Emerging from these broad brush issues, the specific frameworks which are used by counsellors and therapists, particularly in the UK are:

1   Behavioural and cognitive-behavioural approaches.
2   Person-centred and psychodynamic approaches.
3   Attachment theory approaches: also referred to as emotionally focused work.
4   Systemic (family group) approaches.
5   Sex therapy.

It is important to present examples of each of these where there is research evidence to evaluate their effect, but we will consider first reviews of work done across these approaches that has been systematically studied. There have been a number of such reviews over the past five years or so, but one by Christensen and Heavey (1999) is very significant. It summarises all of the more recent shorter summaries and adds additional material. It is particularly helpful for a wider readership because it is published in a context other than the specialist couple and family journals.

The authors ask the question, 'Does couple therapy work?' and they answer the question swiftly by reporting that there are 'dozens' of scientifically competent studies that report unequivocally that counselling and therapy increases couple competence and satisfaction significantly more than couples offered no intervention. They state that at least 65% of couples improve with treatment compared with 35% of those offered no intervention.

Within this number they make an important distinction. This is between those couples who, whilst improved, do not achieve levels of relationship competence like those of problem-free control couples: and those couples who do achieve levels of functioning comparable with the apparently normal people. The authors report that just less than half of the treated couples improve to the level of being considered normal and well-functioning.

Christensen and Heavey continue by asking whether these improvements are sustained over time and report that few studies have followed up the couples involved for more than one year. Given this shorter time frame they nevertheless conclude that up to 6–12 months following the intervention the couples maintain the improvements, with a tendency for the insight and emotionally focused approaches to sustain slightly higher levels of improvement. One striking study by Snyder et al. (1991) compared an 'insight' approach with a behaviour therapy approach. Remarkably, they were able to extend their follow-up period to four years. They studied the state of the couples' relationships four years after the intervention and found a significant difference in favour of the insight approach. But we need to enter some caveats about this study. First, that the couples had a substantially longer intervention than most studies allow. In fact people were seen for a mean of 19 sessions. Second, that follow-up over this length of time has not yet been repeated in another similar study.

Apart from this work by Snyder et al., the review concludes that the differences between the treatment modalities are not great, and that for the most part each approach seems to yield very similar rates of improvement. Couple counselling and therapy does differ in one important respect from studies of psychological intervention in other disorders like depression and anxiety states. This is that there is very little attempt to match couples to therapeutic technique. For example, it could make a lot of therapeutic sense for therapists to first offer a couple the opportunity to explore the history of their relationship through insight-oriented or emotion-focused approaches. They may then be likely to benefit more quickly from, say, an ensuing cognitive-behavioural focus which would focus attention on the actual deleterious components of their current patterns of daily interaction.

The exception to this is obviously sex therapy, in which the specific disorders are generally clearly stated and there may be specific treatment modes for specific disorders such as erectile dysfunction. In those cases treatment may be limited to the man in the couple and therefore the couple relationship may receive little attention. Generally, however, sexual dysfunction clinicians request – or even require – the partners to attend together because of the relationship dimensions of all couple sexual activity.

Specific therapies

Behaviour and cognitive behaviour therapy   This is the method that has probably been most closely studied. So much so that Shadish and her colleagues concluded that there was no need for further studies to demonstrate that behavioural marital therapy worked – and this was in 1993 (Shadish et al., 1993). The early behavioural approaches to couple problems were based very much on the precise social skills the couple actually used in interacting with each other. Therapists paid little or no attention to either the natural history of the relationship, nor to the mutual perceptions of each partner. The methods adopted were those of generic behaviour therapy and included behavioural instruction, modelling and rehearsal together with 'homework' which the couple should use between the sessions. They were especially concerned with communication skills – both verbal and non-verbal. As in other behaviour therapy approaches, the couple and therapist contract to work over a given period of time, which is likely to be between five and ten sessions.

Cognitive behaviour therapy for work with couples followed the development of these methods in dealing with individual problems. Here the work is equally concerned with demonstrated skills (or lack of them) and the thought processes which lie behind the behaviour. There is presumed to be a complex three-way process between the way in which each spouse thinks about each other's behaviour as well as how they actually behave. Therefore the changes which the counsellor or therapist is seeking to help the couple achieve lie equally in the planning and construction of physical acts as well as in the behaviour itself. In cognitive behaviour therapy the emotional experience of the partners is also considered, provided it can be verbalised.

Person-centred and psychodynamic approaches   The therapeutic purists would not accept the coupling of these approaches together but they draw on common concepts which state that the couple needs to understand the internal subjective world which he or she brings to the encounter as being of prime importance in understanding a failing relationship. The chief difference between the two approaches is that a psychodynamic therapist is likely to explore much more fully the psychological history of both the couple and the individuals involved. Although both types of practitioners are of course going to use the psychological experience which the couple displays in a treatment session, both will also leave the work of understanding and integrating any change to the couple. The experience is much more 'hands off' than the behavioural approach because the practitioner believes that the couple have to see for themselves how destructive behaviour comes about before they can bring about change.

Originally these approaches did not set a time limit for the number of sessions. However increasingly – and in line with contemporary counselling and psychotherapy practice – the practitioners often establish a period of time for the therapeutic encounters. Yet this type of work is still undertaken within the tradition of the therapeutic work period not being decided in advance. The work 'takes as long as it takes'. Thus, for example in a study of Relate counsellors using a modified person-centred approach, counsellors saw their clients for up to 30 sessions – although the median number was rather smaller (McCarthy et al., 1998). In addition, therapists using this approach are prepared to work with one partner if need be. The behavioural methods (by definition) need both partners present for optimum effect. In the Relate research already referred to, 50% of the interviews were with one partner alone. This presumably also included those cases in which the counsellor had elected to see one of the partners on his or her own for clinical practice reasons. This study was also unusual in including co-habiting couples in the research sample, who formed 13% of the total. But in the detailed analysis of the research results no attempt has been made to differentiate the outcome separately for each couple group.

Attachment theory models   This approach is derived from the psychodynamic fold, but relies substantially on the work of John Bowlby (Bowlby, 1980). Adult intimate couples are seen as becoming attached in a similar way to the attachment process which takes place early in life between the child and the primary caregivers. Bowlby based his work both on human subjects but also on research on animals to demonstrate that attachment was a powerful biopsychological process. The attachment approach differs from some psychodynamic work in insisting that human beings are primarily relationship-seeking rather than instinct-driven.

The therapeutic method is similar to the psychodynamic approach in that it relies on conversations between the therapist and the couple, but with the explicit task of helping the couple to understand the nature of their attachment to each other. This will have a psychohistorical context, and the therapist aims to help the couple recognise, accept and understand the nature of earlier attachments where they appear to be damaging the contemporary adult relationship. This theory could well begin to tease out why second marriages often seem to be repeat versions of first marriages. Perhaps, too, why second marriages are much more prone to breakdown than first marriages.

Because the concepts of the theory are clear, they have been able to be made operational for research purposes, which gives some support to the idea of the importance of earlier attachments. The theory proposes that there are 'secure' attachments, and three types of 'insecure' attachment modes which are drawn from research studies. The insecure modes are called *preoccupied, dismissing* and *fearful,* and together with secure attachment, they yield ten pairings of attachment style. Therapists then describe how, in order to neutralise the incompetent couple attachment, they strive within the therapeutic situation to construct a transitional 'secure' attachment with the individuals. This relatively new approach has been shown to be effective in properly conducted trials, and much more detail is provided in a volume edited by Clulow (2001).

Systemic (family group) therapy   It is clear that in family therapy, the parental couple is included. But family therapists have also included their particular approach as a remedy for couple difficulties alone. Much couple counselling and therapy using other theoretical approaches is also implicitly systemic therapy since the practitioner is regarding the couple as a particular group of two people in interaction. But the systemic approach is almost exclusively preoccupied with the group properties and not at all with the individual issues of each partner. Within family therapy there are also competing models of explanation and approach which it is not necessary to spell out here since they all subscribe to the concept of the system. They differ in the actual techniques which are used, but mostly in detail. A number of family therapists have developed a work culture in which the therapist works with a consultant who is behind a one-way glass screen and who is able to communicate with the working therapist by means of an ear 'bug'. It is also common practice for the therapist to take time out in order to go to the other side of the screen to consult with her/his colleague. An additional technique is to help a family display its problems by means of sculpting, in which the family is physically posed in the consulting room into a representation of a particular real life problem. The 'sculptor' can then explain how the grouping they have created reflects their perception of the family issues.

It is difficult to evaluate the service delivery or efficacy of the service because the agency is usually called a 'family and marital clinic' and it seems that the entry point is much more likely to be a parental problem than an intimate couple problem. In addition, results reported from client surveys often conflate the adult couple *qua* couple with the responses of the adults as parents. Reimers and Treacher (1995) give a refreshingly open and critical account of some of these issues and particularly of the importance of listening to the client's view about the structure of therapy. More could be done to integrate some of the family therapy theory and method into the other modes of helping couples.

Sex therapy Sexual relationships are clearly fundamental to healthy adult couples. But dealing with sexual difficulties was not prominent in the early years of couple counselling and psychotherapy. It formed part of the work which was done with the couple within the techniques of the particular practitioner. It needed a paradigm shift to make sex therapy more effective and more soundly based in a theory of sexual behaviour. This was the contribution of Masters and Johnson in their original work in 1970 which led to widespread use of the methods of intervention and education which they proposed. These methods have been adapted and changed but almost always are a mixture of behavioural and non-behavioural approaches with a good dose of sexual education included. Sex therapists find that, by and large, sex education is still left to hearsay and magazines and is therefore often faulty.

There has been no definitive randomised controlled trial of sex therapy which unequivocally demonstrates its value, but there are some important surveys on the approach which are well summarised by Wilson and James (1991) and which report improvement rates of 65% or more.

An interesting study is reported from Relate's sex therapy service (McCarthy and Thoburn, 1996) in which the authors report on 3,693 cases. This data reveals that as well as the presenting sexual problem, over a third of the clients reported further problems not related to the immediate sexual difficulty. Of these, the commonest were previous sexual abuse; health/psychological problems and relationship problems. In the light of this multi-problem scene it is not surprising that 53% of the people did not go beyond the initial assessment sessions. Of those who completed treatment, over 80% reported an improved or much improved sexual relationship as well as an equally improved more general relationship. Because of its specificity it is surprising that an appropriate rigorous study of sex therapy's efficacy has not yet been completed. Following the very high rates of success reported in their original study by Masters and Johnson (1970), clinicians have reported more modest but still positive results for problems in couples – problems which at one time were thought to be intractable.

Relationships broken by death of a partner

We will finally consider evidence for the psychotherapeutic assistance offered to a bereaved partner as being a special form of couple therapy. We have spelt out in the first part of this chapter the social and personal consequences of couple breakdown. Separation through death also leads to deleterious consequences for the partner who is left. This ranges from the extreme of an accelerated death rate for survivors, through many forms of physical and psychological disturbance (Stroebe et al., 1993). The outcome of the grieving process in terms of disorder and disability is varied and linked to a number of personal and interpersonal factors. Survivors are more at risk if the death has been sudden and/or catastrophic; are younger rather than older; have a pre-existing health deficit; and had an ambivalent or conflictful relationship with their dead partner. All writers emphasise that grieving in one form or another is the proper human response to the loss of a close attachment figure and, although often painful, is necessary to the successful continuance of the bereaved partner's personal life.

Some of the pre-bereavement risk factors are now clear. It should, then, be possible to offer help to the vulnerable survivor on a proactive basis. Parkes reports an interesting attempt to offer such a service to people identified through their contact with a hospice. Sixty-seven 'high risk' survivors were identified and half of them were offered bereavement counselling and the other half were offered no service beyond simple support. On a number of health and adjustment measures, the un-counselled had a significantly poorer outcome 20 months later than the counselled (Parkes and Weiss, 1983). Other studies have shown that therapeutic intervention for bereaved partners may be successful in diminishing pathological responses, but without any specific model for determining which is the 'right' treatment approach. Raphael and her colleagues (1984) have summarised much of this research, but they conclude that few of the studies have set clearly defined therapeutic goals. They also comment that the specific form of intervention which should be offered to specific groups of people remains quite unclear.

This specificity of provision may actually be premature because there is not at present sufficient fundamental research to enable a proper understanding of bereavement to be linked to appropriate treatments. Given the common, indeed universal, experience of bereavement, it is surprising that there is not considerably more systematic study of bereavement reaction, both normal and abnormal. The vast majority of bereaved adult partners are middle-aged or elderly and 86% of adult deaths occur in those aged 65 or over. Could it be that this segment of broken relationships in society receives less than a fair degree of psychological attention – despite the known consequences – because of an age prejudice?

Lesbian and gay couples

Same-sex couples have so far received much less research attention than hetero-sexual couples. The nature of the couple relationship may well be intrinsically different and therefore require a different therapeutic approach. In an interest-ing comparative study by Kurdek and Scmitt (1986), the authors report on the differences between heterosexual and homosexual couples. They found that love of partner was actually weakest as a relationship factor in heterosexual part-ners, but that the homosexual couples had less barriers to leaving a specific rela-tionship thus, perhaps, increasing instability. Patterson (2000) also reports that in some samples reported by her, lesbian and gay relationships were rather more likely than either married or co-habiting heterosexual couples to fail.

There are virtually no adequate studies of the efficacy of treatment for gay and lesbian relationships, but Green (2000) has presented a series of important papers which outline the tasks of delivering a therapeutic service to homosexual couples.

Some conclusions

The reader has now been introduced to a wide range of models and methods which have been used to help people with relationship difficulties. There is now good evidence, which is summarised in the preceding sections, to demonstrate that intervention into the troubled lives of adult couples which is competently undertaken leads to statistically significant improvement as compared with comparable couples who do not have any help.

Within the models of therapy, the evidence is less strong for work with sexual problems and also approaching couple problems through systemic family therapy. In the first case, however, there is good client survey evidence to give grounds for believing again that treated sexual relationships are better than untreated relationships. The area which is less well researched, yet perhaps of no less importance, is that of counselling and psychotherapy with bereaved individuals. This is not to say that in a time of extreme distress, bereavement counsellors do not bring much consolation. They clearly do, but the question of whether this actually leads to an improved state of well-being as compared with no support remains to be established. The ethical issues are sharp here, but not without precedent.

But how does a couple choose the model of intervention that is going to be most suitable for their problems? This is part of the much broader question for all clients and patients undertaking any form of counselling or psychotherapy and is now receiving the serious attention which it deserves. The issue is actu-ally two-fold. First, there is the question of how a troubled couple can be allocated to an intervention which is appropriate for their problems. But secondly there is the issue of how couples can be moved from first-line treatment to a more skilled and sophisticated treatment mode. It seems at present as if the couple are taken on by an agency for help but that if that help proves ineffective, the couple are simply allowed to leave without further thought about whether a different approach would be of more value. Thus the attrition rate is quite high.

For example, in the Relate study (McCarthy et al., 1998), which is the largest study of couple counselling that we have at present, nearly 40% of those who became clients did not go beyond the first interview. Twenty per cent said that, nevertheless, they were satisfied with a single interview. But 20% were not. So one in five of the clients apparently received no help and were not then enabled to go elsewhere. Information from other services is not easily available and so it may be that some of those are better at following through and finding an alternative treatment for a couple. We clearly need some good naturalistic studies – difficult to do – which would plot the career of contemporary troubled couples more closely to establish what paths they follow in their search for help and how all-too-frequently this is not available.

At the commencement of the chapter the case was made for the social and psychological impact of breakdown in adult couple relationships and the damage which is also done to the development of some children. The situation is actually worse than this because people who re-marry re-divorce at twice the frequency of first-time marriages. This pattern of marriage breakdown appears set to continue, so everything possible should be available to help prevent breakdown in the first place. Measures should then be readily available to help those whose relationships fail to recover competently.

We then laid out in some detail the reasonably strong evidence for the benefits of the psychotherapeutic approach. Yet in a major recent study with which the author was involved, only 25% of a sample of over 8,000 people seeking information about divorce had actually approached a counselling agency (Walker, 2001). It does not of course follow that the other 75% would have used a couple counselling service, but in-depth interviews in the same major study revealed that many respondents thought that people in troubled relationships should have access to a service much earlier on. This view was reinforced by Hart (1999) in his review and this is therefore a challenge to practitioners and policy-makers alike. Finally, the practitioners must become more flexible and open in approach so that the right treatment or series of treatments can be offered for the appropriate problems. Services for troubled couples or survivors of broken relationships are seriously underdeveloped in the UK. In the light of the present state of research, enhanced and increased services are badly needed for both individuals, and couples, and for society.

References

Baker, R., Allen, H., Penn, W., Daw, P. and Baker, E. (1998) *The Dorset Primary Care Counselling Service Research Evaluation*. Dorset: Dorset Health Care NHS Trust.
Bowlby, J. (1969, 1973, 1980) *Attachment and Loss*, 3 Vols. London: Hogarth Press.

Bradbury, T.N. (ed.) (1998) *The Developmental Course of Marital Dysfunction*. Cambridge: Cambridge Univeresity Press.

Christensen, A. and Heavey, C.L. (1999) Interventions for couples. *Annual Review of Psychology*, 50, 165–90.

Clulow, C. (ed.) (2001) *Adult Attachment and Couple Psychotherapy*. London: Brunner–Routledge.

Corney, R. and Jenkins, R. (eds) (1993) *Counselling in General Practice*. London: Routledge.

Fincham, F.D. and Beach, S.H.R. (1999) Conflict in marriage: implications for working with couples. *Annual Review Psychology*, 50, 47–77.

Gottman, J. (1994) *What Predicts Divorce? The Relationship Between Marital Processes and Marital Outcomes*. Hillsdale: NJ: Lawrence Erlbaum.

Green, R.-J. (ed.) (2000) Gay, lesbian, and bisexual issues in family therapy; special section. *Journal of Marital and Family Therapy*, 26, 407–68.

Hart, G. (1999) *The Funding of Marriage Support*. London: Lord Chancellor's Department.

Hendersen, S., Duncan-Jones, P., McAuley, H. and Ritchie, K. (1979) The patient's primary group. In P. Williams and A. Clare (eds) *Psychological Disorders in General Practice*. London: Academic Press.

Hill, C.T. and Peplau, L.A. (1998) Premarital Predictors of relationship outcomes: a 15-year follow up of the Boston couples study. In T.N. Bradbury (ed.) *The Development Course of Marital Dysfunction*. Cambridge: Cambridge University Press.

Hinde, R.A. (1981) The bases of a science of interpersonal relationships. In S.W. Duck, and R. Gilmour (eds), *Personal Relationships*. London: Academic Press.

Jacobsen, H.S. and Addis, M.E. (1993) Research on couples and couple therapy: What do we know? Where are we going? *Journal of Consulting and Clinical Psychology*, 61, 85–93.

Karney, B.R. and Bradbury, T.N. (1995) The longitudinal course of marital quality and stability: a review of theory, method and research. *Psychological Bulletin*, 118, 3–34.

Kurdek, L.A. and Scmitt, J.P. (1986) Relationship quality of partners in heterosexual married, heterosexual cohabiting, and gay and lesbian relationships. *Journal of Personality and Social Psychology*, 51, 711–20.

McCarthy, P. and Thoburn, M. (1996) *Psychosexual Therapy at Relate*. Newcastle: Relate Centre for Family Studies.

McCarthy, P., Walker, J. and Kain, J. (1998) *Telling It As It Is: The Client Experience of Relate Counselling*. Newcastle: Newcastle Centre for Family Studies.

Masters, W.H. and Johnson, V. (1970) *Human Sexual Inadequacy*. London: Churchill.

Parkes, C.M. and Weiss, R.S. (1983) *Recovery from Bereavement*. New York: Basic Books.

Patterson, C.J. (2000) Family relationships of lesbians and gay men. *Journal of Marriage and the Family*, 62, 1052–69.

Raphael, B. (1984) *The Anatomy of Bereavement*. London: Hutchinson.

Reimers, S. and Treacher, A. (1995) *Introducing User-Friendly Family Therapy*. London: Routledge

Reis, H.T., Collins, W.A. and Berscheid, E. (2000) The relationship context of human behaviour and development. *Psychological Bulletin* 126, 844–72.

Rogers, B. and Pryor, J. (1998) *Divorce and Separation: The Outcome for Children*. York: Joseph Rowntree Foundation.

Shadish, W.R., Montgomery, L.M., Wilson, P., Wilson, M.R., Bright, I. and Okwumabua, T. (1993) Effects of family and marital psychotherapies: a meta-analysis. *Journal of Consulting and Clinical Psychology*, 61, 992–1002.

Simons, J. (1999) How useful is relationship therapy? In J. Simons (ed.), *High Divorce Rates: The State of the Evidence* (Vol. II). London: Lord Chancellors Department. Research Series No. 2/99.

Snyder, D.K., Wills, R.M. and Grady-Fletcher, A. (1991) Long-term effectiveness of behavioural versus insight-oriented marital therapy: a 4-year follow-up study. *Journal Consulting and Clinical Psychology*, 59, 138–41.

Stroebe, M.S., Stroebe, W. and Hansson, R.O. (1993) *Handbook of Bereavement.* Cambridge: Cambridge University Press.

Walker, J. (ed.) (2001) Information Meetings and Associated Provisions within the Family Law Act 1996. Final Evaluation Report. London: Lord Chancellor's Department; and Newcastle: Centre for Family Studies.

Wilson, K. and James, A. (1991) Research in therapy with couples. In D. Hooper and W. Dryden (eds), *Couple Therapy: A Handbook.* Milton Keynes: Open University Press.

6
THERAPEUTIC BENEFITS FOR PEOPLE WITH BORDERLINE PERSONALITY DISORDER
Eva Burns-Lundgren

This chapter will address the potential benefits of therapy for a group of people with problems that often impede their getting access to, or making full use of, therapies available within the NHS and other services. As a condition, it is one that often causes controversy and conflict, as has been seen in recent reporting of high profile court cases. Many psychiatrists understandably do not consider its treatment as part of their legally required remit, or a priority in the current highly pressurised and often under-funded NHS. This is especially so as, until recently, there have not been seen to be many clinically effective treatments to offer this group of patients, but rather only management problems and frustrations at the failure of offered or available services. Its sufferers nevertheless make up around 15% of psychiatric inpatients (Winston, 2000), and they are often 'unsatisfactorily maintained as psychiatric outpatients, where successive generations of trainee psychiatrists prescribe them successive generations of antidepressant or antipsychotic drugs' (Ryle, 1997). They also put high demands on Accident and Emergency departments after episodes of self-harm, as well as on substance abuse services and general medical services. It is likely that 'the overall prevalence (and cost to the health service) of untreated borderline personality disorder in various treatment settings is considerably higher than is recognised' (Ryle, 1997).

The chapter begins by looking at what is meant by the term borderline personality disorder, or BPD, and this will include an overview of its aetiology, both as seen generally, and specifically from the perspective of cognitive analytic therapy (CAT). I will then attempt to provide an overview of different treatment models, which have been developed specifically for this client group, and their relative merits as they have been reported in recent research publications. I will return to the specific contribution made to this field by CAT, in terms of the theoretical understanding of the development of the disorder, and as a model of treatment, before the chapter finishes with an overview of general treatment benefits and essential treatment features.

Definitions

What do we mean when we say that someone has a borderline personality disorder? It appears to me that it is a term that is much mis-used, often in a jargon-driven way or to cover up therapeutic short-comings or lack of client progress. If we state that someone has a BPD, we can perhaps justify any lack of achievement, without having to look too closely at our therapeutic practice. We can also blame the institution where we work, or the lack of government funding, for the fact that we don't have the ability to provide the undefined long-term treatment that we assure the listener is the only way to work with these problems. The term BPD often also seems to carry some kind of magical or mystical connotations, which add a certain grandiosity and specialness to our therapeutic endeavours, putting colleagues in awe and perhaps rendering them less likely to ask awkward questions.

Because it is for the people concerned already such a personally and socially destructive, disruptive and often distressing 'condition', we do however owe it to our clients/patients to be clearly aware of what its characteristics and prognosis are. We need to know what can reasonably and most effectively be achieved in our work, so as not to raise false expectations, which would only feed into the common cycle of idealisation leading to inevitable let-down or rejection, and so to further damage and despair.

Classifications

In his review of recent developments in BPD, Winston (2000) states that BPD has an estimated prevalence of up to 2% in the general population and 15% among psychiatric inpatients. According to the two most commonly used international psychiatric manuals of classification in their most recent editions, the World Health Organisation's ICD-10, and the American Psychiatric Association DSM-IV, BPD involves pervasive and longstanding patterns of 'instability of interpersonal relationships, self-image and affects' (APA, 1994). BPD usually affects several areas of functioning, for example, 'affectivity, arousal, impulse control, ways of perceiving and thinking, and style of relating to others' (ICD-10). Relationships are often intense, and characterised by alternation between idealisation and devaluation, with frantic efforts to avoid (real or imagined) abandonment. It commonly includes a markedly and persistently unstable sense of self as well as self-damaging impulsivity, often expressed through angry attacks on others, or suicidal behaviour, gestures or threats. These difficulties tend to occur against a background of chronic feelings of emptiness. They sometimes include transient paranoid ideas and 'dissociative' symptoms, where the person tends not so much to repress unmanageable feelings or conflicts, but to dissociate, cut off from them, and switch abruptly from one state of mind to another. Fonagy (1991: 639–40) describes this very instability as 'a stable and central characteristic of borderline functioning', a 'stable lability'. Overall, women are much more frequently diagnosed than men. The very ability of this client group to cause anxiety in the clinician, and the intensity and confusion in the counter-transference, are often indicators of the presence of a BPD.

As we all know, even at the best of times, and with our wits about us, life is not necessarily easy to make sense of or to deal with. Living with all these difficulties, it therefore does not come as a surprise that people with BDP also suffer a great degree of distress and unhappiness, and that psychiatric conditions 'are a virtually universal accompaniment of BPD' (Ryle, 1997). Depression features for a large number, though its cause, quality and response to medication may differ from the usual range in depressive illnesses. Other conditions commonly found include substance abuse, eating disorders and somatisation disorders.

Causative factors

There is no singular agreed 'cause' for BPD, but there are certain features that commonly figure in the picture of BPD. It is, for example, generally accepted that there can be important biological and genetic determinants, which may influence both an individual's specific capacity to learn and mature, and the impact she or he has on caregivers and on their willingness or ability to provide appropriate care (Kernberg, 1967, as reported in Fonagy, 1991). Stone (1993: 310) states that 'personality disorders ... derive, in part, from patterns of thought and behaviour that appear to be "hard-wired" into the central nervous system ... during the first five or six years of life', and describes the varying impact of certain childhood experiences on adult outcome of BPD. These experiences are summarised by Ryle (1997) to include physical violence and sexual abuse, as well as loss, deprivation and trauma, with high percentages of each reported by Winston (2000). He also quotes the claims by van der Kolk et al. (1994) that the earlier this abuse takes place, the more damaging an effect it is likely to have, both in terms of ability to modulate emotion, and its correlation with self-mutilation (Herman et al., 1989). Fonagy (1991: 651) similarly quotes numerous studies that indicate childhood presence of repeated trauma, physical abuse of a sexual or aggressive kind, as well as more general failure by parents or caregivers to provide 'adequate support, attention, involvement and protection'. He also stresses the negative impact of this failure or absence on the development of mental structures and processes, which leads to an absence in the individual of a 'theory of mind', or a poor comprehension of, and ability to reflect upon, his or her own mental state and that of others.

Ryle (1997) has developed this aspect of the aetiology of BPD further from a more cognitive perspective in CAT, where there is seen to be damage to three levels of development. *Level 1* involves a restriction or distortion of the repertoire of 'Reciprocal Roles', or habitual ways of perceiving and relating to self and others, which are available to the individual. *Level 2* involves the 'incomplete development or disruption of higher order procedures responsible for mobilising, connecting and sequencing Level 1 procedures' (Ryle, 1997: 34). In CAT this is not seen to result from conflicts between intrapsychic forces, but rather from being exposed to 'incoherent, neglectful and contradictory experiences' in the absence of relationships with caring others, who in normal development would provide ways of linking and creating meaning out of these events. There is also additional 'trauma-induced dissociation' in the face of abuse or other emotionally unmanageable experiences, which adds further pressure to the process of disconnection and results in various degrees of separation between split-off aspects of the self. *Level 3* finally involves the 'incomplete development or disruption of self-reflection', which includes narrow attention and deficient vocabulary for thoughts and feelings, as well as 'discontinuity of experience and memory' (Ryle, 1997).

Course

Paris (1993) stressed the chronicity of BPDs, and stated that recovery tends to occur only after 10–15 years. Even when improved, patients with BPD 'continue to have serious problems later in life, and remain at risk for relapse' (Paris, 1993: 145). Paris, like Higgitt and Fonagy (1992) saw no clear predictors for outcome of BPD in terms of level of functioning or suicide, nor did he find evidence that treatment has an effect on long-term outcome. However, Stone (1993) demonstrated that outcome is more favourable than was previously thought, with two-thirds of patients 'clinically well' after follow-up periods of 10–30 years, and about a fifth leading symptom-free lives. The condition does, however, remain a very serious one, with suicide rates in the range of 8–10% reported (Paris, 1993; Ryle, 1997; Stone, 1993). Stone (1990) extracted as factors linked with worse outcome in terms of suicide, those of 'continuing alcohol abuse, chaotic impulsivity and a history of parental brutality or sexual molestation'. Factors negatively affecting overall outcome include a history of parental brutality, a history of father–daughter incest, 'schizotypal' and anti-social features (Ryle, 1997; Stone, 1993), as well as severity or ingrainedness and 'inordinate anger' (Stone, 1993). However, and importantly, Stone (1993) was also able to indicate as attributes or factors connected with better outcome: intelligence, attractiveness, artistic talents, obsessive–compulsive traits and, in the case of alcoholics, adherence to Alcoholics Anonymous (AA). He also reported favourable responses to psychotherapy, but with efficacy depending less on variety and length of therapy than on key patient variables such as 'the positive personality traits of motivation, the strength to face weakness, the confidence to trust another person, and the flexibility to weigh and select among contingencies'. Other positive attributes included candour and introspection, and the ability to accept responsibility for contributing to interpersonal difficulties. Paris (1996) has suggested that patients with a good work history do better.

Treatment challenges

Bearing in mind the damage, pain and complexities involved, working with people who have a BPD is going to be highly challenging, for counsellors and therapists, never mind for the client who is being asked to face some very painful feelings and experiences. It will involve being together on an emotional roller-coaster, with many highs and lows, and abrupt switches between these. So what should be borne in mind when considering whether to offer treatment to someone with a BPD, and if offered, what do those involved need to be prepared for during the course of that process?

First of all one needs to think carefully in terms of *selection and assessment.* Does the person possess enough in terms of the attributes outlined by Stone and Paris, above, in order for the venture to be of a constructive nature, for client and therapist alike? Are the manifestations of the BPD too severe and ingrained? Are there other personality disorders also present which would increase the risk of poor outcome (Dolan et al., 1995)? Is there substance abuse in the picture, and what is the attitude of the client to this? Does this abuse need to be dealt with first, in order for the therapy to have any chance, or can it be dealt with as part of the treatment offered? Are the general social and cultural influences (for example, income, educational level and experience of work) favourable enough, and is there sufficient personal and social support? Attention has to be paid to the potential for violence, and the safety of the treatment setting. If there are too many negative indicators at the outset, and bearing in mind what the therapist's specific setting can realistically offer, a firm and appropriately explained refusal of treatment is likely to be more 'thera-peutic' and less abusive than a possible later repetition of abandonment or rejec-tion and failure.

If treatment is offered, it is for these same reasons important to think clearly in terms of *realistic goal-setting* and avoidance of therapist heroics, both in terms of treatment goals and length of treatment offered. It is also likely to be most helpful for a *focus* to be developed in terms of resolving problems in the present (Paris, 1993), and to establish a clear 'contract' or working agreement. We should not expect psychological-mindedness from the outset, as this is often the very capacity that is lacking, but rather offer some new understanding and see if or how it can be used.

Once work starts, what is likely to be encountered? First of all there is a well-documented tendency towards high drop-out rates. In their review, Gunderson et al. (1989) report a drop-out rate of between a quarter and two-thirds of patients in psychodynamic therapy in the first 6 months. So one of the first tasks is that of establishing a firm working, or therapeutic, alliance as early as possible, which engages and enlists the cooperation of the client in the task ahead.

By these high drop-out rates, are clients perhaps also trying to tell therapists that extended therapy is not the automatic panacea and unquestioned solution that it is often held out to be? In the absence of research evidence, Paris (1993) encourages us to treat these claims with scepticism. He quotes various studies pointing to most therapy benefit being achieved within 10–12 weeks, with there being few benefits to continuing for longer than 25 sessions, and only certain circumscribed personality traits being affected by between 25 and 50 sessions.

What are therapists then likely to face once into therapy with someone with a BPD? Ryle (1997: 41) puts it very starkly: 'The main challenges posed by borderline patients are their tendency to destroy what they most need, their use of anger to conceal or defend against vulnerability and the persistence of their dissociation'. So the challenge is considerable, not least in terms of our view of ourselves as competent, caregiving professionals. Fonagy (1991) describes people with BPD as being interpersonally hypersensitive, whilst, or perhaps because, they at the same time often lack the 'as if' quality in the experience of relationships with others. He sees it as an absence of the ability to think of fantasies or feelings between people as 'mental' processes rather than actual events. This is perhaps both caused and maintained by an underdeveloped capacity to reflect on events and feelings, as well as the person having no accessible emotional vocabulary (Ryle, 1997). It is easy to see how this would increase interpersonal vulnerability, making the person very dependent on the capabilities of the 'other' in relationships and therefore further fearful of intimacy.

This clearly has very considerable implications for the therapy relationship, and the potential for the use thereof. Therapists are, at least initially, easily seen in the transference as (and seduced by the view of themselves as) idealised others, 'perfect' rescuers, which usually leads the client/patient to be on the look-out for, if not to provoke, abandonment or abuse. And once the perceived 'abandonment' has occurred, through inevitably 'less than perfect' understanding or gratification of needs, the punishment is usually swift and can feel highly taxing of therapists' inner resources. There is a tendency to polarise aspects of the self and of other people, with fluctuations from one extreme to another. Gabbard and Wilkinson (1994: 5) point out how 'borderline patients possess an uncanny ability to tune in to the therapist's vulnerabilities and exploit them'. This is a skill the client has no doubt observed and been at the receiving end of, during early years of attack and neglect, as well as one she or he has carefully honed in order to survive and/or extract punishment and revenge. Sandler (1976: 44) describes how 'the patient attempts to prod the analyst into behaving in a particular way and unconsciously scans and adapts to his perception of the analyst's reaction'. This can be seen as part of the search for complementary roles to those in which clients perceive themselves and thus to create predictable, even if painful, interactions and interrelationships. An illusion of control is thus maintained, where at least clients can feel able to pre-empt potential abuse and abandonment by getting in there first and doing it themselves.

This unsurprisingly tends to lead to parallel and very powerful countertransference feelings and responses in the therapist, prominent among which are 'guilt feelings, rescue fantasies, transgressions of professional boundaries, rage and hatred, helplessness, worthlessness, anxiety, and even terror' (Gabbard and Wilkinson, 1994: 19). Much attention is also paid in therapy literature to the prolific use by people with BPD of the processes of projective identification and splitting, whereby unmanageable feelings are cut off from awareness, and considerable pressure is put on the therapist and others to experience and perhaps even act on these. In order for this experience not simply to remain another damaging repetition of past destructive relationships, the task is then for the therapist to hold these emotions and relationships and to bring them into awareness, where new ways can be found and learned about how to name, process and act on them (e.g. Fonagy, 1991; Ryle, 1997; Sandler, 1976). This task is especially crucial when the therapist or counsellor works as part of a team, where the patient can elicit highly contrasting responses from different members of staff, who then find themselves forced into polarised positions, usually always to the detriment of the client (Gabbard and Wilkinson, 1994). Recent attempts have been reported where CAT diagrams have been used within staff groups and organisations to contain and metabolise these processes (Kerr, 1999).

One issue, apart from the risk of violence, that tends to arouse particular anxiety, concerns that of suicide threats and attempts, which are common with this group of patients (Stone, 1993). This can to some extent be pre-empted by the establishment of a clear 'contract' at the outset of therapy, with agreements made about self-harming behaviour and emergency procedures (Ryle, 1997). It does, however, raise core issues such as limits to responsibility and professional boundaries, and therapists need to watch out lest they set themselves unrealistic and unattainable tasks.

This points to a final, and crucial, issue when working with BPD individuals, namely that of the need for supervision (Gabbard and Wilkinson, 1994), and for institutional support. The anxieties inevitably raised can then gradually be diluted at each step up the organisation: 'the patient feels safe with the therapist, because the therapist feels safe with the supervisor, who feels safe with other clinical colleagues' (Ryle, 1997: 96). It is not uncommon for a parallel process to occur, where feelings evoked in the therapist by the patient, also get evoked in the supervisor by the supervisee. This affords an additional opportunity to understand and make sense of what is occurring, which can then be brought back to therapy.

It may seem that this chapter has thus far paid an unnecessary and inordinate amount of attention to the challenges for therapists in this venture, perhaps to the exclusion of focusing on the therapy benefits for BPD clients. Unless these issues are clearly thought about, however, and addressed at an early stage of any therapeutic endeavour with this client group, the task could easily become an unmanageable one, for client and therapist alike. This would lead to very little therapeutic benefit for the client, if not even an actual repetition of harm done, and further confirmation of the client's already negative expectations of human relatedness.

Treatment models and their outcome

So what are the different therapeutic models that have been developed for working with this client group, and what results have they achieved so far? Although the studies by Paris (1993, 1996) concluded that there was 'no evidence that treatment has an effect on outcome', Higgitt and Fonagy (1992) in their review of the effectiveness of a range of treatment methods found that most had some impact, especially on less severely disturbed patients. Since the time of these publications, a number of studies have been undertaken, recently reviewed by Winston in *Advances in Psychiatric Treatment* (2000), which causes him to be more cautiously optimistic about the improving 'outlook for this challenging group of patients' (p. 215). Bateman and Fonagy (2000) have similarly found evidence for the effectiveness of psychotherapy for personality disorders, and summarised effective treatment components.

For their study, Stevenson and Meares (1992) developed a 'coherent, consistently applied, and identifiable treatment approach', based on a psychology of self, which was delivered for 12 months, on a twice weekly basis, by closely supervised trainee therapists. The authors concluded that 'a specific form of psychotherapy is of benefit for patients' with BPD. They point to reductions in impulsivity, affective instability, anger and suicidal behaviour, and found that only 70% of the subjects fulfilled diagnostic criteria for BPD at 12 months follow-up. Sabo et al. (1995) monitored changes in self-destructiveness in their follow-up study of 37 female inpatients with BPD receiving individual psychotherapy. They were able to report a clear and significant decline in suicidal behaviour, though not in self-harm behaviour, which was seen to be an independent variable.

The approach that has received most attention in the past decade is that of dialectical behaviour therapy (DBT), where Linehan et al. (1991, 1994) have offered a comprehensive cognitive-behavioural intervention with specific treatment targets, and followed patients up in randomised controlled trials. Skilled practitioners in an intensive outpatient programme used a combination of individual and group approaches, centring on the patient–therapist relationship. In their own words, the results were mixed, with a reduction at the end of a year's treatment in the number and severity of suicide attempts and in the use of inpatient services. However, the approach did not reduce the level of depression or hopelessness, that is 'subjects in the dialectical behaviour therapy group acted better but were still miserable' (Linehan, 1994: 1775). In contrast, Piper et al. (1993) achieved significant treatment results in terms of 'interpersonal functioning, illness symptoms, self-esteem, life satisfaction and defensive functioning' as quoted by Bateman and Fonagy (1999), in a psychodynamically group-oriented treatment programme involving partial hospitalisation.

In the UK, Dolan et al. (1997) evaluated the impact of 12 months' psychotherapeutic inpatient treatment at the Henderson Hospital therapeutic community. Therapy included a formal daily programme of group meetings and more informal 'sociotherapy' deriving from the social milieu. There was more active participation of patients in their own treatment and that of their peers, as well as in the day-to-day running of the community. The authors found that there was a significant reduction in Borderline Syndrome Index (BSI) for the admitted treatment group, compared to the non-admitted group. Length of stay in treatment was correlated with improvements in borderline psychopathology at follow-up. Recent studies also found reductions in service use and costs in three NHS therapeutic communities (Winston, 2000).

A more recent study has been undertaken by Bateman and Fonagy (1999), comparing the effectiveness of psychoanalytically oriented partial hospitalisation with standard psychiatric care, for patients with BPD. They report a significant decrease on all measures for the treatment group compared to the controls, citing specifically reduction in depressive symptoms, decrease in suicidal and self-harming acts, and improvement in social and interpersonal functioning. While their partial hospitalisation programme seems to have advantages over both possibly more costly inpatient treatments and general psychiatric treatment, the question remains for the authors as to whether it is better than intensive, specialist outpatient treatment approaches.

This is where cognitive analytic therapy may have a role to fill and potential answers to give. These have been outlined by Ryle (1997), and are described in a recent study by Ryle and Golynkina (2000). A randomised, controlled trial (RCT) of outpatient CAT with BPD patients is also in process at Dorset Healthcare Trust, which will be reported in due course. Another RCT comparing CAT with standard treatment for adolescents and young adults at a Health Service centre in Melbourne is now in its early stages, where an attempt is being made to explore whether early intervention with CAT can help prevent the development or reduce the severity of BPD.

Cognitive Analytic Therapy

CAT as a theoretically and therapeutically integrated, brief treatment model, has been developed over the past two decades by Antony Ryle. Even though the model is only now being formally researched in randomised, controlled studies, it has throughout been based on, and lent itself to, research evaluation, both in terms of general outcome and through looking at specific therapeutic components. In his chapter on 'The Evolution of Cognitive Analytic Therapy', Ryle (1997: 12) states:

> CAT originated in an integration of cognitive and psychoanalytical ideas in which a main influence was my use of repertory grid techniques (Kelly, 1955) to measure and describe change in the course of psychodynamic psychotherapy. In the course of this research patients were involved, at the start of therapy, in working with the therapist at the task of identifying and describing clearly what had brought them to therapy (their target problems or TPs) and in elaborating descriptions of the ways in which these were caused and maintained (target problem procedures or TPPs).

I chose to quote this passage both because it clearly illustrates the evaluative stance mentioned above, and because it demonstrates the strong collaborative approach, which is at the core of CAT. It also highlights the use of specific targets, or a focus, which therapy is aimed at, as well as how links are consistently made between these and the (usually) interpersonal procedures which maintain them and make them resistant to revision and change. In view of the influence and prominence of dissociation and splitting in the aetiology of BPD, this is one of the aspects of CAT which particularly recommends it to work with this client group.

The joint descriptive 'reformulation' process was found to be very therapeutic in itself, and has been refined and developed into a core component in the form of the Reformulation Letter, which is usually completed at around session four, and which is accompanied or preceded by a visually descriptive diagram, an 'SDR' or Sequential Diagrammatic Reformulation. This is a particularly containing tool when working with clients with BPD, as it provides a very immediate way of making sense of otherwise disconnected and unmanageable feelings and experiences. It provides this understanding in a descriptive manner, usually jointly arrived at, rather than in the form of interpretations from an 'expert' aimed at a comparatively powerless client/patient, already vulnerable and sensitive to the potential for control and abuse. It has therefore proved to be of clear value in the process of engagement and in prevention of drop-out from treatment.

CAT offers a model for understanding human development, which incorporates object relations and attachment theory, as well as paying attention to the social and cultural formation of mind and the crucial significance of transmission of 'signs' and meaning (Ryle, 1997). Key concepts for the understanding of early personality development are provided by the definition of Reciprocal Roles. These are understood to be acquired in the earliest interactions with mother and other caretakers, and an individual's repertoire of roles is the product of the child's temperament in interaction with the procedures of significant others. These role patterns are endowed with meaning according to their specific context, and internalised, and are seen to provide the template for later interactions with others, and also for inner dialogue and self-care. In CAT theory, splitting is seen to result from 'contrasting, polarised Reciprocal Role patterns and of separate self states' (Ryle, 1997: 18), and projective identification as a particular example of a general tendency to elicit reciprocal responses from others (Ryle, 1994; Sandler, 1976). In BPD, Reciprocal Role patterns are seen to be dissociated into separate 'self states', with access only to a limited role repertoire in each, and with little or no awareness while in each, of the existence or content of other states.

The task for therapy with clients with a BPD then becomes to identify these different 'self states', and for transitions between them to be monitored on a specialised version of an SDR. The client can in this way be helped to feel more in charge of relationships and events, by realising what procedures emanate from which state, and by learning what might trigger a switch from one state to another. This fills a connecting function whereby the client can eventually learn how all the states are aspects of his or her singular self. A typical BPD diagram tends to contain the components shown in Figure 6.1, where the × stands for a flash or trigger point.

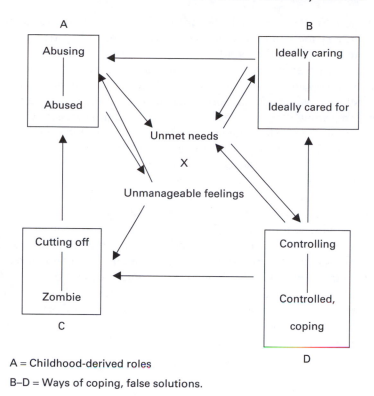

A = Childhood-derived roles

B–D = Ways of coping, false solutions.

FIGURE 6.1   *Sequential diagrammatic reformulation for borderline personality disorder*

Via location on the diagram, therapeutic use can be made of how reciprocal roles are enacted not just externally, but most importantly, in the therapeutic relationship. I find that the diagram is a crucial tool in any therapy, and particularly when working with people with BPDs. It helps to neutralise and make sense of otherwise potentially overwhelming transference and countertransference reactions, which can now be seen to be part of a larger picture, with the therapy relationship as only another example of pervasive patterns. It helps me not to react defensively but to remain open to 'learn from my patient', and also in the development of my 'internal supervisor' (Casement, 1985).

The SDR similarly provides a guiding hand when devising 'homework' assignments to be carried out between sessions. These should always be related to the TPs, with the aim of self-monitoring, and of practising and transferring newly acquired skills to the client before the predicted end of the brief (usually 24 sessions for BPD) therapy. The diagram also helps to predict and deal with reactions to termination, which is actively kept in mind throughout the therapy, and is an invaluable tool in supervision. At the end of therapy Goodbye Letters are exchanged, which offer an opportunity for both to appraise the benefits of the therapy, as well as to look forward to challenges ahead and how best to utilise the new tools and experience to face these. For BPD patients follow-ups are offered at 1, 2, 3 and 6 months, to review and help maintain progress.

In order to pre-empt a common observation from therapists unfamiliar with this model, I would stress that this seemingly reductive and formal structure is intended as a holding and supportive framework, to help guide therapist and client alike through the complex and at times painful process of therapy. It is perhaps only when we feel properly psychologically held and contained that we can take the risk of allowing something intense and scary to happen between the two human beings in the room, and to refuse to be recruited into repeating old, damaging patterns. CAT clearly recognises the uniqueness of each client and therapist, and encourages us not to adhere too rigidly to the format, but to use our judgement and 'push where it moves'. Every CAT has to recreate the tools anew with each patient, and only in this way can we achieve what Yalom (1999) describes, namely that 'the project of constructing a new, unique therapy was the therapy itself'. This respectful joint creation is something utterly unfamiliar to most people with BPD, and likely to join the ranks of one of Yalom's 'curative factors' (Yalom, 1995). However, a balance clearly has to be found, in that research by Bennett and Parry (1996) and Bennett and Parry (in press) has indicated that adherence to the model enhances the therapy, and that this is reflected in better overall outcomes. Or as one could say, 'the cattier the CAT, the better the outcome'.

Therapy benefits for BPD

Having described the specific contribution CAT may have to make in the field of working with BPD, I now round up by returning to the general benefits of counselling for BPD clients, and to what are likely to be the most effective components of such counselling. In summary, the outcome of recent studies appears to indicate a more positive outlook for the potential for real benefits from therapy for people with BPD, even to the point where clients no longer meet the criteria for the disorder. Most of the studies point to a reduction in self-harm and suicidal behaviour, as well as a reduction in hospital admissions and overall use of services and medication. A decrease in violent and impulsive behaviour can be achieved, as well as lowered depression, while self-esteem, affective stability and general social and interpersonal functioning can improve. Improvements have also been maintained at follow-up, which points to continuing treatment effect. Overall, it thus appears that offer of therapy rather than non-therapy is indicated for a population that is associated with potentially high levels of harm to self and others.

For a condition characterised by changeability and inconsistency of self and relationships, the major aim has to be that of integration. It is therefore not surprising that the therapy approaches which appear to have most impact are those with a clear and cohesive model and treatment format, which with good supervision can be provided also by trainee therapists. Bateman and Fonagy (1999, 2000) summarise the essential features of an effective treatment programme for BPD as: a structured and theoretically coherent treatment approach, with a clear focus and with attention paid to a strong relationship between client and therapist, enabling the latter to take a relatively active stance. In their view it needs to be applied consistently and 'relatively long term', though this is not clearly defined, and be well integrated with other services. Most of these criteria are clearly core characteristics of CAT, and in agreement with Ryle (1997), the authors stress that these permit crucial attention being paid to factors (in CAT thought of as procedures) that might otherwise disrupt the therapy relationship and interfere with the possibility for change. It echoes Holmes' (1994: 14) statement in his review of brief dynamic psychotherapy (BDP), that 'to be effective, therapists should learn and stick within a particular model of therapy'.

More research clearly has to be undertaken regarding optimal length of treatment and whether this is best provided on an out-, day- or inpatient basis. I would echo the challenge in Phillips' (2000) book *Promises, Promises* for us as therapists not to enter the arena with our minds already made up, and to dispute the perhaps collusive belief that our clients' difficulties have to be completely understood and worked through before they can move on. Perhaps it is better to leave people with 'unfinished business', but with a strong enough experience of a relationship that has been sufficiently different for new avenues to have been opened up, and with enough conceptual and practical tools for them and us to trust their capacity to take the work further on their own. Or as one of my past clients said in her Goodbye Letter: 'At the moment it feels good to be trusted with my own future.'

References

American Psychiatric Association (1994) *Diagnostic and Statistical Manual of Mental Disorder IV* (DSM-IV). Washington, DC: APA.

Bateman, A. and Fonagy, P. (1999) Effectiveness of partial hospitalization in the treatment of borderline personality disorder: a randomized controlled trial. *American Journal of Psychiatry*, 156, 1563–9.

Bateman, A. and Fonagy, P. (2000) Effectiveness of psychotherapeutic treatment of personality disorder. *British Journal of Psychiatry*, 177, 138–43.

Bennett, D. and Parry, G. (1996) The accuracy of reformulation in Cognitive Analytic Therapy: a validation study. *Psychotherapy Research*, 8, 84–103.

Bennett, D. and Parry, G. (in press) 'Maintaining the therapeutic alliance: resolving alliance-threatening interactions related to the transference'. In D. Charman, *Core Concepts in Brief Psychodynamic Psychotherapy: Training for Effectiveness*. Mahwah, NJ: Laurence Erlbaum.

Casement, P. (1985) *On Learning from the Patient*. London: Tavistock.

Dolan, B., Evans, C. and Norton, K. (1995) Multiple Axis II diagnoses of personality disorder. *British Journal of Psychiatry*, 166, 107–12.

Dolan, B., Warren, F. and Norton, K. (1997) Change in borderline symptoms one year after therapeutic community treatment for severe personality disorder. *British Journal of Psychiatry*, 171, 274–9.

Fonagy, P. (1991) Thinking about thinking: some clinical and theoretical considerations in the treatment of a borderline patient. *International Journal of Psycho-Analysis*, 72, 639.

Gabbard, G. and Wilkinson, S. (1994) *Management of Countertransference with Borderline Patients*. Washington, DC: American Psychiatric Press, Inc.

Gunderson, J.G., Frank, A.F., Ronnington, E.F., Wachter, S., Lynch, V.G. and Wolf, P.J. (1989) Early discontinuance of borderline patients from psychotherapy. *Journal of Nervous and Mental Diseases*, 177 (1), 38–42.

Herman, J.L., Perry, C. and Kolk, B. (1989) Childhood trauma in borderline personality disorder. *American Journal of Psychiatry*, 146, 490–5.

Higgitt, A. and Fonagy, P. (1992) Psychotherapy of narcissistic and borderline personality disorder. *British Journal of Psychiatry*, 167, 23–43.

Holmes, J. (1994) Brief dynamic psychotherapy. *Advances in Psychiatric Treatment*, 1, 9–15.

Kelly, G. (1955) *The Psychology of Personal Constructs*, Vol 1 and 2. New York: W.W. Norton.

Kernberg, O. (1975) *Borderline Conditions and Pathological Narcissism*. New York: Jason Aronson.

Kerr, I. (1999) Cognitive analytic therapy for borderline personality disorder in the context of a community mental health team: individual and organisational psychodynamic implications. *British Journal of Psychotherapy*, 15, 425–38.

Linehan, M., Armstrong, H.E. and Suarez, A. (1991) Cognitive behavioural treatment of chronically parasuicidal borderline patients. *Archives of General Psychiatry*, 48, 1060–4.

Linehan, M., Tutek, D.A., Heard, H.L. and Armstrong, H.E. (1994) Interpersonal outcome of dialectical behavior therapy for chronically suicidal borderline patients. *American Journal of Psychiatry*, 151, 1771–6.

Paris, J. (1993) *Borderline Personality Disorder: Etiology and Treatment*. Washington, DC: American Psychiatric Press.

Paris, J. (1996) *Social Factors in the Personality Disorders*. Cambridge: Cambridge University Press.

Phillips, A. (2000) *Promises, Promises*. London: Faber.

Piper, W.E., Rosie, J.S., Azim, H.F.A. and Joyce, A.S. (1993) A randomized trial of psychiatric day treatment for patients with affective and personality disorders. *Hospital Community Psychiatry*, 44, 757–63.

Ryle, A. (1994) Projective identification: a particular form of reciprocal role procedure. *British Journal of Medical Psychology*, 67, 107–14.

Ryle, A. (1997) *Cognitive Analytic Therapy and Borderline Personality Disorder: The Model and the Method*. Chichester: Wiley.

Ryle, A. and Golynkina, K. (2000) Effectiveness of time-limited cognitive analytic therapy of borderline personality disorder: factors associated with outcome. *British Journal of Medical Psychology*, 73, 197–210.

Sabo, A., Gunderson, J., Najavits, L., Chauncey, D. and Kisiel, C. (1995) Changes in self-destructiveness of borderline patients in psychotherapy. *Journal of Nervous and Mental Disease*, 183 (6), 370–6.

Sandler, J. (1976) Countertransference and role-responsiveness. *International Review of Psycho-Analysis*, 3, 43.

Stevenson, J. and Meares, R. (1992) An outcome study of psychotherapy for patients with borderline personality disorder. *American Journal of Psychiatry*, 49 (3), 358–62.

Stone, M. (1990) *The Fate of Borderline Patients*. New York: Guilford Press.

Stone, M. (1993) Long-term outcome in personality disorders. *British Journal of Psychiatry*, 162, 299–313.

van der Kolk, B.A., Hostetler, A., Herron, N. et al. (1994) Trauma and the development of borderline personality disorder. *Psychiatric Clinics of North America*, 17, 715–30.

Winston, A. (2000) Recent developments in borderline personality disorder. *Advances in Psychiatric Treatment*, 6, 211–18.

World Health Organisation (1992) *The ICD-10 Classification of Mental and Behavioural Disorders. Clinical Descriptions and Diagnostic Guidelines.* (ICD-10) Geneva: World Health Organisation.

Yalom, I. (1995) *The Theory and Practice of Group Psychotherapy*, 4th edn. New York: Basic Books.

Yalom, I. (1999) *Momma and the Meaning of Life: Tales of Psychotherapy*. London: Piatkus.

PART TWO

ENHANCING PERSONAL EFFECTIVENESS AND SOCIAL COHESION

7
CONSUMERS' VIEWS OF THE BENEFITS OF COUNSELLING AND PSYCHOTHERAPY

Colin Feltham

Surely the single most crucial focus of therapy and reflection on therapy is the client or consumer, the person seeking help or guidance, out of real need or serious aspiration. Ultimately most formal research rests on the views of clients about their satisfaction with the therapeutic or growth-promoting services they have received (sometimes alongside observations and corroboration by others). After all matters of theory, training, supervision, quality control, costing and so on have been scrutinised, refined and continuously debated, it is ultimately in the changed or changing experience and behaviour of consumers or seekers where the most important effects of this work are found. For these reasons, this chapter is dedicated to examining some of the reports made by consumers about the benefits they have received. I do not intend to dwell on problematic linguistic nuances but note here that use of the terms 'consumer' and 'benefits received' should not be taken to imply that therapy or psychological growth is a passive matter.

Let us not pretend that some consumers have not been markedly *dissatisfied* with the counselling and psychotherapy they have received. Accounts of such negative observations have been slowly emerging in published form (Alexander, 1995; Heyward, 1994; Masson, 1991; Sands, 2000; Sutherland, 1987) and are a source of concern and impetus for improvement. Certain texts examining both the negative and positive views of consumers demonstrate a balanced evaluation of the benefits of therapy: some consumers are highly critical, some highly enthusiastic; some have clearly received damaging treatment and some consider they have been helped immensely (Dinnage, 1989; Howe, 1989; Lott, 1999; Mearns and Dryden, 1990; Oldfield, 1983). Some consumers concede that they benefited from therapy in spite of finding it painful and frustrating and some have moved on from an unsatisfactory experience to a beneficial one, often implying that any fault might well lie with a particular therapist or therapist–client mismatch, rather than with therapy itself (e.g. Grierson, 1990; Sands, 2000). Readers interested in such complex variables and the difficulty these make in researching therapy effectively might consult Kline (1992).

Consumers may often have quite a different take on therapy from that of their therapists (Feltham, 2000; Howe, 1989). Without denying the existence and importance of negative and ambivalent observations (unfortunately, many pro-therapy accounts have erred towards the naïvely and prematurely positive, or uncritically Pollyannaish), this chapter focuses mainly on some of the reported *positive* experiences of consumers, drawn from a range of sources: empirical research, consumer writings, clinical experience and anecdotal evidence. Space is also devoted here to original material from three people who have agreed to provide their testimonials to the benefits of therapy.

What have clients said about their therapy?

Looking back now, I can see that I was able to incorporate, very gradually, new ways of being myself. Instead of struggling just to cope with my life I experienced my self being brave and not being scared to take risks with my personal relationships. I was able to be clearer in my mind about what I needed in my life and to use that clarity to help me get it. I stopped being manipulative and could ask for what I needed. (Grierson, 1990: 39)

Analysis helped me with psychosomatic difficulties – anorexia, difficulty in breathing, back pain, exhaustion, things like that. And it helped with very bad sexual difficulties, which I know were caused by sex abuse. ('Philip' in Dinnage, 1989: 185)

Incredibly I never realised how anxious and depressed I'd always been. I have spent years trying to solve all my problems through thinking. This was a great defense against feeling how much I was hurting. ... I'm starting to ask for help – to accept that I need it. It was instilled in me very early on not to ask – to be strong and not show any signs of weakness. Now it's such a relief to be able to be human at last. To be able to cry and sob about all my pain. ('Nolan' in Janov, 2000: 127–8)

I was able to get a job and have done well. In fact, I have grown from a person who was unable to handle the most routine tasks at times, into a confident, cheerful person. ... I have rediscovered excitement and adventure in my life. (A client in Oldfield, 1989: 90)

When you talk about things, you start to understand what you're really feeling.

It helped me to face my friend instead of putting up with what she was doing.

I think counselling helped me to learn to like myself and respect myself. (Children's and young people's views in Capey, 1998: 39)

Examples of positive testimonials can be found throughout the literature. They are also in abundance in anecdotal form. A woman has nothing but praise for the counselling she had just after she was diagnosed with breast cancer. Another woman is sure that had she not had counselling when her marriage was falling apart she would have 'cracked up completely'. A man who received short-term counselling at his doctor's surgery is delighted that he has been able to come off medication for depression and start making real progress with his life for the first time in years. A woman who had been receiving a variety of psychiatric inputs for 30 years found the counselling she was finally offered did more to normalise her life and gain satisfaction in less than a year. Usually, humble endorsements of the benefits of counselling and psychotherapy are private, one line, perhaps idiosyncratically expressed, statements on a one-to-one basis; they do not make headlines, nor is their vital personal significance easily captured by any large-scale research. But arguably these capture the very purpose and effectiveness of therapy. It is encouraging, therefore, that at least some of this evidence is honoured – as 'grey literature' (see Hemmings, 1999) – and shows patient satisfaction rates ranging from 66% to 93%. People represented in these reports were by no means the much-maligned 'worried well' but included many with high and enduring levels of clinical distress prior to counselling/therapy. Counsellors and psychotherapists, and their clients, know all this for themselves but the necessarily confidential nature of the work prohibits disclosure. I know as a supervisor who regularly listens to therapists reporting on their work that sometimes they themselves are astonished at some of the unexpected, dramatic changes that occur when people are respectfully, non-judgementally and skilfully listened to, given time, interest and judicious suggestions for deepening their understanding and expanding their life choices (Chernin, 1996; Levin, 1989).

Consumers/clients reflect on their gains

Three accounts of the self-perceived benefits of counselling or therapy are now given. I believe they speak loudly enough for themselves not to require introduction or analysis by me, but the third account (Olvia) is taken from a tape-recorded interview and my own notes rather than being written directly by her.

Case studies

Jean Clark

It is time to go then, to pick up the pilgrim staff and take the road ... to the place of unknowing ... a place where you are strange and a stranger and lonely and because of that afraid.' (West, 1971)

It was 1972. I only intended to see Mary [the therapist] for a few sessions. A family crisis had blown up just weeks after I had taken on a pioneering role, setting up a new counselling service for students. I needed support at a time of great stress. Well, I *thought* that was my intention, yet when Mary said to me, 'How far do you want to go?' I remember responding, 'As far as there is to go.'

Journeys of exploration had always fascinated me; as a child Scott and Shackleton were my heroes. So maybe at some level I did know I wanted to make an inner journey – though at the time I was not aware of what that might mean. Mary was a Jungian psychotherapist, who had retired from her work as one of the earliest student counsellors. She was a wise and fearless companion as I travelled through unknown territories, during the following six years.

It is a long time ago, and I do not recall in detail the things we talked about, beyond the complexities and demands of family life, but I know that she was interested in my dreaming and the images in my inner landscape. I painted pictures of volcanoes, and trapped energies and the pressures grew. I dreamed some powerful dreams and was encouraged to record them and bring them to therapy. My journal writing began and has continued to this day. I recall a night when I could not sleep, and did not know what to do with my restless energies; I went downstairs with my journal and began to write. … 'I am feeling something but I do not know what it is … something is going to happen …'. And then a poem began to emerge.

The images changed to the side of a mountain, and the spring which broke out of the rock; it was as if my energies had at last found their source and a means of expression – and of understanding. The poetry poured out onto the pages of my journal and seemed often to tell me things I had not yet named.

I realised that I had had two frightened parents and had, unconsciously, taken on a burden of fear which was not mine; though it took years before I laid that burden down. I recognised that my liveliness and creativity had been controlled by a domineering Victorian father whose attitude was always, 'You are not doing that right; don't do it that way,' and a mother whose message was 'Be careful'. My play tended to be about cages, or an imagined safe hiding place under the floorboards.

As therapy progressed, so I moved through the barren landscape of volcanic peaks, and the sense of being trapped inside a plugged crater waiting to explode, and became water pouring down the mountainside. I remember seeing a film at this time, in which the snows were melting in spring, and began to trickle and then flow more and more powerfully down the rock faces – and I sat in the cinema weeping for joy at the release of that part of me which had been frozen.

When I was thirteen, because of wartime evacuation, my parents and I had moved from the suburbs of London to North Wales, on the edge of Snowdonia. My external landscape was now one of the sea in all its moods, and mountains, torrents, lakes. The freedom and wildness of nature were a liberation, and continue to be so. In therapy, in my dreams and drawing and poetry, these were the images which emerged and symbolised the stages of my journey. I became very focused on that place where the river meets the sea and wrote a poem about death:

> Now the great, the final fear
> the dragon that comes in dreams
> fear of the final end of life,
> of all that I have known and loved
>   The river flows
>   now to its meeting ...
>   it is the sea ... rolling out
>   to unimagined distances ...
> Now the drops of water begin
> to merge, transform, transmute,
> become one ... with the sea

Only now, writing this paper, have I realised how recent had been my father's death – only 18 months before I entered therapy – and how much this will have triggered the process of release in me. But at the time the focus was on my anger with him, and the remembrance of the frustration expressed in childhood dreams where I beat on walls with my fists. I was still in the conflictual stage of trying to prove to him that I was of worth, and this went on for some years after his death.

I look back now on the six years of my therapy as a releasing of the trapped energies 'under the volcano', which initially erupted in ways which I found very frightening. Mary was a very holding presence at this time. I remember feeling that whatever experiences and confusions and explosive energies I brought to sessions, she would calmly accept them – and I would have the sense of her as a woman who sat carding wool, so that the threads would untangle and lie sheer – and so it would be at a deep level of my psyche. I remember longing for a time when perhaps instead of my creativity 'Thrusting up through layers of arduous rock' (poem 'Well Spring', 1975) it might be like a spring bubbling up. In fact it was eight years after I ended therapy that I finally left my marriage, and moved to a new place, both geographically and in my life, and the wellspring of my creative energy began to bubble and flow.

For, yes, that was another theme which emerged, the growing space between myself, (she who was growing into being a counsellor, and more importantly, growing into becoming the person she desired to be), and my husband of more than 24 years who was finding my growing both threatening and alienating. It was a sad discovery, for I had never envisioned that I would leave my marriage; I tried to deny those feelings of being trapped in a situation where I also had children growing up. I wrote poetry which I tried not to understand:

> Each moment drifts like weed beneath the waves
> The ties that bound us move out on the tide
> The words we speak float past and leave no trace
> Upon the bleak wind blowing from the shore behind

So let us take our ways where they will go
My own path, further yet, beside that sea
And you … impatient, wanting to be done …
Turn back and drive to town along the road   (1976)

But within the period of my therapy, I did not make the choice to separate. It was not yet the time. I was gaining the strength I would need, I was developing both professionally and personally. I was avoiding taking a step which felt so painful.

Although within the therapy we did not work with the transference, I was aware that Mary took the role of the wise mother from whom I would be able to separate, and this was immensely important. My own mother was an unhappy and needy woman, who had always told me, 'I nearly died when you were born', and it felt that she demanded payment for this trauma in her life. She would say with pride when I was an adolescent, 'People say we look like sisters', and I felt that my expected role was that I would never upset her, would take care of her and would take her side and listen to her complainings about her unhappy marriage to my father. To have a therapist who did not make demands, who rejoiced in my growing, who valued my need to separate when the time came, was extraordinarily healing. As my gift to her at the end of therapy, I wrote:

> [To a Mother]
>
> I can manage on my own
> I know how to look after myself
> You have shown me
> how to express and how to restrain
> my emotions, how to understand
> the meaning of silence
>
> I have to leave now
> I need to open the door
> and walk out, and say
> 'I am sure I shall be alright
> even if it goes wrong,
> I shall be able to handle it'.
> Anyway it is only for a time
> my lifetime.
>
> There is pain in saying this
> but it feels appropriate
> The kind of pain you feel
> when the train pulls away
> from someone you love,

at the station, when one of you
is going on a journey
a necessary journey.

Wanting sometimes to come
And say 'This is who I am'
'Look what I have done'
'I know how to love
because of you'

Wanting to meet sometimes and say,
'These are my created works of art –
look upon them and rejoice, because
you are in their making'

Wanting to call sometimes and say
'This is what I am doing,
I wonder if you can advise me
out of all your life experience
what best I could do now ...'

Maybe sometimes needing to meet
and say 'Just for this hour I am a child
confused – but tomorrow I shall be again
standing separate and free,
a woman grown'.   (1978)

I never did call Mary for any further sessions, for it felt that our work together was complete, but we still exchange letters at Christmas and I am always aware of that unconditional valuing of me as a person, which my parents were never able to give me. I know I have built upon the foundation she gave me, and the confidence she had in my abilities, and the sharpness of her perceptions. And I still write poetry.

I was very fortunate to have worked with Mary so soon after the beginning of my counselling career. She gave me a sense of safety in which I could go deep and not be afraid, for she was not afraid. Through my work with her I discovered creative energies in myself and was able to give them expression. All this has enriched my work as a therapist.

Anna Sands

Psychotherapy is something I have very mixed feelings about. I have had two radically different experiences of it, the first damaging and the second helpful. Whatever one's starting point, I imagine that, in order to benefit overall from therapy, a certain scepticism is necessary. Ironically, this also has to go along with a kind of faith that it will be worthwhile – one of the many paradoxes inherent in the whole endeavour. It seems to me that psychotherapy is a great deal more complex than many clients realise at the outset, with all kinds of pitfalls and unforeseen reactions and repercussions. I suspect that the outcome depends much more on the person one goes to and the chemistry between client and practitioner than on the particular approach used.

My first experience of therapy went badly wrong and ended in a breakdown; my second, which was undertaken primarily to deal with the first, was generally positive and ended up lasting for six years. I was still in a state of shock when I went to Kate – my second therapist – and needed help with that. At a more general level, the most obvious benefit was that she provided a space in which I could explore who I am, my feelings, thoughts and problems in a concentrated manner, without having to worry too much about other people's needs, and in a context that felt relatively clear and uncluttered. What made that time and space seem worthwhile was that I rarely left a session without feeling I had learned something, that I had come away having experienced something useful. Kate helped me to see things in a different way, to broaden and deepen my perspective on life and to understand more coherently what it is that makes for a constructive and respectful relationship. The way the therapy was conducted, the way Kate was with me, provided a kind of model for this.

I think when we are young, we often don't have models of what a good, loving relationship between two adults is. Certainly my parents did not provide this. We think we know what it means to behave with respect, love, understanding, sensitivity, consideration and all those things, but we don't necessarily; and living it, of course, is not something that comes easily for most of us. For me, therapy should be about both experiencing and practising that mode of being.

Although I used to make notes for my therapy sessions, I did not keep a retrospective journal. I have sometimes regretted this, and wish that I could write down the things that I learnt. But they have blurred and melted, even though the moments of conscious awareness – which often did not occur during an actual session – were precise and vivid at the time.

The factors that come to mind when I look back on the sessions themselves are inevitably influenced by my perception of the problems in my first experience of psychotherapy, and aspects of that no doubt go back to things in the past. But I also believe that, regardless of one's past, therapy needs to have some kind of meaningful, ethical framework, that the encounter itself should have a 'moral' dimension, and be as conscientious as possible.

When I first met Kate, it was a relief to be with someone who behaved in a relaxed and ordinary fashion and I immediately felt at ease with her. I particularly remember how, when we went into her room, she asked if I would prefer to sit in the chairs or on the cushions on the floor. This might seem to the reader an irrelevant detail, but it was significant for me because, in my first experience of therapy, I felt I just had to go along with my analyst's way of doing things, that I had no choice. This simple offer (I chose the cushions) made me feel I had some control over our encounter.

The ongoing element of negotiation and choice was a key one for me. It not only felt empowering but also acted as a reminder that I shared responsibility for the work. That nothing was cut and dried, that both of us were fallible and vulnerable was an ever-present strand. Kate suggested having three sessions to see how things went, and then a mutual assessment to talk about whether I wanted to continue. Again, this seemed very different from before. My analyst had said at the end of the first session that we should meet again before deciding which direction to go in, then at the end of the second announced that he thought I could do with some therapy. He did not invite me to give him my view. I felt I had been assessed and diagnosed as faulty.

With Kate, how things were between us, how I felt in the therapy room, were an integral part of the work. Before, I had felt that my attempts to discuss how the therapy was going were thrown back at me, further evidence of my problems. As a result, I began to fall further into a black hole. With Kate, this never happened, and she always pulled me back to reality when necessary. I felt I was being accompanied rather than merely observed and commented on.

We were on a joint learning curve – that was something that was often reiterated, and it was said with sincerity rather than trotted out as part of a package. I felt I had something to contribute, something to give which was of value. We talked about psychotherapy a lot, and I felt confident that Kate would always take responsibility for her part in the process – for me that was vital. Her readiness to acknowledge that therapy can be harmful, and to explore how and why this might be so, was invaluable for me. Discussing therapy also meant we were talking about something concrete that was actually happening and to which we were each an equal witness. This meant that our respective notions about roles and responsibilities, our expectations, our hopes and fears, were in a constant state of review and 'analysis'.

I initially went to a psychotherapist/analyst because of problems in my marriage. I knew that something needed to change in me, though the prospect of doing psychotherapy terrified me in many ways. Although my childhood was quite fraught in some respects, I didn't feel the need to rake through it all. I can't remember clearly what my parents were like with me much of the time, and I am wary of making too many connections between my childhood and the way I am now, because so much water has poured under the bridge since then. With Kate, although we did make links between the present and the past, this was not a central focus of the work, so I did not find myself worrying about what something may or may not have signified – as I had done in the previous analysis. What was more helpful, for me, was her concentration on how I felt in the present, her persuading me to move out of my head and into my body and my feelings. This emphasis on what is going on right now in the present, rather than making spurious assertions about the past, helped me to be more aware of my emotions, and of the way I experience other people and respond and act towards them.

I felt able to disagree with Kate, to challenge and to question her – though this took time to develop. She never evaded my questions. I learnt that challenge can be dealt with in an easy and matter-of-fact way. The opportunity to get lucid feedback, knowing that I could ask some difficult questions and get relatively objective answers, from someone whose main agenda was that of truth and clarity, was one of the things I valued above all. At the end of a session in which I had disagreed with what she did or said, Kate would thank me for what I had brought. The first time this happened I was taken aback by it; I was not used to being thanked for disagreeing or for raising potentially awkward issues. It enabled me to feel more comfortable about upholding my own position over something, as well as to deal better myself with challenge and with negative feedback from others. It helped me to begin to learn how to climb out of something sufficiently, so that one is not thrashing around in it, not overwhelmed by hurt or anger, losing sight of what is actually going on.

Tied in with this, the therapy was also, for me, about allowing within myself at a gut level a range of feelings that I had protected myself from – to truly know what it is like to feel rejected or ridiculous or ashamed or whatever. I suppose it was what is often referred to as 'shadow work'. This not only gave me greater clarity about myself; it meant being more able to appreciate the feelings of others, so that one stops acting in a way that might exacerbate another person's problem. I think sometimes therapy concentrates too much on how other people make us feel and, inherent in that, how others made us feel in the past, and then we neglect to explore how we affect others – something which is every bit as important.

One of the things that mattered most to me was that Kate seemed genuinely to like me. With my previous analyst, I had no idea what he thought of me. Kate's positive view of me helped me to regain my faith in myself, to trust my feelings and intuition; and she encouraged me to honour the feminine side of my nature. She seemed to be truly interested in what I said and in things that I wrote, to value our time together, to enjoy my company. I don't think this can be manufactured through training, it comes from a deep place inside and one senses when it is or is not genuinely there. I felt I could be myself, rather than squashing myself into someone else's way of working.

I don't suppose I would have been so conscious of these aspects of the therapy had I not experienced at first hand (and later read about) a 'blank screen' approach when I went to an analytic practitioner. The first time around, I believed I could cope perfectly well with such practice, but the experience left all my insecurities amplified and raw. Although, with Kate, I used to say sometimes that certain things were the case only because I was paying her, I still felt her care for me was genuine. There was no pretension, and no pretence. I felt she was there for me, to serve me as best she could; there didn't seem to be anything else bubbling around. She didn't seem concerned about issues of power or image or ego or about doing things her way. Since these are all things that worry me, and which crop up in so many of our encounters, it was a great relief to be with someone who was – in the therapy room, at least – unfettered in this way.

Kate was, I felt, very skilled in her work and, at the same time, had great humility. She was assiduously honest – and because of this, I trusted her. She was not secretive or evasive about herself, and I also trusted her because she allowed me to get to know her enough to know that her values and ideas were – from my point of view – honourable and sound. She was never defensive, never arrogant, and this was wonderfully liberating. The concept of 'loving kindness' was central to the way she worked. Our exchanges felt authentic, spontaneous and natural, and they had an ethical and spiritual undertow which created a frame, a context.

Kate did not have the psychoanalyst's penchant for doubting the authenticity of what clients tell them, and she listened with great respect. Everything she said was offered as a possibility, tentatively, and I was always invited to tell her if it rang true or not. I never felt foolish with her; that was something I so much valued, because with my previous analyst I had felt unusually ill at ease. We laughed together and cried together and our shared sense of humour was as important as our shared pain. I knew I could ask for things and that reasonable requests would be responded to rather than analysed. The response, and the absence of comment, enabled me to identify for myself what the request might be about, if there was an unconscious motive.

Kate was flexible and open to doing things differently, depending on how I felt and what I wanted. We were physically affectionate when we met and parted. She sometimes held me when I felt particularly upset, and was not averse to sharing an occasional cup of tea. The physical contact between us helped to relax me, and I suppose it made me feel cared about. I remember, nevertheless, that I used to feel nervous when I climbed the stairs to her room (except on the final occasion that I did so).

A key factor for me was Kate's skill in using language, and her ability to make fine distinctions between things which were two sides of the same coin. She had a knack for suggesting a concept or sometimes providing just a single word or phrase that helped me to see something from a different angle, something which pulled me out of my narrowness or stuckness and presented a richer picture. She did not use psychoanalytic jargon or trite phrases; our dialogue was simple yet urbane. She referred to myth, story and books and sometimes to concepts which her own therapist had suggested and which she had found revealing. She described ways of being and patterns of behaviour – and the paradoxes contained within them – in a way which helped me to see more clearly and completely, with a keener and more generous appreciation of both my own and another person's perspective.

Whatever we talked about, she showed great respect for the other people who featured in our discussions. Something which was crucial in my case was that she agreed to have some sessions with me and my husband together. These were useful in themselves, but also because after that I did not feel I was talking about him 'behind his back'. They enabled Kate to get to know him, and to see what I was like with him – to see me at my worst in some instances. She met my children too, during chance encounters when we were out together. This meant she had a picture of the people we were talking about independently of the impression I may have given her of them, and I found this reassuring.

The fact that I experienced Kate as a part of my day-to-day life gave the whole thing more meaning somehow, and she was always very aware that, at the end of sessions, I had to go back outside into a busy life. I never left a session feeling unduly upset or disorientated because she made sure that that did not happen. There had been times towards the end of my previous therapy when I had left feeling in a complete daze, yet I still had to get into the car and return to 'normality', attend to my children and my work and try to be clear-headed.

At one point, she gave me a great deal of extra time and for a long while I felt guilty about this; the realisation that she did so because she chose to – that she actually wanted to give me more time – was very heartening. I found it amazing that I was important to Kate. I knew I was important to my children, but had more difficulty with this idea when it came to other adults.

I don't know how much I had strong 'transference' feelings towards Kate; I don't suppose one can ever be entirely clear about this. There were occasions when certain emotions regarding her would come into my awareness, but I felt sufficiently detached to be able to talk about it and see what it was about, and then move on in some way. Generally, though, it felt good to be in a relationship where there were relatively few 'transference' problems. Things felt clear, I could see what was what. I had no need of my defences and was able to act from a more essential and enduring place inside.

I don't think I had too many illusions about Kate, she was always a very 'real' human being. I knew a bit about her private life, and I knew that many of the things we talked about were, in practice, as hard for her at times as they were for me – whereas before, when my analyst said something, it sounded somehow as if he felt he had worked it all out. I realise that may have been only in my mind, but it still resulted in my feeling increasingly inadequate. Therapists, of course, do have enormous power, because the client is so sensitive to what they say; one feels so exposed and bare. Kate used that power in a positive way.

Our work also enabled me to see that difficulties are containable, that it is possible to have a relationship where things go wrong but where there is still value and the possibility of moving on. There were times when I deeply disliked doing psychotherapy but my feelings about the work felt separate and distinct from those I had about the practitioner, and I always found Kate pleasant to be with.

In practice I have not changed as much as I would have liked. I also believe that, if one becomes too conscious of one's feelings, monitoring them constantly, then it destroys spontaneity and, to a degree, instinctive sensibility and compassion. I feel I have had a kind of emotional education (though I am not at all sure that psychotherapy is the best forum for this), particularly regarding how relationship with another can be when one is not so caught up in the tangles. Of course, it is impossible to reproduce what happens in therapy in our other relationships, but if the model is there, it is at least something to aim for, and a kind of emotional and behavioural dictionary to which one can refer. Sometimes I would have liked a little more hard-headed analysis but, in general, I think the quality of the encounter enabled me to define and redefine my boundaries, to own better what is mine and leave aside more readily what belongs elsewhere.

I am disappointed, in a way, that I still find certain things so difficult, but I hope I am more able to see that aspects of feeling and behaviour are not stuck together with Superglue as they seemed to be before, to say that 'that is a separate issue', tease out the different strands. I suppose I have a greater sense of separateness and objectivity. I think I was lucky with Kate, she was someone with real integrity and intelligence, and the courage not to hide behind theories or techniques when things felt wobbly.

For me, my considerable scepticism about therapy, and about therapists, set alongside having a positive experience of therapy with Kate, taught me an important lesson in itself – that one can learn from something without necessarily embracing the whole package unreservedly. Living with ambiguity is not something that comes easily for me, so accommodating the ambiguity I feel about psychotherapy was actually quite constructive. I learnt that there often aren't answers, one just has to manage as best one can and there is no easy way through. I think I knew that as a child, and I believe that psychotherapy should be a reassertion of that early wisdom and strength.

Olvia

Olvia sought a psychotherapist in Greece, her then home country, following the deaths of her brother and mother, the loss of her job and the development of a very low level of self-esteem. There were also 'hidden, subtle traumas'. She felt that she 'had no skin' (she was feeling very raw), she felt 'totally devastated and abandoned', she was in danger of losing faith in life and sometimes wished she could 'pass away' so the suffering could end. She didn't want antidepressant medication even though life was hell. She believed that 'families create monsters and ... therefore people need outside help'. Although she had 'trouble accepting authority', she wanted a well-qualified psychiatrist/ psychotherapist. She had previously seen a therapist for five or six weeks but without much resolution of her troubles. This therapist had said that she was 'working psychoanalytically' but this had meant nothing to Olvia. Olvia had, however, found the therapist 'somehow false in a vague but persistent way'. Nevertheless, she claimed that 'something can be learned even from awful therapy', in this case that Olvia's instinct about this therapist was subsequently vindicated as correct.

It was important to Olvia that she went with her instinct in accepting her new therapist, who she paid privately. She wanted a male therapist. He was 'non-typical' in being 'very tender', 'spiritually tender' and 'very honest' with a 'childlike quality' and a sense of 'inner peace'. Although he 'had no answers' and even appeared 'timid', he seemed 'at peace with his own inadequacies' and 'genuine'. He exerted no pressure, was never astonished or frustrated and Olvia could bring anything she wanted – dreams, stories, etc. – for the nine months she saw him. He responded to her cues rather than having any agenda. However, he was not, and the process was not, 'airy-fairy'. She experienced, more than the therapist's genuineness, a 'shared humanity' that helped to 'unlock' things; she came to feel comforted and enabled.

Olvia has come to believe that six sessions (a fairly typical time limit now being offered by many counselling services) would have done nothing for her; indeed, that would have felt like a violation. While not idealising therapy or therapists, she believes that therapy is 'one remedy among others' that can 'make the world a better place'. It is a 'safety valve' and should be seen as a 'health provision, not a luxury'. For Olvia, therapy enabled her to trust her own instincts and, also, providence. Part of her instinct was to move from Greece to Britain in order to pursue further study.

What do we learn from consumers?

These three examples of consumers' therapeutic experiences and reflections suggest that the qualities of acceptance, attention, understanding and due flexibility are indeed central. Contrary to some criticisms of consumer perceptions, a clear ability to sense therapists' limitations is evident, along with clients' willingness to accept their therapists' humanness rather than expertise or advice. (See, however, Walker and Patten, 1990 for some evidence of conflict between client and therapist orientations in belief.) A sense of 'journey' is also a common factor among many clients; an appreciation that there is much to learn that even several years of therapy cannot entirely elucidate. Consumers are also seen here as informed and persistent; even if some of their information comes from disappointing therapeutic experiences, this does not necessarily deter them. People are usually driven to therapy by some degree of crisis or discomfort but may find such crises pivotal in making significant life changes. Finally, all are clear that being skilfully accompanied in their self-exploration helped them at many levels: practical, existential, spiritual, emotional. Therapy appears to support increasing self-knowledge and growth in independence.

Key themes readily discernible from the above examples, and also from other sources, are that counselling and psychotherapy don't always go smoothly and indeed may be quite painful; it is important that the therapist is accepting, genuine, interested and flexible; the qualities of the therapist are possibly more important than theory and training; and, for all the hope invested in therapy, it may often be experienced to some extent as disappointing or more modest in its outcomes than expected. The other side of this coin of modesty is that many have reported life-changing experiences, dramatic reversals of fortune, ability to avoid suicide, drugs and other life-threatening phenomena, observable and valued changes in behaviour and enduring lessons for living a more satisfying life. Greater self-acceptance and confidence in living are, too, commonly reported gains.

Among those who have sought to conceptualise what can be learned from consumers themselves, Howe (1989, 1993) is a prominent researcher who believes a common therapeutic sequence is detectable: 'accept me, understand me, talk with me'. However elaborate the theory, consumers' needs and perceptions seem to return to such 'simple' phenomena. McLeod (1990) summarised research into clients' experiences and concluded that there was at that time a dearth of such work (a certain amount had been undertaken within social work) but what could be extrapolated confirmed clients' perceptiveness about the value of the therapist's genuine interest, encouragement, understanding and instillation of hope, among other factors. It has also been shown that clients commonly derive a great deal of benefit from reflecting on their therapists and on therapists' words between sessions and after therapy has ended (Orlinsky and Geller, 1993). Recent client reports confirm many of the above statements and help to establish a powerful case for therapy as desired and effective; and even for more research and publication opportunities to be given to consumers or mental health service users themselves (Etherington, 2001;

Foskett, 2001; Seligman, 1995). To some extent consumer complaints and reports have been responded to in the form of consumer guides written by therapists and counsellors, for example the comprehensive 700 page work of Engler and Goleman (1992) and Dryden and Feltham (1995).

While more and more conventional research studies cite the positive reports of clients on their therapy, McLeod (2001) reminds us that it is time for a more concerted organisation and understanding of clients' views.

Acknowledgements

I am deeply grateful to Jean and Anna for their written accounts and to Olvia for spending time telling me about her experiences and views.

References

Alexander, R. (1995) *Folie à Deux*. London: Free Association Books.

Capey, M. (1998) *Counselling for Pupils and Young Adults: Examples of What LEAs and Schools Provide*. Slough: EMIE/National Foundation for Educational Research in England and Wales.

Chernin, K. (1996) *A Different Kind of Listening: My Psychoanalysis and its Shadow.* New York: Harper Perennial.

Dinnage, R. (1989) *One to One: Experiences of Psychotherapy*. Harmondsworth: Penguin.

Dryden, W. and Feltham, C. (1995) *Counselling and Psychotherapy: A Consumer's Guide.* London: Sheldon.

Engler, J. and Goleman, D. (1992) *The Consumer's Guide to Psychotherapy*. New York: Simon & Schuster.

Etherington, K. (2001) Research with ex-clients: a celebration and extension of the therapeutic process. *British Journal of Guidance and Counselling*, 29 (1), 5–19.

Feltham, C. (2000) Consumer views. In C.Feltham and I. Horton (eds), *Handbook of Counselling and Psychotherapy*. London: Sage.

Foskett, J. (2001) What of the client's-eye view? A response to the millennium review. *British Journal of Guidance and Counselling*, 29 (3), 345–50.

Grierson, M. (1990) A client's experience of success. In D. Mearns and W. Dryden (eds), *Experiences of Counselling in Action*. London: Sage.

Hemmings, A. (1999) *A Systematic Review of Brief Psychological Therapies in Primary Health Care*. Staines: Counselling in Primary Care Trust and The Association of Counsellors and Psychotherapists in Primary Care.

Heyward, C. (1994) *When Boundaries Betray Us: Beyond Illusions of What is Ethical in Therapy and Life*. San Francisco: Harper Collins.

Howe, D. (1989) *The Consumers' View of Family Therapy*. Aldershot: Gower.

Howe, D. (1993) *On Being a Client: Understanding the Process of Counselling and Psychotherapy*. London: Sage.

Janov, A. (2000) *The Biology of Love*. New York: Prometheus.

Kline, P. (1992) Problems of methodology in studies of psychotherapy. In W. Dryden and C. Feltham (eds), *Psychotherapy and its Discontents*. Buckingham: Open University Press.

Levin, D. (1989) *The Listening Self*. London: Routledge.

Lott, D.A. (1999) *In Session: The Bond Between Women and their Therapists*. New York: Freeman.

Masson, J.M. (1991) *Final Analysis: The Making and Unmaking of a Psychoanalyst.* London: Harper Collins.

McLeod, J. (1990) Client experience: literature review. In D. Mearns and W. Dryden (eds), *Experiences of Counselling in Action.* London: Sage.

McLeod, J. (2001) Introduction: research into the client's experience of therapy. *Counselling and Psychotherapy Research*, 1 (1), 41.

Mearns, D. and Dryden, W. (eds) (1990) *Experiences of Counselling in Action.* London: Sage.

Oldfield, S. (1983) *The Counselling Relationship: A Study of the Client's Experience.* London: Routledge.

Orlinsky, D.E. and Geller, J. (1993) Patients' representations of their therapists and therapy: new measures. In N.E. Miller, L. Luborsky, J.P. Barber and J.P. Dochery (eds), *Psychodynamic Treatment Research: A Handbook for Clinical Practice.* New York: Basic Books.

Sands, A. (2000) *Falling for Therapy.* London: Palgrave.

Seligman, M. (1995) The effectiveness of psychotherapy. The Consumer Reports Study. *American Psychologist*, 50: 96–104.

Sutherland, S. (1987) *Breakdown: A Personal Crisis and a Medical Dilemma.* London: Weidenfeld & Nicolson.

Walker, L.G. and Patten, M.I. (1990) Marriage guidance counselling II: What counsellors want to give. *British Journal of Guidance and Counselling*, 18 (3), 294–307.

West, M. (1971) *Summer of the Red Wolf.* London: Heinemann.

8
VISIONARY DEEP PERSONAL GROWTH
Juliana Brown & Richard Mowbray

There must be more to life than this ...

The human potential movement

Not all work that may be referred to as 'therapy' is offered primarily as remedy for problems of a psychological nature. This chapter will explore the benefits of work that explicitly espouses the development of awareness as its main goal. Such work, which may specifically eschew the label 'therapy' and its variants on the grounds of inappropriateness, largely owes its existence to the advent of the human potential movement.

In the USA in the 1960s, a 'heady' mix of ingredients combined to form a new movement. The openness to experimentation that existed in California and to a lesser extent elsewhere in the USA at that time provided a conducive environment for the integration of influences from Asia, Britain and continental Europe along with those that were 'home grown'. These included imported eastern religions and mysticism, an interest in consciousness expansion (resulting in part from experimentation with psychedelic drugs), a throng of ideas and practices brought to the USA by people such as Moreno, Reich and Perls who had sought refuge from the attentions of the Nazis in the 1930s, the teachings of British 'mystical expatriates', notably Aldous Huxley and Alan Watts, and the work of American humanistic psychologists Maslow and Sutich and encounter group pioneers Rogers and Schutz. Huxley's 1960 lecture 'Human Potentialities' gave a name to the movement and inspired Richard Price and Michael Murphy to turn the latter's inherited spa property into the first 'growth centre' – Esalen (Lawson, 1988).

Bill Swartley was one of the less well-known figures involved in the early days of the human potential movement, although he started one of the earliest growth centres, the Centre for the Whole Person in Philadelphia in 1962, and later was a founder of the International Primal Association. Writing in 1971, Swartley reflected on the formation of the human potential movement as follows:

> In general, psychotherapy has ignored normal people and has exhibited even less interest in people who have super-normal mental health, or who I call super-sane. This has left a scientific gap which during the last eight years has begun to be filled by members

of a new profession. The practitioners of the new profession do not even have a generally accepted name yet. Usually we are called encounter group leaders. Our infant science is usually called the Human Potential Movement. The place we practice our new profession is called a growth centre. The normal people with whom we work are called group members. I like to call myself a humanologist or one who practices the science of humanology. Humanology, I define as the science of becoming fully human. In statistical terms, humanology is the science of helping average people continue to mature into a state of super-normal mental health …

[The client] who is attempting to grow (or mature) psychologically retains the responsibility for her own growth … To make the contrast with psychotherapy as clear as possible, humanologists do not even try to make a diagnosis and have no therapy to offer. (Swartley, 1971)

The human potential movement fostered opening and release rather than suppression. It favoured 'experiencing it' and catharsis – 'letting it out', with both bodily and vocal expression rather than just verbal 'talking about'. Screaming and vigorous expression tended to be encouraged rather than inhibited.

The human potential movement pioneered numerous techniques that have subsequently gained more mainstream acceptance and have been adopted in areas such as business management, the school system and in psychotherapy training institutes – although the more expressive techniques do not necessarily fit too snugly with conventional institutions.

Some of the methods used in the human potential movement were revivals of active and body-oriented approaches that had been discarded in the early days of psychoanalysis as the latter movement sought recognition and respectability (just as many parts of the humanistic world are doing today). Catharsis, touch, bodily approaches and direct work with primary processes were not methods that could readily be fitted into the respectable version of psychoanalysis.

Such active, expressive techniques may be taken to be hallmarks of the human potential movement, but they do not represent its essence. Its essence is more a question of the particular model espoused, the model of 'self-actualisation' or 'personal growth', a model which we will refer to as the 'holistic growth model'. This is a model which stands in marked contrast to what is commonly referred to as the 'medical model' (or metaphor) and its analytic and behaviourist associates.

The medical model

The 'medical model' presupposes a state of 'sickness', 'illness' or 'disorder' on the part of the 'patient', a state of 'dis-ease', as it is fashionable to emphasize. The 'patient' is 'unwell'. The practitioner will make a 'diagnosis' of the patient's condition on the basis of his or her 'symptoms' and apply an appropriate 'diagnostic label' to the 'disorder' or 'syndrome'. The practitioner will then 'treat' the patient by administering an appropriate 'therapy' as a 'remedy', thereby hopefully 'curing' the condition or counteracting the disease process and restoring the patient to normal health – seen as the absence of the 'disease' or 'disorder'. This is a model which is about 'normalising' and carries an implicit or explicit notion of 'normality'. The absence of any proven disease process underlying many so-called 'mental illnesses' (Breggin, 1991; Grof, 1985; Parker et al., 1995) means that the treatment of them under a medical model will often be a question of treating the 'symptoms' rather than the disease. That is, suppressing or counteracting them in some way.

Under the medical model, the patient is not expected to have full adult responsibility in relation to his (or her) treatment. Some of this is passed over to the practitioner – the patient does not treat himself. Either his illness renders him incapacitated, or the treatment of his illness involves procedures that he may not fully understand or be able to carry out for himself. There is likely to be some form of legal or 'official' recognition of this special status of being 'unwell' in the form of eligibility for treatment under the state or private health insurance and also the possibility of being relieved of the need to work via a 'sick note' from a doctor. The patient's role here is quite passive. He is 'in the care of' the practitioner with whose treatment he is expected to co-operate. By contrast the practitioner's role is rather more active in the sense of it being he who diagnoses, prescribes, advises and does things to and for the patient to make the patient better. He has the status of an expert, who takes responsibility for the patient; takes care of the patient (Parsons, 1953). 'The doctor–patient relationship as defined by the medical model ... reinforces the passive and dependent role of the client. It implies that the solution of the problem depends critically on the resources of the person in the role of scientific authority, rather than on the inner resources of the client' (Grof, 1985: 319). This authoritative status is typically endorsed by the state in the form of statutory registration of the practitioner's profession (Mowbray, 1999: 206).

Elements of a medical model attitude, as regards both symptoms and the practitioner–client/patient relationship, are to be found in numerous forms of psychotherapy including psychoanalysis, behaviour therapy and hypnotherapy (see, e.g., Rowan, 1983: 3, 57). Given their pervasiveness, medical model attitudes are also to be found in the minds of many practitioners and clients/patients, whatever the approach, even when a different premise appears to be involved in the approach in question. Witness the widespread adoption of the *Diagnostic and Statistical Manual of Mental Disorders* (DSM), modelled on the *International Classification of Diseases* (ICD), even by humanistic practitioners. The DSM also provides the basis for the majority of psychotherapy outcome research (Roth and Fonagy, 1996: 26–9).

In addition to underlying medical metaphors, our Western culture is saturated with conceptions of mental ill health which have an underlying *malfunctioning machine metaphor*. A person is as likely to be referred to as having 'maladaptive' responses or 'dysfunctional' behaviour these days as they are to be labelled as suffering from a 'neurosis' or 'nerves'. Along with this is an associated ethos of problem-solving and 'repair' – the 'technical fix' – for a machine needing repair or 'adjustment' to deal with patterns of faulty learning. In our secular, machine- and computer-dependent age, the medical model of 'cure' (with earlier echoes of salvation and Jesus performing miracles) coexists with this model of us as machines or computers in need of fault correction and restoring to smoothly efficient functioning. Behaviourist approaches that, in the extreme, bypass the issue of consciousness altogether are particularly prone to such a mechanistic conception, as apparently also are cognitive approaches (Rowan, 1988: 243).

These medical and mechanistic metaphors merge and overlap and indeed they have common roots in a Newtonian world-view. The notion of the psyche being generated by organic processes which may fail, leading to psychological disorders (biodeterminism), mates with the machine metaphor to produce an incestuous offspring – the 'human bio-computer'. Your computer has 'crashed' – is it a hardware problem (genetic, neural or biochemical abnormalities) or a software conflict (bugs in your early 'programming')?

Whether of the 'cure', 'repair' or 'reprogramming' variants, the remedial world-view informed by these sorts of model is so culturally ingrained that it is often very hard for people to think outside of it in relation to what may emerge from the psyches of themselves and others. The self-actualising orientation is all too easily occluded by the prevailing cultural norms. The terminology that people adopt or drift into using, and the associations that those terms have in the culture, can exacerbate this tendency. Terms such as 'clinical', 'treatment', 'symptoms', 'diagnosis', 'disorder', 'psychopathology' and 'therapy' associate to prevailing medical metaphors, as do phrases like 'getting better'.

The holistic growth model

The holistic growth model offers an alternative perspective which assumes that everyone has an inherent potential to experience processes of inner development resulting in a continuous process of 'becoming'. Such a process of moving towards wholeness is known by many names, including: 'self-actualisation', 'individuation', 'self-realisation', the 'growth process' or the 'primal process'. It is concerned with the process of 'emergence' or 'unfoldment', with experiencing as fully as possible, with expression and integration. The 'goal' in a holistic growth model is a path rather than an end-point; a journey rather than an arrival. It is about 'knowing yourself' more; about fulfilling more of the potential to be who you really are, rather than narrowly focusing on the cure of a 'disorder', the relief of symptoms or the resolving of a problem. It is about 'B' (for Being) values rather than 'D' (for Deficiency) values' (Maslow, 1968).

A holistic growth model usually involves the acceptance of an existing state of being. Acceptance of that state is what is usually required for growth to occur anyway. The sort of psychological or emotional phenomena which under a medical model would be labelled as 'symptoms' would under a holistic growth model be regarded as manifestations of consciousness and part of the 'self' and their meaning for the person explored rather than efforts being made to cure, suppress or eliminate them. Thus at any level such phenomena can be seen in the light of a growth model and 'owned', opened to and experienced, or seen through the lens of a medical model, regarded as defects to be got rid of and disowned, 'treated', 'cured' or suppressed. In the absence of sound indications that such experiences are indeed manifestations of a true organic disease process, their designation as symptoms should be regarded as presumptive and due to an application of the medical metaphor rather than as 'fact' (Parker et al., 1995). From a holistic growth model point of view, many such 'symptoms' would be seen as forms of communication, means of defence, signs of regression, 'altered states', or as 'stages of a transformative process in which the client has become arrested' (Grof, 1985: 329) – rather than illness.

The holistic growth process is spontaneous and unfolds in a unique way for every individual. It has its own dynamic pressure and pace. Caron Kent (1969) has referred to 'growth forces' driving the process. The question of change is one of allowing these inherent forces to function more fully. The question of facilitation is largely one of providing an environment that is conducive to the spontaneous emergence of these 'growth forces' and which maximises the opportunities for their expression – rather than the application of elaborate technique.

There are arguably two basic levels of this facilitation consistent with a holistic growth orientation: work that assumes and requires adequate adult functioning on the part of the client and work that does not.

Human potential work – facilitation with SAFAA

We will refer to the first of these levels as 'human potential work', though it may be practised under various labels of greater or lesser appropriateness to its nature. This is a form of work intended for *'average maturing adults'* to use Swartley's phrase (Swartley, 1975), or *'autonomous functioning adults'* to use Kelley's phrase (Kelley, 1989). That is, it is a form of work for people who are regarded and regard themselves as 'normal', or 'ordinary' rather than in some way less autonomous than the average level prevailing in the society. This of course begs the question of whether 'normal' is 'healthy', but does correspond to society's recognition of the status of 'adulthood' with respect to responsibility and choice, except in certain specified cases such as when one is 'sick' and a degree of diminished responsibility is usually allowed. Thus it is a necessary pre-condition for human potential work that clients have *Sufficient Available Functioning Adult Autonomy (SAFAA)*. At and beyond this level of functioning, *healing* could be said to become *'wholing'* and it is to this that human potential work addresses itself (Mowbray, 1995: 265–6; 1997: 40).

The SAFAA criterion is not determined by the *presence* of intensely experienced feelings or distress but rather by the *absence* of access to a functioning 'adult' self. The requirement of a sufficiently available 'adult' in the sense of 'here-and-now-self' and ability to be in contact with 'here-and-now' and 'consensus' reality does not, for example, preclude the exploration of states of regression and of projections and transference feelings. The trick is that such feelings are explored on a 'twin-track' basis, that is, on the basis of an adult-directed journey – exploring things from the past while maintaining contact with the present and allowing one's 'inner child' (or whatever) out, in the presence of one's 'adult'. Being an 'average maturing adult' engaged in a 'wholing' process does not preclude having deep life issues that may be addressed thereby.

In consequence of the combination of these two criteria, the roles of client and practitioner in human potential work differ markedly from those in a medical model activity. First, the decision as to whether the SAFAA requirement is met is one for mutual agreement between potential client and practitioner. Furthermore, unlike in the case of activity operating from a medical model where the practitioner is the expert who takes responsibility for the treatment of the patients, in human potential work the practitioner does not apply treatments to the clients. Instead, whilst the practitioner may have experience of a general nature, the clients are seen as the 'experts' – on themselves. Hence the client directs the exploration – the process is one of self-exploration and the client does the 'work'. In human potential work clients retain responsibility for their growth process, their actions and their feelings – which they are encouraged to 'own'. The practitioner's role is to facilitate, to 'be with', to sit alongside. As Swartley put it, in human potential work the practitioner is to be the 'patient', the one who waits with calmness (Swartley, 1971).

The relationship between practitioner and client is a non-hierarchical partnership between adults with differential roles rather than the practitioner having the status of a 'healer' and the client being regarded as in need of the practitioner's healing actions. Clients are not regarded as being sick or unwell, rather they are 'average maturing adults' concerned to 'know themselves', capable of taking responsibility for themselves and of being self-directing. They have sufficient 'adult' functioning – a *good-enough adult*, as Winnicott might have said. In human potential work the client is not 'in the care of' the practitioner. That does not mean that the practitioner does not care about the client or has a licence to be 'careless' but rather that the practitioner is not in any sense 'in charge' of the client. The basis for relationship is one of 'informed agreement to explore' rather than 'informed consent to treatment' as in the 'new' medical model. The 'client' role is equal, contractual and more active than that of the 'patient', however well informed the latter's 'consent to treatment' may be.

The practice of *Primal Integration* provides an example of the practical application of these principles. The work typically takes place in a group environment, which is highly unstructured and free and yet has very firm ground rules and boundaries for participation. To ensure safety for all concerned, terms and conditions apply. A wide range of avenues for expression is available and allowable – verbal, vocal and physical and artistic. A high degree of self-responsibility and self-regulation is called for on the part of the participants, who by and large retain the initiative in their self-exploration. The work is not even labelled as 'therapy' or 'psychotherapy' lest potential clients are misled as to what is expected of them by the assumptions commonly adhering to those terms. The role of the facilitators is not to direct or lead in the conventional sense but rather to 'follow' and not get in the way. Ideally the application of active techniques by the facilitators is kept to a minimum. All participants are interviewed before being admitted to ensure that they meet the SAFAA criterion. Participants need to be willing and able to respect and abide by the preconditions for attendance and to contain strong feelings when necessary rather than act them out destructively towards others or themselves. Subject to participants meeting these requirements, the broad range of experiences which may emerge is welcomed, including deeply traumatic ones. The setting is inclusive of such experiences but not exclusively focused upon them (Brown and Mowbray, 1994, 1996).

Spiritual emergency

When the process of growth becomes so intense and rapid that it interferes with normal daily functioning, a state of what Christina and Stanislav Grof have termed 'spiritual emergency' exists. 'Spiritual emergencies' are 'critical and experientially difficult stages of a profound psychological transformation that involves one's entire being' (Grof and Grof, 1990: 31). By default, such states do not meet the SAFAA criterion.

Spiritual emergencies can be triggered by a wide range of events including near-death experiences, strong emotional experiences such as the loss of a loved one, childbirth, the use of mind altering drugs and involvement in various spiritual practices.

A wide range of phenomena may emerge in the course of such crises, such as the awakening of kundalini, shamanic crises, peak experiences, near death experiences, past life memories, visionary states and possession states. Despite a lack of adult containment, all of these experiences would be regarded from this perspective as indicative of an intense period of personal transformation rather than pathological phenomena (Grof and Grof, 1989: 13–26).

The 'emergency' exists more in relation to the person's *outer* life than the inner process, which though it may be stormy, frightening, painful and prolonged, remains in essence a positive healing one – a process of renewal (Perry, 1974). Risks that await someone in such a state include those that await anyone who is not in sufficient contact with their adult mode of consciousness to safely and effectively negotiate the physical world and 'consensus reality'. There are dangers, amongst others, of accident and involvement with the police. There is a risk of hospitalisation and the abortion of the unfolding process by drug-based interference which can make the process more difficult to complete (Perry, 1974, 1999) and lead to psychiatric labelling, dependence on medication with harmful side effects, social stigma, reduced job opportunities and reduced access to financial services such as insurance.

There are also internal risks, however. Not everyone can 'trust the process' or sustain the pain. The various forms of addiction are a significant hazard for anyone in the throes of such a transformational crisis who lacks appropriate support and understanding and who succumbs to temptation.

In cases where there is evidence of acting out, excessive projection, delusions of persecution or active attempts at bodily self-harm or suicide then, whether or not a spiritually emergent process is under way, a medical approach involving medical treatment aimed at suppression may be inevitable if not preferable since whatever inner process may have been involved has been detrimentally 'hooked' onto the outer world. In a sense there may be too much outer orientation and involvement for whatever inner healing process there is in play to function with safety. As with dreaming, such an inner process at this level works most safely when the active capacities of an adult body are temporarily withdrawn from involvement in what is a highly symbolic inner journey.

In sum, the inner process may be trustworthy so long as it remains an inner process that does not get too confused with the current outside world and so long as it can be borne. However, there are problems for the person undergoing it regarding the social and political context in which it occurs and the extent of supportive resources available.

Holistic growth on the 'NAS'?

Practical forms of assistance for people undergoing spiritual emergencies that support rather than suppress such processes may be hard to come by. There is arguably a great need for alternatives to hospitalisation and/or medication for people going through an intense growth experience who are out of touch with an 'adult mode' and cannot therefore be assumed to be capable of self-responsibility and safe functioning in 'here and now' reality. Likewise, to some extent, for people who are just about able to so function, but *want* to opt out for a while because they are too preoccupied with pain and suffering – with 'problems of being'.

It is possible to go through a spiritual emergency at home with the support of friends and relatives (Podvoll, 1990). However, the helpers in such ad hoc arrangements can easily become exhausted by the intensity and duration of such episodes which may go on for days, weeks or months and have scant respect for conventional patterns of living.

The ideal arrangement for addressing spiritual emergencies would seem to be the establishment of non-hospital 'blow out' centres ('episode centres'?) specifically intended to meet this need: 'This service would provide a unique atmosphere based on the attitude that the Individual's experience is an "altered state of consciousness" to be explored, and not a sickness to be immediately put to a finish' (Perry, 1974: 154). Such 24-hour care centres would provide a genuine sanctuary for people in these crises – an environment where the process could be allowed to proceed unhindered (Grof and Grof, 1989, 1990).

Similar such centres have existed before, for example the Laingian experiment at Kingsley Hall in the east end of London in the 1960s (Berke, 1979) or 'Diabasis', John Weir Perry's Jungian-oriented facility in Berkeley, California during the 1970s (Perry, 1974, 1999). Some, such as the Arbours Centre in

London, still remain (Berke, 1979). Most however have tended to founder on the rock of financing (Breggin, 1991; Grof, personal communication, 1988). The DSM now recognises the existence of spiritual and religious problems which it does not classify as mental disorders and it is conceivable that medical insurance might extend to cover them. However, this would involve the practice of psychiatry and allied professions taking on quasi-spiritual or religious functions. It seems more appropriate that funding (and hence control) should involve separate public or private institutions which accept that the fostering of the evolution of our consciousness by this route is a valuable concern and no less vital to the well-being of our society and culture than, say, public funding of the arts.

Such residential and non-residential retreat centres – genuine asylums with medical support staff but not necessarily subject to medical authority – would provide a service that is accepting of people in an 'altered state of consciousness' or 'non-ordinary state of consciousness'. People benefiting from this service would be funded by others and looked after by others through state or other third party funding. Staffing could be largely on the basis of a 'non-credentialed' registration system since conventional licensing systems based on academic qualifications will be of little relevance to effectiveness in this milieu and unnecessarily exaggerate the cost of service provision (Mowbray, 1995: 209–12; 1997). Those who are most suitable to support others going through such 'crises of renewal' may well be people who have been through such crises themselves rather than 'licensed professionals' who have not (Perry, 1974: 152–7).

Such a 'National Asylum Service' (NAS) would be a service for 'holistic growth' below the SAFAA margin (Mowbray, 1995: 189; 211–12). Human potential work ('wholing') being above that margin requires no state involvement and indeed its provision is liable to be adversely affected by state intervention in the usual form of the statutory licensing of practitioners (Mowbray, 1995, 1999).

Just as the human potential movement can be seen as occupying a distinct societal area between other conventional institutions (education, the health service/medicine, the arts and religion) for activities involving participants who fulfil the SAFAA criterion (Brown and Mowbray, 1990), so such an NAS could be a separate form of public service, somewhere in between education and the health service rather than subsumed by either.

Questions of choice – spiritual emergency or a SAFAA route?

There is an issue of choice in relation to spiritual emergency. Why do some people's inner journeys involve total preoccupation with the outpourings of their unconscious day and night for weeks, requiring others to take responsibility for their care with all the attendant risks and burdens, whilst other people manage to grow without letting go of responsibility for their daily lives?

In the more accepting social climate that now exists for spiritual emergencies in some quarters, some people may unconsciously take permission for this type of path without sufficient resources really being in place to sustain it. Others may consciously yearn for it as a hopefully more rapid alternative to their current path – usually in vain in our experience. However, to embark on such a process in a cultural environment which is generally antipathetic if not hostile to it may in itself represent an acting out of self-destructive urges. How can the emergent urge be steered towards less hazardous paths? Whilst giving due attention to the inner process going on, how can one temporarily contain it when necessary, in order to maintain one's outer life? How can one live in two worlds at once? How can one integrate the experience with the rest of one's life?

A partial answer lies in familiarity. Whilst differing modes of consciousness are best kept boundaried, like waking and dreaming, acquainting oneself with the deeper aspects of one's nature and finding space for the deeper aspects of the growth process in one's daily life allows for an ease of movement between these states in a way that a practice of rigid separation and exclusion does not. Hence deliberate 'working on/with oneself' at depth with a SAFAA criterion can cultivate a familiarity with negotiating different modes of consciousness which allows for a true self-regulation that encompasses deep levels of being as well as an outer adult orientation. The emergent process can thereby be grounded in both forms of reality.

Some pitfalls on the growth path

Selfishness
The pursuit of personal growth can too easily become corrupted into an exercise in advanced self-centredness. Any personal growth that does not increase the capacity for love of others and for relatedness and social responsibility is not worthy of the label and is merely self-inflation.

Idealism and unrealistic expectations
Once fulfilling potential is accepted as an option, what we are (and have) may seem inadequate and lacking in value compared with what we now aspire to. Setting over-ambitious standards can easily slide into a pursuit of perfection at the expense of acceptance of one's self as one is and others as they are. Compared with the possible, we are all rather poor shadows of what we might be for ourselves and those we relate to. Over-avid pursuit of the possible may undermine the ability to live an ordinary life with balance and with the grace to accept and appreciate the available. Moreover, human potential assumptions adopted with naïveté can lead to confusion between how things in the world might possibly be and how things actually are now, leading to unrealistic decisions and major errors of judgement.

Mistaking disease for growth
It is unwise to assume that all psychological and emotional 'symptoms' are simply expressions of consciousness rather than signs of a genuine physical disease

process. The consequences of such an assumption are regarded by Striano as: 'the foremost hazard of faulty therapy: the neglect of physical illness (for example diseases of the endocrine glands, notably the thyroid) as the source of 'mental' symptoms' (Striano, 1988: 4).

In the case of spiritual emergencies, although the concept of mental disease may have been inappropriately extended to include many states that, strictly speaking, are manifestations of a natural and evolutionary process rather than a disease process, it is a mistake to assume that *all* those who are labelled psychotic are really in the throes of a spiritual opening and that mental conditions requiring psychiatric treatment and care do not really exist. It is thus important to differentiate between spiritual emergencies and genuine psychiatric disorders – is this a disease process going on or one of meaningful emergence? Is this a medical matter or a case for 'transformational crisis' facilitation (Grof and Grof, 1990: 252–7)?

Conclusion

Pitfalls aside, rather than work of a psychological nature being the 'privilege' of a minority regarded as 'disordered' or in need of 'help', the benefits for society of 'average maturing adults' engaging in deep work to expand their awareness and to 'know themselves' better are potentially huge since the 'middle ground' of society is arguably where the real limits to political and social evolution lie.

Likewise, providing possibilities for those in the throes of spiritual emergencies to resolve such crises in a way that is inclusive of their depths rather than suppressive of them would enhance their capacity for wholeness to the benefit of all.

References

Berke, J. (1979) *I Haven't Had to Go Mad Here*. Harmondsworth: Penguin.

Breggin, P. (1991) *Toxic Psychiatry*. New York: St Martin's Press.

Brown, J. and Mowbray, R. (1990) Whither the human potential movement? *Self and Society*, 18 (4) 32–5 (Reprinted in Mowbray, 1995: 223–7).

Brown, J. and Mowbray, R. (1994) Primal Integration. In D. Jones (ed.), *Innovative Therapy – A Handbook*. Buckingham: Open University Press.

Brown, J. and Mowbray, R. (1996) Primal Integration: deep personal growth work. *London and South East Connections*, Issue No. 16 (Dec. 1996/Mar. 1997) 6–7.

Grof, S. (1985) *Beyond the Brain*. Albany, NY: State University of New York Press.

Grof, C. and Grof, S. (eds) (1989) *Spiritual Emergency: When Personal Transformation Becomes a Crisis*. Los Angeles: J.P. Tarcher.

Grof, C. and Grof, S. (1990) *The Stormy Search for the Self: Understanding and Living with Spiritual Emergency*. Los Angeles: J.P. Tarcher.

Kelley, C. (1989) Radix and psychotherapy. *Chuck Kelley's Radix Newsletter*, Issue No. 3 (August 1989). (Available from the author at 13715 SE 36th St, Steamboat Landing, Vancouver, WA 98684 USA.)

Kent, C. (1969) *The Puzzled Body*. London: Vision Press.

Lawson, M. (1988) 'Growing up lightly: rascal-gurus and American educational thought. *Educational Philosophy and Theory*, 20 (1): 37–49.

Maslow, A. (1968) *Towards a Psychology of Being*, 2nd edn. New York: Van Nostrand Reinhold.

Mowbray, R. (1995) *The Case Against Psychotherapy Registration: A Conservation Issue for the Human Potential Movement*. London: Trans Marginal Press.

Mowbray, R. (1997) Too vulnerable to choose? In R. House and N. Totton (eds), *Implausible Professions: Arguments for Pluralism and Autonomy in Psychotherapy and Counselling*. Ross-on-Wye: PCCS Books. pp. 33–44.

Mowbray, R. (1999) Professionalization of therapy by registration is unnecessary, ill-advised and damaging. In C. Feltham (ed.), *Controversies in Psychotherapy and Counselling*. London: Sage. pp. 206–16.

Parker, I., Georgaca, E., Harper, D., McLaughlin, T. and Stowell-Smith, M. (1995) *Deconstructing Psychopathology*. London: Sage.

Parsons, T. (1953) Illness and the role of the physician. In C. Kluckhorn and H. Murray, (eds), *Personality in Nature, Society and Culture*. New York: Knopf.

Perry, J. (1974) *The Far Side of Madness*. Englewood Cliffs, NJ: Prentice–Hall.

Perry, J. (1999) *Trials of the Visionary Mind: Spiritual Emergency and the Renewal Process*. Albany, NY: State University of New York Press.

Podvoll, E. (1990) *The Seduction of Madness: A Revolutionary Approach to Recovery at Home*. New York: Harper Collins.

Roth, A. and Fonagy, P. (1996) *What Works for Whom? A Critical Review of Psychotherapy Research*. New York: Guilford Press.

Rowan, J. (1983) *The Reality Game: A Guide to Humanistic Counselling and Therapy*. London: Routledge and Kegan Paul.

Rowan, J. (1988) *Ordinary Ecstasy*, 2nd edn. London: Routledge.

Striano, J. (1988) *Can Psychotherapists Hurt You?* Santa Barbara, CA: Professional Press.

Swartley, W. (1971) Defining the status of a patient, Transcript of a presentation given at Hahnemann Medical College and Hospital Symposium: The Encounter Movement and Psychiatry, 16 June 1971.

Swartley, W. (1975) *Primal Integration*. Philadelphia: Centre for the Whole Person. (Reprinted in *Self and Society*, 15 (4), July 1987, 159–65.)

9
THE BENEFITS OF PSYCHOTHERAPY TO SPIRITUALITY
Shahid Najeeb

In the minds of some, psychotherapy and spirituality are worlds apart, and in the minds of some, they are related. For those who work in psychotherapy, spirituality is often seen as a kind of alien, emotional mumbo-jumbo. Likewise those in the spiritual sphere often see psychotherapy as a kind of pseudo-scientific pseudo-spirituality, ill suited to the needs of the individual or the community. On the other hand, there are others who see that psychotherapy and spirituality are related intimately to each other, for both are about the non-material, but substantial, aspects of our lives. Some might even go so far as to say that psychotherapy is the spirituality of our age.

The view that I will develop here is that psychotherapy and spirituality are related but separate human endeavours and that psychotherapy can aid the development of spirituality. This will mean first going through related areas like some of the reasons for psychotherapy's mistrust of spirituality and how psychotherapy can function as a religion. I will also need to explain what I understand by spirituality. Only then will it become clear why I think psychotherapy can benefit the development of spirituality.

Psychotherapy's mistrust of spirituality

Although there are many kinds of psychotherapies, I will talk only about psychoanalytic psychotherapy, or psychoanalysis, for that is my background. For me there is little distinction between psychoanalytic therapy and psychoanalysis and I use the terms interchangeably.

We know Freud was not particularly sympathetic towards religion, regarding it as 'the universal obsessional neurosis of humanity' (Freud, 1927). Psychoanalysis has generally continued along this track, regarding religious practices as being symptoms of unresolved internal problems. Psychoanalysis has probably been more strident in its criticism of religion, because of its defined symptomatology, than it has been of spirituality *per se*. But the implicit criticism of spirituality is nevertheless there. Psychoanalytic criticisms of religion are basically along two lines.

The first is that psychoanalysis regards religious beliefs as being largely delusional. There is no rational reason for the beliefs of religion and every aspect of religious belief and practice can be understood as expressions of one's unconscious internal world. Humans need a long time to grow and develop. A unicellular organism is fully formed the moment it is created, but humans seem to spend almost a quarter of their lives being dependent on their parents and before they can be regarded as fully fledged adults. This long dependency inevitably has psychological sequelae in the form of one's dependence on one's parents being replaced by one's dependence on God or gods, that provide the same functions of safety, discipline and protection that parents once gave. God is talked and prayed to in exactly the same way as one's parents. Indeed God is often regarded as being 'God the Father'. Since psychoanalysis is about exposing delusions and hypocrisies, it must necessarily expose the delusional and hypocritical aspects of religion. It must show us that God is not an external and supernatural figure, but actually an internal and perfectly natural figure. It must demonstrate our irrational and infantile dependence on this figure and show us how, when we are in this frame of mind, we regress to magical and primitive modes of thinking that are qualitatively different from our usual adult modes of thinking. This is the business of psychoanalysis. Of course this does not mean that psychoanalysis necessarily achieves this aim, for we all know that there are aspects of our thinking and fantasy life that are virtually impregnable to the most detailed and painstaking of analyses. But this is at least the aspiration and general attitude of psychoanalysis.

The second line of implicit psychoanalytic criticism of religion and spirituality stems from religion tending to interfere with people's ability to take responsibility for themselves and their lives. By constantly deferring to religion and by being dependent on it, religion creates a kind of cul-de-sac in which we may get hopelessly trapped. This entrapment prevents us from being able to assume a mature and adult position in our affairs. Since psychoanalysis is about freedom and responsibility, it is implicitly critical of anything that restricts personal freedom or prevents us from taking responsibility for ourselves.

Psychoanalytic views about spirituality are a bit different from those about religion. The reason is that spirituality is generally not as organized a belief system as religion. Nor is the mode of thinking as uniform as what one generally associates with religion. There is probably such a thing as 'religious spirituality', where the beliefs of spirituality are formulated and contained within the overall container of religion. In fact, for many, this spirituality would be the essence of religion. If religious spirituality exists, then there must be such a thing as non-religious spirituality, which is not so organized or contained. The thinking of non-religious spirituality is consequently much more diffuse and heterogeneous than that of organized religion. The psychoanalytic criticism of spirituality is consequently much softer for it is not so much a criticism, as an attempt to expose the unconscious and fantasy elements of spirituality. If spirituality exists outside organized religion, spirituality does not generally interfere with people's sense of responsibility, nor is there the powerful deference seen in organized religion. But it still stems from one's internal world and, not being seen as such, is externalized. A sense of inner connection nevertheless remains. The thinking of spirituality can still be very primitive and magical. The job of the psychotherapist is thus to expose it for what it is and thereby to enhance the individual's sense of reality and responsibility and to replace irrational and immature thinking with rational and mature modes of thinking.

Religion's mistrust of psychotherapy

I do not think religion has been particularly concerned with the advent and development of psychotherapy in our modern age. The religious perspective is such that it is not particularly curious about or interested in the development of human ideas except in so far as they impinge on religious or spiritual practice. With dwindling church attendances and the blossoming of all kinds of psychotherapies, organised religion has probably been forced to regard psychotherapy as a kind of competitor for the human need to seek refuge and find solace in wisdom and a compassionate understanding. I do not think there is a uniform religious attitude towards psychotherapy. Amongst the less informed it is probably regarded as the work of the devil. Amongst the better informed, it is probably seen not so much as a threat as a tool that can be used skilfully and to good effect in ministering to the needs of the parish.

Psychotherapy as the religion or spirituality of our age

Probably psychoanalysis, more than psychotherapy, can be considered a modern religion. The reason for this is that psychoanalysis is probably more structurally organised, has a single defined originator, the works of whom have, over time, acquired almost scriptural veneration in some quarters. But all psychotherapies offer themselves today as a kind of modern spiritual alternative.

I do not think any school of psychotherapy does this deliberately or consciously. It is something that seems to happen because of the nature of the psychotherapeutic process. This may be because psychotherapy sets itself up as being diametrically opposed to materialism, for it offers a different perspective from that which materialism offers. What seem absolute and irreducible values of wealth and power are taken apart by psychotherapy and exposed for what they are. This is similar to what religion does, when it replaces a transient reality with a more enduring or eternal reality. Psychotherapy does this by turning to an internal reality, which is more enduring than the fleeting events of everyday life.

This internal reality involves one's emotional life, including one's relationship with oneself and with those one is closest to. This internal life is seen as coexisting with but also as being different from and more important than the vagaries of ongoing external life. The sense of smallness in comparison with the power of external events can be reinterpreted as a childlike sense of smallness in relation to powerful and omnipotent parents. One also becomes aware that these powerful parents exist much more powerfully internally than externally. For it is only within ourselves that we preserve their awesome power and our initial sense of impotence, exactly in the way it once was.

Externally we can see individuals, including our parents, a bit more realistically. These powerful internal figures can be a source of comfort or threat. When we feel intimidated or threatened by them, we try to overcome them by becoming more powerful than them, for instance by amassing power and wealth. We confuse an internal situation with an external one, or we try to solve an internal problem with an external solution. These external solutions usually do not succeed. They are addressed much more effectively through psychotherapy.

It is through the process of psychotherapy that we become aware of the nature of our problems. When we can understand the nature of our problems and how they are related intimately to our internal relationships with our internal figures, we can obtain a sense of relief. Moreover, we can address and try to rectify our relationships externally and internally. If we can understand that our problems are basically with our internal figures, then we can, through emotional insight, try to improve the internal situation. If we are able to do so, we can feel more at peace with ourselves. When we can feel these internal relationships are not as threatening, the lust for power and wealth is not as pressing.

Psychotherapy unravels the nature of relationships, external and internal, and by doing so focuses interest within, on the human spirit. It sets up a distinction between external and internal reality, between materialism and spirituality, in much the same way that religion and spirituality do. But by doing so, I think psychotherapy does not realise that it is performing the function of spirituality. It provides a sense of inner security, comfort and protection. Instead of seeking material security, the individual turns to and finds inner sources of security and comfort. External materialism is replaced by an inner spirituality. Now when psychotherapy does this, it is functioning as a *de facto* religion or spirituality. It names the generators of religious and spiritual functions, yet it of itself usurps their functions and performs them itself.

Psychological underpinnings

We have touched on the psychological meanings of spirituality at several points, and it might be useful to make them more explicit now. The hints for the inner psychological meaning of spirituality come from three directions:

1　Spirituality is generally considered 'otherworldly', that is, separate and different from our everyday lives.
2　It seems to involve something that is much bigger than us.
3　It provides a way in which we can reconcile ourselves to our birth and our death.

Psychoanalytically speaking, I think we would tend to understand 'spirituality' as a special aspect of our inner world. Our inner worlds reflect our outer world and we have a relationship with our inner figures, just as we have a relationship with our external figures. Prominent in our inner world are our internal parents and most, if not all our relationships with other people are heavily influenced by these inner relationships. We are generally not aware of these internal figures or our relationship with them, but the everyday work of any in-depth psychotherapy makes them and our relationship with them very apparent. It becomes clear that they and our relationship with them are always present in every action.

The internal relationship with our internal parents is extremely complex and not easy to understand. In a gradual development over the past few decades we have come to understand something about the nature of these relationships. The way we experience our internal relationship with our internal parents goes something like this. We experience ourselves as being very small and impotent, in contrast with which we experience something 'other' as being very powerful and omnipotent. This 'other' gets easily gathered into the concept of a personal God, who is imbued with all the characteristics of a parent. We have come to understand that all feelings of apprehension, anxiety and panic are related to our troubled relationship with these internal figures. When they are in conflict with each other or with us, our world falls apart. We experience intense anxiety and at times panic, especially when we feel that everything that we depended upon is falling apart and there is nothing that can be relied upon. When the relationship between them and us is harmonious, the world becomes a content, secure and happy place. Gone is the feeling of threat and danger. In our internal phantasy our internal parents are felt to be in a state of loving contact with us and amongst themselves. We experience their loving contact with each other as being a kind of loving, sexual union. They are felt to be the true generators of our lives and us. We feel that it is they that create not us. Since we feel child-like in our relationship with them, we feel that our productivity and creativity is at best a simulation of their real and joyous creativity. We often have a feeling of an enormous debt of gratitude that we owe them for our very existence, its meaning and our productivity. When the time comes for us to die, we hope, in our phantasy, that we can return to them and their safekeeping, which is again interpreted by religion as a return to God and his safekeeping. These are the underpinnings of our emotional life and of the work of any psychotherapy. Of course the different schools of psychotherapy formulate these internal truths in the manner most congenial to them and their theoretical frameworks, but these are the basic internal emotional facts, stated simply and rather baldly.

However, as briefly mentioned above, we are certainly not always in a state of loving and harmonious contact with these internal parents. There are many variations in the nature of our relationships with them. We have seen that when they are in conflict with each other or with us, the security of our world is shattered. Our external world too feels broken, tormented and meaningless. We struggle to gain control of this chaos and by doing so, try to gain control of these powerful, but out of control, parents. They in turn are felt to be dangerous to us and to our state of well-being. There is rivalry, competition and destruction all round. In order to gain control of the situation, we start believing that *we*, rather than they, are all-important. We start to feel that we rather than they, are the centre of the Universe. It is only us that matter, not someone else that we owe our existence to. This defensive dominance of our internal world, with ourselves, obliterates all other relationships and replaces them with us in a central position. Yet we know clinically that this can never be completely so, for the existence of internal parents cannot be completely eliminated. They remain waiting, as it were, in the wings. They are thus sometimes felt to be hidden but highly dangerous persecutors watching and waiting to pounce. Or alternatively, if there is a recollection of a time when we were in loving contact with our internal parents, before conflict and rivalry set in, we have a sense of a golden or fabled past, which we try perpetually to re-establish.

Another kind of relationship that we can have with our internal parents is that they still preserve their importance to us, but this importance and indeed their very presence, seems in danger of being lost. This presence is of vital importance when we feel lost, persecuted and at a dead end. We thus consciously and deliberately build a temple for these important figures and our relationship with them. We build these temples to keep alive and preserve what is so easily and so often lost. We go to these temples with our prayers, our hymns, our devotion and our promises to be good and worthy of their love. We sing songs of joy and gratitude. We light candles to symbolise keeping alive the presence of these important people. We ring bells, produce music and light incense at the thought of them and whisper respectfully in their august presence. Sometimes the relationship with these internal parents might not be so formalised, as happens in spirituality. For instance they may be seen to be represented by forests, rivers and the great ocean. Great creatures of the sea are apt symbols. Or our relationship with them may be formulated in vague and mysterious rituals and practices.

Material spirituality

'Material spirituality' seems something of an oxymoron, but I think such a thing does exist. We are all aware of the importance of material gain and success. Our everyday lives are preoccupied with it. 'If only I had a bit more money, I could have a better house or go on a lovely holiday.' 'If only I gained some recognition, I would not feel my life and my efforts were wasted', and so on. These and similar thoughts run through our minds the whole time. But occasionally, very, very occasionally, we think that maybe these things aren't everything. We think that there is another dimension to life that is not covered by material success. We feel that this dimension is something deeper, and far greater than any material dimension. We locate it sometimes within ourselves, sometimes somewhere in the heavens and sometimes in both heaven and us.

This is the spirituality that we have been talking about. It is the opposite of materialism and offers comfort in times of stress, especially when things are not going well for us. We can always think that even if we do not have material success, it really does not matter in the wider scheme of things. We can say to ourselves that there is something far greater than all the money or power in the world and if we can be successful in this dimension then we do not have to worry about material things. If we can be successful spiritually, we can feel richer and more powerful than any materialist could possibly feel. Or even better, if we are successful materially we can still aspire to be successful spiritually, for then we have covered all contingencies. Then we cannot be assailed, not in life and not in death, neither in this world nor in the next. What a wonderful position to be in! Power hungry humans find this very appealing. It is wonderful to feel protected by an infinite power that protects one in every aspect of one's life and which protects one in death as well.

Traditionally priests, as intermediaries between this great power and us, have benefited enormously from our great fear and our infinite lust for benefit and gain. But the power of priesthood has always been undermined, whenever there is a suggestion that part of that enormous power is to be found within oneself in the form of a spirit or soul. This idea is even more powerful than what the priests so jealously guard. For it suggests that within ourselves, *we* house this great power, for *we* are a part of it. We are connected and allied to the most powerful thing in the universe. It is absolutely wonderful to feel so regally related!

What I want to draw out from this is my impression that spirituality so understood is little different from materialism. Certainly we start off from different premises and the realms they encompass are of course totally different. One is all about the substantial and material world that we live in and the other is about the non-substantial and spiritual world. But the aims and aspirations in one seem to match closely the aims and aspirations in the other. Both seem to be about amassing benefit, promoting personal gain and generally making one less vulnerable to the vagaries of life. They are the same goals and aspirations, now dressed as materialism, now as spirituality. When we see them in this way, can we claim that they are really distinct entities? Just because the language of discourse changes, does that mean that the discourse is thereby different? I do not think so. To my mind, it is best to call this 'material spirituality'.

Spiritual spirituality

Earlier I described what were the psychoanalytic roots of spirituality and religion. Now I want to talk about the roots of spiritual spirituality. Though they are hinted at in material spirituality, they go far beyond. Likewise, though we may understand them psychologically, they go beyond our psychoanalytic understanding. What I shall be describing is basically a Buddhist understanding of spirituality, but this understanding is more implicit than is explicitly stated in Buddhist literature. Nor is this the formulated understanding of any particular school of Buddhism, though it is part of the overall understanding of all major schools.

The spirituality I want to describe is intimately connected with evolution of the human mind. Charles Darwin has most cogently stated the modern theory of evolution in the following few sentences:

As many more individuals of each species are born than can possibly survive; and as, consequently there is a frequently recurring struggle for existence, it follows that any being, if it vary however slightly in any manner profitable to itself, under the complex and sometimes varying conditions of life, will have a better chance of surviving, and thus be naturally selected. From the strong principle of inheritance, any selected variety will tend to propagate its new and modified form. (Darwin, 1859)

The Buddhist theory of evolution disappears into the distant mists of ancient human thinking. The Darwinian model has chance, genetic mutation and environmental adaptation as the central thesis of the theory. Since the Darwinian model would be familiar to all readers of this book, I shall concentrate only on the Buddhist model. The Buddhist model of evolution is purposive, with an infinite number of determinants. The Buddhist theory goes something like this. Life on Earth is one enormous seething cauldron of life. All forms of life are the expressions or different faces of life and hence all forms of life are interconnected. (This is most clearly formulated by the Hua Yen School of Buddhism, e.g. Chang, 1971; Cleary, 1993; Cook, 1977.) All forms of life move purposefully, though blindly and without any conscious awareness, to greater and greater development. This development is driven by a craving impulse for life inherent in all organisms:

In the theory of biological evolution it is assumed that from simple beginnings more and more complex organisms come into being over innumerable generations, and science is content to explain the process by the allied theory of natural selection. But to give a thing a name is not to explain it. Nobody has yet revealed exactly what is the driving force behind natural selection. It cannot be by mere chance that a single-cell protoplasm becomes more highly organised, more sensitive and more completely master of its environment until it becomes the higher animal and eventually the human being. On the other hand, the evolutionary urge produces too many errors and failures in its progress to be the result of a consciously directed plan from the mind of a higher intelligence. It exhibits the features of a blind, groping desire towards some incompletely defined goal. And these are precisely the features we would expect it to show if it were motivated by this craving which Buddhism teaches is the generating energy of life. It is illuminating to interpret the selective processes of biological evolution in this light. Dispensing with the obsolete theological trappings of God and soul, Buddhism shows that the whole pattern of evolution is based upon the blind craving impulse, which works through the natural biological processes towards a progressively realised result. (Story, 1975)

The more developed forms of life are more differentiated and more specialised than lower forms of life. The highest forms of life have consciousness as one of the features of their existence. The highest forms of consciousness have an awareness of consciousness as a central feature. In these features, the model is identical to the Darwinian model. Life in both models is moving from lower to higher forms, in the one because it is more adaptive, in the other because it is driven by craving. This craving is initially merely to survive, then it becomes a craving for more life and finally it is a craving for greater consciousness.

This process of evolution and development is inherent in all organisms. They are not aware of it individually yet they are part of it, both individually and collectively. This process of evolution underpins theories of previous existences, for if one understands the process of evolution, one understands that life cannot appear out of nothing. From a chromosomal point of view too we know that individual life is an illusion. Individuals are the individual expressions of an enormous chromosomal pool, that does not die with the death of individuals, but which continues to mutate perpetually. Individuals and their individual chromosomes die, but the chromosomal pool does not. It continues to perpetuate itself, carrying within itself the lessons learnt from previous environmental experiences and the adjustments to those experiences.

Modern scientific theory uses chromosomal DNA as the connecting link of all forms of life. Buddhist theory uses 'craving' and 'consciousness' as the connecting link, if one includes in this 'consciousness', the 'unconscious' striving for awareness of all creatures. There is no end point in the Darwinian model but there is in the Buddhist model. The endpoint in Buddhist theory is a Buddha. A Buddha is a being in whom the craving impulse has come to an end. A Buddha is also a being who is fully enlightened, by which is meant a being who is fully aware of his or her consciousness and all its contents, including past existences. A Buddha is thus the only creature that steps out of the evolutionary cycle and hence is not reborn in any form whatsoever.

Now what does all this have to do with spirituality? Spirituality from this perspective is the proper understanding of this process. It means understanding a number of things:

1 Although we exist individually, we are part of a bigger whole. We may not be able to fully see or understand this greater picture, but we are nevertheless a part of it. We cannot opt out of it even if we choose to.
2 Since we are part of this greater whole, we are connected to everything else. We have an intimate connection with all creatures, human and non-human, animate and inanimate (inanimate matter constitutes the building blocks of all animate matter).
3 This awareness goes beyond all theory. It stands outside psychoanalytic, DNA and 'consciousness' models. It may be expressed in these and other ways, but it transcends them. We can understand our existence in complex ways, some not even dreamt of today, but the facts of our interconnected evolutionary existence stand outside all theory.
4 This understanding has consequences that cannot be ignored. These consequences can be called 'ethical' but it is an ethics that is not circumscribed by postulates of what is good, or by promises of reward and punishment. It is based on the sense of responsibility that awareness and true understanding bring. It means being responsible for ourselves (our development and awareness) and being responsible for the well-being of all that we come into contact with because of our intimate relationship with them.

Maybe what I am describing is something that many would say has nothing to do with spirituality. I call it spiritual, because it is something that exists in us, apart from, yet an intimate part of our material existence. It is the 'inner' life of all of us and it is the 'inner life' of all existence. It can be seen from this that 'spiritual spirituality' or Buddhist spirituality is different both from psychoanalytic understandings and from conventional understandings of spirituality. Now we are better placed to show how psychotherapy can facilitate the development of this spirituality.

Psychotherapy as a spiritual act

Some elements of the above description of spirituality now need elaboration. Anyone who has studied the psychological development of the human infant will know how complex the whole process is. While there are many theories about the process there are some elements that should be common to all theories. These are the biological elements that underpin psychological development.

Sometimes it is assumed that humans are born with a kind of integrated awareness, such that the process of birth can be recollected in a reasonably coherent manner. Neurologically we know this cannot be the case. Many of the sensory pathways are not fully developed and our most acute and important sensory organs, our eyes, do not work together coherently. Our earliest experiences must of necessity be fragmentary and uncoordinated. From this chaotic mass of sensory and emotional experiences, we gradually develop coherence, coordination and order. The enormity of this task is probably underestimated, for we tend to take it for granted. But we know from clinical experience just how fragile this sense of order and coherence is, for it can be easily threatened or lost.

The task of bringing about order and coherence takes place in a big way in the first few weeks and months of extra-uterine life, but it is something that has to take place subliminally all the time throughout life. This is one of the reasons why we take such pains to distinguish ourselves from other objects and people in our environment. There are many other reasons for us to distinguish ourselves from others, such as the powerful fondness and love that we have for ourselves, which we come across repeatedly in the consulting room. This has to do with our emotional development, but it probably has its roots in our survival instincts.

The point I am making is that there are very powerful factors at work that all move in the direction of separating ourselves out from other people and our environment. The importance of these forces and their general direction should not be disparaged, for they are absolutely essential for our coherent emotional and intellectual functioning. However, what they also do is blind us to the bigger picture. The bigger picture is the picture covered by the term 'spirituality' above.

The everyday work of the psychotherapist is concerned with matters of importance to the individual. These are usually very painful issues, like being unable to relate to others or form meaningful relationships with them. Or struggling with feelings of impotence, frustration, emotional poverty, self-denigration and so on. Whatever the issues and whatever the problems, the experience always has two elements. One is the experience of pain and the other is the problem of one's relationship with oneself, including relating oneself to the elements of one's own life or one's relationships with others. They are all problems centred around I, me, myself, my world, my life, my job, my relationships. These are very real problems and the pain experienced in them is very real. That is why these problems need to be addressed seriously and attended to psychotherapeutically, for there is really no other way of being able to ameliorate them effectively. This is the enormous importance and relevance of psychotherapy.

This is not all that there is in life, however. For as we have seen, our individual struggles take place in a much wider landscape. A landscape that we are generally not aware of, but which nevertheless exists. When through psychotherapy we are able to ameliorate the pain the individual suffers, he or she might be able to look around and become aware of the landscape that has always been there. When the individual is able to do that, he or she immediately becomes aware of all the things mentioned above, that is, the interrelationship and interconnectedness of all things, the part one plays in it and the responsibilities it places on us, individually and collectively. When the individual starts moving in this direction, we can say that the spirituality that has always been latently present in the individual becomes manifest. Psychotherapy thus frees the individual to pursue the spiritual journey. If psychotherapy is seen in this way, psychotherapy is itself part of a greater whole. The whole process of psychotherapy can thus be seen as part of a much greater spiritual act, that transcends the individual yet involves him or her essentially.

Summary

The following is an extract from a contribution of mine to a Buddhist newsletter (Najeeb, 2000), which summarises the main points about psychotherapy facilitating spirituality. The term 'Buddhism' can be exchanged for 'spirituality' or anything else that may suit the reader's bent of mind. The terms are not important. The way they form part of an overall picture is.

Buddhism is evolution – evolution of the individual through the practice of Buddhism and evolution in the understanding of Buddhism, within the individual. This evolution takes place moment after moment, month after month, year after year and life after life. When the individual has fully evolved, his or her understanding of Buddhism is fully evolved and there is little distinction between the individual and Buddhism, between truth and its practice, between the individual and all beings. This is Buddha. 'If you can see the Dharma, you can see me.'

Evolution takes place in the individual, but this is not to be understood only as evolution of the individual. Butterflies live only for moments, but they are evolving. Trees live for many years, but they are evolving. Species live many thousands of centuries, but they too are evolving. The whole of creation is evolving. With the evolution of creation, there is evolution of awareness, for awareness is part of creation, part of evolution. When awareness has evolved to encompass the evolving whole of creation, then evolution and awareness become one. This is Buddha. Sometimes Buddha goes by the name of Krishna, sometimes by the name of Moses, sometimes by the name of Jesus and sometimes by the name of Mohammed. Sometimes Buddha goes by the name of flower, sometimes by the name of stone lantern, sometimes by the name of song. Sometimes Buddha goes by the name of candle and incense, sometimes by the name of regret and repentance, sometimes by the name of kindness and generosity. Sometimes Buddha goes by the name of YOU. For you are evolving, as are flowers and butterflies. You may not be able to see it, but evolving you are. So do not disparage forests and mountains, do not disparage hardened criminals and do not disparage yourself. You are part of this great mosaic of life that is ever moving, turning, evolving.

The great river of life moves over rocks and boulders, round corners and over waterfalls. It sparkles in the sunlight and gurgles amongst the ferns and willows. It grows and slows down with time and maturity and it carries much debris from the past. One day it will enter the ocean and become one with it, no longer distinguished by ups and downs, by differences and characteristics, it becomes one with the endless rhythms of the ocean, coming in when the tides come in and going out when the tides go out. However, sometimes the river gets caught in little eddies that swirl and turn and which seem to go nowhere. These circles are about our individual selves. Circles of 'I' and 'me' and 'mine', which revolve round one another. These circles become tighter, the knots harder, and there is no forward movement. This is the dwelling place of psychotherapy. Amongst eddies and whirlpools, amongst debris and weeds, amongst arrested development and regressive currents. Psychotherapy attempts to unravel these tangles of the individual self, so that the river can move forwards again. Forwards to wherever the terrain takes it. Forwards to its union with the ocean.

It might be that some people have a sense of the river and hence are aware of the eddies they get caught in. Others might only be aware of their tiny pool and its endless swirling currents. They feel they are not a part of the river, or the banks or the trees or the blue sky. These little places become their world, their universe. Once they can be freed from this, they might discover the sun and the morning breeze. They might discover the river of which they are and always have been a part.

Evolution is not an individual matter. Evolution involves all beings, including the therapist and client. They are both parts of a greater whole. That is why sometimes the therapist and client are two different beings, sometimes they are within the one person, a single being. The one helping, guiding, supporting and the other being helped, guided and supported ... We help others and we help the stranded parts of ourselves that are entangled and lost. We are guided by others and we are guided by those undamaged parts of ourselves that point to and illuminate the way. For the flame of truth is never damaged, no matter how defective the lamp that burns it. There is no flame without a lamp and a lamp is not a lamp till it has a flame. This is how our understanding heals us and heals those that come to us for help. We owe it to others and we owe it to ourselves to illuminate darkness and to overcome obstructions ... We owe it to others and we owe it to ourselves to facilitate the process of evolution, to permit the river to flow again in untrammeled ease, to flow in peace and dignity to the great bosom of the ocean. This is the tireless work and the gentle music of Buddhas and this is your work, your music, so that you can hear how you are an integral part of it.

> To carry the burden of the instrument,
> count the cost of its material,
> and never to know that it is for music,
> is the tragedy of deaf life.

> (Tagore, 1955)

References

Chang, G.C. (1971) *The Buddhist Teaching of Totality*. London. The Pennsylvania State University Press.

Cook, F.H. (1977) *Hua Yen Buddhism*. Delhi, India: Pennsylvania State University Press.

Cleary, T. (1993) *The Flower Ornament Scripture*. Boston and London: Shambhala.

Darwin, C. (1859) On the Origin of Species by Means of Natural Selection. In M.W. Strickberger, *Evolution*. Sudbury, MA: Jones and Bartlett. p. 25.

Freud, S. (1927) *The Future of an Illusion*, standard edition. London: Hogarth Press. p. 43.

Najeeb, S. (2000) Psychotherapy in the practice of Buddhism. *Dharma Vision*, (2), 3–4.

Story, F. (1975) *Rebirth as Doctrine and Experience*. Kandy, Sri Lanka: Buddhist Publication Society. p. 39.

Tagore, R. (1955) *Fireflies*. New York: Macmillian. p. 202.

10

THE COUCH AND THE BALLOT BOX: THE CONTRIBUTION AND POTENTIAL OF PSYCHOTHERAPY IN ENHANCING CITIZENSHIP

Keith Tudor & Helena Hargaden

As we began writing this chapter, the British government's proposals, originally laid out in its White Paper *Excellence in Schools*, pledging education for citizenship and the teaching of democracy in schools, became statutory for all schools (in September 2000). On 21 January 2001, in his presidential inauguration address, George W. Bush called his fellow Americans to citizenship: 'I ask you to be citizens. Citizens, not spectators. Citizens, not subjects. Responsible citizens, building communities of service and a nation of character.' A couple of weeks earlier, on the BBC radio programme *Start the Week* (8 January), Andrew Samuels, psychotherapist and the author of *Politics on the Couch* (Samuels, 2001a) was attempting to explain to Jeremy Paxman, the show's host, how the psychological or the internal life contributed to notions of citizenship. He was duly misunderstood and predictably patronised by Paxman – who, himself, has written a portrait of *The English* (Paxman, 1999) without any reference to psychology, let alone the internal life.

Although citizenship, understood from a variety of political perspectives, is in vogue, and psychotherapy[1] is the psychological *zeitgeist*, the connection between the two is rarely made. Given the focus of and emphasis in most psychotherapies on the client's intrapsychic world, the notion that psychotherapy contributes – or may contribute – to active citizenship appears counterintuitive, and, given the conservatism of much psychotherapeutic theory and many psychotherapists, even countercultural.

Psychotherapy, across its 'schools' (theoretical orientations) and forms (predominantly individual, 'one to one'), has rightly been criticised for focusing on 'the self' to the exclusion of other/s, and on the individual to the exclusion of context; the monoculturalism of its origins, theory and much of its practice is a prime example of this. Linking this critique of the individualism of psychotherapy to its universality, Kareem and Littlewood (1992: 8) argue that, historically, psychotherapy became accepted precisely *because* it 'was able to ignore social contexts in favour of intrapsychic factors ... [which] helped establish psychoanalysis as a universal (and thus a 'scientific') process'. Whilst Jung is often quoted as telling his students that 'when you treat the individual you treat the culture', this in itself does not sufficiently account for the relationship between individual and culture. Moreover, this formulation separates and distances psychotherapists both from their culture and from their clients.

As an antidote to its conservatism, psychotherapy over the past hundred years can also claim a number of radical traditions, critical of reaction and regulation, individualism and monoculturalism, professional defensiveness, hierarchy and institutionalisation, and offering alternative perspectives on the relationship between internal and external states: the internal world and the external, social world. These include, amongst others and more recently, within psychoanalysis, Kovel (1970, 1988), Richards (1984, 1989), Hoggett (1992) and the practice of 'social action psychotherapy' (Holland, 1988, 1990); within Jungian analytic psychology, Samuels (1993, 2001a); within transactional analysis, the radical psychiatry tradition – see Agel (1971), Roy and Steiner (1988); and, from the person-centred approach, perspectives on personal power and the mutuality of the therapeutic relationship – see Rogers (1978) and Natiello (1990).

Drawing on these traditions, we argue that psychotherapy does contribute – and can contribute more – to enhancing citizenship. In discussing citizenship we do not adopt a particular view or concept; rather, we are concerned with the *process* of citizenship (personally, psychologically and politically) and the ability (or otherwise) of people being, becoming and belonging as active citizens: 'the nation of citizens does not derive its identity from common ethnic and cultural properties but rather from the praxis of citizens who actively exercise their civil rights' (Habermas, 1994: 23). The focus, then, is on how psychotherapy enhances (or detracts from) the *praxis* of citizenship. Taking as our starting point people or citizens as 'subjects', in the first half of this chapter we explore the movement from subjects to subjectivity and then from subjectivity to intersubjectivity. This also reflects and represents the two mutually contradictory interpretations of active citizenship which derive, respectively, from the liberal tradition of natural law as interpreted by the English philosopher John Locke, and the communitarian understanding which derives from the work of the Greek philosopher Aristotle. In the second part we discuss therapy and citizenship through arguments about the importance and significance of therapists as citizens and citizens-as-therapists.

From subjects to subjectivity

Unlike our counterparts born in, or who are, citizens of countries that are republics, British people are (lowercase) *subjects* of Her (uppercase and upperclass) Britannic Majesty. Whilst some of us eschew the monarchy and monarchism (and, with Tony Benn, refer to the period of English history, 1649–1660 as the Commonwealth and not 'the Interregnum') and experience shivers down the spine at the playing of some republican anthems, being (passive) subject is, politically and psychologically, deeply embedded in the psyche of British subjects. Even in applying for a British passport, which may be viewed as defining citizenship, the application forms are held by 'Crown' post offices! These historical and political facts are reflected in people's psychological experience and permeate the therapeutic relationship, especially as regards power.

The implicit agenda in most therapy is to increase consciousness. Could extended consciousness be linked to the development of conscience? Damasio (1999) certainly thinks so and makes impressive claims for our increased ability to care more for others as a result of the process of becoming more conscious: it is

> the ability to suffer with pain as opposed to just feel pain and react to it; the ability to sense the possibility of death in the self and in the other; the ability to value life; the ability to construct a sense of good and of evil distinct from pleasure and pain; the ability to take into account the interests of the other and of the collective; the ability to sense beauty as opposed to just feeling pleasure; the ability to sense a discord of feelings and later a discord of abstract ideas, which is the source of the sense of truth. (1999: 230)

He highlights two further abilities: 'the ability to rise above the dictates of advantage and disadvantage imposed by survival-related dispositions and the critical detection of discords that leads to a search for truth and a desire to build norms and ideals for behavior and for the analyses of facts' (1999: 230).

Is this list too idealistic? We think not. However, the critical detection of discords requires the therapist to be mindful of the economic, social and political world as well as the psychological – and the discords between these worlds. How can we understand these claims, for instance, in the context of the United States of America, long the home of psychotherapy, when we hear of America's resistance (embodied in her President) to cooperating with the international task force and treaty on global warming?[2] Nor do we notice a shift, as a result of any psychotherapeutic influence, in its attitude towards health for all its citizens or increased compassion towards children, the homeless, or dispossessed indigenous First Nations peoples.

Turning our critical gaze towards Britain, we observe that interest in and practice of psychotherapy has grown at the same time as a rise in individualism and materialism, together with the emergence of an urban underclass, namely, a population of homeless people. Whilst we see some change in the form of a generalised increased consciousness about therapy itself, this is often ambivalent and disputed – and, in any case, focusing on therapy *per se* (rather than its effects or its contribution) may be viewed as somewhat narcissistic (a diagnosis perhaps reflective of the state of our Western nations). Our present task, as therapists and writers, is to translate such ideas and ideals into clinical practice which is critical, which connects and which enhances the possibilities of active citizenship and social inclusion. We begin this task by considering the phenomenon of transference – literally, the 'carrying across', usually from the past to the present – or 'transference attitudes' and their contribution to the understanding of conscious and unconscious processes.

The co-creation by therapist and client of the therapeutic and transferential relationship connects both in an unconscious bond that necessarily implicates the therapist in who she is as a person and therefore who she is as a citizen – and so too, the client. In this context we think that it is the history, personality and imaginative capacity – in short the *person* who is the therapist – which informs the extent to which the client's potential for awareness is increased and allows a vision for possibilities to emerge without (as Keats put it) 'an irritable searching after fact and reason' (Gittings, 1979). In societies that value empiricism, materialism and the idea of certainty, the transferential relationship offers an opportunity to make a distinction between our conscious intentions and unconscious life:

> There are more things in heaven and earth, Horatio,
> Than are dreamt of in your philosophy.
>
> (Shakespeare, *Hamlet*, I.v. 166)

In the transferential relationship the logic of the imagination gains a higher status than it occupies in the material world. The purpose of transference is that it provides the possibility for the client to use the therapist to change something that cannot be changed by rational, cognitive-behavioural means alone. Such a relationship offers the client the possibility to travel through his own psychic country, to release his own imaginative capacities and to make psychic – and social – change.

There are several domains of transference, some or all of which may evolve in the therapeutic relationship. For instance, transference can take the form of an *unconscious longing* and need for a perfect other. In such a scenario the therapist becomes idealised and clearly this carries responsibilities linked to power and control. At the same time such a situation affords potential for significant psychic change. In the following example 'Rosa' sought to introject the therapist as an unconscious psychological striving towards health and autonomy: 'introjection is both a defence and a normal developmental process; a defence because it diminishes separation anxiety, a developmental process because it renders the subject increasingly autonomous' (Rycroft, 1995: 87).

Rosa had spent several years in therapy. One day she arrived for her session and almost immediately commented upon the therapist's diary, which lay on a small table. The client said that she had one just like that. The therapist noted a different tone to the session. It was chattier and she began to feel as though she was on the phone to a friend. This tone was sustained over several months. During this time Rosa consistently made reference to the therapist's choice of clothes, the furniture, the presence of a computer in the study next to the consulting room and so on. When analysing the transference the therapist hypothesised that Rosa was seeking a sense of twinship (Kohut, 1977). It was as though she wanted to recognise herself in the therapist, who was a strong, attractive woman. The therapist recognised that the client was seeking to see herself as an autonomous woman, who could be attractive and smart and who mattered in the world. Rosa's mother had used sex and a stereotyped femininity to retain power in the world. From an early age Rosa had felt critical of her mother. She had resisted identifying with her mother as much as possible but was left empty and without a sense of her identity or complexity as a woman.

The position of women as citizens has, of course, been compromised, historically. As Fraser and Gordon (1994: 90) put it, discussing the power of the words citizen and citizenship and the meaning and emotion of the French word *citoyen* – 'a word that condemned tyranny and social hierarchy, while affirming self-government and status equality; that was a moment when even women succeeded in claiming address as *citoyenne* rather than as *madame* or *mademoiselle*'. The liberation from internalised tyranny and hierarchy and the reclaiming of personal power is essential for personal development as a subject and citizen – a process that can be facilitated in the therapeutic dyad where working through, in this case unconscious identification, is made possible by a conscious psychotherapist.

For some clients the transference takes on a more volatile dynamic. When trapped in an internal world of conflict, therapy can offer an opportunity for relief and a reworking through of the conflict in the safety of the relationship.

John often experienced himself as 'between a rock and a hard place'. Often finding himself in conflict with his environment, he believed that people were more against him than for him and he suffered too from enormous anxiety. A union representative, John was in a permanent state of agitation, aggravation and resentment about the way society had changed. In therapy, he would often report on bitter arguments and conflicts he had with people in his life whom he blamed for the many faults he perceived about life, the government, the country, the world and so on. The therapist privately thought that John must appear to be an aggressive and intimidating adversary. (Much later in the therapy she was able to share this perception with him.) In the transference situation he found some relief. Sometimes he made the therapist his ally where he found relief from the apartheid world of 'them' and 'us', which was the psychological terrain of the world that he mostly inhabited. At other times he gained relief from making the therapist his adversary. When the therapist misunderstood John, or made an interpretation that did not fit (or perhaps because it did), John would become enraged. The therapist's capacity to sustain these attacks in a benign and tolerant fashion enabled him eventually to regulate his own internal world of conflict and tolerate feelings and experiences from which he had sought to escape most of his life. As he worked through this inevitably painful process with his therapist the quality of his relationships in the world changed for the better. He became more effective in all of his communication and was enabled to make some radical changes in his workplace in an atmosphere of relative calm.

A more subtle transferential process is one that happens when the client needs the therapist to understand him by 'making' her feel the way that he feels. In many ways this is the most intangible of transferential processes. The Jungians describe it as a type of alchemical process that is not easily available to concrete language. Yet it also offers exciting potential for the therapist and client. We think that the capacity to be as truly human as we are can only be arrived at through a relational process that involves us in emotional exchange. This is now well documented and recently supported by neuroscientists such as Schore (1994). When the early relationship is insufficient to activate the infant's innate capacity for autonomous expression then he is left with a type of 'mangledness' inside, leaving him unable to reap the benefit of who he really is. There is something truly tragic about those people who potentially have much to give yet find themselves unable to connect emotionally with their community and who therefore feel a concomitant sense of deep dissatisfaction and alienation.

Peter was a clever, warm and interesting man. He had suffered with anxiety and depression all his life and could not understand why. He had no memories of pain, abuse or difficulties except that things had gone wrong in late adolescence when his mother had died and his father had withdrawn. Although much recovered from his depression, and now in middle age, he still suffered from anxiety, which had prevented him from realising his potential. Within a relatively short time the therapist noticed that she began to feel under pressure from Peter. For instance when she offered minor interpretations he refuted them as though they were absolute rubbish. When she tried explanations Peter would ignore her. She began to notice that she felt constrained and controlled and became more and more careful about how she phrased her responses. His apparent lack of interest in her psychological observations made her feel as though she should 'pretend' not to be a psychotherapist. Alongside this she began to feel despised.

In analysing her countertransferential response she hypothesised that Peter was trying to communicate with her how he felt inside – but he did not have the words to say it. It was the inarticulate speech from a deeply hurt person. When she realised how awful he felt, instead of feeling defensive and irritated with him she found empathy for his state and understood too that what he needed most was the articulation and validation of his feelings. She could quite easily now suggest to him some of what he felt, since she had felt the feelings so intensely herself. Each time she offered an emotional sense of what he may be feeling, she was moved to notice how he often wordlessly received her words, nodding quietly – at last someone could understand.

As Peter reclaimed his capacity to feel and to know and express his true sense of himself he became more open and less controlling. Consequently he was able to be more accepting of his children's less positive expressions such as their competitiveness, and angry and hurt feelings about which he had previously complained. He gained insight into his need to rationalise, which helped him to accept his feelings, and as this happened he became lighter inside, more satisfied and less controlling – also, the therapist intuited – with his wife. He also became more satisfied in his work situation because he could give and receive more interpersonal emotional support.

These three domains of transference are taken from and developed in Hargaden and Sills (2001) in which they distinguish (respectively) between *introjective, projective* and *transformational* transference.

Of course, it is incumbent on the psychotherapist to understand and work with such transference or transferential attitudes, however this is understood theoretically. In doing so, it is important to acknowledge the positive intention and aspirational aspect as well as the necessity of political activity: it is not always and not only a pathological defence against anxiety. We challenge reactionary theory and practice which pathologises notions of rebellion and revolution, for example, in transactional analysis the concept of the archaic 'Rebellious Child', a term which infantilises and patronises opposition and resistance. Both authors have worked with a number of overtly political citizens/clients for whom therapy has provided the forum in which they have been able to reflect on the personal (intrapsychic) meaning of their extrapsychic political activism.

Supporting clients to become psychologically and socially aware, emotionally literate, assertive and to own their personal power are, of course, aspects of psychotherapy which influence the development of active and participatory citizenship.

When a black woman arrived for psychotherapy the therapist began to realise that the client had little understanding or information about her own race and culture. Using explanation and interpretation the therapist helped bring alive dormant aspects of her client's sense of self (see Stern, 1985 and below). The white therapist quoted passages from Alice Walker's *In Our Mother's Gardens*, sharing a knowledge of race and culture which began to stir in her client a need and desire to know more. As a direct result of the therapy this client joined a black consciousness-raising class and became more aware and powerful even as she became more vulnerable within the therapy.

These examples have focused on the dynamics of the 'subject' and have described an important movement from passive subject to active subjectivity: a reclaiming, as it were, of personal human rights and citizenship. We now consider a further movement from subjectivity to '*intersubjectivity*' which acknowlegdes that subjective phenomena are also experienced by others and, indeed, that the focus of human enquiry (including psychology and psychotherapy) is on the other – 'the natural functioning of the person is other-oriented and not self-oriented' (Brazier, 1993: 84) and on the 'in between' between people. As Crossley (1996: 11) puts it: 'human subjectivity is necessarily directed towards alterity'.

From subjectivity to intersubjectivity

'The goal [of psychotherapy] must be nothing less than a shift from radical individualism to a notion of citizenship based on a more complex understanding of individual and social happiness' (Bellah et al., 1991: 107). Bellah and colleagues challenge us as psychotherapists to involve ourselves in the shift from individualism to an understanding of our – and our clients' – interconnectedness and interdependency as human beings and our social roles, responsibilities and duties as well as rights as citizens. In order to promote this movement from individual subject (and individualised subjectivity) to *inter*subjectivity, through the development of 'more complex understanding', it seems to us that group psychotherapy offers the most relevant forum for this. Indeed, the move from individual to group therapy is, in itself, a move towards greater intersubjectivity and, potentially, to active citizenship. Steiner (1971) argues that extended individual psychotherapy '*silently colludes with the notion that people's difficulties have their source within them while implying that everything is well with the world*' (p. 280; original emphasis), and Tudor (1999) suggests that group therapy (rather than individual therapy) may be viewed as the therapy of choice. In his book on group psychology and political theory, Alford (1994) views the group and not the individual as the most fundamental reality in society – and, interestingly, argues that political theory needs to draw on insights from group pyschology and leadership.

Taking Yalom's (1995) 'therapeutic factors', which describe the contribution of group therapy to the improvement of a client's condition, we identify five (of the eleven) as of particular relevance to the understanding of intersubjectivity and citizenship:

- *Universality* – the notion that we are not unique, alone or isolated in our 'wretchedness'. From this we take and argue the importance of psychotherapists being interested and active in the world. Samuels (2001a), for instance, argues that economics is important to a 'psychologically inflected approach' to politics and psychology (in terms of ethics, influence and credibility). The current political debates in Britain and Europe about people seeking asylum and citizenship may be viewed in terms of universality, that is, that not the individual immigrant, nor the citizen nor the host country is alone – or, in individual terms, that the causes and consequences of migration and immigration are the isolated or isolating problem of the individual asylum seeker and the individual host nation.

- *Altruism* – the notion that people receive through giving support, reassurance, suggestions, insight, etc. There is a dynamic correspondence between giving and receiving empathy; indeed, research in the past 20 years on child development suggests that giving (love and understanding) is as, if not more, important than receiving (see, for instance, Stern, 1985). Indeed, it is only through the other that we know ourselves. In this context, the conclusions of the Council of Europe's Commission Against Racism and Intolerance (2001) that asylum seekers and refugees in Britain experience problems of xenophobia, racism and discrimination, fuelled by a largely conservative and intolerant media and the tone of much political discourse, are a serious indictment of people's ability to be extensional and inclusive in their frame of reference. Some of the responses to the presence of people seeking asylum in particular towns (ports of entry) in Britain may be seen as to do with a lack of altruism due to both internal and external dynamics, that is, feelings of scarcity and invasion, lack of resources and relations, racism, etc.

- *Interpersonal learning* (both in terms of input and output) – and gained, according to Yalom, primarily through transference and insight. From this we take the view of the therapist as facilitator of such learning; indeed, Giesekus and Mente's (1986) research suggests that it is the *clients'* empathic understanding of each other which is the most important therapeutic factor in psychotherapy groups. Interestingly, whilst there is considerable literature concerned with the 'acculturation' of incomers to society and citizenship, there is little about what the indigenous population can learn and gain from its immigrant fellow citizens.

- *Group cohesiveness* – which encompasses '*the patient's relationship not only to the group therapist but to the other group members and to the group as a whole*' (Yalom, 1995: 48; original emphasis). This may be taken as both reflecting and as analagous of the relationship between client and society (both in terms of its members and as a whole). Just as Rogers (1973) viewed the group as organism; equally the psychotherapy group may be viewed as society; moreover the group also *is* society. In our view, more psycho-social work could be done in mixed psychotherapy groups, the mix comprising the antagonistic relationships present in society.

- *Existential factors* – defined as 'responsibility, basic isolation, contingency, the capriciousness of existence, the recognition of our mortality, and the ensuing consequences for the conduct of our life' (Yalom, 1995: 88). From this we emphasise the importance of political material in the consulting room (see Samuels, 1993) as well as issues of morality (see Doherty, 1995). In this sense, the 'couch' is never far away from the 'ballot box' and indeed, can and should contribute to our understanding of the issues involved in what the ballot box represents. In choosing the ballot box as a metaphor for participatory citizenship we are emphasising the rights, even duty, to vote, whilst holding or promoting no illusions about particular forms of democracy or the outcome of voting.

In a group, members are required to take account of others, to understand and work with their projections and see and mirror themselves in each other. As Semyonova (1993: 91) puts it: 'macrosocial events, such as political changes, mass rebellions or violent ethnic conflicts intrude upon, penetrate and determine the content of the interactions between group participants'. Semyonova writes in the context of the change in what was formerly the USSR and, whilst we may not think our cultural experiences to *be* as dramatic as this, the social upheavals in this country and the pace of social change can *feel* equally dramatic and sometimes as catastrophic, and can certainly affect if not determine interactions in group psychotherapy.

The death of Stephen Lawrence, a young black man killed by a group of young white men, in 1993 impacted vividly in one of the authors' practices, instigating heated discussion and debate about racism and how the group members understood themselves within the context of the subsequent report on institutionalised racism (McPherson, 1999). For one white member of the group it seemed particularly gruelling and difficult to understand the significance of difference. For her, such acknowledgment of difference poised a threat to her fragile and narcissistic sense of self. Working with this the therapist needed to acknowledge the individual injury of the client as foreground whilst also working with the reality of racism as it evolved and was understood by other group members, some of whom were black:

> in respect to most of these [external] influences, the group setting can function as a barrier, stopping them for a moment, making them objects of conscious discussion. In this way these events become accessible to reflective awareness, to investigation, mirroring and change. (Semyonova, 1993: 91)

Stephen Lawrence's death and the ensuing, unfolding awareness of institutionalised racism brought the group members into painful conflict with each other; such awareness intensified the meaning of difference and forever changed each member as they recognised within themselves and each other their own internal conflicts and their connection with the external world of conflict. Through a process of over a year the group mourned the loss of illusions, and former identities were changed and lost forever in a growing and more mature understanding of our inter-connectedness as humans and the inevitability of difference: 'to truly connect with each other, individuals must manage their most compelling emotions – anger, fear, sadness, grief, [envy] – the very emotions that drive behaviour' (Kohlreiser, 1999: 1).

At some point in any and every psychotherapy group the issue of *belonging* will surface for most people, as illustrated in this case example.

In a mixed psychotherapy group this issue came out more strongly than usual when a new man joined the group. X had a history of being bullied and rejected but had done some significant analytic therapy in which he had gained much insight and strength. He was also quite conversant with his vulnerability and able to show it. He joined the group in order to learn how to tolerate his – and others' – feelings without being overwhelmed by anxiety. Some of the group he joined were, in many ways, more frightened of their vulnerability and unused to expressions of feelings than he was. Over a period of six months it became clear that X could easily be excluded and become *persona non grata*. He played into this by enacting some of the bullying he had experienced and introjected. At the same time what became most evident to the therapist was that X's vulnerability was frightening to others, and for one man in particular – Y – it became the reason that X 'should' be excluded from the group. This became clear when X did not attend a particular group meeting at which Y expressed pleasure and, again, a desire to exclude the incomer.

The therapist offered the group a thought about Gypsies and how, as a group, they were (are), almost universally, the most despised, feared and hated ethnic group. The therapist offered this socio-political observation as a way of understanding a human tendency to project on to others (Other), and invited the men to think about what and how they projected on to the absent man. This intervention seemed to work as an invitation to look at themselves personally without them, in turn, feeling too persecuted and hounded or even hated by the therapist.

This is a particularly pertinent example, as the application for and achievement of citizenship has always reflected a dynamic of inclusion – exclusion – which may be understood in personal, psychological and political terms. Indeed, the issue of social exclusion – and, therefore, inclusion – is very much on the current political agenda in Britain in terms of health and education policy. There is a specific echo in the above example as, originally, a *persona grata* was defined as 'acceptable' only to a person of patronage (originally a monarch). The unacceptable person, therefore, is not officially recognised and, ultimately, remains stateless. Currently, in relation to people seeking asylum in Europe, this is a political 'hot potato', in which context citizenship becomes a scarce and exclusive commodity which, in turn, exacerbates defensiveness and projection.

In terms of psycho-educational and psycho-social strategies in the clinical setting, we suggest that the use of such approaches in the therapeutic relationship could be referred to as 'empathic interventions' or 'empathic transactions' (see Hargaden and Sills, 2001, 2002). Such interventions or responses always need to be pitched in such a way that the client can hear them – and hence the emphasis upon empathy. Nevertheless, the therapist has a broad spectrum of empathic responses from which to choose. In particular, the use of the therapist's sociological and political understanding can be communicated through the use of empathic explanation and interpretation.

When a white male client entered therapy, the therapist recongised how very hurt he was. Thomas looked miserable and seemed depressed. As the therapist got to know Thomas he communicated a bitter, resentful, deep-seated sense of hostility. Outwardly he appeared taciturn and uncooperative and it became clear to the female therapist, from his complaints about his workplace, that he was in danger of being scapegoated by colleagues who perceived him as particularly irritating. It seemed that because many of his colleagues identified as feminists, he felt anxious that he would be – or would be perceived to be – 'politically incorrect', yet much of the time he felt angry and victimised by them.

The therapist understood his communication on an ulterior level as well as at a social level (see Berne, 1961). She recognised that in one way he was telling her how he experienced her. This was reflected in the historical relationship with his parents. His mother had been very depressed and had been in a deeply antagonistic relationship with his father, who sounded brutal and who had humiliated both his wife and son. Whilst not wanting to collude in his sexism, the therapist understood that he needed to feel that she was on his side and could hear his rage and hatred before he was able to engage with a rational understanding of his predicament.

It was some time before Thomas could move on to a political and social understanding of his situation. Through his relationship with the therapist he learned to identify that some of his depression and sadistic attitudes towards women were actually more to do with his parents' feelings which they had projected into him. He connected with the grief of feeling so rejected and unloved by parents who seemed particularly self-absorbed.

As Thomas gained insight and confidence through the therapy he was able to discuss more openly and effectively with the therapist how to avoid becoming a scapegoat in the work situation. Understanding so much more about his vulnerability, gaining insight into his internal world and, most importantly, recognising that the therapist was neither depressed and downtrodden like his mother, nor brutal and humiliating like his father, supported his growing sense of robustness and confidence in his sexuality and maturity. The therapeutic relationship eventually evolved into quite open and interesting discussions about femininity and masculinity, as a result of which Thomas was able to understand his position of privilege and male benefit, without feeling diminished or ridiculed by the therapist. On the contrary, he felt empowered for, at heart, he had no particular argument with feminists and could see more clearly how he, too, could be more empowered by positively engaging with his colleagues.

Rowan (1997: 12), describing the patriarchal system as one in which 'everything female is devalued', asserts that patriarchy is hugely problematic and that, although there are exceptions to it, broadly speaking it continues to be a strong pervasive pattern in society.

Finally, on the subject of intersubjectivity, we offer a developmental view, based on Stern's (1985) work, which considers, and, in some ways summarises, citizenship as part of the domains of (inter-)relatedness. Challenging traditional, sequential 'stage' theories of infant and human development, Stern proposes an account, based on an organising principle which concerns the subjective sense of self in relation to self-and-other, comprising four senses of self and domains of relatedness which build one upon the other (see Figure 10.1). Whilst there are formative phases in the development of self (up to and around 15 months), 'once formed, the domains remain forever as distinct forms of experiencing social life and the self. None are lost to adult experience' (Stern, 1985: 32). Thus, they may be used to describe the development of citizenship.

We view Stern's work as applicable to the praxis of citizenship – whether in the social, political or clinical setting. Table 10.1 applies Stern's senses of self and domains of relatedness to citizenship and, of course, given the nature of the theory, should be read (top to bottom) cumulatively and not as alternative options or competing concepts of citizenship. This schema is also consitent with van Gunsteren's (1994) point that the neo-republican concept of citizenship includes elements of the other concepts (that is, liberal individualistic and communitarian), also noted in the table.

Therapy and citizenship – therapists as citizens

Tjelveit (1999: 237) suggests that: 'society supports psychotherapy because it believes the pursuit of the well-being of individual clients benefits the society'. This is an interesting supposition which seems to be more true at some times than at others. In the case of the white woman mentioned above who felt so challenged by difference in the wake of the Stephen Lawrence inquiry, the therapist involved worked closely with her on the detail of her discomfort. The client blamed the therapist for being 'too politically outspoken', thus causing her unease – as a result of which the therapist felt thoroughly blamed and at fault. However she was able to put her defensiveness to one side, to avoid any righteousness and to stay with the client's discomfort in a way that was both

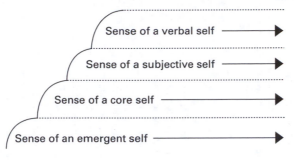

FIGURE 10.1   *Senses of self (Stern, 1985)*

empathic and supportive, without giving up on her own political perspective. Over time it became possible for client and therapist, working also in individual sessions, to discuss the problem more openly and equally. Eventually the client accepted that there was such a thing as racism, that it was problematic and that she had found such an acknowledgement too challenging at the time. As a result of this therapeutic work the client was able to be more effective in her own work and social community and began to report observations she had made about difference and how it worked in her life. This enhanced her own life immeasurably and she began to embrace a sense of otherness in a way that brought value and meaning into her life: 'what one is never not, establishes the life space within which one may hope to become uniquely and affirmatively what one is -- and then to transcend that uniqueness by way of a more inclusive humanity' (Erikson, 1969: 266).

This case suggests the benefits of plurality, not only in relation to external realities but towards an awareness of the plurality of our psyches and the possibilities therein for all of us to benefit from such interconnectedness. For Samuels (1989: 1) this involves us in an attempt 'to hold unity and diversity in balance ... to hold the tension between the one and the many'. In this case the client was enabled to move from a rather chronic dissatisfaction with life towards a more qualitatively satisfying life experience through her involvement with the 'other' and a move away from self-preoccupation. The encouragement of such preoccupation through self-reflection marks most therapy, essentially, as a narcissistic enterprise; however, when the therapeutic endeavour is connected to the macrocosm, that is, the wider field, it can be seen to benefit both individual and society.

In the first part of this chapter we described the movement from passive subject to active, intersubjective being, operating in a number of domains of relatedness (self–others). Implicit in our argument is the desirability, paralleled in the currently popular notion of 'joined up government', of the intersubjective, interconnected, 'joined up' therapist who has, reflects and promotes an integrated sense of 'the personal and the political'. Despite this being an influential and still popular slogan, disintegration and splitting between personal and social states, roles and responsibilities is still rife. In an article discussing the implications for counselling practice of *The 1998 Human Rights Act*, Hardy and

TABLE 10.1 *Self, relatedness and citizenship*

Capacities/qualities	Sense of self	Domain of relatedness	Self as citizen	Qualities/capacities of citizenship
Vigorous goal-directedness to assure social interactions which produce affects, perceptions, sensorimotor events, memories, etc.; the emergence of organisation	Emergent self	Emergent relatedness	Emergent citizen — May describe someone who is perhaps unsure of their eligibility for particular citizenship	Emergent organisation of self and the state, bearer of rights and preferences (Liberal individualistic)
and				together with
Coherent, physical entity with unique, affective life	Core self	Core relatedness	Core citizen — Describes someone who has a coherent (though perhaps unarticulated) sense of themselves as citizen	A sense of belonging to a developed community, judicious action (Communitarian)
and				together with
Subjective mental states (feelings, motives, intentions)	Intersubjective self	Intersubjective relatedness	Intersubjective citizen — Descibes someone who experiences a sense of belonging as a citizen	Autonomy, capacity for judgement, the facilitation of mutual interaction, the organisation of pluralism (Neo-republican)
and				together with
Personal world knowledge and experience which can be objectified and rendered as symbols with meanings	Verbal self	Verbal relatedness	Verbal Citizen — Describes someone who has an articulated and well-developed sense of themselves as citizen	The political possibility of equality and office, to be governed and governor, including the tolerance of unknowing (Neo-republican)

Source: Based on Stern, 1985

Hill (1999) express their hope that 'our primary professional responsibility will continue to be to our clients and [that] the protection of the economic well-being and moral life of the country can be entrusted to other professionals such as politicians, police and clergy' (1999: 372). Apart from the obvious point that it is naïve to trust the economy or morality to politicians, law, order, justice or the right of free association to police, and morals to the clergy, this statement supports the dangerous disassociation of counsellors and psychotherapists from economics and morals – and politics and citizenship. One might as well trust human rights to governments ...

Doherty (1995: 19) argues that 'psychotherapy at its best ... can be a profoundly humanizing experience that increases our moral capacity' and views psychotherapy as an ideal 'moral laboratory'. From this, he voices the view that psychotherapists should be less avoidant of grasping moral issues and of being clear about their own moral standards. This echoes the concept of cultural intentionality (see Shweder, 1990). Indeed, we assert that therapists need to be *intentional* – culturally, socially, politically and morally – and that these subjects or arenas are too important to leave to the tender mercies of external 'experts' (such as politicians), too interconnected to attempt to separate them from other 'professional issues', and too much a part of the human condition not to allow their discussion on and from the couch.

If as therapists we are to be integrated and intentional citizens, then, notwithstanding the radical tradition cited earlier, we need to tackle the deep conservatism of therapy and therapists. As Samuels puts it:

> what interests me about the therapists is how conventional they are! They are happier with straight people. They are happier with nuclear families. It is a very odd thing that we deal so much with the unconscious – we deal with the kinky – and yet we are a very conventional group of people. (Samuels and Williams, 2001: 3)

This conservatism, conventionality and conformism has roots:

- The *history* of psychoanalysis and psychotherapy is characterised by a strong conservative tradition which generally sought acceptance by the medical/psychiatric establishment; indeed, most of the founding fathers [*sic*] were a part of that establishment. This is echoed in current debates in favour of the statutory regulation of the profession of psychotherapists – for a critique of which see Mowbray (1995).
- Those practitioners and theoreticians who have been or are identified as being radical, critical and even explicitly espousing left-wing *politics* were (are) often marginalised and pathologised (see, for instance, Robinson, 1969).
- Much of the *theory* of therapy reflects this conservatism, from the roots of psychoanalysis in natural science (see Schwartz, 2000), through the widespread adoption and application of the medical model 'diagnosis→treatment→cure', to psychotherapy (for a critique of which, see Sanders and Tudor, 2001), through to notions of 'therapeutic neutrality', transference and the therapeutic relationship, much of which perpetuates the view of the psychotherapist as expert and guru.

- Similarly, the *education* of therapists, which (despite a radical education tradition drawing inspiration from writers and practitioners such as Paulo Freire, Carl Rogers and John Holt) favours the traditional 'banking' concept of imparting knowledge and 'teaching' and, with it, the infantilisation of adult learners; and thus has not necessarily or sufficiently encouraged critical independence of thought and practice in therapy.
- Following from this, the fact that the predominant global *economy* is capitalism encourages competition rather than cooperation between psychotherapists: 'in capitalist society, the leading ideological edge of Internalized Oppression is *individualism* – the set of beliefs which places the individual above the collective. Behavior inspired by individualism takes a certain form ... and that form is *competition*' (Costello, et al., 1988: 55).
- The widespread private practice of psychotherapy means that, in *cultural* terms, therapy and therapy training is viewed and, indeed, *is* inaccessible to large numbers of people and is open to accusations of being the domain of white, middle-class privilege (see Kearney, 1996).

As described here, our view of therapists as citizens is communitarian, a concept of citizenship which emphasises the citizen as member of a community (see van Gunsteren, 1994). Castel, Castel and Lovell (1982) most clearly describe the therapeutic and social implications of this:

> this kind of therapeutic method demands ... that [therapists] be immersed in the same milieu as their clients. If therapists and clients truly form an endogamous community, then the boundaries between personal problems and social problems vanish; the personal and social become merely polar points on a spectrum, and therapy can deal with the whole spectrum by working to transform the individual and his surroundings at the same time. (1982: 160–1)

Therapy and citizenship – Citizens-as-therapists

Samuels (2001) has developed the notion of 'citizens-as-therapists' from 'political clinics' or workshops at which participants are invited to consider a political theme and to imagine themselves as the therapist and the political theme or issue as the client. For Samuels such appreciation of the problems of the world 'constitutes a radical shift in what we expect or imagine a citizen to be ... Why should one not try to do politics like a therapist? In such a case, the citizen-as-therapist approaches politics in the same ethos of unknowing and humility that characterizes all good clinical work' (2001a: 166).

Of course, the need for psychotherapy to address the social world and include psycho-social and psycho-educational strategies is not new. In his study of a therapeutic community, Rapoport (1960) identified what he viewed and described as four sociological principles – permissiveness, communalism, reality confrontation and participation – at work. These have become four principles which are widely adopted in therapeutic communities and may equally be applied to communities which are, are not or could be therapeutic. Thus, in local or national and even international politics, we could see the emergence of the citizen-as-therapist-as-activist.

For us, such appreciation and the possibilities of citizen as 'reflective practitioner/activist' have roots, some of which extend back beyond the last hundred years of therapy – despite which, according to Hillman and Ventura (1992), the 'world's getting worse'. This includes the notion that, by virtue of the existence of a state, there is a 'social contract' between its members. Tudor (1997) explores the difference for the practice and association (free or otherwise) of counsellors and psychotherapists in adopting the different views of society which derive from the French philosopher Jean-Jacques Rousseau and the English philosopher Thomas Hobbes – differences, centring on being ruled and being free, which equally stand for the citizen adopting the role of therapist with its concomitant therapeutic and social responsibilities.

Finally, in order to promote the notion and practice of citizen-as-therapist/activist, we briefly consider three areas: the *status* of citizenship; the *concept* of citizenship being promoted through the British government's education for citizenship; and the *sense* of citizenship.

The status of citizenship

We cannot be citizen-therapists if we are not citizens. A person's economic, domiciliary and political status with its ensuing rights and responsibilities is basic and crucial. In applying psychological concepts and theory to issues of citizenship, we do not overlook the fact that there are too many people in Britain today with no legal status, stateless, homeless and in the proverty trap of not being able to work legally and thereby being exploited. The status of citizenship is sometimes seen as a 'problematic' in relation to *admission*, *membership* and *pluralism*, all of which reflect an inclusion/exclusion dynamic:

- *Admission* concerns immigration and citizenship (as discussed above). To paraphrase the German theologian Dietrich Bonhoeffer (who thought the test of the morality of a society was what it does for its children), perhaps the test of a civilised society is how it treats its immigrants (rather than subjecting them to Norman Tebbit's infamous and divisive 'cricket test' by which he linked national loyalty and, by implication, citizenship, to support of a/the national side).
- *Membership* appears straightforward except for the fact that certain citizens are excluded from active, participatory citizenship by virtue of their 'disability': the physically impaired[3] are largely segregated from an architecturally challenged environment; and the mad (patients compulsorily detained under the Mental Health Act 1983 in England and Wales) and the bad (prisoners) are excluded from the electoral register and, therefore, the vote. The excluding category of 'madness' is due to be extended to include (in the next Mental Health Act) people with personality disorders, who are seen as both mad and bad – and dangerous to know.

- *Pluralism* in terms of citizenship is certainly problematic. Different countries take different perspectives, for instance, on the status and identity of people who wish to reassign their gender. More generally, Samuels comments:

> if you take something like equal opportunities legislation ... the statistics show that, while some things have changed, it has not achieved as much in 25 years as something so centrally positioned in society and backed by government should have achieved. And I'm wondering if that is because the psychological dimensions have been overlooked. It's a male dominated society. And, are men going to give up their power that easily? ... the point is that government is terribly unhappy with thinking about citizens being sexed citizens. (Samuels and Williams, 2001: 3)

Education for citizenship

As we referred to in our introduction, the British government considers that:

> citizenship and the teaching of democracy ... is so important both for schools and the life of the nation that there must be a statutory requirement on schools to ensure that it is part of the entitlement of all pupils. It can no longer sensibly be left as uncoordinated local initiatives which vary greatly in number, content and method. (Advisory Group on Citizenship, 1998: 7)

In a critical study of this government report, Flew (2000) analyses what he sees as the fear of the ad hoc nature of life without state intervention which lies behind this initiative and identifies a five-fold argument implicit in the report which he summarises thus:

1. Education for citizienship is highly important.
2. 'Uncoordinated local initiatives' are not enough to provide it.
3. Therefore, government must impose a national curriculum for citizenship on all students.
4. Such a curriculum is best learnt in schools.
5. Such government intervention will be more effective at creating effective citizens than without it.(2000: 5)

Again, the notion of education for citizenship is not new. Chartism, the nineteenth-century movement for universal suffrage, emphasised education as the necessary training for the responsibilities of citizenship. However, it did so through local initiatives, many of them not necessarily coordinated. Furthermore, there is real and present danger in the government taking a curriculum-centred view of citizenship (and of education generally) in that it seeks to produce 'common citizenship', that is, citizens defined by the government, for the government – and certainly not independent citizens/therapists/activists. This is revealed clearly (and with synchrony as we finished writing this chapter) in the vitriolic reaction on the part of David Blunkett, the then Minister for Education, to teachers taking industrial action – action which is, of course, a right of the citizen. In an age of postmodernism and pluralism, we need to be thinking in terms of education for (being, becoming and belonging as) the intersubjective citizen and, thus, in terms of development (Raghavan, 1987), the 'good enough citizen' (Samuels, 2001b) and 'emotional literacy' (Steiner, 1984; Antidote, 2001).

The sense of citizenship

Given that the *sense* of citizenship, based on a developing sense of self, is so important to the pursuit of intersubjective well-being and active, participatory, critical citizenship, it is surprising (or perhaps unsurprising) that so little has been written about it. In a rare if not unique reference, the Scottish Council Foundation (1998) talks in terms of 'civic well-being': 'markers of good health should include feeling valued, having a sense of purpose and control over life, feeling connected to a larger community and enjoying life' (p. 17). Such a curriculum, based on sound appreciation of the needs and development of children (rather than political expediency and ignorance of psychology) would revolutionise schools and society – which is why David Blunkett would not admit it. The Foundation's document, titled *The Possible Scot*, also includes references to the importance of 'emotional intelligence' and safe and supportive social environments in promoting a holistic concept of health. It will now be clear that we favour a communitarian concept of citizenship, based on political philosophy which, in turn, derives from Aristotle, a philosophy and practice in which

> the citizens are integrated into the political community like parts into a whole; that is, in such a manner that they can only form their personal and social identity in this horizon of shared traditions and intersubjectively recognized institutions ... in [which] citizenship can only be realized as a joint practice of self-determination. (Habermas, 1994: 25–6)

Citizenship, like human rights, is much too important to be confined to the discipline of a distinct – and, the government would have it, 'taught' – subject or left to experts. In our praxis, citizenship, along with human rights, becomes a psychological and social attitude (as well as identity), and, importantly, an active, participatory and co-creative social and therapeutic relationship with other intersubjective subjects.

Notes

1 We use this term (and, at times 'therapy') generically to stand for psychoanalysis, counselling, counselling psychology and other psychological therapies – and both psychotherapist and therapist to stand for the practitioner. For ease of reading, we generally refer to the therapist as 'she' and the client as 'he', although of course the terms should be regarded as interchangeable.

2 This chapter was completed before 11 September 2001 and subsequent, related events. To date, we have yet to see whether the building of an international alliance against terrorism will have any political or psychological effect on US isolationism and unilateralism.

3 We use the phrase advisedly and in the political tradition of The Union of Physically Impaired Against Segregation (UPIAS) (see UPIAS, 1981).

References

Advisory Group on Citizenship (1998) *Education for Citizenship and the Teaching of Democracy in Schools*. Sudbury: Qualifications and Curriculum Authority.

Agel, J. (ed.) (1971) *The Radical Therapist*. New York: Ballantine Books.

Alford, C.F. (1994) *Group Psychology and Political Theory*. New Haven, CT: Yale University Press.

Antidote (2001) *Emotional Literacy*. Notes available on http://www.antidote.org.uk

Bellah, R.N., Madsen, R., Sullivan, W.M., Swidler, A. and Tipton, S.M. (1991). *The Good Society*. New York: Knopf.

Berne, E. (1961) *Transactional Analysis in Psychotherapy*. New York: Grove Press.

Brazier, D. (1993) The necessary condition is love: going beyond self in the person-centred approach. In D. Brazier (ed.), *Beyond Carl Rogers*. London: Constable. pp. 72–91.

Castel, R., Castel, F. and Lovell, A. (1982) *The Psychiatric Society*. New York: Columbia University Press.

Costello, J., Roy, B. and Steiner, C. (1988) Competition. In B. Roy and C. Steiner (eds), *Radical Psychiatry: The Second Decade*. Unpublished manuscript. pp. 55–67.

Council of Europe Commission Against Racism and Intolerance (2001) *Report on the United Kingdom*. Available on www.ecri.coe.int

Crossley, N. (1996) *Intersubjectivity: The Fabric of Social Becoming*. London: Sage.

Damasio, A. (1999) *The Feeling of What Happens*. London: Heinemann.

Doherty, W.J. (1995) *Soul Searching: Why Psychotherapy Must Promote Moral Responsibility*. New York: Basic Books.

Erikson, E.H. (1969) *Gandhi's Truth: On the Origins of Militant Nonviolence*. New York: W.W. Norton.

Flew, A. (2000) *Education for Citizenship*. Studies in Education No. 10. London: Institute of Economic Affairs.

Fraser, N. and Gordon, L. (1994) Civil citizenship against social citizenship? On the ideology of contract-versus-charity. In B. van Steenbergen (ed.), *The Condition of Citizenship*. London: Sage. pp. 90–107.

Giesekus, U. and Mente, A. (1986) Client empathic understanding in client-centered therapy. *Person-Centered Review*, 1, 163–71.

Gittings, R. (1979) *John Keats*. Harmondsworth: Penguin.

Gous, J.S. and Wheeler, R.L. (2000) The detection of shame in group psychotherapy: uncovering the hidden emotion. *International Journal of Group Psychotherapy*, 50 (3), 381–96.

Habermas, J. (1994) Citizenship and national identity. In B. van Steenbergen (ed.), *The Condition of Citizenship*. London: Sage. pp. 20–35.

Hardy, S. and Hill, A. (1999) Human rights in counselling practice. *Counselling*, 10 (5), 371–3.

Hargaden, H. and Sills, C. (1999) The Child ego state – an integrative view (an exploration of the deconfusion process). *ITA News*, No. 54, pp. 20–4.

Hargaden, H. and Sills, C. (2001) Deconfusion of the Child ego state: a relational perspective. *Transactional Analysis Journal*, 31 (1), 55–70.

Hargaden, H. and Sills, C. (2002) *Transactional Analysis: A Relational Perspective*. London: Brunner-Routledge.

Hillman, J. and Ventura, M. (1992) *We've Had a Hundred Years of Psychotherapy and the World's Getting Worse*. San Francisco, CA: Harper Collins.

Hoggett, P. (1992) *Partisans in an Uncertain World: The Psychoanalysis of Engagement*. London: Free Association Books.

Holland, S. (1988) Defining and experimenting with prevention. In S. Ramon and M.G. Giannichedda (eds), *Psychiatry in Transition: The British and Italian Experiences*. London: Pluto Press. pp. 125–37.

Holland, S. (1990) Psychotherapy, oppression and social action: gender, race and class in black women's depression. In R. Perelberg and A. Miller (eds), *Gender and Power in Families*. London: Routledge. pp. 256–69.

Kareem, J. and Littlewood, R. (eds) (1992) *Intercultural Therapy: Themes, Interpretations and Practice*. Oxford: Blackwell.

Kearney, A. (1996) *Counselling, Class and Politics: Undeclared Influences in Therapy*. Manchester: PCCS Books.

Kohlreiser, G. (1999) The Kosovo refugee crisis. *The Script*, 29 (5): 1–2.

Kohut, H. (1977) *The Restoration of the Self*. New York: International Universities Press.

Kovel, J. (1970) *White Racism: A Psychohistory*. New York: Pantheon Books.

Kovel, J. (1988) *The Radical Spirit: Essays on Psychoanalysis and Society*. London: Free Association Books.

McPherson, W. (1999) *The Stephen Lawrence Inquiry*. London: HMSO.

Mowbray, R. (1995) *The Case Against Psychotherapy Registration: A Conservation Issue for the Human Potential Movement*. London: Transmarginal Press.

Natiello, P. (1990) The person-centered approach, collaborative power, and cultural transformation. *Person-Centered Review*, 5 (3), 268–86.

Paxman, J. (1999) *The English: A Portrait of a People*. London: Penguin.

Raghavan, J.V. (1987) Education: a major instrument for development. In S.R. Gupta and U.W. Schöttli (eds), *Good Citizenship: Rights, Duties, Responsibilities*. New Delhi: Cizitenship Development Society. pp. 94–101.

Rapoport, R.N. (1960) *Community as Doctor*. London: Tavistock.

Richards, B. (ed.) (1984) *Capitalism and Infancy: Essays on Psychoanalysis and Politics*. London: Free Association Books.

Richards, B. (ed.) (1989) *Crises of the Self: Further Essays on Psychoanalysis and Politics*. London: Free Association Books.

Robinson, P.A. (1969) *The Freudian Left*. New York: Harper and Row.

Rogers, C.R. (1973) *Carl Rogers on Encounter Groups*. Harmondsworth: Penguin.

Rogers, C.R. (1978) *Carl Rogers on Personal Power*. London: Constable.

Rowan, J. (1997) *Healing the Male Psyche*. Routledge: London.

Roy, B. and Steiner, C. (eds) (1988) *Radical Psychiatry: The Second Decade*. Unpublished manuscript. pp. 29–35.

Rycroft, C. (1995) *A Critical Dictionary of Psychoanalysis*, 2nd edn. London: Penguin.

Samuels, A. (1989) *The Plural Psyche: Personality, Morality, and the Father*. Routledge: London.

Samuels, A. (1993) *The Political Psyche*. London: Routledge.

Samuels, A. (2001a) *Politics on the Couch: Citizenship and the Internal Life*. London: Profile Books.

Samuels, A. (2001b) Towards transformative citizenship: the good enough citizen. Notes of a discussion, available on http://www.antidote.org.uk

Samuels, A. and Williams, R. (2001) Andrew Samuels in conversation with Ruth Williams. *Transformations*, 13 (Supplement).

Sanders, P. and Tudor, K. (2001) This is therapy: a person-centred critique of the contemporary psychiatric system. In C. Newnes, G. Holmes and C. Dunn (eds), *This is Madness Too: A Critical Look at Psychiatry and the Future of Mental Health Services*. Llangarron: PCCS Books. pp. 147–60.

Schore, A. (1994) *Affect Regulation and the Origin of the Self*. New York: Lawrence Erlbaum Associates.

Schwartz, J. (2000) *Cassandra's Daughter: A History of Psychoanalysis*. London: Penguin.

Scottish Council Foundation (1998) *The Possible Scot*. Edinburgh: SCF.

Semyonova, N.D. (1993) Psychotherapy during social upheaval in the USSR. *Group Analysis*, 26 (1).

Shweder, R.A. (1990) Cultural psychology – what is it? In J.W. Stigler, R.A. Shweder and G. Herdts (eds), *Cultural Psychology*. Cambridge, MA: Cambridge University Press.

Steiner, C. (1971) Radical psychiatry manifesto. In J. Agel (ed.), *The Radical Therapist*. New York: Ballantine Books. pp. 280–2.

Steiner, C. (1984) Emotional literacy. *Transactional Analysis Journal*, 14 (3), 162–73.

Stern, D. (1985) *The Interpersonal World of the Infant*. New York: Basic Books.

Tjelveit, A.C. (1999) *Ethics and Values in Psychotherapy*. London: Routledge.

Tudor, K. (1997) Social contracts: Contracting for social change. In C. Sills (ed.), *Contracts in Counselling*. London: Sage. pp. 207–15.

Tudor, K. (1999) *Group Counselling*. London: Sage.

Union of Physically Impaired Against Segregation (1981) Aims and policy statement. *Disability Challenge*, 1.

van Gunsteren, H. (1994) Four conceptions of citizenship. In B. van Steenbergen (ed.), *The Condition of Citizenship*. London: Sage. pp. 36–48.

Yalom, I. (1995) *The Theory and Practice of Group Psychotherapy*, 4th edn. New York: Basic Books.

11
FOSTERING EMOTIONAL INTELLIGENCE
Hilde Rapp

In this chapter I will explore the following questions:

1 The 'what for' of emotional intelligence: what is it needed for and why does it matter?
2 The 'what' of emotional intelligence: what do we mean by it?
3 The 'how' of emotional intelligence: how does it develop, how does it work and what does it do?
4 The 'why and how' of emotional intelligence, i.e. what do we know about how to manage our emotions in a reasonably aware and reflective manner and why is this a good thing?

The 'what for' of emotional intelligence: what is it needed for and why does it matter?

Using emotional intelligence to get things done with others

Since the groundbreaking books by Daniel Goleman (1995, 1998) on emotional intelligence, many initiatives have recognised the overwhelming importance of the capacity for managing our emotions in a modern society. Whether at home, at school or at work, so much gets done through personal relationships with others. To work well with others depends crucially on what is meant in this chapter by emotional intelligence.

In a nutshell it is the capacity to know how to:

- Understand and manage one's own feelings and those of others.
- Make contact and establish a good relationship with others.
- Listen and feed back accurately what was understood.
- Agree on prioritising shared tasks.
- Plan how to work together to realise shared aims and values and to achieve joint goals and tasks and how to evaluate outcomes.
- Manage emotions, conflicts and differences regarding ways and means.
- Understand and agree how each participant can personally benefit, grow and learn through doing things together with others.

Work satisfaction depends greatly on a sense of having achieved something of value in joint work with others with whom we have a 'good enough' relationship. We can only truly learn within a trusting and respectful relationship, where we believe that feedback, whether praise or constructive criticism, is honest, accurate and well meant.

Using emotional intelligence to rebuild troubled lives after the Second World War

The more focused and explicit application of methods for fostering emotional intelligence, represented especially by counselling and psychotherapy, arose out of the need to regenerate society after the Second World War. The pain and distress caused by the experience of war to millions of human beings all over the world required the development of ways of fostering greater well-being on a national scale. Especially in North America, behavioural, and later in the UK, cognitive behavioural, programmes addressed themselves to ameliorating more specific problems such as coping with bereavement, recovering from trauma, overcoming phobias and fears and so forth. Person-centred and humanistic ways of working, especially under the name of counselling, were used to reach out into the wider community with low cost or free help with rebuilding troubled lives (Egan, 1990). Psychoanalysis and psychodynamic therapies and counselling were also available to adults, couples, families and children in particularly severe difficulties. Practitioners are drawn from all walks of life, bringing a wealth of personal experience and learning to the task, and many will have a professional background as psychologists, nurses, doctors, social workers, teachers, clergy or psychiatrists.

One might therefore wish to claim that the heartland of studying the conditions for 'emotional literacy', as Susie Orbach (1999) calls it, has traditionally been psychotherapy and counselling. The past 20 years witnessed a mushrooming of therapeutic approaches, both in terms of variety and quantity. A wealth of both 'soft' and 'hard', qualitative and quantitative, research findings illuminate key factors involved in facilitating emotional learning and intelligence. We are beginning to understand more fully how to help rebalance the workings of emotions in disarray. Even more importantly, we know what is needed to help to prevent people, and especially children, from missing out on essential learning opportunities for acquiring emotional intelligence (Greenberg and Pinsof, 1986; Greenberg and Safran, 1987; Greenberg et al., 1993; Rapp, 1998).

Why does emotional intelligence matter even more today?

Poverty and social exclusion The decline of inner city communities is strongly associated with lack of opportunities for learning the social skills needed for emotional well-being. Social isolation interacts with material disadvantage and increasing poverty and deprivation. A vicious cycle is created: poor environments engender poor social skills which lead to poorer social and emotional relationships. Friedli (2001) convincingly shows that this has a detrimental effect on health and mental health overall and her review of conditions in the UK confirms the validity of many earlier studies conducted in the US, as well as those carried out under the auspices of WHO, which show the deadly interaction between loss of productivity through lack of social capital leading to a vicious spiral of poverty and emotional illiteracy.

Building social capital through realising our human potential   The cost of poor emotional intelligence is unacceptably high for individuals, families and society at large. The untold human misery of being and feeling socially excluded is heartbreaking. In addition, social isolation means that the participation of increasing numbers of people is lost each year in the creation of the social, cultural and economic wealth of our society.

Writers such as Fukuyama (1995, 1999) have written about this broader context in terms of social capital. A society will only thrive if its members trust one another, look out for one another, have shared values, goals and aspirations, or at least a thoroughgoing respect for significant differences in outlook and way of life. The tragic interracial tensions in the Midlands and North of England and the persecution of refugees, especially in deprived housing estates in Glasgow, witnessed during the hot summer of 2001 in Britain, are glaring examples of a breakdown of social capital, directly related to poor emotional intelligence.

Within education, there has been a strong humanistic commitment to creating opportunities for 'lifelong learning'. A raft of policy initiatives have made a public commitment to develop new incentives and new vehicles which will increase social capital by encouraging and enabling all people to realise their potential and to raise their level of attainment and achievement (DfEE, 1999).

This significantly involves the acquisition of so-called key skills which directly implicates the use of emotional intelligence with respect to the capacity for 'working with others' and to 'managing own learning' (CPCAB, 1999b).

In the UK citizens will now have access to so-called 'personal learning accounts' which are serviced by 'Local Skills Councils', which provide funds for each citizen to contribute towards courses and other learning opportunities of their own choosing.

An educated workforce is part of the creative capital of a society. And, equally importantly, educated citizens ensure the very life of a potentially fair, just, healthy, wealthy and vibrant society in which citizens are resourced to manage their own learning (DfEE, 1999). Keith Tudor and Helena Hargaden's chapter, in this volume, on enhancing citizenship (Chapter 10) explores these issues in more depth.

Commerce   Within the management literature targeting the business world, understanding the value of emotional capital is recognised as second to none when it comes to the success and profitability of a business venture (Cooper and Sawaf, 1997; Thomson, 1998; Weisinger, 1998). Most of modern commerce depends on the ability to negotiate desired outcomes successfully with other people (Fineman, 1993; Kofman and Senge, 1995). Factors such as supply and demand, availability of natural resources, or the conditions of manufacture, increasingly have a smaller effect on the pricing and movement of goods around the globe than management skills, leadership skills, the recruitment, motivation and retention of key staff, and what is called 'market sentiment'.

Business decisions crucially depend on people's ability accurately to assess or read the emotional qualities and signals of others. Is this person trustworthy? Is their faith in the management capabilities of company X based on an accurate assessment of the chief executive's leadership qualities and flair in motivating his workforce (Belbin, 1981)? Is this person a bit down today, and will their mood adversely affect their judgement of the market situation (Adair, 1995; Senge, 1990; Thomson, 1998; de Geus 1997)?

Psychometric instruments used by human resources directors and recruitment consultants in the selection of staff (insofar as they are used at all) include measures of the capacity to show empathy, to listen well, to give accurate motivational feedback, conduct an appraisal process, manage uncertainty and contingencies, and deal with conflicts calmly and wisely (CPCAB, 2001; Kleyn, 2000). Similar qualities are measured by leadership skills assessment tools used in business, industry and in the public sector alike. Many companies routinely offer training, and personal coaching and mentoring in these skills to their staff.

About 20 per cent of the workforce make use at one time or another of company-sponsored employee assistance programmes to help them to address emotional challenges. If what can be learnt in management packages and course programmes that foster the growth of emotional intelligence no longer suffices to address difficulties, personal counselling picks up the tab. Chapter 13 in this volume, by Cary Cooper and Carolyn Marchington-Yeoman discusses these developments in depth.

Health and social care   In the field of health and social care many key policy documents focus on the value of personal communication and relationships. Berwick (2001) and Botelho (1998) for example have advocated, both in North America and now in the UK, that people across all functions of local government, the voluntary and independent sector, the police and the criminal justice system and the health and social care economy, need to work together in partnership to really understand and meet the needs of people temporarily or permanently in need of help and support.

In the UK a new White Paper sets out the vision for services for people with learning disabilities under the title *Valuing People* (2001). We cannot value people if we do not understand what they are trying to tell us about who they are, what matters to them and how they would like to be helped. Asking the right questions, really listening to the answers, picking up unexpressed distress, helping to formulate plans for action – all these activities require the considered application of emotional intelligence (see also Chapter 12 in this volume by Graham Curtis Jenkins on counselling in primary care settings).

These are the skills which are now explicitly named in official strategic documents, and their corresponding local implementation plans, especially where training and workforce development needs are concerned (Workforce Action Team, 2001; Rapp, 2001c). The most recent reforms in the British National

Health Service are in part a response to the recognition that NHS staff are still not well enough equipped, either at a structural, organisational level, or individually, to resolve racial tensions and interpersonal difficulties (DOH, 2001).

Spiritual teaching and philosophy   It would be foolish not to build on the vast storehouse of philosophical and spiritual teachings which have for thousands of years guided human beings in understanding and managing their emotions. Anyone drawn to a particular spiritual teaching will know how through examples, metaphors, parables and sustained moral exploration, very detailed guidance has been made available about diverse paths to self-knowledge. An excellent volume by West (2000) and Chapter 9 in this volume by Shahid Najeeb explore these issues more fully.

All spiritual teachings are quite explicitly designed to foster emotional intelligence. However, in my view, these paths are to be followed, not to be written about, and they should certainly not be written about from outside the tradition that gives them meaning.

The creative arts   The same can be said for the most emotionally literate of all human endeavours, the creative arts, whose sole purpose is to engage with the complexities of human emotion in all its myriad forms. As we immerse ourselves in novels, plays, poetry, paintings, sculpture, installations, television and film, we expose ourselves, raw and questing on the 'slopes of the human heart' as the poet Rilke so aptly puts it. Already Aristotle (ca 310 BC) in his *On the Art of Poetry* (1965: Ch. 6), recommended thorough participation in the whole gamut of emotions as they are stirred up in us by engaging with drama because he thought this would cleanse, refine and educate our emotions (*catharsis*: purification). Theatre directly fosters emotional intelligence. This point is made forcibly by the renowned British playwright Edward Bond (1990, and personal communication).

The 'what' of emotional intelligence: what do we mean by it?

Context

After the explicit divorce between art, religion, magic and science, following the so-called Enlightenment in the eighteenth century, different traditions and disciplines have endeavoured to increase our understanding of emotional intelligence and emotional life. Each has been focusing on a particular question, with its own philosophy of enquiry, drawing on its own traditional sources, and applying its own methodology.

This involves defining and describing the differences between such concepts as, for example, emotion, motivation, feeling, drive and affect. This includes attempts at understanding and explaining the neurophysiology and neurochemistry of emotion and motivation, the wider determinants for disturbances in our emotional functioning, and the study of how we might learn to better understand and manage our emotions (Depue, 1996; Ekman et al., 1983; Frances et al., 1992).

For instance, social and intercultural psychologists have studied how we express and display emotions in different contexts and cultures. Ethnologists and developmental psychologists have studied how we learn to understand our own emotions and how we make sense of how other people feel and act across the life span. The work of Ekman et al. (1975) and Collett (1977) has become the mainstay of academic research into how people of all ages, across a wide range of cultures all over the world, recognise primary emotions or families of emotions.

Given the diversity of traditions involved, there are lively debates about how to categorise, classify, describe and verbally define the different terms used to refer to aspects of our emotional life in the fast growing field of psychology, anthropology and psychotherapy. It is beyond the scope of this chapter to engage with these debates. Interested readers might wish to refer to the work of authors such as Millon and Davis (1996) where the complexities of definitional and theoretical issues are addressed in greater depth. I will present my own working definitions, which are of course tied to my own theoretical assumptions, and which are therefore open to challenge.

There is reasonable consensus that emotional intelligence involves combining our relatively detached understanding of the bio-psycho-social facts *about emotion*, motivation and affect with *our living understanding of our own inner experience of feelings* (Strasser, 1999). This means learning to become aware of subtle mutual perceptions and the mutual attribution of beliefs and behavioural intentions. Both virtuous and vicious cycles are possible here (McCullough Vaillant, 1997).

We need to learn to check out whether our 'reading' of the other person's affective expression is accurate, whether our fantasy of what they are about to do is justified. This is part and parcel of becoming aware ourselves of what we want, what we are feeling, and how we communicate this to the other person. Mutuality means that we are each a contributory cause for the other's behaviour, and that some of what we do is a direct effect of the actions of the other. If we learn to become reflective in this way, then we can transmute a reflex action, driven by the 'inner brain' (see 'The "how" of emotional intelligence' below), into a considered and thought-through response which reflects our values, beliefs and personality.

However, we know, if not from experience then certainly from study and research, that in many situations we do not have the luxury and space to stand back and reflect. We act spontaneously, and *in extremis*, most certainly with all the instinctual resources of the 'inner brain' (MacLean, 1973; see 'The "how" of emotional intelligence' below), which directs our orienting reflex to the source of danger, raises our eyebrows and dilates our pupils to let in maximal light for perception, mobilises adrenaline, oxygenates our muscles, releases other hormones which bring a mixture of fear and courage, and gives us access to memories of perception-judgement-behaviour-outcome sequences which have worked in similar situations before.

Emotion, motivation, curiosity and survival

'Emotion', as used in this context, designates the whole gamut of biological, social, cultural and psychological factors involved in our subjective experience, our social behaviour and its cultural interpretation. 'Emotion' refers to our subjective experience of feelings and thoughts, judgements and intentions to act in certain ways, as well as the presumed underlying biological givens, physiological and psychological states, and associated reflexes and reactions.

There is a vast array of differentiated emotions with their associated vocabulary which describes difference nuances, which vary across different cultures. I refer to these culturally and socially interpreted differentiated emotional states as '*affects*'.

There is, on the whole, fairly general agreement that the following emotions should be considered as the basic families of psycho-bio-social forces which move human beings to social action in order to meet their basic human needs. As mentioned above, there is still considerable controversy about what we might mean by basic emotions, how many categories and families of emotions there are and so forth. The wide scope and variety of socially differentiated '*affects*' collected within each category or family is defined in terms that are highly laden with cultural meanings, customs, conventions and interpretations, and they should therefore be seen as '*affective terms*'.

However each '*affect*' derives its energy to move us to action (hence e-*motion*) from the underlying evolutionary function of the family. It could be argued that the '*motive*' for choosing a particular socially constructed response – if there is time to respond rather than to react in an emergency – is itself rooted in the cultural interpretation of the situation that has given rise to the emotion (see further below).

Eight families of emotions

1 **Anger:** acrimony, aggression, animosity, annoyance, disapproval, disparagement, exasperation, fury, hatred, hostility, indignation, irritability, outrage, resentment, violence, wrath ...
2 **Disgust:** abhorrence, aversion, contempt, disdain, distaste, loathing, rejection, revulsion, scorn ...
3 **Fear:** apprehension, anxiety, concern, consternation, disquiet, dread, edginess, fright, misgiving, nervousness, panic, phobia, qualm, terror ...
4 **Joy:** amusement, bliss, cheerfulness, contentment, delight, ecstasy, enjoyment, euphoria, excitement, gratification, hilarity, interest, mania, pleasure, rapture, satisfaction, thrill, whimsy ...
5 **Love:** acceptance, adoration, affinity, agape, attention, devotion, empathy, esteem, friendliness, kindness, infatuation, interest, mercy, pity, sympathy, trust, warmth ...
6 **Sadness:** cheerlessness, dejection, depression, despair, disappointment, gloom, grief, loneliness, longing, melancholy, nostalgia, pining, self-pity ...
7 **Shame:** chagrin, contrition, exposure, embarrassment, guilt, humiliation, mortification, regret, remorse ...
8 **Surprise:** amazement, astonishment, shock, wonder ...

Although it is clear that cultures differ with respect to so-called 'display rules', that is, which emotions it is acceptable to express openly and fully in public, all healthy normal human beings do recognise these eight families of emotions and know how to express them (Ekman et al., 1975, 1983; Ekman and Davidson, 1994; Howell, 1991; Collett, 1985, 1993).

The 'how' of emotional intelligence: how does it develop, how does it work and what does it do?

Hindsight, midsight and foresight

Clinical, social and developmental psychologists have studied how constitutional and environmental factors interact in distorting the range of our emotional repertoire, destabilising our emotional life (Plutchik and Kellerman, 1986).

Over the past 30 years, clinicians and researchers have been alarmed at the rate at which younger and younger people seem to get into patterns of problematic relationships with others and to adopt more and more dysfunctional ways of caring for themselves. Daniel Goleman (1995) has collected an impressive array of research which clearly shows that depression, addiction to drugs and alcohol, eating disorders, antisocial behaviour and violence, self harm and even teenage pregnancy seem to be directly related to problems in recognising, expressing and managing these eight families of emotions (see also Rapp, 1998).

Emotional intelligence can be equated with the capacity to learn from experience (Rapp, 2001a). Crucially this means that we look back at what happened in situations, we reflect on available knowledge with *hindsight*, we examine what choices we may have had, but did not act on, and we reconsider how we might want to deal with such situations in the future. Even little children do this through make-believe, through stories, through day-dreaming. If we do learn, then the next time round we may well have time to recognise what we are confronted with, and with *midsight* we may already be able to use some of the knowledge gained last time. The 'third' time, as it were, we may well be able to see it coming, we may well have time to stand back briefly and we may be able actually to plan a considered response with *foresight*. This is precisely what psycho-educational programmes teach children, adolescents and adults, who act impulsively, and who may, in addition, be addicted to fast, but inappropriate 'cures' for anxiety, misery or boredom (Rapp, 1998).

We know from research that trust, empathy, synergy, pleasure, or perhaps a sense of achievement (if the shared task was not a pleasant one) will be the outcome of such a reflective and aware approach. We know equally well that mistrust, chaotic interaction and conflict, misery and eventually isolation will be the likely outcome of interactions where we have not checked out our own feelings, or not bothered to find out where the other person is really coming from (Rapp, 2001b).

Our understanding of how affects are culturally interpreted in the form of different rules and meanings is utterly crucial to avoiding misunderstandings between people and organisations from different cultures (Hofstede, 1991; Rapp, 2000; Trompenaar and Hampden-Turner, 1997).

Our contemporary understanding of emotions and emotional intelligence requires a thorough understanding not only of the socio-cultural determinants of our affective behaviour, but also of the biological foundations of our emotional responsiveness (Depue, 1996).

Two recent books by John Birtchnell (1994, 1999) address the growth and development of human emotions and human relating from an evolutionary perspective and a third book is in progress which focuses in on the role of the brain more specifically.

There is a vast literature from developmental psychology and studies in developmental pathology about the bio-psycho-social development of our capacity to express, recognise and make use of emotionally laden communication (Harris, 1989).

The 'inner' and the 'outer brain'

Birtchnell (1994), like Maslow (1954), and indeed before them Sigmund Freud (1889, 1911) and Anna Freud (1937), posits that human emotional intelligence is a composite of activities mainly carried out by the evolutionarily older paleomammalian brain, the 'inner brain', and the newer neo-cortex, the 'outer brain' (Birtchnell, 1999; MacLean, 1973).

The 'inner brain' is largely concerned with our immediate personal survival needs and it is also involved in ensuring the long-term survival of the species. The so called *'instincts'* or *'drives'* of classical psychoanalysis would be servants of the 'inner brain', in that they are primarily working in the service of the survival of the species (Dawkins, 1989). This means they regulate in a global way that we seek conditions of safety, that we ward off sources of danger, and that we reproduce. Activities which serve these three goals are themselves dependent on a fine balance between curiosity and accessing prior learning. This balance is crucial to our ability to find new solutions to managing unknown situations, where it is initially unclear whether they are safe, perilous, or conducive to productive human relationships. Curiosity is therefore also sometimes thought of as a *'drive'*.

Drives and affects

Somewhat tentatively, I use the term *'drive'* to refer to the presumed underlying psycho-biological 'driving forces' (*Triebkraefte*) which give basic shape and direction to those emotional interactions with the world which ensure our survival as individuals and as a species. There is much controversy in the field about the use of such theoretically laden terms, which cannot be done justice in this chapter. I therefore present my personal understanding of what I believe to have been Freud's original use of the word *'Triebe'*: to signpost the evolutionary function of *drives* as the underpinning *motivational forces* which direct us towards what is life-sustaining and away from what is life-threatening.

In the animal world, by and large, natural habitats still exist which contain information, enough of which has remained fairly stable over time. This allows animals to survive on the basis of *drives* and *instincts* which are largely pre-patterned with respect to sequences of behaviour that ensure the animal's survival.

However, urban foxes and domestic or captive animals will have to do a huge amount of new learning to adapt to wholly new environments and we do not yet understand how this is reflected in the working of their brains. In the human life-world we depend less and less on information organised via *'drives'* and the inner brain, and more and more on *affectively laden*, socially and culturally constructed forms of social organisation which create conditions of safety, deal with danger, and manage the social reproduction of society. This is the work of the 'outer brain', which is itself the product of our increasing need to make use of such new information, and in that sense, it could be said that it is to a large measure a function of our curiosity. Novel ethical dilemmas are the order of the day, be they to do with changing family structures, reproductive technology, forms of cultural definition of identity, new technologies and radically different service economies.

Curiosity directed at the human life-world could therefore be said to be constitutive of emotional intelligence, which is, in itself, the developmental stimulus for the development of the 'outer brain'.

The 'why and how' of emotional intelligence: what do we know about how to manage our emotions in a reasonably aware and reflective manner and why is this a good thing?

From drives to affects

What was the work of drives which are to a large extent continuous with similar bio-social mechanisms in the animal kingdom, has become the work of affects. 'Hot cognitions' and 'hot learning' (Abelson, 1963; Greenberg and Safran, 1987; Safran and Greenberg, 1986) is another popular term for what I mean by 'affects', that is, the blend of arousal, state dependent perception, memory and learning, emotional tone, social-cognitive appraisal and interpretation, and the production of a behavioural intention to act in a certain way. We use *affect*, defined in this way, to regulate social and personal relationships between individuals who define themselves much more in terms of their cultural identity than in terms of their biological nature.

Affects then are the socially directed and culturally interpreted gestures of human relating which have their origin in the eight families of emotion, six of which Ekman et al. (1975) made famous in the wake of Darwin's original descriptions (Darwin, 1872, 1916). I have given some examples of affect terms above. A good thesaurus or a good read of contemporary literature or indeed listening to youth culture music will yield a rich harvest of affective terms.

Most developmental psychologists now agree that as our perceptions about the relationship between infants and caregivers have changed, so a much greater degree of social responsiveness is encouraged in infants and young children – that is, if all is well. Where these are available, play groups and nurseries, team work in schools, the wealth of clubs and after-school activities, create rich opportunities for some children to relate with peers and adults while they engage in a multitude of, hopefully, stimulating shared tasks. All these activities require the use of emotional intelligence (Weare, 2000).

The crucial role of opportunities for affective learning

Children as young as 3 develop what is known as a theory of mind (or other minds) and can work out whether someone is lying or misleading, guess at people's true motives, work out how to negotiate playground conflicts, get the emotional drift and moral of a story and so forth. Good introductions to this literature can be found in Harris (1989) and in Whiten (1991).

Unfortunately, for many children these opportunities are not available. Levels of relative poverty in the US and in the UK are higher than 40 years ago, and the way this is blighting children's lives is a cause for alarm. It is precisely because the increasing complexity of our society is such that manual jobs are on the decline and managerial jobs on the increase, that opportunities to acquire and develop emotional intelligence in preschool, school and after-school community projects are so vital. There was a real push in the United States in the 1970s to set up early intervention programmes which foster the growth of emotional intelligence. Goleman (1995) gives a very good summary of these programmes. In the UK, the Natural Birth Movement, the push for breast feeding, the Preschool Playgroups movement and the radical bent of primary school education took a similar, if not even more radical line to boost social and emotional literacy, focusing on attachment, play space, creativity and productivity (Rapp, 1998).

The links between social and emotional deprivation, poor emotional intelligence and subsequent personality disorders, relationship difficulties, a pull towards drugs, alcohol, addictions and crime are well documented, and also significantly associated with a failure to find work and to remain connected to socially meaningful networks (Rapp, 1998).

Ordinary everyday emotional literacy

Emotional intelligence is really the *capacity to learn from direct social experience, taking into account the whole of our declarative and procedural knowledge about the wider world and the contexts of human decision-making.*

Intersubjective understandings of the meaning of emotionally charged personal experiences are combined with what we know from reading, academic study, participation in workshops, immersion in art and so on regarding explanations of externally observable behaviour.

Intuitive, popular, implicit, as well as scientific (by whatever understanding of science) theories of the role and function of emotions are part of our everyday knowledge base. Rocketing sales of self-help books, agony aunt columns in popular magazines, and Susie Orbach's *Guardian* articles, collected in book form (Orbach, 1999) are a good example of the popular appeal of talking more openly and intelligently about our emotions. This is why children, adolescents and young offenders can and do benefit from psycho-educational input, provided it is combined with hands on experiential work, and where necessary supported by counselling and psychotherapy (Greenberg and Pinsof, 1986; Greenberg et al., 1993; Rapp, 1998).

That insight and understanding constitute only half of emotional intelligence was the major breakthrough from psychotherapy research and counselling training, especially within the experiential and humanistic tradition and the human potential movement. The other half consists in learning to change through learning from direct experience and practising of novel ways of behaving and relating (Greenberg and Paivio, 1997). Psychoanalysis also has been much concerned with learning from experience, but in a rather different way (Rapp, 2001b), focusing more on 'inner action', rather than on overt behaviour.

A note of warning: emotional intelligence crucially requires that we are aware of our own darker and more passionate and violent feelings, sometimes referred to by Jungians as 'the shadow'. This can be frightening and dangerous work. Here, psychoanalysis, psychotherapy and counselling truly have their place.

This is not the place to give a cookbook run-down of tried and tested ways to foster emotional intelligence. A few examples have been given throughout the chapter. There are many excellent workbooks, including one by Daniel Goleman (1998), and popular, yet deep engagements with how emotional intelligence informs how we reflect on how we feel and how this can and should lead to more aware, ethical action. All therapy and counselling trainings address this area in some form or other.

Here we come full circle to what I said about spiritual traditions and the arts. Fostering emotional intelligence is something one needs to do, live, in a safe, supportive yet challenging learning environment with peers, coaches, mentors, teachers or counsellors and therapists, risking oneself, learning to grow through live feedback.

What needs to be learnt on the hoof is how to relate to others in ways that maximise our human potential (Bohart and Tallman, 1999). I have run workshops and courses for pre-schoolers, adolescents, adults in community settings, therapists, students and managers in industry, provided group and individual therapy, counselling and supervision. What I have learnt in all these different settings is that people want to find out how we and those we interact with manage our search for contact, privacy, safety, freedom of self expression, understanding, belonging, support, challenge, intimacy, space to be alone, opportunities to be productive in a valued role, and a sense of identity, achievement and worth.

Emotional intelligence is to know both from experience and from study what sorts of things get in our way of fulfilling such ordinary human aspirations and how we can overcome these barriers (Rapp and Davy, in press).

Self-help groups, workshops, modules in schools, ways of relating in nurseries, parent education, varieties of management training programmes, and of course psychotherapy and counselling are all ways of fostering emotional intelligence.

What we can learn to different degrees in all these settings is how complex affects are constructed in the context of cultural rules and meanings, built on the foundations of our biological makeup, and how we might learn to master them so that we do not act in ill-considered, impulsive and harmful ways.

References

Abelson, R.P. (1963) Computer simulation of 'hot cognitions'. In S. Tomkins and S. Messick (eds), *Computer Simulations of Personality*. New York: Wiley.

Adair, J. (1995) *Not Bosses but Leaders*. London: Kogan Page.

Aristotle (1965) On the Art of Poetry. In *Aristotle, Horace, Longinus. Classical Literary Criticism* (trans. T.S. Dorsch). London: Penguin.

Belbin, R. Meredith (1981) *Management Teams – Why they Succeed or Fail*. London: Heinemann.

Berwick, D. (2001) (personal communication) Don Berwick is working with the NHS Executive in collaboration with the Institute for Health Care Improvement (IHI), Boston, the European Forum on Quality Improvement in Health Care and the new annual Asian-Pacific Forum in Sidney, to make the commitment to 'patient-centred services', relying on emotionally intelligent communication central to all NHS work.

Birtchnell, J. (1994) *How Humans Relate: A New Interpersonal Theory*. Westport, CT: Praeger.

Birtchnell, J. (1999) *Relating in Psychotherapy: The Application of a New Theory*. Westport, CT: Praeger.

Bohart, A.C. and Tallman, K. (1999) *How Clients Make Therapy Work. The Process of Active Self-healing*. Washington, DC: APA.

Bond, E. (1990) Notes on post-modernism. In *Two Post-Modern Plays*. London: Methuen Drama.

Botelho, R.J. (1998) Negotiating partnerships in healthcare: contexts and methods. In A.J. Suchman, R.J. Botelho and P. Hinton-Walker (eds), *Partnerships in Healthcare: Transforming Relational Process*. Rochester, NY: University of Rochester Press. pp. 19–51.

Collett, P. (ed.) (1977) *Social Rules and Social Behaviour*. Oxford: Blackwell.

Collett, P. (1985) History and the study of expressive action. In K. Gergen and M. Gergen (eds), *Historical Social Psychology*. New York: Erlbaum.

Collett, P. (1993) *Foreign Bodies. A Guide to European Mannerisms*. London: Simon and Schuster.

Cooper, Robert and Sawaf, Ayman (1997) *Executive EQ: Emotional Intelligence in Leadership and Organisations*. New York: Putnam.

CPCAB (1999a) CoDAS (Counsellor Development and Assessment System). This framework is regularly updated. Information from: CPCAB (Counselling and Psychotherapy Central Awarding Body). e-mail:info@cpcab.co.uk; website: www.cpcab.co.uk.

CPCAB (1999b). Developing a Learning Society: A Radical Strategic Perspective. Feedback to second report of the National Skills Task Force.

CPCAB (2001) International Leonardo Research Project into the use of Human Relating Skills in Small to Medium Sized Businesses. Information from: CPCAB (Counselling and Psychotherapy Central Awarding Body). e-mail: info@cpcab.co.uk; website: www.cpcab.co.uk; address: PO. Box 1768, Glastonbury, Somerset BA6 8YP.

Darwin, C. (1872, 1916) *The Expression of Emotion in Man and Animals*. New York: Appleton & Co.

Dawkins, R. (1989) *The Selfish Gene*. New York: Oxford University Press.

De Geus, A. (1997) *The Living Company: Growth, Learning and Longevity in the Business World*. London: Nicholas Brealey.

Department of Health (2001) *Shifting the Balance of Power within the NHS: Securing Delivery*. London: DoH.

Depue, R.A. (1996) A neurobiological framework for the structure of personality and emotion: implications for personality disorders. In J.E. Clarkin and M.F. Lenzenweger (eds), *Major Theories of Personality Disorder*. New York: Guilford Press.

DfEE (1999) *Delivering Skills for All*. Skills Task Force second report. London: DfEE.

Egan, G. (1990) *The Skilled Helper: A Systematic Approach to Effective Helping*, 4th edn. Pacific Grove, CA: Brooks/Cole.

Ekman, P and Davidson, R.J. (eds). (1994) *The Nature of Emotion: Fundamental Questions*. New York: Oxford University Press.

Ekman, P., Levenson, R.W. and Friesen, W.V. (1975.) *Unmasking the Face: A Guide to Recognising Emotions from Facial Clues*. Engelwood Cliffs, NJ: Prentice-Hall.

Ekman, P., Levenson, R.W. and Friesen, W.V. (1983) Autonomic Nervous System activity distinguishes among emotions. *Science*, 22, 1208–10.

Fineman, S. (1993) *Organisations as Emotional Arenas: Emotion in Organisations*. London: Sage.

Frances, A., McKinney, K., Tayna, H., Rosenthal, N. and Hall, W. (1992) Levels of emotional awareness and psychotherapy integration: problems and prospects.

Freud, Anna (1937/1966) *The Ego and the Mechanisms of Defence*. London: Hogarth Press.

Freud, S. (1889/1911) Formulations Regarding the Two Principles in Mental Functioning (trans. M.N. Searl). *Collected Papers*, Vol. 4. London: Hogarth Press. pp. 13–21.

Freud, S. (1895/1950) Project for a scientific psychology. *Standard Edition*, Vol. 1. London: Hogarth Press.

Friedli, L. (2001) *Making it Happen. A Guide to Delivering Health Promotion*. London: Department of Health. (A report by Mentality, co-sponsored by the Sainsbury Centre for Mental Health.)

Fukuyama, F. (1995) *Trust: The Social Virtues and the Creation of Prosperity*. New York: Free Press.

Fukuyama, F. (1999) *The Great Disruption: Human Nature and the Reconstitution of Social Order*. London: Profile Books.

Gardner, Howard (1983) *Frames of Mind – The Theory of Multiple Intelligences*, (10th Anniversary edn.) New York: Basic Books.

Goleman, D. (1995) *Emotional Intelligence: Why It Can Matter More Than I.Q.* London: Bloomsbury.

Goleman, D. (1997) Interview. *Journal of Business Strategy*, March/April.

Goleman, D. (1998) *Working with Emotional Intelligence*. London: Bloomsbury.

Greenberg, L.S. and Paivio, S.C. (1997) *Working with Emotions in Psychotherapy*. New York: Guilford Press.

Greenberg, L.S. and Pinsof, W.M. (eds) (1986) *The Psychotherapeutic Process: A Research Handbook*. New York: Guilford Press.

Greenberg, L.S. and Safran, J.D. (1987) *Emotion in Psychotherapy*. London: Guilford Press.

Greenberg, L.S., Rice, L. and Elliot, R. (1993) *Process-Experiential Therapy: Facilitating Emotional Change*. New York: Guilford Press.

Harris, Paul L. (1989) *Children and Emotion*. Oxford: Blackwell.

Hofstede, G. (1991) *Cultures and Organisations*. London: Harper Collins.

Howell, S. (1991) 'Art and Meaning', in S. Hiller (ed.), *The Myth of Primitivism*. London: Routledge.

Kleyn, Peter (2000) *The Comprehensive Personality Profile (CPP). Psychometric Assessment Tools and Skills Tests*. Woking: White House Training and Distribution Ltd.

Kofman, F. and Senge, P.M. (1995) *Communities of Commitment: The Heart of Learning Organisations*. Portland, OR: Productivity Press.

MacLean, P.D. (1973) *A Triune Concept of Brain and Behaviour*. Toronto: University of Toronto Press.

Maslow, A. (1954) *Motivation and Personality*. New York: Harper & Row.

McCullough Vaillant, L. (1997) *Changing Character: Short-Term Anxiety-Regulating Psychotherapy for Restructuring Defenses, Affects and Attachment*. New York: Basic Books.

Millon, T. and Davis, R. D. (1996) An Evolutionary Theory of Personality Disorders. In J.E Clarkin. and M.F. Lenzenweger (eds), *Major Theories of Personality Disorder*. New York: Guilford Press.

Orbach, S. (1999) *Towards Emotional Literacy*. London: Virago.

Plutchik, E. and Kellerman, H. (eds) (1986) *Emotion: Theory, Research, and Experience*. Vol. 3: *Biological Foundations of Emotions* New York: Academic Press. pp. 173–97.

Rapp, H. (1998) Healthy Alliances to Promote Mental Health and Social Inclusion. A BIIP Discussion Paper. London: British Initiative for Integrative Psychotherapeutic Practice.

Rapp, H. (2000) Working with difference: culturally competent supervision. In B. Lawton and C. Feltham (eds), *Taking Supervision Forward. Enquiries and Trends in Counselling and Psychotherapy*. London: Sage. pp. 93–113.

Rapp, H. (2001a) Learning from Experience. Learning from Wilfred Bion. Paper presented at the 17th SEPI Congress, Santiago, Chile, 16 June 2001.

Rapp, H. (2001b) Working with Difference and Diversity: The Responsibilities of the Supervisor. In S. Wheeler and D. King (eds), *Supervising Counsellors: Issues of Responsibility*. London: Sage. pp. 131–53.

Rapp, H. (2001c) A–Z of Government Policy, Organisations and Terms of Reference Relevant to Health and Social Care. CPCAB website www.cpcab.co.uk

Rapp, H. and Davy, J. (in press) *Barriers and Defences*. Oxford: Open University Press.

Rice, L.N. and Greenberg, L.S. (eds) (1984) *Patterns of Change. Intensive Analysis of Psychotherapy Process*. New York and London: Guilford Press.

Safran, J.D. and Greenberg, L.S. (1986) Hot cognition and psychotherapy process: an information processing/ecological approach. In P. Kendall (ed.), *Advances in Cognitive-Behavioural Research and Therapy*, Vol. 5. New York: Academic Press.

Salovey, P. and Meyer, J. (1991) Emotional Intelligence in *Psychology Today*, New York.

Senge, P.M. (1990) *The Fifth Discipline: The Art and Practice of the Learning Organisation*. New York: Doubleday.

Strasser, F. (1999) *Emotions. Experiences in Existential Psychotherapy and Life*. London: Gerald Duckworth & Co.

Thomson, K. (1998) *Emotional Capital. Capturing Hearts and Minds to Create Lasting Business Success*. Oxford: Capstone.

Trompenaar, F. and Hampden-Turner, C. (1997) *Riding the Waves of Culture*. London: Nicholas Brealey. pp. 13–14.

Valuing People (2001) A New Strategy for Learning Disability for the 21st Century. A White Paper. Presented to Parliament by the Secretary of State for Health by Command of Her Majesty. March 2001.

Weare, K. (2000) *Promoting Mental, Emotional and Social Health: A Whole School Approach*. London: Routledge.

Weisinger, H. (1998) *Emotional Intelligence at Work: The Untapped Edge for Success*. San Francisco: Jossey–Bass.

West, W. (2000) *Psychotherapy and Spirituality. Crossing the Line between Therapy and Religion*. London: Sage.

Whiten, A. (ed.) (1991) *Natural Theories of Mind: Evolution, Development and Simulation of Everyday Mindreading*. Oxford: Blackwell.

Workforce Action Team (2001) Mental Health National Service Framework (and the NHS Plan). Workforce Planning, Education and Training: Underpinning Programme: Adult Mental Health Services. Final Report by the Workforce Action Team: Special Report.

PART THREE

THERAPEUTIC SETTINGS AND ARGUMENTS FOR EFFECTIVENESS

12

GOOD MONEY AFTER BAD? THE JUSTIFICATION FOR THE EXPANSION OF COUNSELLING SERVICES IN PRIMARY HEALTH CARE

Graham Curtis Jenkins

Introduction

For the past 15 years counsellors have been gaining an ever stronger foothold in primary health care in Britain. In 1999 80% of primary care groups in England reported that at least some of the general practices in their group 'had' a counsellor (Wilkins et al., 1999). The national survey of over a thousand counsellors working in primary care carried out in 1999 (Mellor-Clark, Simms-Ellis and Burton, 2001) suggested that, in over 50% of all general practices, counsellors were working as members of the primary health care team (PHCT). It also revealed that, contrary to the powerfully expressed views of some (Sibbald et al., 1993), for the most part they were adequately trained and supervised. Eighty-seven percent were women with an average age of 48 years and an average of 6 years of experience of working as a primary health care counsellor. The counsellors reported that the predominant working core model was person-centred but many counsellors working in primary health care – like psychological therapists in other settings – had learned what worked from their contact with general practice patients and used a variety of psychotherapeutic treatment approaches (Table 12.1).

The patients counsellors see often arrive in distress, sometimes with feelings of dismissal and even angry but frequently apprehensive about what will happen in the counselling session. However, patients are usually clear that they want relief from their unpleasant feelings of distress and confusion. The referral decisions made by GPs are often meant to be governed by complex guidelines and protocols of do's and don'ts issued by service providers, health authorities and trusts (for example, Camden and Islington Medical Audit Advisory Group, 1996; and see Table 12.2).

However, the reality is that intuition and experience of the referring GP that 'something is going on' in this patient's life and he or she (the GP) is not the

TABLE 12.1   *Patients with depression: theoretical models in forming treatment approach (n = 1031)*

Cognitive-behavioural therapy alone	11%
In combination with other treatment approaches	36%
Psychodynamic therapy alone	19%
In combination with other treatment approaches	41%
Person-centred therapy alone	21%
In combination with other treatment approaches	48%

Source: J. Mellor- clark (2000), National Survey of Counsellors Working in Primary Care: Interim Report to Counselling in Primary Care Trust

TABLE 12.2   *Suggested referral guidelines for GPs*

Problems to refer to counsellor
1   Crisis of limited severity or duration
2   Adjustment disorders including newly diagnosed post traumatic stress disorder
3   Behavioural problems, anger management
4   Relationship difficulties
5   Anxiety/depression
6   Grief or loss reactions
7   Adjustment to diagnosis of major illness
8   Somatic fixation
9   Psychosexual problems
10   Collaborative management of chronic pain
11   Substance misuse

Problems likely to require referral to mental health services
1   Patients with severe suicidal or homicidal intention
2   Psychotic illness
3   Substance misuse*
4   Sexual abuse*
5   Phobias
6   Eating disorders*
7   Sexual difficulties*
8   Problems resistant to change

*Some counsellors working in primary care are competent to work with patients with these conditions.
Source: Counselling in Primary Care Trust, *Supplement* No. 2 (1996)

best person to help (whereas maybe the counsellor can) seems to be the commonest reason for referral. An uninterested or overextended NHS secondary care mental health service or one with a 6 month waiting list for assessment for suitability for psychological therapy ensures that once the GP's habit of referral starts, it is hard to break. As experience grows so the referrals become increasingly sophisticated as GPs learn exactly what the counsellor can or cannot do. GPs often realise that their counsellor is good at some things and not others, or like working with specific client groups, and GPs find that their counsellor makes their life 'easier': 'I don't know how we managed without [her]' is typical of GP comments about 'their' counselling service and an often-repeated sentiment in many studies of GP satisfaction with services (Bunker and Ward,

2000). The complex reasons for the acceptance of the counsellor's work by GPs are well covered by many authors (Pietroni and Vaspe, 2000). Every counsellor and GP has a different story to tell of the success (and sometimes failure) of this relationship (Curran and Higgs, 1993; Lees, 1999).

While the services remained ad hoc and practice-based, dependent on the relationship between the counsellor, the GP, the patients and the rest of the primary health care team, counsellors developed their work in many creative ways. Some GPs and counsellors agreed to target frequent attenders or patients on long-term antidepressant medication (e.g. Heal, 1997). These patients frequently commented that finally someone was listening to them and this reduced their consultation rates with GPs, and often their medication too. Some counsellors started running anxiety reduction sessions or family therapy and group therapy services (e.g. Page and Wood, 2000). These different initiatives were dependent on the creativity of the counsellors, their skills, time and inclination coupled with an ability to 'take' the rest of the PHCT with them as they developed new ways of working. The fund holding practice experiment (terminated in 1999 by the Labour government) allowed for the ability to find and use 'pots' of funding from various budgets which meant that the more creative and innovative general practices succeeded in developing services in a variety of ways with totally unexpected side effects – reduction in referrals to the Community Mental Health Services (Coe et al., 1996), reduction in GP consultation rates and reductions in psychotropic medication prescribing (Bunker and Locke, 1998).

But where was the evidence to support this growth of counselling in primary health care? Like many other innovations in health care, there were many clear psycho-social reasons for the expressed need for such services. GPs didn't wait for the evidence of worth before allowing counsellors with a variety of training and backgrounds to join their primary health care teams. This is not the only time this has happened in the NHS in recent years. There are other examples, like routine mammography for the early diagnosis of breast cancer (Baum, 2001; Miller, 2001). Mammography was introduced as a result of strongly felt beliefs amongst groups of very influential individuals and organisations. These groups were in far too much of a hurry to introduce such services to wait for an evidence base that justified the setting up of such services in the first place. Political will and media pressure overwhelmed the small but insistent voices of perhaps wiser individuals asking for evidence of worth before investing in the very expensive initiative. The result is that it is now clear that the advantages argued by the proponents to justify this enormously expensive health care screening intervention have become sometimes difficult to discern. From what evidence we have, the effect of the intervention appears to be equivocal in actually reducing the incidence of breast cancer for a variety of reasons. However, the service is currently now unstoppable and has entered the public's mind as a 'good thing'. So it was with the growth of primary care counselling.

As is typical with any new development in health care in the UK, there were proponents and opponents. On the one side were the GPs, counsellors and patients who claimed to have found how valuable such a service was. A large number of audits and clinical trials (mostly non-randomised) seemed to indicate that patients benefited, took less medication and reduced the number of consultations they had with GPs (Hemmings, 2000). Unfortunately, many of the studies were methodologically flawed, which created great uncertainty about the actual effect that counsellors were having on patients.

On the other side were two groups, opponents and proponents – the psychotherapy and counselling researchers and the very powerful mental health lobby made up of psychiatrists, psychologists, community psychiatric nurses and mental health managers, both groups guilty of equally flawed studies attempting to prove their case.

As positive reports of the strengths of primary health care counselling services did become available, the more insistent were the voices of opposition. Harris (1994) was typical of the genre. The criticism unsurprisingly centred on the largely imagined lack of training of counsellors and their supervision (Sibbald et al., 1993) and the potential damage that counsellors might apparently be doing to severely distressed patients. 'Overmedicalising misery' and the lack of 'real' evidence that counsellors were 'effective' also figured in the carpetbag of accusations levelled at counsellors working in primary care.

However, the lack of evidence of the right kind, which met the criteria of the modern 'evidence based health care' (Rowland and Goss 2000), was the most severe criticism (Friedli et al., 1997; King et al., 1994).

The modern gold standard in evidence-based health care is the randomised controlled trial (RCT) (Sibbald and Rowland, 1998). If there is no evidence of worth, no money should be spent on providing services – this is the criterion by which the National Institute for Clinical Excellence (NICE) makes its decisions. This is as it should be in what Cochrane called *cure* conditions, like treatments for diabetes, heart disease or cancer (Cochrane, 1999). However, the application of the similar gold standard to evaluating *care* conditions, like Community Mental Health Services or social work (and counselling), as Cochrane pointed out, is fraught with problems, apart from the obvious ones like challenges to the external validity of even carefully performed RCTs to demonstrate the value of one intervention over another. This is particularly important in small-scale randomised trials where almost inevitably the numbers of patients in research and control arms are rarely large enough to produce statistically reliable findings.

One problem is bias – a 'one sided inclination of the mind' – and there tends to be in many areas of health care research a systematic disposition of certain trial designs to produce results that are consistently biased one way or the other.

Wherever bias is present, it usually means that the effects are overestimated and poor trial design or its implementation can make 'treatments' look better or worse, or can even show that a treatment is working when it patently is not (Ernst and White, 1998). This is the problem inherent in uncritically believing the conclusions of non-standardised Systematic Reviews and why the 'Cochrane' registered Systematic Review of counselling in primary care (Rowland et al., 2000), like all the other Systematic Reviews currently produced by the Cochrane Collaboration (1994), are governed by strict guidelines that attempt to eliminate bias. Whether it succeeds is open to question. These guidelines, for instance, ask reviewers to measure the effect of different research trial designs to see if they affect the results in such reviews. Not only is this advice sometimes ignored by those carrying out reviews in health care but it is also ignored by policy-makers who can make eventually wrong decisions based on information that is subsequently shown to be incorrect or subject to statistical bias as a result of further data becoming available which changes the picture. Even worse, the health care professionals of all kinds are slow to adopt the recommendations of well-performed Systematic Reviews of high quality. It is important to understand this process because it is both the use and misuse of research results that govern policy-making and subsequent implementation of any new service or intervention in health care (Khan et al., 1996).

What are the special problems that relate to counselling research?

First and foremost, the process of randomisation causes problems. We know from a number of researchers what can go wrong (Fairhurst and Dowrick, 1996). Selection of patients and controls can be easily manipulated in a variety of ways, particularly if those responsible on the ground for ensuring whether patients receive the 'research' intervention or fall into a 'placebo' or 'treatment as usual' group are convinced that the intervention does work (and often believing that they can manage without the need for tiresome procedures like randomisation in proving so).

Some practitioners have been known to manipulate the opening of the treatment allocation envelopes or the shaking of the dice or whatever other form of randomisation procedure has been chosen by the researchers (Hemmings, personal communication, 1998). Researchers have tried a number of techniques to overcome the difficulty. One, Bradley and Brewin's patient preference randomisation model (Brewin and Bradley, 1989; Silverman and Altman, 1996) has been shown to be useful in overcoming at least some of the difficulties. Despite criticism, a recent research project where 102 patients were traditionally randomised and 203 were randomised according to their choice (the patient preference model) to either antidepressants or counselling for depression (Bedi et al., 2000) demonstrated that at baseline and at outcome there was absolutely no difference in the two groups, each group responded equally well to either eight weeks of counselling or eight weeks of antidepressants. Yet, it is still probably important that findings like this must always be replicated before assuming that this is invariably the 'truth'. Unless randomisation is adequately performed and concealed, the final results are bound to be biased. For instance, odds ratios can be exaggerated in trials where treatment allocation is not properly concealed (Schultz et al., 1995).

It could be argued that, because there is so much difficulty in performing reliable randomisation, non-randomised trials ought to be included in Systematic

Reviews. Unfortunately, the truth is sobering, especially in studies of alternative therapies like acupuncture for chronic back pain. The outcome of randomisation is meant to ensure that the observer is 'blind' and does not know which treatment the patient has received. Knowing or suspecting which patients got what treatment tends to lead to overestimation of treatment effects (Ernst and White, 1998). This is especially important when counselling and psychotherapy researchers have to design, for instance, an acceptable 'active' counselling placebo instead of the actual counselling. This has proved very difficult in practice and has resulted in totally unexpected effects that also usually threaten the hidden randomisation procedure too (Burton et al., 1991).

There are also other threats to the veracity of research findings. It has been estimated that just getting the same research published in a number of different journals will result in an overestimate of the outcomes by 20% between journals (Tràmer et al., 1997).

Sample sizes are also critically important and too few patients in either the randomised or control group can cause overestimation of effects. This is an ever-present hazard to research into counselling in primary care which normally fails to attract funding of sufficient size to ensure that the numbers of patients in the sample 'arms' are large enough to prevent this happening (Rowland et al., 2000).

As far as counselling research evidence is concerned, upon which the policy-makers and managers can make or break services, all the above factors are present. However, there are other factors that are peculiar to psychotherapy research when performed by non-psychotherapists, like psychiatrists or researchers who use the medical model of cure and who believe counselling is a drug to be used to 'cure' patients of their ills (Hemmings, 1999).

'Counselling' is not a drug that can be titrated in appropriate measured doses to a consistently behaving patient with a specific problem to measure the effect, unlike research that measures the effect of, say, a new drug at a specified dose level on a specific form of diabetes in a particular age group of patients. The problem is that experienced therapists have always known that when they have worked for any length of time, particularly in primary health care, they have to use 'what works' tailored to each individual patient, which is usually a brief form of therapy and which for the most part must meet the patient's immediate needs. Counsellors also report that they use a combination of 'therapeutic' approaches (Cummings and Sayama, 1995). This does not mean that they have to 'buy into' the core theoretical model or school from which each is derived. Failure to understand this way of working by some researchers has had unfortunate side effects. Some try to control the type of therapy intervention, believing it can be standardised, even person-centred therapy (Friedli et al., 1997; Ward et al., 2000). Yet, the reality is that most psychotherapy researchers now reluctantly agree that therapists themselves are more likely to be the cause of outcome variance than the style or type of therapy offered (Asay and Lambert, 1999).

This causes great difficulties of interpretation of results in small-scale RCTs of efficacy using a small number of therapists. Two or three therapists could have up to half of the total treatment effect of the other therapists involved in such a study. It is often quite erroneously argued by researchers, unwilling to accept the possibility or ignorant of such an effect, that this or that treatment has 'an evidence base' on which to make commissioning decisions about what sort of therapists delivering particular forms of therapy to employ in a given service to achieve given outcomes – which is patently absurd. In one recent well-publicised research study, three of the counsellors involved saw 50% of the patients in the counselling arm, yet the researchers claimed that counselling was as effective as cognitive-behavioural therapy in the care of depressed patients in general practice – a very unsafe conclusion in the circumstances (Ward et al., 2000). I believe it is important to make sure that the therapists delivering the therapy intervention are closely monitored. This would ensure that, if there is a variation in the way a specific therapy is delivered, it will supplement the outcome data representativeness of patients, therapy and process and can also give insight into how the results claimed were achieved.

The only way to overcome this problem would be to use a cluster RCT format. However, the costs would be totally prohibitive because of the large numbers of patients and therapists required.

Further problems can arise when, despite the best efforts of editors and peer reviewers, papers are published which claim findings that are not borne out by the results presented. 'Significance' is a case in point. Some authors claim success in their study even when the results are not statistically significant due to small numbers, inappropriate statistical tests and even data manipulation (which is very difficult to spot) and which can cause great difficulties in interpretation. Finally, there is publication bias. Some publications refuse to publish any non-randomised research papers and some journals carry much more prestige than others.

Bias takes many forms and it will not go away in the foreseeable future, and lack of funding is likely to ensure that researchers will continue to implement inappropriate research designs with insufficient numbers of patients recruited to reach significance.

Because of the many factors I have described, the evidence base for the promotion of brief psychological therapies in primary health care by counsellors will be always be vulnerable to vociferous criticism from sceptics unless both the quality of the research method and the funding necessary to perform large enough cluster RCTs becomes available. This is unlikely. A recent RCT published in the *British Medical Journal* in December 2000 (Ward et al.) cost £500,000 (King et al., 2000), at a cost of £2,000 per patient in the psychological therapy treatment arm.

So what information and research results can be used to persuade policymakers and managers in the NHS that counselling services should be expanded in primary health care?

Recently, the development of a standardised audit and outcome system has come to be seen as a possible way out of the impasse I have described (CORE System Group, 1998; Mellor-Clark et al., 1999).

The use of audit in counselling in primary care

For many years critics of primary care counselling complained that few if any counsellors routinely audited their work. However, the introduction of the CORE system has now made it possible to audit the management and outcome of counselling in primary care in ways that few previously thought possible (Mellor-Clark, 2000).

The CORE system (CORE System Group, 1998) is founded on the belief that the psychotherapy works and takes into account most of the preconditions necessary for a beneficial psychological change over time, namely trust, alliance, shared strategy and patient or client effects on outcome (Hubble et al., 1999). The system now in routine use in many parts of the NHS and counselling and psychotherapy services in universities and industry measures those changes reported by patients thought to be indicative of benefit, assuming that the therapist routinely works, to a greater or lesser extent, using and activating the preconditions I have already described. The working alliance, motivation and psychological mindedness of the patient are also measured. (However, from the thousands of randomised controlled trials of psychotherapy and counselling it is clear that these so-called common factors are present in varying degrees wherever effective therapy takes place.) The components of the system include (1) a patient report questionnaire, which includes assessment of the domains of well-being, symptoms, life and social functioning and risk, (2) therapist completed assessment and end of therapy forms and (3) the administrative checklist and support service for feedback and evaluation, currently provided by the Psychological Therapies Research Centre at the University of Leeds.

From the preliminary analysis much useful information has been gained about the difference between providers of services, the effect of waiting times on outcome and the overall effects of counselling interventions in primary care (Mellor-Clark, Connell and Barkhan, 2001). It will also be possible in the future to compare directly the results from secondary and tertiary level NHS psychological therapy with services in primary care. From the CORE System dataset derived from over 2000 clients completing their 'counselling episodes' in primary care, it is apparent that more than 75% who completed the CORE Outcome Measure (Barkham et al., 2001) before they saw the counsellor scored at/or above the predetermined clinical cut-off level for a clinical population and showed a reliable and clinically significant change by the end of therapy (59% moving from a clinical to a non-clinical population). Seven per cent of patients seen deteriorated after seeing the counsellor. The most frequent problems that patients presented with were categorised as depression and anxiety by counsellors (see Table 12.3) but this fails to catch the complexity of associated problems and concerns experienced by patients. This will be captured in future analysis when the emerging therapy issues associated with depression, anxiety and other 'symptoms' or labels are teased out of the data.

Trauma and abuse was identified as an issue for almost one in five of patients seen, highlighting the complexity of the work of the counsellor in general

TABLE 12.3   *Patients' presenting problems and concerns (n = 2,042)*

Depression	71%
Anxiety	78%
Interpersonal problems	60%
Self-esteem	50%
Bereavement and loss	32%
Physical problems	19%
Trauma and abuse	19%
Work	19%
Living and welfare	13%
Addictions	6%
Other	13%

Source: J. Mellor-Clark and J. Connell (2000) *Exploring Service Quality with CORE system Data.* Report to CPCT, July 2000

practice. We should not be surprised at these outcomes. As the vast majority of counsellors working in general practice are appropriately qualified, supervised and experienced (Mellor-Clark, Simms-Ellis and Burton, 2001), it is to be expected that the therapeutic intervention delivered by these counsellors working in primary health care should be capable of producing such clinical changes. We know that between a third and a half of the counsellors used a mixture of at least two therapeutic approaches, which demonstrates clearly the variety of sophisticated therapeutic approaches used by the counsellors, who tailored their therapeutic approach to the patients' needs.

However, it is also clear that there are wide variations between services, which can have both moderating and mediating effects on the effectiveness of the service in terms of patient outcome. For instance, waiting times, as already mentioned, have a number of effects. We know that, as patients wait, they often tend to deteriorate. This could easily be demonstrated if required in analysis of services by waiting times using CORE (see Table 12.4). Those services in the first quartile of waiting times (1–14 days) might report that between 90% and 100% of patients are appropriately referred (decided by counsellors). In this first quartile of services, between 77% and 80% might have both reliable and clinical change. In the fourth quartile, however (waiting time 43–56 days), it could be that less than 70% of clients were appropriately referred and only between 65% and 68% of patients might show reliable and clinical change. Such findings would be very useful in informing providers about their service efficiency.

There are many other factors that need to be taken into account when reviewing such results and using them to commission services. In the reactive environment of primary health care, general practitioners see patients on demand and need to have referral services like A&E or medical and surgical admission services available 'on tap', 24 hours a day. Any service that makes patients in crisis wait longer than a few days is either not used at all or reserved for patients who the GP reckons are not ill or distressed enough to merit emergency referral to a second tier service. Counselling services with long waiting lists are comprised, then, of referred patients who GPs feel will not suffer from the three or four month wait to be seen. That is the perception that many GPs

TABLE 12.4   *Effect of waiting on service delivery*

Service provider	Waiting times (days)	Appropriate referral (%)	Planned endings (%)	Reliable and clinical change (%)
1st quartile	1–14	100–90	75–66	77–80
2nd quartile	15–28	89–80	65–56	74–76
3rd quartile	29–42	79–70	55–46	69–73
4th quartile	43–56	69–60	45–36	65–68

Source: Hypothetical core data: J. Mellor-Clark and J. Connell (2000) *Exploring Service Quality with Core System Data.* Report to CPCT, July 2000

share. However, the CORE system might show what happens to patients on waiting lists. There is ample evidence that nearly half of patients with a chronic psychological problem are still suffering many years later (Lloyd et al., 1996).

We also know from the preliminary CORE system dataset analysis (CORE Audit Management Group, 2000) that there are wide variations in premature endings and attendance failures between services and between individual therapists. These must influence the effectiveness of the services. However, we do not yet know why or to what extent they matter. There is a lot of evidence from North American managed care that patients decide for themselves when they can leave off seeing the therapist, and only return when distress levels rise again (Hoyt, 1995). Indeed, Cummings, in his famous Bill of Rights for Patients (Cummings and Sayama, 1995) is clear: 'Patients are entitled to relief from pain, anxiety and depression in the shortest time possible with the least intrusive intervention', which is a reality for many UK counsellors and their patients in primary health care.

There are many misconceptions about the nature of this form of therapy and whether it matters if patients prematurely terminate their therapy before they have completed the 'set' number of sessions. Talmon (1990), in his study of clients who attended for therapy only once, showed how counterintuitive are the findings when the outcomes of patients who prematurely terminate therapy are examined. Those clients for instance who remembered the one and only session two years later and who spoke of the benefits made such statements as 'It really made me think and I can't thank the therapist enough'. The psychotherapist's contemporary notes of these clients often indicated that the therapist felt confused and was not clear about what was going on! Some clients, however, claimed they had never even seen a therapist despite the fact that the therapist's own notes of the one and only session seemed self-congratulatory and often mentioned 'catharsis and movement'. It is likely that for those unplanned or unrecorded endings reported in the CORE system research findings similar outcomes are likely.

There are other problems which can affect the efficiency of services. If the GP 'makes' the appointment for the patient to see the counsellor – rather than inviting the patient to make an appointment themselves – there is anecdotal evidence that these 'doctor made' appointments are much more likely to end in a 'no show' than when patients make the appointment themselves. So, the style of the service and the customs of the general practices in which counsellors work can sometimes have profound effects which can remain undetected by audit. Where all the primary health care team know the counsellor, value the work done and 'know' that counselling works, the placebo effect is greatly enhanced. The patient receives consistent and positive comments from nurses, reception staff and doctors and enters the therapeutic session greatly advantaged and expectant that relief is at hand. Where there is a lack of belief in the effectiveness of counselling in a primary health care team, a senior partner perhaps, who thinks 'counselling is bunk' and tells all who listen of his beliefs, can greatly undermine a service – even influencing the choice of accommodation provided for the counsellor. Broom cupboards and photocopying rooms have been mentioned by counsellors trying to struggle to establish a service in such undermining environments.

It is inevitable that widespread routine use of the CORE system as the preferred audit tool for psychological therapy services will throw up variations in services that cannot easily be explained. Services where perhaps the counsellors and their supervisors use a single core theoretical model of therapy might be identified either as over- or under-performers as they try to make every patient 'fit' their preferred core model. Services that exclusively use trainees or newly trained counsellors with minimal experience might be unable to demonstrate results that match the national or local audit results.

Services that are underfunded, services that use triage (sorting) of patients to arbitrarily decide who 'deserves' therapy are also likely to have poorer results as nearly half of patients who are referred to such triage services, often located away from the general practice, refuse to attend for the assessment because they do not consider themselves 'mentally ill' (McEvoy, 1999). Triage services run by community mental health staff in a mental health centre or psychiatric department in a distant hospital are especially prone to this. One such service in Manchester reported that just under half of all patients referred to a triage service manned by CPNs failed to attend (McEvoy, 1999). Different practice populations with large numbers of non-English speaking patients also influence outcomes in a variety of ways.

I believe that, on the basis of current information flowing from audit of counselling services in primary care, there is supportive evidence which helps to justify the further development of efficient brief psychological therapy services delivered by counsellors. The services must be prepared to change in response to the audit data they generate and identify strengths and deficiencies. It is imperative that routine audit of services sets targets regularly upgraded to ensure that the service provided is:

- *Effective*, with short waiting lists and appropriate referral of patients, satisfactory falls in levels of psychological distress and disorder in patients seen by the services that are either as good as or better than the national average.
- *Accessible*, where the patient's autonomy is respected and the responsibility for making and keeping appointments is the patient's (with a small contribution from the counsellor), and the service is available at times that suit the patient.

- *Acceptable*, when patients feel their needs are being met ethically and culturally and where the service reflects any special local, social or mental health needs.
- *Appropriate*, where the counsellors are appropriately trained and supervised so that they are able to work in a way that meets patients' needs, and where appropriate referral to other services can be made if patients have been inappropriately referred to them or are found to have complex and difficult problems that the counsellor feels unable to handle.
- *Equitable*, ensuring that the service meets the needs of all the adult population (avoiding at all costs the current managerial solution to dismantle all the existing counselling services in general practices in a primary care group or team – on the principle that if some cannot have it then none should).
- *Efficient*, which is probably the most important because efficiency, or its lack, can affect every aspect of a service.

Funding should be sufficient to make sure that only professionally trained and experienced counsellors, preferably with membership of a properly regulated professional association, are employed, with agreed targets for waiting times and for falls in psychological distress in patients seen, and with provision for training needs of counsellors, where identified, to be met on a regular ongoing basis. Outliers, those counsellors who consistently under- or over-perform in a service, need be identified so that the over-performers can be deployed to meet the needs of patients with special or extraordinary problems and the under-performers are invited to consider how their professional development needs can be met to bring them up to the standards of the rest of the service (however threatening that might be).

These are enormous challenges. Few in the nursing or medical profession have come anywhere near to meeting anything like them. Yet, counsellors using the CORE system are in a position to lead the way in the NHS.

It is essential that the enormously exciting and potentially threatening standardised audit tools like CORE are held emotionally and intellectually within the profession. The data generated is likely to be of a far higher quality and relevance than any other data accessible to health workers in the NHS and its use by all in the profession will ensure that counselling and psychotherapy will not only continue, but will develop and improve to meet the psychological needs of the population if these challenges are met head on and overcome.

When services become fine tuned, primary care groups and health service trusts will learn how to deploy counsellors in new and exciting ways. Reducing the inappropriate prescription of psychotropic medication (Ashworth et al., 2000), reducing referrals not just to community mental health services but to other secondary health care services, will be seen as a normal and satisfactory outcome of the provision of appropriate and professional counselling services.

Medical cost offset will be seen as part of the normal evidence of worth for services of this kind (Spurgeon and Barwell, 2000). In AD 942 Galen commented that more than half the patients who consulted him had predominantly a psychological basis for their symptoms. Patients have not changed. If counsellors working with the rest of the primary care team could divert just a few of the patients seeing a variety of health care professionals with somatic (bodily) symptoms of illness, yet whose cause is in part psychological, we could generate savings to the NHS that would not just fund the entire cost of a nationwide primary care counselling service but generate additional savings which could be diverted into other areas of health care (Cummings et al., 1993).

Finally, and most important, unless counsellors working in primary health care adopt a system of audit like CORE for the services they provide, it is likely that siren voices will get ever louder that there 'is no evidence', and anybody can do the work with minimal training (like the current proposals for a graduate primary care mental health worker with a first degree in psychology and 30 days of training).

Routine audit of services like counselling and psychological therapy and community mental health services will ensure the continuing development of counselling in primary care and will preserve, develop and promote the provision of this most valuable addition to primary health care in the United Kingdom.

References and futher reading

Asay, T.P. and Lambert, M.J. (1999) The empirical case for common factors in therapy. In M.A. Hubble, B.L. Duncan and S.D. Miller (eds), *The Heart and Soul of Therapy*. Washington, DC: American Psychological Association Press. Chapter 2.

Ashworth, M., Wastie, J., Reid, F. and Clements, S. (2000) The effects of psychotherapeutic interventions upon psychotropic prescribing and consultation rates in one general practice. *Journal of Mental Health*, 9, 625–35.

Barkham, M., Evans, C., Margison, F., McGrath, G., Mellor-Clark, J., Milne, D. and Connell, J. (1998) The rationale for developing and implementing CORE outcome batteries for routine use in service settings and psychotherapy outcome research. *Journal of Mental Health*, 7, 34–47.

Barkham, M., Margison, F., Leadi, C., Lucock, M., Mellor-Clark, J., Evans, C., Benson, L., Connell, J. and Audin, K. (2001) Service profiling and outcomes benchmarking using CORE. OM. Towards Practice based evidence in the psychological therapies. *Journal of Consulting and Clinical Psychology*, 69 (2), 184–96.

Baum, M. (2001) Survival and reduction in mortality from breast cancer. *British Medical Journal*, 321, 1470.

Bedi, N., Chilvers, C., Churchill, R., Dewey, M., Duggan, C., Fielding, K., Gretton, V., Miller, P., Harrison, G., Lee, A., and Williams, I. (2000) Assessing effectiveness of treatment of depression in primary care. Partially randomised trial. *British Journal of Psychiatry*, 177, 312–15.

Brewin, C.R. and Bradley, C. (1989) Patient preferences and randomised clinical trials. *British Medical Journal*, 299, 313–15.

Bunker, N., and Locke, M. (1998) South Kent NHS Primary Care Counselling Service 1997–98. Report to South Kent Community NHS Trust, Dover.

Bunker, N. and Ward, J. (2000) Current Evidence and Future Development Primary Care Counselling Service Annual Report, 1999–2000. East Kent Community NHS Trust, Dover.

Burton, M., Parker, R. and Woolner, J. (1991) The psychological value of a chat. A verbal response modes study of a placebo attention control with breast cancer patients. *Psychotherapy Research*, 1 (1), 39–61.

Camden and Islington Medical Audit Advisory Group (1996) *Counselling and Psychological Therapies: Guidelines and Directory*. London: Family Health Services Authority (FHSA).

Cochrane, A.L. (1999) *Effectiveness and Efficiency. Random Reflections on Health Services.* London: RSM Press.

Cochrane Collaboration (1994) *The Cochrane Collaboration Handbook.* Oxford: Oxford University Press.

Coe, N., Ibbs, A.H. and O'Brien, J. (1996) *The Cost Effectiveness of Introducing Counselling into the Primary Care Setting in Somerset.* Taunton: Somerset Health Authority.

CORE Audit Management Group (2000) Provisional Dataset Analysis. Report to the Counselling in Primary Care Trust. University of Leeds: Psychological Therapy Research Centre.

CORE System Group (1998) *CORE System Information Management Handbook.* Leeds: CORE System Group.

Cummings, N. and Sayama, M. (1995) *Focused Psychotherapy.* New York: Brunner Mazel.

Cummings, N.A., Dorken, H., Pallak, M. and Henke, C. (1993) Medicaid, managed behavioural health and implications for public policy: a report of the HCFA – Hawaii medicaid project. *Healthcare Utilization and Cost Series* Vol. 2. San Francisco: Foundation for Behavioral Health.

Curran, A. and Higgs, R. (1993) Setting up a counsellor in primary care – the evolution and experience in one general practice. In R. Corney and R. Jenkins (eds), *Counselling in General Practice.* London: Routledge. pp. 75–88.

Ernst, E. and White, AR. (1998) Acupuncture for backpain. A meta analysis of randomised controlled trials. *Archives of Internal Medicine,* 158, 2235–41.

Fairhurst, K. and Dowrick, C. (1996) Problems with recruitment in a randomised controlled trial of counselling in general practice: causes and implications. *Journal of Health Service Research and Policy,* 1, 77–80.

Friedli, K., King, M., Lloyd, M. and Horder, J. (1997) Randomised controlled assessment of non-directive counselling versus routine general practitioner care. *Lancet,* 350, 1662–5.

Friedli, K., King, M.B., Lloyd, M. et al. (1997) Randomised controlled assessment of non-directive psychotherapy versus routine general practitioner care. *Lancet,* 350, 1662–7.

Harris, M. (1994) Magic in the Surgery. *Counselling and the NHS – a Licensed State Friendship Service.* Research Report No. 20. London: Social Affairs Unit.

Heal, M. (1997) Introducing a counselling culture to general practice. *Journal of Institute of Counselling and Psychotherapy,* 6, 15–19.

Hemmings, A.J. (1998) Personal Communication.

Hemmings, A.J. (1999) *A Systematic Review of Brief Psychological Therapies in Primary Health Care.* Staines: Counselling in Primary Care Trust Publications.

Hemmings, A.J. (2000) Counselling in primary care. A review of the practice evidence. *British Journal of Guidance and Counselling,* 28 (2), 233–52.

Hoyt, M.F. (1995) *Brief Therapy and Managed Care Reading for Contemporary Practice.* San Francisco: Jossey–Bass.

Hubble, M.A., Duncan, B.L. and Miller, S.C. (1999) Directing attention to what works. In M.A. Hubble, B.L. Duncan and S.C. Miller (eds), *The Heart and Soul of Change.* Washington, DC: American Psychological Association Press. Chapter 14.

Khan, K.S., Daya, S. and Jadad, A.R. (1996) The importance of quality of primary studies in producing unbiased systematic reviews. *Archives of Internal Medicine,* 156, 661–6.

King, M., Broster, G., Lloyd, M. et al. (1994) Controlled trials in the evaluation of counselling in general practice. *British Journal of General Practice* 44, 229–32.

King, M., Sibbald, B., Ward, E., Bower, P., Lloyd, M., Gabbay, M. et al. (2000) Randomised controlled trial of non-directive counselling, cognitive behaviour therapy and usual practitioner care in the management of depression as well as mixed anxiety and depression in primary care. *Health Technology Assessment Report,* 4, 19.

Lees, J. (ed.) (1999) *Clinical Counselling in Primary Care.* London: Routledge.

Lloyd, K., Jenkins, R. and Mann, A. (1996) Long term outcome of patients with neurotic illness in general practice. *British Medical Journal,* 313, 26–8.

McEvoy, P. (1999) Drawing the line. *Health Services Journal,* 30 September, pp. 28–9.

Mellor-Clark, J. (2000) Developing practice and evidence for counselling in primary care: the agenda. *British Journal of Guidance and Counselling,* 28 (2), 253–66.

Mellor-Clark, J., Barkham, M., Connell, J., and Evans, C. (1999) Practice based evidence and the need for a standardised evaluation system: informing the design of the CORE system. *European Journal of Psychotherapy, Counselling and Health*, 2 (3), 357–74.

Mellor-Clark, J., Connell, J. and Barkham, M. (2001) Counselling outcomes in primary health care. A CORE system data profile. *European Journal of Psychotherapy, Counselling and Health*, 4 (1), 65–86.

Mellor-Clark, J., Simms-Ellis, R. and Burton, M. (2001) *National Survey of Counsellors Working in Primary Health Care. Evidence for Growing Professionalisation*. Royal College of General Practitioners. Occasional paper 79.

Miller, A.B. (2001) Effects of screening programme on mortality from breast cancer. *British Medical Journal*, 321, 1527.

Page, P. and Wood, P. (2000) Group work in primary care counselling. *Counselling in Practice*, 4 (1), 9–10.

Pietroni, M. and Vaspe, A. (2000) *Understanding Counselling in Primary Care*. London: Churchill Livingstone.

Rowland, N. and Goss, S. (2000) *Evidence Based Counselling and Psychological Therapies. Research and Applications*. London: Routledge.

Rowland, N., Godfrey, C., Bower, P., Mellor-Clark, J., Heywood, P. and Hardy, R. (2000) Counselling in primary care: a systematic review of the evidence. *British Journal of Guidance and Counselling*, 28 (2), 215–31.

Schultz, K.F., Chalmers, I., Haynes, R. and Altman, D.G. (1995) Empirical evidence of bias. Dimensions of methodological quality associated with estimates of treatment effects in controlled trials. *Journal of the American Medical Association*, 273, 408–11.

Sibbald, B. and Rowland M. (1998) Why are randomised controlled trials important? *British Medical Journal*, 316, 201.

Sibbald, B., Addington Hall, J., Brennaman, D. and Freeling, P. (1993) Counsellors in English and Welsh General Practices: their nature and distribution. *British Medical Journal*, 306, 29–33.

Silverman, W.A. and Altman, D.G. (1996) Patient preferences and randomised trials. *Lancet*, 347, 171–4.

Spurgeon, P. and Barwell, F. (2000) Personal responsibility empowerment and medical utilisation. A theoretical framework for considering counselling and offset costs. *European Journal of Psychotherapy, Counselling and Health*, 3, 229–44.

Talmon, M. (1990) *Single Session Therapy: Maximizing the Effect of the First (and often only) Therapeutic Encounter*. San Francisco: Jossey–Bass.

Tràmer, M., Reynolds, D.J.M., Moore, R.A. and McQuay, H. (1997) Effect of covert duplicate publication on meta analysis: a case study. *British Medical Journal*, 315, 635–40.

Vickers, A. and Smith, C. (2000) Incorporating data from dissertations in systematic reviews. *International Journal of Technology Assessment in Healthcare*, 16, 711–13.

Ward, E., King, M., Lloyd, M., Bower, P., Sibbald, B., Farrelly, S., Gabbay, M., Tarrier, N. and Addington Hall, J. (2000) Randomised controlled trial of nondirective counselling, cognitive behaviour therapy and usual general practitioner care for patients with depression I: Clinical effectiveness. *British Medical Journal*, 321, 1383–8.

Wilkins, D., Gilliam, S. and Leese, B. (1999) *The National Tracker Survey of Primary Care Groups and Trusts: Progress and Challenges*, 1999/2000. London: King's Fund.

13

THE BENEFITS OF COUNSELLING AND EMPLOYEE ASSISTANCE PROGRAMMES TO BRITISH INDUSTRY

Carolyn Marchington-Yeoman &
Cary L. Cooper

Very few empirical studies exist looking at workplace counselling or employee assistance programmes (EAPs). One of the best estimates of effectiveness is obtained by reviewing a broad range of studies of counselling and psychotherapy carried out in mental health and educational settings (Lambert et al., 1986; Shapiro, 1989). The findings reveal the average person receiving help to be better off, psychologically, than up to three-quarters of those not receiving help. Research looking at counselling for work-related problems has found similar results (Firth and Shapiro, 1986). Obviously these benefits are worthwhile, but research shows that average figures conceal wide variations, in that not all individuals receiving counselling will benefit substantially. There thus remains considerable room for improving the effectiveness of counselling (Shapiro et al., 1993).

One of the only evaluations of workplace counselling to take place in Britain was carried out in the Post Office (Cooper and Sadri, 1991). The counselling service was an open access service located within the occupational health service, staffed by clinical psychologists. The research systematically assessed the impact of stress counselling among postal workers, from shopfloor level to senior management. Sickness absence and questionnaire data before and after counselling were compared, and these changes were compared with a control group matched in terms of age, sex, grade and years of experience. The sample was 250 employees who had counselling over a one-year period.

The research found that there were significant declines, from before to after counselling, in sickness absence days and events, clinical anxiety levels, somatic anxiety and depression, and increases in self-esteem. The control group showed no changes over the study period. However, despite this improvement, the mental health and absence levels of the average client remained worse after counselling than that of a typical member of the control group. There were no changes in job attitudes during the counselling. Reported health behaviours (not measured in the control group) changed over counselling, with decreased use of smoking, eating, coffee and alcohol, and increased use of relaxation, exercise and humour.

There is thus promising evidence that worksite counselling is effective. However, most of the evidence is indirect, based on evaluation of similar methods in other settings, where the client and their presenting problems may be quite different from people seen at the workplace (Shapiro et al., 1993).

The evaluation of employee assistance programmes (EAPs)

Kim (1988) describes methods for evaluating EAPs. However, there are relatively few published EAP evaluation studies. They differ from research on counselling and psychotherapy in placing greater emphasis on cost savings rather than measures of psychological well-being.

Since most US and British EAPs were created in an era of increased account-ability and because of their relationship to cost-conscious, profit-directed organisations, one would expect EAPs to have generated many evaluation studies. In fact, researchers (Knott, 1986) in this field seem to be still searching for identity, direction, methodologies and information. Most EAPs attempt to assist employees in a variety of ways, with a mixture of hard and soft benefits, and their simultaneous provision to the same employees makes the identification of a clear 'outcome-orientated by intervention' model difficult, if not impossible. As a consequence, the greater the vagueness of interventions and services provided to employees, the greater the vagueness of defining the impact and outcome of such interventions.

In the USA, the financial and other benefits of stress-care are widely recognised and most of the Fortune 500 companies have employee counselling services in place. British companies are now also recognising that by helping employees to cope with stress, they may be able to reduce absenteeism, improve morale, and ultimately boost profitability. Most larger companies in Britain are therefore beginning to see EAPs not as an additional cost, but as a possible investment. This is almost certainly true in the medium to long term, although conclusive measures of the benefit are not yet available relating to Britain. For that reason, some British employers are sceptical about the benefits, particularly financial, of stress counselling schemes.

In the UK, evaluations of EAPs tend to be almost exclusively qualitative in nature, other than basic statistical reports on usage rates and the like. However, in the USA there has been a move away from such anecdotal evidence of EAP effectiveness towards insisting upon hard data: 'Almost every company with an EAP in the USA is subjecting it to close scrutiny in terms of cost-benefit, utilisation and success rates. All sorts of bottomline questions are being asked' (Bickerton and Stern, 1990). In the future, this type of hard data is likely to be demanded by UK companies as well.

US studies

A number of evaluations have been conducted in the USA, with varying degrees of scientific rigour. The McDonnell Douglas Corporation (1989) commissioned a financial impact study which was an independently conducted, scientifically valid cost-benefit analysis. It involved the longitudinal analysis of the costs associated with health care claims and absenteeism for a 4-year period (1985–88), before and after an EAP intervention. Each client was matched to ten other employees on six demographic variables, thus establishing an appropriate control group.

The research did not try to measure the financial impact of factors that could not be objectively and concretely measured – soft dollar items such as productivity, job performance level, replacement labour costs and other subjective data were ignored. The result was therefore the most conservative possible study on outcome. The overall saving for the EAP population (compared to control) was $5.1 million and the dollar return on investment was 4:1.

One of the most ambitious and sophisticated cost-benefit evaluations was undertaken by the US Department of Health and Human Services Employee Counseling Service (ECS) Program. It required the cooperation of ECS programmes in 16 operating units throughout the USA, which provided services to the Department's 150,000 staff. ECS counsellors saw in excess of 2,500 troubled employees during the 30-month period of evaluation. The evaluation had a number of important aspects: confidentiality of clients was guaranteed; the evaluation was compatible with existing policies and procedures; the minimum burden was placed on EAP staff; feedback was given to management to aid decision-making; the design was rigorous so that results were credible (this was achieved by collecting individual level data); and the emphasis was on outcome (i.e., cost-benefit). Employees who had not used the EAP were the control group and were selected in terms of unit, sex, age and salary level. Cost-benefit analyses revealed that the estimated cost per client was $991; the estimated benefit in 6 months was $1,274 saved per employee, and for every dollar spent the return in 6 months was $1.29. A 5-year return of $7.01 per dollar invested was extrapolated from these figures, on the assumption that the level of benefit measured over 6 months would continue undiminished over 5 years (Maiden, 1988).

Nadolski and Sandonato (1987) examined the work performance of employees referred to the EAP for counselling over a 6-month period at the Detroit Edison Company. The measures used were lost time (instances and number of days), health insurance claims, discipline warnings and accidents – all of which are generally accepted as valid measures of work performance. A measure of work productivity was also developed for use with those clients referred by their supervisor. A longitudinal, comparative study was used and data were collected for employees at initial entry to the EAP (for 6 months up to that point) and for 6 months following treatment. A sample of 67 employees was used – 31 supervisory referrals and 36 self-referrals. Instances of lost time reduced by 18% and the number of lost days reduced by 29%. There was a reduction in health insurance claims of 26% and written warnings diminished by 13%. There was also a 40% decrease in suspensions and a 41% reduction in the number of job-related accidents. In addition, the quality of work improved by 14%, the quantity of work by 7%, peer relationships by 7% and relationship with supervisor by 13%. Unfortunately, no control group was used with this piece of research.

McClellan (1989) reports on the cost-benefit study carried out as part of an overall evaluation of the Ohio State EAP. There were no benefits in terms of reduced accidents, theft, sick leave, or turnover, or increased productivity. The sensitivity of EAP measures to these effects may have been diminished by State policies: for example, sickness absence was considered an entitlement to additional leave.

In addition, the EAP itself was highly diffuse, comprising a central administrative and training unit, linked to 30 local community service centres, dealing in total with 44 health insurance plans and 86 service vendors. Accounting systems were imprecise and individuals' contacts with the EAP atypically long, suggesting later intervention than is ideal. All in all, the direct financial savings of the Ohio State EAP probably did not offset its cost to the State government. The employees, however, were very satisfied with the service, and so as an employee benefit, it had some value.

The General Motors Corporation reported a payoff of 2:1 for its EAP and HARTline (Florida), comparing pre-EAP figures with post-EAP figures, found accidents had declined by 50%. The time an employee had taken off work (a week or two) was counteracted by the counselling time at the EAP. Workers' compensation claims dropped from 60 to 49 and liability expenses, such as bodily injury and property damage, shrank from $1 million to $29,951.

Chicago Bell credits its EAP for slashing its poor customer performance ratings from 28% to 12%. In 1984, the EAP saved the company almost $500,000 in reduced sickness and disability absences (Pope, 1990). Masi (1984) summarises that, overall, EAPs average a 3:1 return on the dollar.

The varied results of these evaluations show that the cost-effectiveness of EAPs, whilst promising, cannot be taken for granted. The findings also point to factors conducive to success. For example, McDonnell Douglas' tightly managed and well-focused EAP fared better than the more diffuse Ohio State programme.

UK studies

Even though findings from US studies have indicated generally positive outcomes, calls for good quality, independent evaluative research of EAPs are increasing. Despite the wide scale potential benefits of services, there is still a paucity of information about these services in Britain, and an even greater lack of robust research substantiating their effectiveness.

Intuitively, one would expect that if a significant proportion of employees are reporting the early resolution of potentially serious problems and returning to work, then this must show up on the bottom line. It is a virtual impossibility to obtain purely quantitative proof, and so the decision to institute an EAP is still more often a leap of faith than a measured decision. Given that many employers in Britain are not just concerned with showing a return on investment, this is likely to remain the case. Many British companies are, quite rightly, primarily concerned about the human factor, rather than a simplistic pay-off decision.

Much of the occupational stress research over the past two decades has explored the causes and consequences of stress (Cooper and Payne, 1988; Ivancevich, 1986; Sauter et al., 1989). More recently, researchers have turned their attention to strategies that might be used to remedy the problem (Cooper, 1987; Murphy, 1988). However, there has been very little research evaluating the comparative usefulness of primary, secondary and tertiary interventions.

The bulk of the small amount of stress intervention research which has been conducted has focused on secondary interventions or stress management techniques (Marshall and Cooper, 1979), with very little research having been undertaken which evaluates tertiary interventions, such as EAPs.

An Employee Assistance Programme is one human resource strategy that may help to combat the now well-recognised human and organisational costs of workplace stress. With the growing acceptability and use of counselling in British organisations, there is an increasing demand for information on the effectiveness of EAPs. Although organisations are beginning to see the assets that counselling can bring to organisations and are testing counselling as a means of employee support, it is not yet being seen as a direct means of competitive advantage by many organisations. However, some UK companies are now recognising that by helping employees cope with stress, they may reduce absenteeism, improve morale and ultimately boost profitability.

Most larger companies in the UK are, therefore, beginning to see EAPs not as an additional cost, but as an 'investment'. This is almost certainly true in the medium to long term, although convincing measures of the benefit are not yet available in the UK. In the UK there is still a lack of knowledge about EAPs, but at the same time organisations are beginning to seek out information about them and are keen to learn what EAPs claim to accomplish.

The potential strength of EAPs/counselling services in industry is that 'they function to minimise the damaging consequences of personal distress to the mutual benefit of the individual employee and employing organisation'. Providing professional assistance to the employee – in the form of short-term, focused, confidential counselling or referral to a specialist resource where appropriate – means early intervention and control over issues that may otherwise develop into a crisis. This could help to avoid unnecessarily damaging consequences, both for the individual concerned and the organisation as a whole.

Potential benefits for the individual include improved mental well-being, improved functioning at work, and increased job/life satisfaction. At the organisational level, evaluations of programmes, mainly in the USA, have reported significant improvements in absenteeism, time-keeping, accidents and injury, medical visits, sickness benefits, surgical costs, disability claims, disciplinary action, grievances, interpersonal conflict, unwanted terminations and so on, all with the associated positive changes in work concentration and performance (Murphy, 1994).

The American research which has been highlighted is mainly of a cost-benefit nature and there has been little real quantitative evaluation of EAPs in the USA. There is an even greater paucity of research in the UK. In response to this, a large scale study was carried out which utilised both quantitative and qualitative research methodologies. This research aimed to fill the gap in evaluation which exists for British EAPs, and it is this study which forms the focus of the remainder of this chapter.

The objectives of the research

The objectives of this quantitative impact study were:

1 To evaluate what effects EAP counselling has had on individual employees, in terms of: mental well-being; physical well-being; job satisfaction; sources of pressure; and self-reported absence.
2 To objectively substantiate the impact of counselling at the organisational level, using individual sickness absence records.

The aim of the research was to assess the effectiveness of EAP counselling at the organisational and individual levels. Since very little was known about UK EAP providers, and their numbers have dramatically increased over recent years, it was decided that there was a need to assess the effectiveness of these services at both the individual and organisational levels.

A quantitative methodology was employed. Questionnaire data and sickness absence statistics were collected for individuals who attended face-to-face counselling, and in addition a survey of all employees who had access to an EAP was conducted.

Results and discussion

Individual questionnaire data

There were six key findings in relation to the pre-counselling, post-counselling and follow-up psychological measures. This section will look at each in turn.

1 After receiving counselling (and at follow-up) clients report significantly improved general and context-specific (i.e. work-related) mental well-being and physical well-being, compared to before counselling. However, there are no reported changes for job satisfaction or sources of pressure.

To a great extent, this finding is not surprising. Counselling, whether internal or external to the organisation, is aimed at helping individuals cope with their personal and work lives better. As such, one would hope to find some change in a client's mental and physical health after receiving counselling. However, job satisfaction is concerned with an individual's satisfaction with various aspects of their job, and the sources of pressure scales are concerned with where employees perceive stress as originating from within the organisation. None of these things is likely to change as a result of going for counselling, because counselling services are not organisational interventions and it is therefore unlikely that specific organisational issues are addressed. This results in the organisation staying the same and the individual changing.

Hence, one cannot expect to see an impact on job satisfaction or sources of pressure. In effect, the individual still views the workplace the same as they did before (because it is the same as it was before), so no changes result for job satisfaction or sources of pressure. However, individuals are able to cope better and therefore should be more mentally (and probably physically) healthy.

The fact that similar findings were obtained when comparing pre-counselling and follow-up scores, suggests that any psychological changes resulting from counselling are likely to be sustained over a period of at least 3–6 months after counselling. This is to be expected. Indeed, it was suggested earlier that the effects of counselling might continue well after counselling ends and therefore greater effects may be seen at some later stage.

The findings for mental health and job satisfaction are the same as those found in the Post Office study (Cooper et al., 1990). Even though different measures of mental health and job satisfaction were used, the Post Office study also found an improvement in mental well-being from before to after counselling, but no change in job satisfaction.

2 There are some differences in terms of the results for internal and external services. The data from this research suggest that it is mainly the internal counselling services which are having the effects described above.

This may be due to some extent to the greater ability of internal services to deal with workplace issues, as highlighted in the first section of this report. If an individual is counselled as a person within the workplace context and all the culture, policies and procedures of the organisation are known to the counsellor, one would expect the counsellor to be more effective at helping the person to cope with both their work and home life. This more effective coping can be expected to have an effect on the person's mental and physical health. This may well be the case with internal counselling services.

In contrast, as highlighted earlier, EAPs are less able to deal with organisational issues, primarily because the counsellors do not know enough about the organisations involved. Thus, clients seeing an EAP counsellor are likely to be counselled as individuals, but not within the context of the workplace. Therefore, the whole of the person's life is not being addressed. If only the individual's personal problems are being dealt with and they are no better able to cope with work-related issues, then a significant effect on mental and physical health is unlikely.

The somewhat surprising finding is that if internal services do have the ability to feed back organisational issues to the company, as they purport to do, one would expect there to also be an effect on the other variables contained in the questionnaire (i.e. job satisfaction and sources of pressure). The fact that this was not evident may be explained in at least three ways.

First, the pre- and post-counselling questionnaires were completed by individuals at the start and finish of counselling. The time period between completion of the two questionnaires is therefore quite short (on average about 10 weeks, according to clients). Even if an organisational problem was picked up by a counsellor and fed back to the company it is unlikely that any changes at the organisational level would be instituted before the client finished counselling. Therefore, one could not expect to see an impact on the job satisfaction and sources of pressure scales.

Secondly, although internal counsellors do indeed have the opportunity to feed back issues of employee concern to the organisation, it may well be that they do not actually do so in practice. It is quite possible that they use their knowledge of the company to help individual clients (hence the effect on individual well-being scores), but do not then feed back issues to the organisation for them to address. If this is the case then obviously no impact on job satisfaction or sources of pressure can be expected.

Thirdly, it may be the case that even if the counsellor does feed back problems and organisational issues to the company, these may not be addressed by the organisation. So, although the counsellor has picked up on these issues and fed back on them, the organisation may choose not to do anything about them. If this is the case then obviously there would be no impact on an individual's job satisfaction or sources of pressure.

A further explanation for the differences found between the internal and external services might be to do with the sample sizes. It was possible to collect much more data from the internal services than from the EAPs, so the sample sizes, and hence the likelihood of significant findings, are much greater for the internal services.

3 An unmatched control group of a sample of all employees within two companies showed no changes on the mental and physical health scales where changes were detected for counselled employees.

Whilst these two groups of employees were not ideal as controls, they were considered to be suitable for this use, given the fact that we were unable to collect data from matched controls from within the same organisations as the clients. The fact that the scores of these individuals showed no changes for the scales on which the client group did show changes, suggests that the effects found for counselled employees are likely to be due to some extent to the counselling process.

4 There were no significant differences from post-counselling to follow-up (3–6 months after counselling) on any of the mental and physical health measures. However, clients did report significantly more stress as coming from the 'organisational structure and climate'.

There is a belief that counselling may well continue to have an effect for some time after counselling itself has ended. This suggestion is not borne out by the results of this research, because no improvement in mental or physical health was found from post-counselling to follow-up. However, at follow-up clients did report significantly more stress as coming from the 'organisational structure and climate'. Therefore, the longer-term impact of counselling may have been obscured by the perception of more stress. Indeed, if employees are reporting more stress from work, but their psychological health has been unaffected, this is positive in itself, as one would have expected to see a reduction in mental health when more stress is being experienced.

It might also have something to do with the continued failure of organisations to address organisational issues giving rise to stress. The individual is mentally better able to cope with stress in general, following counselling, but the failure of the organisation to take effective action is then likely to prove even more frustrating and hence stressful.

5   The introduction of an EAP does affect the individual being counselled but not the whole employee population, in terms of mental and physical health, job satisfaction and sources of pressure.

This finding is not surprising since, as discussed earlier, an EAP is an individual not organisational intervention. Hence no organisational impact can be expected. In order to have an organisational effect, an organisational level intervention would need to be introduced, in addition to the counselling.

An organisational level intervention would enable the organisation to identify its sources of stress and, where possible, to address them appropriately. Simply introducing an EAP in an attempt to affect organisational indicators is unlikely to work, since an EAP does not have any global effect on the organisation, although it does help individuals psychologically and reduce their absenteeism.

Whilst this research offers support to the argument that a healthier workforce is likely to lead to a healthier organisation (if we count sickness absence as an indicator of this), the company-wide data do not suggest that an EAP has any effect on the organisation, other than reducing absence in those who use the service. This is not surprising, since if an organisation is to manage stress effectively it is essential to intervene at both the individual and organisational levels.

6   Individuals who have access to an EAP, but do not use it, do not benefit psychologically, or in terms of their job satisfaction or perceived sources of pressure from knowing that it exists.

This finding is in direct opposition to what some organisations and/or providers believe, which is that simply knowing help is available should it be needed can reduce stress. This is not supported by this data, which shows no effect on individuals who have not had counselling. In fact, the employees in one of the companies involved reported being less job satisfied and seeing more stress as coming from 'organisational structure and climate' following the implementation of the EAP.

Sickness absence data

With regard to objective sickness absence data the main findings were as follows.

1   There was a significant reduction in both the total number of days absence, and the number of absence events, from before to after counselling. However, there was no such reduction for the matched control group.

The findings from the objective sickness absence data are in line with the self-reported sickness absence given by clients on the questionnaires. The self-report absence statistics reveal that, after counselling, fewer people were absent from work in the previous 6 months, and those who were absent had fewer days off.

These results are also identical to those found in the Post Office study, where the number of days absence and total absence events fell in the 6 months following counselling compared to the 6 months preceding counselling.

2   The absence statistics (days and events) for the control group and client group were identical at the pre-counselling stage, but differed significantly at the post-counselling stage, when the client group showed significantly less absence compared to the matched controls.

These sickness absence results can be considered in conjunction with the questionnaire results on psychological health, in that essentially what is happening is that going for counselling is having an effect at the individual level.

It is the individual's health (i.e. mental and physical well-being) and health behaviours (i.e. sickness absence) which appear to be affected by counselling, rather than organisational indicators (i.e. job satisfaction and sources of pressure). This is to be expected, because counselling is essentially an intervention that focuses on the individual (not the organisation), where the emphasis is on changing the individual's response to stress rather than changing the organisational sources of stress. It is therefore likely that the greatest effect will be shown for individual outcomes i.e. absence, mental well-being and physical well-being.

Implications for research and practice

Stress management interventions at work

DeFrank and Cooper (1987) classify workplace stress interventions into three levels, focusing on the individual, the individual/organisational interface, and the organisation. Currently British EAPs and workplace counselling programmes are focused purely at the individual level, although this does not have to be the case. They can also target the organisation. Indeed, a comprehensive stress management programme should attempt to identify and reduce (or eliminate) stressors at each of the three levels (Cooper et al., 1990). To employ interventions that focus purely on the individual, which most EAPs do, is to make the individual responsible for their problems, even if they are work-related.

However, individual level interventions do have a very important role to play because individuals may suffer stress from both their personal and work life and this will impact upon an employee's performance at work and their psychological well-being.

The key is that, whilst the introduction of a counselling service may well be of benefit to individuals, psychologically, there is unlikely to be any impact at the organisational level, unless an intervention targeted at changing the organisation is also in place.

Cooper and Cartwright (1994) assert that it is necessary to broaden the conceptualisation of stress management interventions (including employee counselling programmes), because activities aimed solely at individuals' reactions to stressful circumstances, and not also targeted at modifying the circumstances themselves, will not be sufficient to avoid negative legal ramifications. Workplace counselling has an important part to play in extending the individual's psychological and physical resources, but its role is essentially one of 'damage limitation', often addressing the consequences rather than the sources of stress that may be inherent in the organisation's structure and culture.

Any EAP or workplace counselling programme needs to be positioned in order to maximise the value of the benefits in the human resource and organisational areas. The service needs to function as an integral, yet independent part of the organisation, and needs to ensure that it offers support to all involved in change and other company developments.

There is also a need to consult with the organisation, where developments and events impact on the well-being of employees, and to respond promptly to requests for counselling programmes to address organisational needs. The EAP should report any relevant organisational trends distilled from problems presented by users of the service, to a key person in the organisation, and be proactive in suggesting steps that a public/private sector company might take to reduce or at least minimise the adverse impact of organisational change.

However, the problem here is that once the decision to introduce an EAP or counselling service has been made, responsibility for the service is usually passed down to someone in a non-senior position within the company. This is not really the most appropriate level at which feedback could lead to action. Someone in a senior position is far better placed to institute changes as a result of feedback.

Murphy (1995) suggests that in practice 'EAPs provide very limited feedback to the organisation. Usually feedback is restricted to information about how many employees were seen by the EAP and the general types of problems encountered.' He goes on to point out that EAPs have tended to focus on characteristics of employees, not characteristics of the job or organisation, which may be causing employee stress. Cooper and Cartwright (1994) agree with Murphy and point out that occupational stress is likely to present a major threat to the financial health and profitability of organisations.

Organisational preoccupation with the outcome of the stress process has tended to detract from the more proactive approach of addressing the source or causal factors. Rather than focusing exclusively on what the organisation can provide for employees to help them cope with stress more effectively, organisations would be well advised to consider what the organisation can do to eliminate or reduce workplace stressors (Cooper and Cartwright, 1994).

Too often EAPs are treated as tertiary interventions, as remedial reactions to be invoked after something has happened, as simply and solely a safety net. However, this devalues the potential of EAPs to prevent the escalation of problems at an early stage (a secondary level intervention), when judicious practical guidance and brief counselling is all that is needed. It also ignores the proactive role which EAPs can play in supporting line and HR managers in performance management, through training courses and through assistance with individual cases. An EAP can also play a role at the primary level of intervention in terms of supporting strategic organisational changes, not only through the continual stream of management information that organisations need in order to modify such developments in policy and strategy.

For the future there is certainly value in finding out how cost-effective, in financial terms, EAPs are. Egan (1994) has suggested finding methods of costing psychological and social problems. His advice is, since personal misery and social disruption almost always detract from productivity, to calculate the loss to the company of such misery in financial terms: for example, the loss of a key employee through sexual harassment; the hospitalisation of a manager for clinical depression; the low morale that indicates that ten employees are working at 80% of their potential; the breakdown of a significant relationship that means a high-level manager is only 50% productive for 3 months. Add to this the financial cost as low morale is spread, as customers meet less than excellent service, as opportunities are lost, and the cost escalates out of all proportion (Carroll, 1996).

Egan (1994) also notes that prevention is financially more rewarding than cure. There is little point in saving money on a project that ends up costing more in personal disruption and morale. Finally, according to Egan (1994), lost opportunity costs should also be calculated: for example, the time a manager puts into dealing with a suicidal member of staff is time lost for other issues.

Most of the existing data supporting the effectiveness of EAPs can be challenged on one or more methodological issue. However, while it is essential to remain aware of these potential pitfalls, it is also important to realise that, from a more pragmatic point of view, service consumers (employees), sponsors (employers) and providers (EAP staff) generally express high levels of satisfaction with these programmes. The increasing prevalence of EAPs among organisations is an indication of this general level of satisfaction.

EAPs are now spreading rapidly in the UK. It is therefore becoming urgent to have additional, properly controlled investigations of their effectiveness and cost-effectiveness so as to supplement the meagre database currently available.

There is a need to define clearly the measures that will be used in evaluating the success of the EAP. It is impossible to collect data on every conceivable measure and it is paramount to be clear from the outset as to what outcome measures will be collected.

Wider acceptance of EAPs will only come when their effect has been substantiated by research. As EAPs become more established, it would be useful if future EAPs endeavoured to integrate research into practice. Unfortunately, few companies have either the time or the inclination to develop long-term research of this nature.

However, academic institutions are increasingly taking the initiative in linking up with the business community in order to examine the effectiveness of counselling in the workplace. Collaboration of this kind is vital if good research is to be translated into better practice (Lee and Gray, 1996).

To date there is no theoretical basis to counselling in organisational settings, including EAPs. There is no text that struggles with what types of counselling are best suited to organisations or that evaluates the various counselling models *via-à-vis* applications to particular organisations and settings (Carroll, 1996).

Conclusion

In the UK, counselling in the workplace has suddenly expanded over the past few years. However, these programmes have tended to be employee- rather than organisation-directed, with the focus being on changing the behaviours of the individual and improving their lifestyles and/or stress management skills (Cooper, 1993).

The interactionist approach (Cooper et al., 1988; Cox, 1978) depicts stress as being the consequence of a 'lack of fit' between the individual and their environment, in this case the workplace. However, most workplace interventions (including workplace counselling programmes) emphasise improving the adaptability of the individual to the workplace. This is often described as the 'band aid' or inoculation approach, the implicit assumption being that the organisation will not change and will hence continue to be stressful, so the individual must be helped to strengthen and develop their resistance to stress. There seems to be much less concern with adapting the organisation to 'fit' the individual. One reason for this may be that the professional 'interventionists', the counsellors etc., are more comfortable with changing individuals rather than changing organisations (Ivancevich et al., 1990).

There is a need for workplace counselling programmes to become much more of a business tool and to help organisations to address sources of stress within the company.

References

Bickerton, R. and Stern, L. (1990) Why EAPs are worth the investment. *Business and Health*, May, 14–19.

Carroll, M. (1996) *Workplace Counselling*. London: Sage.

Cooper, C.L. (1987) *Stress Management Interventions at Work*. Bradford: MCB University Press.

Cooper, C.L. (1993) Finding the solution – primary prevention (identifying the causes and preventing mental ill health in the workplace). In R. Jenkins and D. Warman (eds), *Promoting Mental Health Policies in the Workplace*. London: HMSO.

Cooper, C.L. and Cartwright, S. (1994) Healthy mind, healthy organisation – a proactive approach to occupational stress. *Human Relations*, 47 (4), 455–71.

Cooper, C.L., Cooper, R.D. and Eaker, L. (1998) *Living with Stress*. London: Penguin Books; New York: Viking/Penguin (2nd printing 1993).

Cooper, C.L. and Payne, R. (1988) *Causes, Coping and Consequences of Stress at Work*. New York and Chichester: John Wiley.

Cooper, C.L. and Sadri, G. (1991) The impact of stress counselling at work. In P.L. Perrewe (ed.), Handbook on Job Stress. Special Issue. *Journal of Social Behaviour and Personality*, 6 (7), 411–23.

Cooper, C.L., and Sadri, G., Allison, T. and Reynolds, P. (1990) Stress counselling in the Post Office. *Counselling Psychology Quarterly*, 3 (1), 3–11.

Cox, T. (1978) *Stress*. London: Macmillan.

DeFrank, R.S. and Cooper, C.L. (1987) Worksite stress management interventions: their effectiveness and conceptualisation. In C.L. Cooper (ed.), *Stress Management Interventions at Work*. Bradford: MCB University Press. pp. 4–11.

Egan, G. (1994) *Working the Shadow-side: A Guide to Positive Behind the Scenes Management*. San Francisco: Jossey–Bass.

Firth, H. and Shapiro, D.A. (1986) An evaluation of psychotherapy for job-related distress. *Journal of Occupational Psychology*, 59, 111–19.

Ivancevich, J.M. (1986) Life events and hassles as predictors of health symptoms, job performance and absenteeism. *Journal of Occupational Behaviour*, 7, 39–51.

Ivancevich, J.M., Matteson, M.T., Freeman, S.M. and Phillips, J.S. (1990) Worksite stress management interventions. *American Psychologist*, Feb., 252–61.

Kim, D.S. (1988) Assessing EAPs: evaluation, typology and models. *Employee Assistance Quarterly* (Special Issue: Evaluation of Employee Assistance Programs), 3 (3&4), 169–87.

Knott, T.D. (1986) The distinctive uses of evaluation and research: a guide for the occupational health care movement. *Employee Assistance Quarterly*, 1, (4), 43–51.

Lambert, M.J., Shapiro, D.A. and Bergin, A.E. (1986) The effectiveness of psychotherapy. In S.L. Garfield and A.E. Bergin (eds), *Handbook of Psychotherapy and Behavior Change*, 3rd ed. New York: John Wiley. pp. 157–211.

Lee, C. and Gray, J.A. (1996). Evaluating EAPs. Unpublished.

Maiden, R.P. (1988) EAP evaluation in a federal government agency. *Employee Assistance Quarterly* (Special Issue: Evaluation of Employee Assistance Programs), 3 (3&4), 191–203.

Marshall, J. and Cooper, C.L. (1979) *Executives under Pressure*. London: Macmillan.

Masi, D.A. (1984) *Designing Employee Assistance Programs*. New York: AMACOM.

McClellan, K. (1989) Cost benefit analysis of the Ohio EAP. *Employee Assistance Quarterly*, 5 (2), 67–85.

McDonnell Douglas (1989) McDonnell Douglas Corporation's EAP produces hard data. *The Almacan*, August, 18–26.

Murphy, L.R. (1988) Workplace interventions for stress reduction and prevention. In C.L. Cooper and R. Payne (eds), *Causes, Coping and Consequences of Stress at Work*. Chichester: John Wiley. pp. 301–39.

Murphy, L.R. (1994) Managing job stress: an employee assistance/human resource partnership. *Personnel Review*, 24 (1), 41–50.

Murphy, L.R. (1995) Managing job stress. Unpublished.

Nadolski, J.N. and Sandonato, C.E. (1987) Evaluation of an Employee Assistance Programme. *Journal of Occupational Medicine*, 29 (1), 32–7.

Pope, T. (1990) EAPs: good idea, but what's the cost? *Management Review*, 79 (8), 50–3.

Sauter, S., Hurrell, J.T. and Cooper, C.L. (1989) *Job Control and Worker Health*. Chichester and New York: John Wiley.

Shapiro, D.A. (1989) Outcome research. In G. Parry and F.N. Watts (eds), *Behavioural and Mental Health Research: A Handbook of Skills and Methods*. Hove and London:

Shapiro, D.A., Cheesman, M. and Wall, T.D. (1993) Secondary prevention – a review of counselling and EAPs. Paper presented to the Royal College of Physicians Conference on Mental Health at Work. London, 11 January 1993.

14
PSYCHOTHERAPY, THE PSYCHOLOGY OF TRAUMA AND ARMY PSYCHIATRY SINCE 1904
Ian P. Palmer

> Medical disorders create complex problems, ones that have extended beyond questions of medical diagnosis and therapy to issues of social attitudes and policy.
>
> (Feudtner, 1993)

I am pleased to say that psychotherapy is alive and well in the British Defence Psychiatric Services. Indeed, the development of psychotherapy and the military is inextricably linked, despite their seeming incongruence as bedfellows. I shall explore their relationship over the past century to contextualise the work of military psychiatry.

It is unlikely that Freud's ideas would have been so eagerly embraced earlier in the twentieth century if it were not for the First World War (Stone, 1985). Indeed, W.H.B. Stoddart, an officer in the Royal Army Medical Corps, undertook the first lecture given in this country on Freud's ideas when he presented the Morrison Lectures to the Royal College of Physicians of Edinburgh in 1915 (Pines, 1991; Stoddart, 1915). Psychotherapy continues to play an important part in military practice, even to this day.

In my opinion, psychotherapy is of benefit to both the individual and the military society. As I will show, soldiers are exposed to stressors that are most unusual in society today. They will require to adapt to the change wrought by such exposure; however, not infrequently pre-existing traumas from the past are equally as important and often require addressing. It is important to remember that although individuals serve within the Armed Forces they are part of a much larger social group, and this colours their experiences, the expression of difficulties and the provision of support.

Psychotherapy is able to help individuals profitably continue in service and provide useful service to the Army. At other times it can be used to strengthen group dynamics. For others psychotherapy may foreshadow the end of a military career but hopefully lead to a frame of mind that will allow them to develop their full potential on exit from service.

As we enter the twenty-first century, society seems to be taking an increasingly negative view of risk-taking and risk-taking behaviours and legislation reflects the growing emphasis on health and safety at work and leisure. Safety has become a preoccupation and exposure to traumatic events is seen as increasingly abnormal and even preventable! If not preventable, then someone must be at fault and therefore to blame. Accompanying this is the feeling that after exposure to such events counselling in some shape or form is *always* required, whether the individual has problems or not. To my mind, this is based upon a complex interplay of issues and beliefs within society rather than any proven benefit to individuals.

It must not be forgotten that soldiers form a specially selected part of society and will not exhibit the normal range of illnesses seen in civilian practice. They are subjected to physical examinations and closely watched during training to see how they handle the transition from civilian to military life – the 'Healthy Warrior' effect.

Definition of terms

The terms psychotherapy – 'treatment of mental disorder by psychological means' *(Concise Oxford Dictionary*, 1990) – and counselling – 'the process of assisting or guiding clients, esp. by a trained person on a professional basis, to resolve especially personal, social or psychological problems' (*Concise Oxford Dictionary*, 1990) – mean many things to many people, and to a large extent they have become somewhat debased terms in society today. Counselling is a particularly value-laden term and nowhere more so than in the Army.

The *Concise Oxford Dictionary* talks about the seeking and the giving of advice by experts. There are a large range of experts within the Army who include not only the medical, nursing and welfare services but also Commanders, Unit Welfare Officers, Regimental Associations, British Legion and so forth. I would never underestimate the importance and power of informal counselling from these experts, especially comrades.

Psychotherapy is nowadays generally of the brief type and has proved to be extremely valuable. There is still, however, a place for more in-depth work with selected cases.

Background to military service

Military society

The Army is an organisation *par excellence* that thrives on risk, the dignity of risk and the excitement of risk. If this were ever to change it would be unable to fulfil its role. This is not to suggest that unsafe practices during training and other situations should be accepted, but training must be as realistic as possible if individuals are to be able to function on a battlefield. Today's Army is drawn from volunteers not conscripts, and hard training is essential to the development of the group processes that bind individuals to their comrades and units.

The Army is a 'can do' organisation that has to push people further than they believe they can go. In this way individuals may grow physically, intellectually and emotionally. Within the Army, particularly within the fighting Arms, an individual altruistically gives up his autonomy for the benefit of the group and receives in return the support and protection of that group, support that should exist for soldiers after traumatic events, and usually does. After operational deployments including combat, many individuals describe a feeling of belonging and achievement, a sense of purpose, increased self-esteem, self-knowledge and insights into the workings of the world. The relationships forged during combat are sometimes stronger and longer-lasting than other personal relationships.

Although the role of soldiers changed in the latter part of the twentieth century, it is still the policy of the British Army to train for Total War, as this may happen at some stage in the future. This means that all the other roles are subsumed to this and due cognisance must be paid to the psychological effects of all types of deployment up to full battlefield combat. Even within Operations Other Than War, such as Bosnia, it is possible to have situations where combat can be extremely intense given the levels of armament available and used by all sides. Although the Gulf War was in military parlance a 'Limited War', it was a high intensity, high-speed war in which vast amounts of ammunition were expended. However, just as in the First and Second World Wars, it still fell to the infantry to 'fight through' and at times engage in hand-to-hand combat.

The military family – a psychodynamic view

The psychodynamic view of why individuals join the Army is a very useful paradigm within which lies the seed of both strength and weakness during and after combat. The explanation runs as follows: individuals looking for psychological 'structure' will find it in the Army, which provides both horizontal and vertical support and a clear understanding of their 'place' within that (military) family and society, through its rules and regulations, boundaries are extremely clear. It is a 'safe' environment for individuals who are looking for this sort of certainty. The Army therefore replaces the individual's biological family membership and the feeling of belonging is paramount to the cohesiveness of this new family.

If individuals entering the service have a realistic understanding of the reasons why the Army exists, of the strengths and weaknesses of such a hierarchical system, then should the Army 'family' fail the individual, it may be easier to understand and accept, after all, that all families have their limitations.

If, however, individuals have come from a dysfunctional background they may unconsciously invest the Army with unrealistic powers. Such idealisation can lead to a 'facultative regression' where everything is provided (food, clothes, wages etc.) and someone else is always responsible. If during combat or other operations things go wrong and the 'family' fails them, the loss of their fantasy is more difficult to accept and adjust to. My experience leads me to believe that a number of individuals who run into difficulties during or after combat may have unconsciously decided to enter the Army in search of an 'ideal' family. Such individuals are much more likely to become angry at the system and blame it for what has happened to them rather than accept the reality of their situation and their responsibilities.

The soldier's lot

The psychological plight of the soldier has been studied fairly extensively (Ahrenfeld, 1958; Binneveld, 1997; Culpin, 1920; Myers, 1940; Rivers, 1916, 1918; Shephard, 2000) and has led to a much deeper understanding of the unconscious mind. Being a soldier requires emotional fortitude. Anyone who breaks down or loses control may feel a personal failure and that his colleagues see him as a failure – which may or may not be true.

The dilemma in which a soldier finds himself is unique. If they stay on a battlefield they may be killed, maimed or psychologically damaged; however, if they escape the battlefield (for whatever reason) then they may feel guilty and ashamed at having let their comrades down. It is well known throughout all Western military literature that soldiers fight for each other rather than for any particular cause. The bonds forged in combat can be extremely strong and emotionally important and it is therefore unusual for individuals not to suffer grief if one of their number is killed. Such grief is not infrequently compounded by guilt. The initial euphoria of having survived an attack soon becomes an unpleasant experience as they realise that their best mate did not survive, indeed he may have died to save them.

I believe the most important and binding concepts of psychological trauma to soldiers are grief and loss (Garb et al., 1987). Obviously the worst outcome of combat is death of friends and maiming of comrades or self. The loss of friendships and relationships may be magnified by a loss of faith in the system and the loss of control of their lives for a period of time with the concomitant feelings of helplessness and the experience of near death (the constant concomitant of exposure to traumatic combat events). There is also a loss of existential omnipotence, a loss of the belief in the continuity and regularity of life. There may be a loss of religious Faith, or faith in organisations, or in others' abilities to do what they say they will do. Body image and self-esteem may be shattered and belief in justice may be lost; whatever happens, change in these individuals' lives is inevitable and irreversible. How the individual, their families, friends and employers accept, assimilate and accommodate to the physical, psychological, cognitive, attitudinal, spiritual and political changes determines the outcome.

Groups

The great benefit of the Army is that soldiers by and large go into combat or other situations in groups. When encountering traumatic events, unlike their civilian counterparts, soldiers have at least trained to know what to expect and have an idea of what to do in such situations. It is recognised that anyone confronted with extreme situations can be unable to function, hence the emphasis on repetitive drills and standing operating procedures (SOPs) to attempt to ensure soldiers have an almost automatic system to fall back on when things get tough.

Soldiers will also deploy with friends who will suffer the same privations, highs and lows, exposures and 'constriction' of their world. They have a military culture from which to draw strength; Regimental tradition; possibly parent(s) who have been in the Regiment or Armed Forces; pride in the uniform, the organisation, their country, their role and abilities. Because they live in a hierarchy there are older, wiser people around who, having shared the same privations and come through the same training, can help them through difficulties, providing good role models who will be acceptable experts. Individuals such as Junior and Senior NCOs, Regimental Sergeant Majors and Officers may, and in my opinion should, be much more important than most mental health personnel.

History of military psychiatry

The First World War and the individual

In the First World War there were no psychotherapists or even psychiatrists as we know them today within the Army but a number of psychologists and neurologists took up the challenge posed by mentally disabled soldiers. Some, such as Rivers (Rivers, 1916, 1918; Myers, 1915, 1940; Shephard, 1991), favoured the work of Freud, were psychologically minded and could be described as an 'Uncoverer', whereas others, such as Yealland (Adrian and Yealland, 1917) followed a more behavioural path and the work of Babinski (Binneveld, 1997), and could be described as 'Coverers'. The other group were the more physical/neurological, e.g. Mott (1919).

The 'Uncoverers' seemed to believe in what is termed 'isolation of affect'. They searched for meaning in combatants' experience and through emotional release sought to empower individuals to accept, assimilate and accommodate their experiences and adapt to change. It is fair to say that most of this work was provided for Officers. Although seen to work in a number of cases, such analysis was too time-consuming for general applicability at a time of national crisis where every available man was required for the war effort.

Thus greater emphasis was put on the application of rapid therapies. The 'Coverers' were in the ascendancy. Their work was based on suggestibility and conditioned responses. It was argued that following exposure to unpleasant events individuals developed a 'learned' response through suggestion and therefore, *ipso facto*, counter-suggestion could remove their symptoms.

Suggestion whilst awake, under hypnosis or drugs, alongside faradism (i.e., the use of electricity, which had been commonplace, and nearly ubiquitous for many complaints and conditions since its discovery), were all used in their work. Not infrequently it seems to have become a battle of wills, but we must be careful in our criticism without contextualisation.

Suggestion, thus conducted, was held to work but there are very few records of just how effective it was, and reading between the lines one felt that individuals cured of one 'hysterical' condition, for example, would come along with another not long afterwards.

Following the First World War Parliament set up the Southborough Committee to examine the condition of shellshock. It reported in 1922 (War Office, 1922). Their recommendations were that soldiers should be better selected, better trained and better educated, whilst accepting it was inevitable that every soldier had his breaking point.

The First World War allowed society to begin to understand, in part at least, the Unconscious and unconscious mental processes. It led to a change in the psychiatrist–patient relationship, the establishment of outpatient psychiatry and the beginning of the move to remove patients from asylums.

Evacuation syndromes

Prior to the First World War, the Russians in their war with Japan (1904/5) found that a number of soldiers who had broken down lost their symptoms when kept close to the front. If, however, they were evacuated back to Moscow (a journey time of weeks) their psychological symptoms became fixed, and they remained unwell for long periods of time. This became known as the 'Evacuation Syndrome' and it holds as much today as in 1905, based as it is on the social construct of a soldier as a soldier rather than as a patient.

Although anathema in today's society, any endeavour to treat a soldier as a patient during combat will mean that he will be withdrawn from combat, unit strength will be diminished and the lives of his comrades, who will have to undertake his duties, will be put at greater risk.

Evacuation of such cases is therefore not necessarily very popular, indeed it almost constitutes a reverse Darwinism, where those who are stoical or mentally 'strong' enough to remain on a battlefield put themselves in grave danger whereas those who are mentally 'weaker' are allowed to escape. There will therefore always be a tension between the organisation and those individuals who break down during combat.

In the early part of the First World War the evacuation of psychiatric casualties to the UK created enormous burdens and pressures on hospitals in the UK, and just as the Russian experience 10 years earlier predicted, these evacuations led to the fixation of symptoms and an extraordinarily large pension bill. Later in the war individuals were kept closer to the front and treated in a more social way, as I shall describe below. It is important to remember that the social dimension of psychiatric illness or psychological reactions is extraordinarily important in the military.

The Second World War and the group

The Second World War required the lessons of the First to be relearned. The analysts had the upper hand and abreaction was used extensively. The Second World War showed an increase in the use of brief therapies based on abreaction using thiopentone or ether, or hypnosis, but other physical treatments such as sleep and coma-therapy were quite popular (James, 1945; Ludwig, 1947; Palmer, 1945; Sargant, 1942).

PIES	7 Rs
Proximity	Recognition
Immediacy	Respite
Expectancy	Rest
Simplicity	Recall
	Reassurance
	Rehabilitation
	Return

FIGURE 14.1   *The principles of battleshock management*

The power of the group in protecting the individual was recognised and clearly demonstrated. Given the large number of psychiatric casualties and the scarcity of psychiatrists and psychiatric nurses, groups were formed based on psychoanalytical ideas and were felt to be very powerful and cost-effective in treating psychiatric cases. This built and extended the interest that followed the First World War in industrial psychology and a more sociological view of psychiatric disorders.

The work of Bion and others is known to us today and continues in the work carried on at the Tavistock Centre and the Institute of Group Analysis (Harrison and Clarke, 1992). From the 1950s, with the advent of more effective medication, biological views have gained increasing importance and status, although the psychotherapies remain the mainstay of management.

PIES and the Seven Rs (Figure 14.1)

Thus far in the story I have concerned myself with those individuals who were deemed to have broken down mentally and their treatment in rear areas, that is, areas behind the forward edge of combat.

It was understood by the Russians and re-learnt by the Allies that by keeping soldiers in their social role (soldier), they retained their comradeship, self-respect, self-worth and their feeling of belonging and many cases could be returned to useful duty.

In 1917 Col. Salmon, an American psychiatrist, was sent to examine the lessons learnt by the Allies prior to America joining the War (Salmon, 1917). He noted that simple interventions proximal to the front undertaken rapidly and in a climate of expectancy of return to duty allowed return of men to duty. The acronym PIES was coined (Proximity, Immediacy, Expectancy and Simplicity) and applies equally well as the basic tenet of First Aid!

With this approach, between 40 and 80 per cent of soldiers could be returned to some form of military duty, although not necessarily to the front line.

The Seven Rs

The 'treatment' is straightforward once the emotional and behavioural sequelae of psychological reactions to combat are recognised as such. Those identified are kept close to the battle whilst at the same time allowing them respite from fighting. They are rested, fed and encouraged to recall their experiences with other individuals who understand what they have been through. They are rehabilitated within a military atmosphere and given jobs to do that would include helping other soldiers in a similar condition. Finally, wherever possible, they would be returned to units with whom they had developed their friendships, their comradeships and with whom they had fought.

Seldom in civilian practice are issues of guilt and shame spoken of. These emotional issues are ever-present in psychological reactions to combat and often underestimated: guilt at leaving their comrades behind if evacuated, guilt at sins of omission or commission and shame at having let their comrades down.

The social aspects of 'breakdown' should never be underestimated and some of the most important 'psychotherapists/counsellors' in the service are other soldiers, and these individuals should not be neglected.

The process of PIES has been used successfully in all wars subsequent to the Russo/Japanese War. It is hardly surprising therefore that military psychiatry felt it had 'cracked' the problems of combat-related psychological breakdown by the end of the Second World War. The provision of psychiatric services in Korea and Vietnam was seen as the model product of this knowledge.

Vietnam and PTSD

Only following the Vietnam War did the debate move on from the intrapsychic processes *during* combat to the psycho-social cost *following* combat. This primarily American debate culminated in 1980 with the formulation of the DSM-III diagnosis of Post-Traumatic Stress Disorder (PTSD). PTSD seemed to offer a valid description and an explanation for the symptoms felt by some of the Vietnam veterans following service in South East Asia (Young, 1997). Coupled with the American societal emphasis on litigation this psychiatric label led to an explosion of medico-legal claims against the Armed Forces, yet none against the Government of North Vietnam! This process continues apace and has spread to the UK. The concept of PTSD has, however, thrown up an immense amount of conflicting data; for example, the traumatic event itself is only felt to account for 30% of the variance in most cases and, at most, 30% of individuals get PTSD following exposure to trauma. It would appear that there is a societal move, especially within legal circles, to subsume almost every human reaction to unpleasant events under the rubric of PTSD. Whilst there may be some biological underpinning of the diagnosis, I fear that its overzealous application is unhelpful.

PTSD is not really common in the military today. Out of a population of 250,000 servicemen and women, the Defence Psychiatric Centre, the specialist PTSD centre for the Armed Forces, sees roughly 100 cases a year.

It is worth remembering that PTSD is only one of a number of post-traumatic mental health outcomes and that there is an 80% chance of having at least two other psychiatric diagnoses if you have the diagnosis of PTSD.

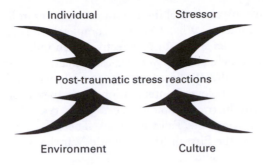

FIGURE 14.2   *The multifactorial genesis of post-traumatic stress reactions*

Post-traumatic stress reactions

I believe psychological reactions to trauma are ubiquitous and are best thought of in a similar way to bereavement reactions as their genesis is multifactorial and related to the interaction between the individual (their strengths and weaknesses), the traumatic event to which they are exposed (with all its attendant variables), the environment before, during and after exposure, and a factor often neglected especially in the West – the culture from which the individual comes and to which he returns (Figure 14.2).

The simplistic view that exposure to trauma entails PTSD is, in my opinion, both dangerous and inaccurate, and does disservice to survivors.

Within the societal debate about the psychological cost of traumatic events, be these sexual abuse, exposure to combat, road traffic accidents, etc., I find the issue, indeed culture, of blame most unhelpful and saddening.

Whilst projection has a rightful place initially as individuals struggle to come to terms with trauma, I fear litigation and the media conspire to maintain blame. Survivors' social worlds become coloured and damaged by this and their illness behaviour only compounds their difficulties. The 'you weren't there so you don't know what it was like' defence is another block to personal growth and is often seen – even within military practice!

It is being increasingly recognised that individuals who blame others excessively and become extraordinarily angry do less well psycho-socially following exposure to traumatic events. My clinical experience to date is that these individuals have often had multiple difficulties stemming back to childhood and this is where depth psychotherapy (short of full analysis) has much to offer.

PIES and psychological debriefing

I would like to dispel the link (or perhaps by now myth) that has crept into the critical incident stress debriefing (CISD) or psychological debriefing debate. It has been postulated by a number of authors that psychological debriefing was used in the First and Second World Wars to good effect. PIES (Proximity, Immediacy, Expectancy and Simplicity) has been put forward as evidence for the benefit of early psychological intervention for all, regardless of whether or not they have symptoms. What has been completely misrepresented is that PIES has only ever been shown to be effective when individuals have defined themselves, or been defined, as psychological casualties. In addition, military personnel conducted the 7Rs in a military environment and culture. To my knowledge early psychological interventions were never offered to combat troops without psychiatric symptoms during the two World Wars, Korea, Vietnam, the Yom Kippur or Falklands wars. There has therefore never been any experience from the First or Second World War that shows such interventions are in any way beneficial.

The Gulf War and post-conflict syndromes

The most recent lesson to be re-learnt has been the development of vague symptoms unexplained by medical science of the day following deployment to combat zones (Hyams et al., 1996). Such symptom complexes rapidly become labelled as syndromes by either the medical establishment or, latterly, the media. Examples include Effort Syndrome, Disordered Action of the Heart, Neurocirculatory Asthenia, Agent Orange Syndrome and Gulf War Syndrome (Rosen, 1975; Wood, 1941). There are many similarities between the symptoms exhibited in these conditions and Chronic Fatigue Syndrome, Fibromyalgia and other recognised, but ill defined, clusters of symptoms seen in civilian practice today. Recent work following the Gulf War has shown that there is an increase in such symptoms following the Gulf War (Unwin et al., 1999) but no fully blown syndrome has been identified (Ismail et al., 1999).

Specific conditions

Combat-related psychological reactions and disorders may be thought of in the following way (see Figure 14.3):

- Those reactions occurring during combat
  Acute stress reactions (ASR)
- Those reactions occurring after combat
  Post-traumatic stress reactions (PTSR)
- Mental illness following combat
  Post-traumatic mental illness (PTMI)
  Depression
  Anxiety
  Phobias
  PTSD
  Substance abuse
  Post-conflict syndromes (PCS)

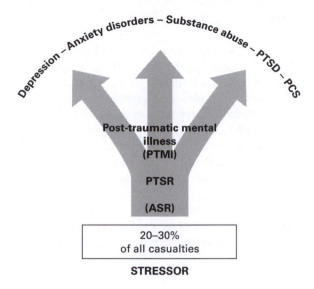

FIGURE 14.3   *Combat-related psychological reactions*

Occupational view

Whilst small groups can be especially intolerant of mental illness, the Army offers a conundrum. It cannot function effectively as a group if psychological breakdown occurs, yet it accepts that combat will create psychological problems for some soldiers and it is interesting to see how this occurs. First, individuals who have served together under difficult situations for long periods of time are much more prepared to accept changeable behaviours in their numbers because they know their compatriots, their seniors and juniors, better. Individuals who are new to a unit and do not fit in are always likely to have more difficulties.

All military doctors are occupational doctors and this is nowhere more obvious than within psychiatry. The individual is extraordinarily important but only in as much as how that individual fits in to the overall group. Rather like a machine, each individual cog is vital for the machine to work. The primary role of military medicine is therefore the maintenance of the fitness of the whole by attention to the individual.

Military psychiatry is tasked therefore to return individuals to duty wherever possible for the benefit of the organisation and the individual, who has invested an immense amount in their social role in becoming a soldier. If, however, they cannot fit in, then it is up to the medical services to ensure that they receive the treatment they require and support following their return to civilian life.

The very nature of post-traumatic reactions, human nature and personality difficulties will always make it difficult to be able to identify and offer such help to all individuals, but it is an aim to which the Armed Forces strive.

Pathways to care

How can an individual get help within the Army? Whilst it is extremely easy to see a mental health worker in the Army, there are pressures that militate against the seeking of help. They include being male, being in the Army, not wanting to lose face and the avoidance inherent in the post-traumatic stress reaction itself. Initially, we would therefore encourage any soldier to talk to his mate or mates, within his platoon, section or Company; his commanders (from Lance Corporal upwards) – in other words, the chain of command. These individuals should know that individual, will have worked with that individual, and know his strengths and weaknesses and should be able to provide the social milieu and support so important to individuals in difficulties. Unfortunately, few civilians have this close psychological network available to them and it is to this network that we would encourage soldiers to turn first, in the same way that it would be right for individuals to turn to their family first after suffering a bereavement.

Psychotherapy

Analytic psychotherapy is not part of military practice, as it is an occupational service and soldiers (employees) are integral to the smooth functioning of the service. Soldiers must be fit (to fight) at any given moment. It is therefore unsurprising that there has been a move towards brief psychotherapeutic interventions that today revolve around cognitive-behavioural therapy models.

Within them it is possible to trace the work of earlier military psychiatrists and the theories of Babinski (Ellenberger, 1970) and Pavlov (Dews, 1981; Wolpe and Plaud, 1997) in terms of suggestion and exposure therapy. Exposure can be in vivo, in imagination, aurally or visually through videos. Work with psychologically injured soldiers requires trust and a good therapeutic relationship to succeed given the level of arousal and emotions triggered by the contemplation of 'revisiting' the traumatic event.

In a similar way to the 'Uncoverers' of the First and Second World Wars, most of the therapy undertaken within the military today involves individuals facing up to their experiences and mastering them *in full consciousness*. We are helped greatly by medication in treating co-existing depression and anxiety which, if untreated, prevent full use and benefit from psychological therapies.

My particular interest is with 'resistant' or difficult cases in which anger, rage and fear form a potent emotional foment. In such cases I am heavily influenced by Winnicott (1965) and feel that the key to therapy is the ability to 'hold' the uncomfortable emotions for the individual until such time that they are able to accept them back, assimilate them and accommodate the changes wrought in them. Seldom, however, have I found myself simply dealing with a traumatic episode without having to examine the developmental antecedents in the individual's past.

Normalisation and stigmatisation

It is intriguing how the military accommodate psychological breakdown. They may be in advance of civilian society by normalising the reaction; in other words, rather than giving individuals psychological labels they give labels such as exhaustion or fatigue.

This must not be underestimated, as the appending of psychiatric labels in a combat scenario is fraught with difficulty. By normalising the reaction military culture can provide support to individuals, and reduce the stigma of psychological difficulties.

Shellshock, for example, in the First World War, was a non-pejorative, acceptable, descriptive term, at least initially, and explained how even a decorated 'hero' could develop psychological difficulties.

In the Second World War a larger number of psychological terms were introduced, of which psychoneurosis was the most common, certainly within the American Armed Forces. Psychoneurosis rapidly became bastardised into 'psycho', which remains a pejorative label today. The process of destigmatisation involved the description of individuals as having either 'fatigue' or 'exhaustion' (combat or battle fatigue or combat or battle exhaustion). These terms were understandable and accepted by the soldiery and the hierarchy, for exhaustion and fatigue were constant concomitants of combat, that is, they had great face validity. Soldiers could therefore have a psychological label to which no stigma was appended. Combat exhaustion or fatigue meant that you had 'been there', 'seen the elephant' (combat – a US Marine term) and had paid the price.

Given the ubiquity of the post-traumatic stress reaction it may be considered as normal. Endeavours to 'normalise' this experience encourage individuals to talk but to talk, as one would in grief, to people who shared that experience, who underwent that change, and not immediately to seek specialist help.

Conclusion

Military psychiatry has shown us that psychological reactions occur during and following combat. However only a minority of soldiers suffer acute breakdowns during combat or go on to develop post-combat mental illness.

Psychological reactions to combat may be conceptualised as those occurring *during* combat (acute stress reactions, ASR), those occurring *after* combat (post-traumatic stress reactions, PTSR) mental illness (post-traumatic mental illness, PTMI – depression, anxiety, phobias, PTSD), post-conflict syndromes (PCS) and substance abuse.

Work from the First and Second World Wars has shown that acute stress reactions (shellshock, battleshock, combat stress reaction) are uncommon and, what is often forgotten, seldom occur without concomitants such as fatigue and exhaustion; hunger and thirst; lack of supplies, including ammunition; poor leadership; worries about family, children etc.

A similar situation occurs with post-traumatic stress reactions, which also have a multifactorial aetiology that is too often neglected.

The social dimension of any breakdown in the military must be addressed in every case and wherever possible the soldier's military identity must be respected and maintained. Inappropriate evacuation can have far reaching implications for the future mental health of the soldier(s) concerned.

Whilst changes in psychiatric practice are reflected in military psychiatry and the move towards a biological view continues with the attendant benefits of precise diagnosis, psychotherapy in its many guises remains the bedrock of the management of post-traumatic stress reactions and mental illness.

A psychodynamic and psycho-social understanding is vital to understanding and managing the traumatised soldier.

Disclaimer

Throughout, the male gender has been used, as the majority of soldiers, especially those engaged in combat, have been men. The majority of the psychiatric observation and research has been undertaken on male soldiers. There is no reason to think that women confronted with combat will react in a vastly dissimilar way.

The views expressed in this chapter are those of the author alone and may in no way be taken to reflect those of the Ministry of Defence.

References

Adrian, E.D. and Yealland, L.R. (1917) The treatment of some common war neuroses. *The Lancet*, 9 June, 867–72.

Ahrenfeld, R.H. (1958) *Psychiatry in the British Army in the Second World War* London: Routledge & Kegan Paul.

Binneveld, H. (1997) *From Shellshock to Combat Stress. A Comparative History of Military Psychiatry*. Amsterdam: Amsterdam University Press.

Concise Oxford Dictionary (1990) 8th Edition (ed. R.E. Allen). Oxford: Oxford University Press.

Culpin, M. (1920) *Psychoneuroses of War and Peace*. Cambridge: Cambridge University Press.

Dews, P.B. (1981) Pavlov and psychiatry. *Journal of the History of Behavioural Science*, 17, 246–50.

Ellenberger, H.F. (1970) Shellshock and the ecology of disease systems. *History of Science*, 31(4), 377–420.

Feudtner, C. (1993) Shellshock and the ecology of disease systems. *History of Science*, 31 (4), 377–420.

Garb, B., Beich, A. and Lerer, B. (1987) Bereavement in combat. *Psychiatric Clinics of North America*, 10 (3), 421–36.

Harrison, T. and Clarke, D. (1992) The Northfield Experiments. *British Journal of Psychiatry*, 160: 698–708.

Hyams, K.C., Wignall S. and Roswell, R. (1996) War syndromes and their evaluation: from the US Civil War to the Persian Gulf War. *Annals of Internal Medicine*, 125 (5), 398–405.

Ismail, K., Everitt, B., Blatchley, N., Hull, L., Unwin, C., David, A. and Wessely, S. (1999) Is there a Gulf War Syndrome? *The Lancet*, 353, 179–82.

James, G.W.B. (1945) Psychiatric lessons from active service. *The Lancet*, 22 December, 801–5.

Ludwig, A.O. (1947) Neuroses occurring in soldiers after prolonged combat exposure. *Bulletin of the Menninger Clinic*, 1, 15–23.

Mott, F.W. (1918) War psycho-neuroses. (I) Neurasthenia: the disorders and disabilities of fear. *The Lancet*, 26 January, 127–9.

Mott, F.W. (1919) *War Neuroses and Shell Shock*. London: Oxford Medical Publications.

Myers, C.S. (1915) A contribution to the study of shell shock. *The Lancet*, 1: 316–20.

Myers, C.S. (1940) *Shell Shock in France, 1914–18*. Cambridge: Cambridge University Press.

Palmer, H. (1945) Military psychiatric casualties – experience with 12,000 cases. *The Lancet*, 13 October, 454–7.

Pines, M. (1991) *A History of Psychodynamic Psychiatry in Britain*. In J. Holmes (ed.), *Textbook of Psychotherapy in Psychiatric Practice*. Edinburgh: Churchill Livingstone.

Rivers, W.H.R. (1916) The repression of war experience. *The Lancet*, 2 February, 173–7.

Rivers, W.H.R. (1918) War neurosis and military training. *Mental Hygiene*, 2 (4), 513–33.

Rosen, G. (1975) Nostalgia: a 'forgotten' psychological disorder. *Psychological Medicine*, 5, 340–5.

Salmon, T.W. (1917) The care and treatment of mental diseases and war neuroses ('shell shock') in the British Army. *Mental Hygiene*, 1 (4), 509–47.

Sargant, W. (1942) Physical treatment of acute war neuroses. Some clinical observations. *British Medical Journal*, 2, 574–6.

Shephard, B. (1991) The early treatment of mental disorders: R.G. Rows and Maghull, 1914–1918. In G.E. Berrios and H.L. Freeman (eds), *150 Years of Psychiatry, 1841–1991*. London: Gaskell.

Shephard, B. (2000) *A War of Nerves*. London: Jonathan Cape.

Stoddart, W.H.B. (1915) The new psychiatry. *The Lancet*, 20 March, 583–90, 27 March, 639–43.

Stone, M. (1985) Shellshock and the psychologists. In W.T. Bynum, R. Porter and M. Shepherd (eds), *The Anatomy of Madness*, Vol. II. London: Tavistock Publications.

Unwin, C., Blatchley, N., Coker, W., Ferry, S., Hotopf, M., Hull, L., Ismail, K., Palmer, I., David, A. and Wessely, S. (1999) Health of UK Servicemen who served in the Persian Gulf War. *The Lancet*, 353, 169–78.

War Office (1922) *Report of the Committee of Enquiry into 'Shell Shock'*. London: HMSO.

Winnicott, D.W. (1965) *The Maturational Process and the Facilitating Environment*. London: Hogarth Press.

Wolpe, J. and Plaud, J.J. (1997) Pavlov's contributions to behavior therapy. The obvious and not so obvious. *American Psychologist*, 52 (9), 966–72.

Wood, P. (1941) Aetiology of DaCosta's syndrome. *British Medical Journal*, 7 June, 845–51.

Yealland, L.R. (1918) *Hysterical Disorders of Warfare*. London: Macmillan and Co. Ltd.

Young, A. (1997) *The Harmony of Illusions: Inventing Post-Traumatic Stress Disorder*. Princetown, NJ: Princetown University Press.

Further reading

Bourke, J. (1996) *Dismembering the Male: Men's Bodies, Britain and the Great War*. London: Granta.

Bourke, J. (1999) *An Intimate History of Killing*. London: Granta.

Freedman, L. (ed.) (1994) *War*. Oxford: Oxford University Press.

Garland, C. (ed.) (1998) *Understanding Trauma. A Psychoanalytical Approach*. London: Duckworth.

Hynes, S. (1998) *The Soldier's Tale. Bearing Witness to Modern War*. London: Pimlico.

Keegan, J. (1991) *The Face of Battle*. London: Pimlico.

Keegan, J. (1994) *A History of Warfare*. London: Pimlico.

O'Brien, L.S. (1998) *Traumatic Events and Mental Health*. Cambridge: Cambridge University Press.

Ritchie, R.D. (1968) One History of Shellshock. PhD Thesis, University of California, San Diego.

15
THE CLINICAL EFFECTIVENESS OF PSYCHOTHERAPY
Stephen M. Saunders

In 1952, Hans Eysenck published a study of the effects of psychotherapy and concluded that there were none. He reviewed 24 studies in which people undergoing psychotherapy were contrasted to people not. He concluded that there was 'an inverse correlation between recovery and psychotherapy; the more psychotherapy, the smaller the recovery rate' (1952: 322). Eysenck concluded that what appeared to be an effect of psychotherapy was simply spontaneous remission: over time, people experiencing mental health problems get better on their own. Being in therapy was merely coincidental to this recovery.

Eysenck was both right and wrong. He was entirely correct to insist that the question of the effectiveness of psychotherapy must be addressed using scientific methods. Eysenck's article launched an active half century of research into the effectiveness of psychotherapy. In that time, the scientific methodology applied to evaluating psychotherapy has been improved and elaborated. Eysenck was wrong, as will be shown, to conclude that psychotherapy is not effective for alleviating mental health problems. There is a huge body of scientifically sound and methodologically rigorous research showing, unequivocally, that psychotherapy is effective. Indeed, psychotherapy is one of the most effective and efficacious health care procedures in the medical repertoire of interventions.

This chapter reviews the principles of scientific enquiry. It shows that the methodology applied to the question of whether psychotherapy is effective has been rigorous and sound. It demonstrates that there is a great deal of evidence to support the conclusion that there is a causal relationship between engaging in psychotherapy and mental health improvement. The chapter concludes with a discussion of one of the most important, unresolved issues facing the field: convincing people in need of psychotherapy to seek it.

The steps in scientific enquiry

At the most rudimentary level, science is a process of developing, testing and revising or eliminating theories. Scientific enquiry starts with a set of observations that are formulated into an idea, model, or theory. Theories generate research questions and hypotheses, which are statements about likely associations between observed events. For example, a clinician might repeatedly observe that emotional trauma leads people to avoid social situations, and theorise that such trauma leads to intense social anxiety. A research question might ask whether there is an association between trauma and mental health, and the associated hypothesis might predict that trauma causes, in some people, mental health problems.

Research questions and hypotheses are translated into experiments and studies, which generate data or evidence. Coming full circle, if hypotheses of a theory are consistently supported by evidence, then the theory is considered plausible. Ultimately, a theory might be generally accepted as a good or accurate model of the sequence of causal events. In contrast, if evidence does not support a theory, the theory is eventually rejected or, perhaps, replaced by another theory. If a theory of causal change is accepted, researchers turn to explicating, first, the generalisability and limitations of that cause and, second, the mechanism of that cause.

In summary, a theory generates hypotheses that are tested, via experimentation and observation, to generate evidence that either does or does not support the theory. It was this methodology that led to the abandonment of theories that schizophrenia is caused by either poor mothering (Fromm-Reichmann, 1948) or double-bind messages (Bateson et al., 1956). Those theories were abandoned in the absence of supportive evidence (e.g., Waring and Ricks, 1965), whereas the causal mechanisms underlying biochemical causes of schizophrenia, postulated by widely accepted theories, are being evaluated (Tsuang, 2000).

It will be shown that psychotherapy researchers have followed all of these steps in the process of scientific enquiry and have, accordingly, generated solid evidence of its clinical effectiveness. Researchers have carefully constructed and defined theories and terms regarding psychotherapy and its effects. Research questions and hypotheses have been translated into experiments and studies. A great deal of research has shown that psychotherapy *per se* (and not some other confounding variable or process) is an effective way to treat mental health problems. The review includes two exemplary, large-scale studies that have established the efficacy of psychotherapy. Research into the generalisability of psychotherapy to the variety of individuals and problems that exist is briefly reviewed, with special emphasis on psychotherapy's application to depression, anxiety, alcohol use problems and the eating disorders. The following review will highlight some of the recent research into the underlying mechanisms and processes of therapy-induced change. Finally, clinicians and researchers will be reminded of a largely ignored challenge to the field: how to encourage people who need therapy to seek it.

Step 1: Theories and operational definitions in psychotherapy

A theory is typically derived from a set of related observations. Theories have two essential purposes. First, theories explain observations. Second, theories generate predictions about future observations. In the case of psychotherapy, for many centuries medical doctors, shamans, and health care providers have observed that listening, being sympathetic, giving advice and suggesting alternative ways of perceiving events had a salubrious effect on both the mental and physical health of people in distress. For example, the ancient philosopher Epictetus noted, 'People are disturbed not by things but by the views which they take of them'. Numerous theories about how to understand these effects have been offered.

Research hypotheses, which are derived from theory, typically predict some association or relationship between constructs. In order to evaluate hypotheses, the constructs under consideration must be operationally defined. An operational definition is the translation of a construct into an entity that can be measured (e.g., defining the construct 'mental health' as the number of distressing emotional symptoms a person reports experiencing the previous week). Operational definitions must be both reliable and valid. Reliable measures are consistent across time, situations and test administrators. Valid measures generate data or scores that fluctuate in accordance with the actual state or amount of the construct. In other words, a valid measure of mental health will fluctuate consistently with actual differences in mental health status. Without valid measurement of constructs, theories cannot be appropriately evaluated. For example, one of the most severe criticisms of Freud's theory of psychosexual development has been the difficulty of measuring his constructs, such as the unconscious, repression and sublimation (cf. Crews, 1996).

Psychotherapy researchers have gone to great lengths to develop reliable and valid operational definitions of mental health problems and psychotherapy interventions. The theory of psychotherapy essentially states that that there is a causal relationship between psychotherapy and mental health improvement. The primary constructs requiring reliable and valid operational definition, then, are mental health problems and psychotherapy. Another construct that required operational definition was improvement or change in mental health. These have been carefully defined by psychotherapy researchers.

Mental health problems

Emotional distress cannot be measured except via self-report, which is prone to all the exigencies of human error, such as forgetfulness, exaggeration, fatigue, denial and social desirability. None the less, hundreds of reliable and valid measures of the severity of specific mental health problems, such as depression, anxiety, alcohol misuse and symptoms of the eating disorders, have been developed (cf. Garfield and Bergin, 1994; Kramer and Conoley, 1992).

The most widely accepted operational definitions of mental health problems in the USA are detailed in the *Diagnostic and Statistical Manual of Mental Disorders*. The DSM is currently in its fourth edition (DSM-IV), reflecting its status as a tool that is constantly being revised, updated and improved. Like the Present Status Examination (PSE; Wing et al., 1974), which provides psychiatric classification according to the criteria set forth in the ninth edition of the *International Classification of Diseases* (World Health Organisation, 1977), structured interviews for making DSM-based diagnoses are available (e.g., Spitzer et al., 1992).

There are other conceptions of mental health problems. For example, the tripartite model of mental health problems asserts that mental health comprises a sense of well-being, an absence of symptoms, and generally adequate role functioning (cf. Howard et al., 1993; Mintz et al., 1992). There are numerous valid and reliable ways to measure these as well (e.g., Howard et al., 1996).

Psychotherapy

In the causal proposition that psychotherapy leads to mental health improvement, measurement of psychotherapy has proved remarkably challenging. While it might seem fairly easy to determine whether psychotherapy has been delivered, brief consideration reveals that it is not. For example, a vexing question for researchers has been 'How many sessions constitute a 'dosage' of psychotherapy?' (cf. Howard et al., 1986). At one extreme, if one session of treatment should be considered psychotherapy, then researchers would have to acknowledge that there are numerous persons who obtained psychotherapy but did not improve. Alternatively, if a patient must obtain at least 25 sessions before he or she is considered to have obtained psychotherapy, then researchers might be accused of selectively attending to a subgroup of patients who received a great deal of treatment and likely did well.

One of the most important accomplishments of the past two decades has been the operational definition of the term 'psychotherapy'. Numerous therapies have been 'manualized' so that different therapists, in different parts of the world, can administer essentially identical treatments for the purpose of examining their effects. For example, Luborsky (1984) developed a manual for psychoanalytic therapy, and several manuals for the conduct of cognitive-behavioural therapy exist (e.g., Beck et al., 1979; Steketee et al., 1982). Research has established that these therapies can be reliably reproduced and are distinguishable (e.g., DeRubeis et al., 1982; Wilson, 1996a).

Change measurement

Change in mental health problems has also proved vexatious to measure. A variety of sophisticated methodologies for evaluating change as the result of therapy have been developed, including growth curve analysis, random regression modelling, and ratings of clinical significance (e.g., Francis et al., 1991; Gibbons et al., 1993; Jacobson and Follette, 1985; Newman and Howard, 1991). These methodologies have been incorporated into evaluations of the clinical effects of psychotherapy, and have bolstered the assertion that psychotherapy causes a predictable sequence of changes.

Step 2: Establish the causal effect of psychotherapy and rule out alternative explanations

Research into theories that posit causal relationships, such as the theory of the effectiveness of psychotherapy, must establish that such a causal relationship does exist. Establishing cause is one of, if not the, most difficult steps in scientific enquiry. Generally speaking, a causal relationship exists if the presence of one variable (i.e., the independent variable) causes a change in another variable (i.e., the dependent variable). The change in the latter may be its appearance, increase, decrease or disappearance. Researchers must also be able to state that the causal influence under investigation, and not some unmeasured or uncontrolled influence, has caused the effect. In other words, researchers must rule out alternative explanations for any observed associations between different constructs. Given the challenging conclusion of Eysenck's (1952) review, for example, psychotherapy researchers also assumed the task of ruling out spontaneous remission as the actual cause (versus psychotherapy) of change in clients.

The following review of research shows that a conclusion that there is a causal connection between psychotherapy and mental health improvement is justified. Research has established the causal link and other explanations have been evaluated and eliminated via high-quality efficacy research (evaluation of whether, under controlled circumstances, a particular procedure produces an effect – cf. Howard et al., 1996; Seligman, 1995). Two examples of such research are reviewed, as are meta-analyses of numerous studies. Specific challenges to the integrity of the conclusion (i.e., ruling out spontaneous remission and the placebo effect) are also discussed.

The randomised clinical trial

The usual procedure for establishing causal effects in psychotherapy is the randomised clinical trial (RCT). In conducting an RCT, patients are randomly assigned to one of two or more interventions to be compared. One of these conditions may be a placebo-attention condition, wherein the putative 'active ingredients' of the intervention under investigation are suppressed or withheld. As there is general consensus that psychotherapy is superior to no treatment and similar agreement that it would, therefore, be improper to withhold active treatment, it is more common for patients to be assigned to competing psychotherapies (e.g., cognitive therapy versus psychodynamic therapy).

In the usual RCT, patient and therapist variability is minimised to the extent possible. Patients are carefully selected to control for excessive patient variability. For example, patients might be carefully screened to determine that they meet diagnostic criteria for panic disorder but not a comorbid substance use disorder. Therapists are rigorously trained to conduct a treatment that has been standardised or 'manualised' in an attempt to limit the variability of the therapeutic intervention. By maximising the integrity of putative therapeutic ingredients and minimising variability of confounding variables, these experiments minimise threats to the conclusion that the one variable causes a change in the other (Cook and Campbell, 1979; Kazdin, 1994).

Two major psychotherapy research programmes utilised RCT methodology to establish the causal effects of psychotherapy. The Treatment of Depression Collaborative Research Project (TDCRP), conducted in the USA, was a large-scale study of the effectiveness of different treatments for depression. The Sheffield psychotherapy research programme in the UK has conducted a variety of studies evaluating the effectiveness of different psychotherapies. These two programmes highlight the methodological sophistication of psychotherapy research.

The Treatment of Depression Collaborative Research Project   The TDCRP studied 230 depressed outpatients randomly assigned to one of four treatment conditions. The primary aim was to compare the efficacies of two well-standardised psychotherapies for depression: cognitive therapy (CT; Beck et al., 1979) and interpersonal psychotherapy (IPT; Klerman et al., 1984). In an attempt to establish that the therapies were specifically responsible for any observed change, the researchers compared these to two other conditions. The 'standard reference condition' utilised a known efficacious agent, the antidepressant imipramine hydrochloride. The final condition was a drug placebo plus clinical management, included to evaluate whether the 'active' treatments would produce change beyond enhanced hope and attention from a clinician. This latter condition included weekly sessions, with a psychiatrist, of general support and encouragement. These four conditions were explicitly specified in treatment manuals and were conducted by experienced therapists. Valid and reliable measures of depression, depressive cognitions and social functioning were collected across the course of the study (Elkin, 1994). Analyses indicated that patients improved in all four conditions, that the psychotherapies were not significantly different, that the psychotherapies were superior to placebo, and that the psychotherapies were not inferior to the drug treatment in reducing symptoms of depression (e.g., Gibbons et al., 1993).

Sheffield psychotherapy studies   Researchers at the University of Sheffield have examined the effectiveness of psychotherapy in a series of studies that emphasise application of scientific methodology. In the Sheffield Psychotherapy Project (Shapiro and Firth, 1987), they assigned 40 persons with either depression or anxiety to 16 sessions of psychotherapy. The treatment involved eight sessions of cognitive-behavioural treatment ('Prescriptive' therapy) followed by eight sessions of relationship-oriented psychotherapy ('Exploratory' therapy), or vice versa. Patients were randomly assigned to either ordering of treatments. The study found that Prescriptive therapy was only somewhat superior.

In another study, Sheffield investigators evaluated the effectiveness of brief therapy (three sessions total) on mild to moderate depression. They assigned 116 clients rated as either stressed or suffering subclinical depression or low-level clinical depression to either cognitive-behavioural or psychodynamic-interpersonal psychotherapy. Results indicated no significant differences between the treatments until one-year follow-up, when cognitive-behavioural treatment showed superior outcomes on one measure. Other evaluations indicated that they are generally equivalent in effectiveness (e.g., Shapiro et al., 1994).

Meta-analytic studies   The best way to summarise the multitudes of studies on the effectiveness of psychotherapy is through meta-analysis. Meta-analysis (cf. Glass, 1976; Rosenthal and Rubin, 1986) is a method for summarising and integrating research. Numerous individual studies are quantified and coded so that they can be compared with one another. Typically, an effect size (ES) is calculated for each study, indicating the size of the difference between the treated and untreated groups.

In perhaps the first application of this methodology to psychotherapy, Smith, Glass and Miller (1980) summarised 475 studies of psychotherapy. They found that the average person who received psychotherapy was better off than 75% of those persons who did not receive psychotherapy (having been assigned to the control condition). Hundreds of meta-analyses of psychotherapy have subsequently been conducted, and they are invaluable in reaching clinically meaningful conclusions about research. Meta-analytic studies have shown, for example, that short-term dynamic therapy is as effective as other treatments (and more effective than no-treatment – Anderson and Lambert, 1995; Svartberg and Stiles, 1991), that therapies with children (e.g., Weisz et al., 1987) and the elderly (e.g., Scogin and McElreath, 1994) are effective, that different types of marital therapy are more effective than no treatment but generally similar to one another (Dunn and Schwebel, 1995), and that psychotherapy alone is as effective as combining psychotherapy and medication for less severe depression, whereas for more severe depression combined treatment was significantly better (Thase et al., 1997).

As noted, there have been hundreds of meta-analytic studies of psychotherapy research. Lipsey and Wilson (1993) conducted a meta-analysis of these meta-analyses. They examined 156 meta-analyses in which treatments were compared to control conditions, which yielded a sample encompassing over 9,000 studies and more than one million patients. They calculated that psychotherapy had a mean 'effect size' that was considerably larger than that of a plethora of widely used, well-established medical interventions, such as heart bypass surgery. Thus, they concluded that 'a strongly favorable conclusion about the efficacy of well-developed psychological treatment is justified' (1993: 1200).

Ruling out spontaneous remission

As will be recalled, Eysenck concluded that time was a confounding variable in the studies he reviewed, that is, that mental health improvement was due to the mere passage of time (spontaneous remission) rather than the psychotherapy intervention. More recent research has contradicted this claim. It is well established that serious mental illness can last for years or even a lifetime in the absence of intervention (e.g., Keller et al., 1992). Most individuals suffer for many years before seeking help for their problems (Saunders, 1993). Finally, researchers have shown that psychotherapy usually achieves in two months what remits 'naturally' in two years (McNeilly and Howard, 1991).

Accounting for the placebo effect

The placebo effect comprises expecting to feel better, feeling more hopeful and experiencing a caring relationship. The placebo effect is a powerful and essential aspect of all effective health care. Medical patients who adhere to treatment, even when that treatment is a placebo, have better health outcomes than poorly adherent patients (see Horwitz and Horwitz, 1993). In summary, outcomes of treatment – whether psychological or medical – are partly due to non-specific therapeutic effects, such as hope and the quality of the relationship between patient and clinician. However, research has shown that the effects of psychotherapy are not due to placebo alone. Whereas patients randomly assigned to attention-placebo conditions tend to improve, patients randomly assigned to psychotherapy do much better (e.g., Elkin, 1994). Lipsey and Wilson (1993) explicitly explored the placebo effect in their meta-analysis and concluded that psychological interventions have an effect above and beyond the substantial placebo effect. The 'placebo effect' needs to be better understood, appreciated, explained and even manipulated (Wilkins, 1986).

Step 3: Establish generalisability and limits of causal relationship

The carefully controlled, experimental research described in step 2 is necessary to evaluate the causal effect of a health intervention (Shadish and Ragsdale, 1996; Wilson, 1998). Controlled conditions are necessary to establish that the intervention, and not some other factor, is responsible for any observed change. The consequence of such control, however, can be limitations on the generalisability of the intervention. Change generated in a controlled, laboratory-based environment may not be achievable outside of that environment. A procedure that effectively eliminates a certain disease but must be implemented in highly controlled, precise conditions may have little practical utility to other practitioners and patients. In other words, psychotherapy treatments developed within the controlled environment of the research laboratory may not reflect psychotherapy as actually practised in everyday settings. Treatments must be evaluated within the uncontrolled, sometimes chaotic world of the practising clinician (Weisz et al., 1992, 1995). Such 'effectiveness' research is the necessary follow-up step to efficacy research, as it asks 'Does this new, experimentally validated treatment work in practice?'

In addition, at this step the limits of the causal relationship are evaluated. Efficacious treatments are not equally effective with all people or all conditions. Some treatments may work better with some people than other treatments. For example, researchers have established that the likelihood of a problem drinker successfully learning to control his drinking behaviour depends on the severity and chronicity of the problem (Rosenberg, 1993). Determining the limitations of psychotherapy's effectiveness is an important aspect of its scientific study.

Generalisability to the real world

There are fairly stark contrasts between efficacy and effectiveness research (cf. Howard et al., 1996). There is little control exerted in effectiveness studies in order to mimic, as closely as possible, actual practice (Clarke, 1995). Effectiveness studies follow the progress of patients who choose their treatment (versus those who are randomly assigned to treatment, as in the RCT). There are few screening procedures, and many patients have more than one diagnosis. Therapy proceeds until the patient, sometimes in collaboration with the therapist, decides to terminate. As a result of these differences, some have questioned whether interventions developed in the laboratory are usable in the clinic (e.g., Shadish et al., 1997).

Weisz and his colleagues have examined this issue explicitly and directly as it pertains to child and adolescent psychotherapy. In a review of meta-analytic studies of this population, Weisz et al. (1992) reported that psychotherapy conducted by practising clinicians in clinic settings 'may not be nearly so positive' as controlled research suggests. They neatly turn the table on the issue, however, by pointing out that clinics should try to improve treatment conditions to approximate better the positive results obtained in laboratories (Weisz et al., 1995).

Other clinic-based studies have generated more positive results. In a type of meta-analysis of effectiveness studies, Howard and colleagues (1986) compiled and reanalysed data available from studies that included over 2,400 patients reported in effectiveness studies covering a 30 year period. They found a lawful linear relationship between the number of sessions and the probability of patient improvement. To be specific, they reported that by about the eighth session, almost half of patients are measurably improved, and that by session 26, half of the remaining patients have improved. This 'dose-effect' finding has been replicated, and researchers have demonstrated that different disorders respond at different rates (e.g., Horowitz et al., 1988; Kadera et al., 1996). For example, Kopta and colleagues (1994) found that over 75% of chronically distressed patients are improved by session 52, whereas less than 60% of characterologically disturbed clients are improved by then. These and other studies (e.g., Seligman, 1995) have established that psychotherapy as conducted in the real world is effective.

Applicability to specific disorders

Research studies have documented the applicability of psychotherapy to a wide variety of emotional disorders, including marital problems (e.g., Jacobson and Follette, 1985), sexual dysfunction (e.g., LoPiccolo and Stock, 1986), obsessive – compulsive disorder (e.g., Steketee et al., 1982), borderline personality disorder (e.g., Linehan et al., 1991), and a variety of childhood and adolescent disorders (e.g., Kazdin et al., 1990). Research establishing its effectiveness to the most common disorders, depression, anxiety, bulimia nervosa and alcohol problems, is now reviewed.

Depression   In a comprehensive review of studies that have compared therapy to either no treatment or another form of treatment, Robinson and colleagues (1990) concluded that depressed patients 'benefit substantially from psychotherapy' and that the benefits endure. Others have reached similar conclusions with regard to suicide attempters (van der Sande et al., 1997) and depression in the elderly (Scogin and McElreath, 1994).

Anxiety disorders   Psychotherapy's effectiveness in ameliorating anxiety disorders is well established. Sherman (1998) reported that psychotherapy for post-traumatic stress disorder (PTSD) was significant both immediately after treatment and at long term follow-up. Abramowitz (1997) reached the same conclusion about psychotherapy for obsessive–compulsive disorder (OCD; see also van Blakom et al., 1994). Taylor (1996) found similar results when reviewing psychotherapy for social phobia, and reported that treatment effects tended actually to increase over follow-up. Panic disorder and agoraphobia respond most consistently and enduringly to psychological (versus pharmacological) treatments (Clum et al., 1993; Mattick et al., 1990).

Bulimia nervosa   Psychotherapy is a relatively new treatment option for the eating disorders, but research data suggests that it may be the most effective treatment. Whittal and colleagues (1999) reviewed nine medication-based and 26 psychotherapy-based RCTs of bulimia nervosa, and they found that cognitive behavioural treatment tended to produce the largest effects.

Alcohol and drug use problems   Alcohol and drug use problems have been largely eschewed by practising psychologists, who tend to see these problems as more appropriate for restrictive environmental conditions and confrontation-based groups. William Miller and his colleagues (e.g., Miller and Brown, 1997) have both argued and demonstrated, however, that psychotherapeutic techniques – such as cognitive restructuring – and basic psychotherapeutic conditions – such as empathy and unconditional positive regard – are highly therapeutic to these populations. In particular, they have developed the technique of 'motivational interviewing', which is a directive, client-centred therapeutic intervention that motivates clients to change problematic behaviour by assisting them in exploring and resolving ambivalence (Rollnick and Miller, 1995). Motivational interviewing has demonstrated efficacy and effectiveness (Westerberg et al., 2000).

Step 4: Delineate the mechanism of action in psychotherapy

After establishing the efficacy and generalisability of a health intervention, research typically is directed at understanding the mechanism of the causal action (e.g., Shapiro, 1995). Based on the accumulated proof that psychotherapy does alleviate mental health problems, a great deal of ongoing psychotherapy research is investigating what aspects of therapy cause what types of changes in patients. For example, Jacobson and colleagues (1996) partitioned cognitive treatment (CT) into cognitive restructuring and behavioural activation (BA). They compared therapies that emphasised either of these techniques, and found that both worked generally well. Addis and Jacobson (1996) contrasted these two treatment modalities to clients' conception of their reason for being depressed. They found that clients who endorsed existential reasons for depression had better outcomes in CT, whereas clients who reported relationship-oriented reasons did worse in CT.

Burns and Spangler (2000) evaluated whether doing homework between sessions was an important aspect of cognitive-behavioural therapy. They found that homework had a causal effect on depression improvement, that is, doing homework was found to be directly related to recovery.

It used to be believed that psychotherapy comprised specific interventions, such as cognitive restructuring (challenging and changing cognitions) and stimulus control (avoiding certain situations). Non-specific factors, such as activation of hope and the experiencing of an empathic and positive relationship, have been found to be as or more important. For example, Saunders (2000) reported that feeling an emotional connection and mutual understanding with one's therapist is an important aspect of recovery.

Other researchers have investigated the shape of change in psychotherapy. As reviewed earlier, whereas almost half of patients are improved by session 8 (Howard et al., 1996), patients with chronic conditions or with personality disorders require significantly more treatment (Kadera et al., 1996; Kopta et al., 1994).

Completing the research cycle

Psychotherapy researchers, although initially resistant, have taken up the challenge of proving the worth of their endeavours to practising clinicians and clinicians (e.g., Beutler et al., 1996). The dominant challenge to psychotherapy researchers at present has not yet been adequately addressed, however. Although psychology and psychiatry have established effective interventions for alleviating the profound personal, family and societal distress associated with mental health problems, the majority of people with such problems do not seek appropriate care. Epidemiologic research into the prevalence and treatment of mental illness indicates that a substantial proportion of both children and adults in the population have suffered, are presently suffering, or will suffer at some time in their life from a diagnosable psychiatric disorder (e.g., Kessler et al., 1994; Regier et al., 1988). One out of five people will personally experience a diagnosable mental illness in any given year, and the lifetime prevalence is one in three. Yet, less than 20% of people with a diagnosable disorder had sought treatment for it within the previous year. Moreover, most of this treatment-seeking was to the general medical sector (Shapiro et al., 1984; Tischler et al., 1975).

There continue to exist profound barriers to adequate mental health care. These include ignorance about mental illness and its treatment (Veroff et al., 1981a; Veroff et al., 1981b) and, most especially, reluctance to attribute problematic behaviour or distress to mental illness (Meile and Whitt, 1981; Saunders, 1993; Whitt and Meile, 1985). It can only be assumed, then, that psychologists and psychotherapists have not adequately addressed or redressed these issues. Despite over five decades of research establishing that therapy is an immediately, profoundly and usually permanently effective way to address mental health problems, the general public hesitates to seek our services. Psychotherapy researchers have established that the intervention works very well. What remains is the promotion of therapy to the people in need of it.

Returning to Eysenck

Eysenck purported, but failed, to use scientific enquiry to evaluate psychotherapy. When psychotherapy is put through the rigours of scientific testing, it is revealed to be an extremely efficacious treatment. Compared to no treatment and alternative treatments (including medicine), it has been shown to be effective. It has been established that it is psychotherapy and not some other confounding variable that accounts for patient change. It has been shown to be generalisable to the real world, and has been shown to be of varying effectiveness with different disorders. It is particularly effective with the anxiety disorders and bulimia nervosa. The mechanisms of such effects are under investigation.

Despite this positive review, it is noted that a good number of patients either fail to improve or improve to an inadequate degree. Understanding treatment failure and broadening the effectiveness of current treatments are critical agendas for the field (e.g., Wilson, 1996b). Psychotherapy researchers need to address the issue of further delineating the characteristics of effective versus ineffective treatments. More importantly, still, psychotherapy researchers must figure out how to convince the general public that their health intervention is an acceptable and beneficial response to mental health concerns.

References

Abramowitz, J.S. (1997) Effectiveness of psychological and pharmacological treatments for obsessive–compulsive disorder: a quantitative review. *Journal of Consulting and Clinical Psychology* 65, 44–52.

Addis, M.E. and Jacobson, N.S. (1996) Reasons for depression and the process and outcome of cognitive-behavioral psychotherapies. *Journal of Consulting and Clinical Psychology*, 64, 1417–24.

Anderson, E.M. and Lambert, M.J. (1995) Short-term dynamically oriented psychotherapy: a review and meta-analysis. *Clinical Psychology Review*, 15, 503–14.

Bateson, G., Jackson, D., Haley, J. and Weakland, J. (1956) Toward a theory of schizophrenia. *Behavioral Science*, 1, 251–64.

Beck, A.T., Rush, A.J., Shaw, B.F. and Emery, G. (1979) *Cognitive Therapy of Depression: A Treatment Manual*. New York, NY: Guilford Press.

Beutler, L.K., Kim, K.J., Davison, K., Karno, M. and Fisher, D. (1996) Research contributions to improving managed healthcare outcomes. *Psychotherapy*, 33, 197–206.

Burns, D.D. and Spangler, D.L. (2000) Does psychotherapy homework lead to improvements in depression in cognitive-behavioral therapy or does improvement lead to increased homework compliance? *Journal of Consulting and Clinical Psychology*, 68, 46–56.

Clarke, G.N. (1995) Improving the transition from basic efficacy research to effectiveness studies: methodological issues and procedures. *Journal of Consulting and Clinical Psychology*, 63, 718–25.

Clum, G.A., Clum, G.A., and Surls, R. (1993) A meta-analysis of treatments for panic disorder. *Journal of Consulting and Clinical Psychology*, 61, 317–26.

Cook, T.D. and Campbell, D.T. (1979) *Quasi-experimentation: Design and Analysis Issues for Field Settings*. Boston, MA: Houghton Mifflin.

Crews, F. (1996) The verdict on Freud. *Psychological Science*, 7, 63–8.

DeRubeis, R.J., Hollon, S.D., Evans, M.T., and Bemis, K.M. (1982) Can psychotherapies for depression be discriminated? A systematic investigation of cognitive therapy and interpersonal psychotherapy. *Journal of Consulting and Clinical Psychology*, 50, 744–56.

Dunn, R.L. and Schwebel, A.I. (1995) Meta-analytic review of marital therapy outcome research. *Journal of Family Psychology*, 9, 58–68.

Elkin, I. (1994) The NIMH Treatment of Depression Collaborative Research Program: where we began and where we are. In A.E. Bergin and S.L. Garfield (eds), *Handbook of Psychotherapy and Behavior Change* 4th edn. New York, NY: Wiley. pp. 114–39.

Eysenck, H.J. (1952) The effects of psychotherapy: an evaluation. *Journal of Consulting Psychology*, 16, 319–24.

Francis, D.J., Fletcher, J.M., Stuebing, K.K., Davidson, K.C. and Thompson, N.M. (1991) Analysis of change: modeling individual growth. *Journal of Consulting and Clinical Psychology*, 59, 27–37.

Fromm-Reichmann, F. (1948) Notes on the development of treatment of schizophrenia by psychoanalytic psychotherapy. *Psychiatry*, 11, 263–73.

Garfield, S.L. and Bergin, A.E. (eds) (1994) *Handbook of Psychotherapy and Behavior Change*, 4th edn. New York, NY: Wiley.

Gibbons, R.D., Hedeker, D., Elkin, I., Waternaux, C., Kraemer, H.C., Greenhouse, J.B., Shea, M.D., Imber, S.D., Sotsky, S.M. and Watkins, J.T. (1993) Some conceptual and statistical issues in the analysis of longitudinal psychiatric data: application to the NIMH Treatment of Depression Collaborative Research Program dataset. *Archives of General Psychiatry*, 50, 739–50.

Glass, G.V. (1976) Primary, secondary, and meta-analysis of research. *Educational Researcher*, 5, 3–8.

Horwitz, R.I. and Horwitz, S.M. (1993) Adherence to treatment and health outcomes. *Archives of Internal Medicine*, 153, 1863–8.

Horowitz, L.M., Rosenberg, S.E., Baer, B.A., Ureño, G., and Villasenor, V.S. (1988) Inventory of Interpersonal Problems: psychometric properties and clinical applications. *Journal of Consulting and Clinical Psychology*, 56, 885–92.

Howard, K.I., Kopta, S.M., Krause, M.S., and Orlinsky, D.E. (1986) The dose-effect relationship in psychotherapy. *American Psychologist*, 41, 159–64.

Howard, K.I., Lueger, R.J., Maling, M.S. and Martinovich, Z. (1993) A phase model of psychotherapy outcome: causal mediation of change. *Journal of Consulting and Clinical Psychology*, 61, 678–85.

Howard, K.I., Moras, K., Brill, P.L., Martinovich, Z. and Lutz, W. (1996) Evaluation of psychotherapy: efficacy, effectiveness, and patient progress. *American Psychologist*, 51, 1059–64.

Jacobson, N.S. and Follette, W.C. (1985) Clinical significance of improvement resulting from behavioral marital therapy components. *Behavior Therapy*, 16, 249–62.

Jacobson, N. S., Dobson, K.S., Truax, P.A., Addis, M.E., Koerner, Kelly K., Gollan, J.K., Gortner, E. and Prince, S.E. (1996) A component analysis of cognitive-behavioral treatment for depression. *Journal of Consulting and Clinical Psychology*, 64, 295–304.

Kadera, S.W., Lambert, M.J. and Andrews, A.A. (1996) How much therapy is really enough? A session-by-session analysis of the psychotherapy dose-effect relationship. *Journal of Psychotherapy Practice and Research*, 5, 132–51.

Kazdin, A.E. (1994) Methodology, design, and evaluation in psychotherapy research. In A.E. Bergin and S.L. Garfield (eds), *Handbook of Psychotherapy and Behavior Change*, 4th edn. New York, NY: Wiley. pp. 19–71.

Kazdin, A.E., Bass, D., Ayers, W.A. and Rodgers, A. (1990) Empirical and clinical focus of child and adolescent psychotherapy research. *Journal of Consulting and Clinical Psychology*, 58, 729–40.

Keller, M.B., Lavori, P.W., Mueller, T.I., Endicott, J., Coryell, W., Hirschfield, R.M.A. and Shea, T. (1992) Time to recovery, chronicity, and levels of psychopathology in major depression: a five year prospective follow-up of 431 subjects. *Archives of General Psychiatry*, 49, 809–16.

Kessler, R.C., McGonagle, K.A., Zhao, S., Nelson, C.B., Hughes, M., Eshleman, S., Wittchen, H. and Kendler, K.S. (1994) Lifetime and 12-month prevalence of DSM-III-R psychiatric disorders in the United States: results from the National Comorbidity Survey. *Archives of General Psychiatry*, 51, 8–19.

Klerman, G.L., Weissman, M.M., Rounsaville, B. and Chevron, E. (1984) *Interpersonal Psychotherapy of Depression (IPT)*. New York, NY: Basic Books.

Kopta, S.M., Howard, K.I., Lowry, J.L. and Beutler, L.E. (1994) Patterns of symptomatic recovery in time-unlimited psychotherapy. *Journal of Consulting and Clinical Psychology*, 62, 1009–16.

Kramer, J.J. and Conoley, J.C. (eds) (1992) *The Eleventh Mental Measurements Yearbook*. Lincoln, NB: Buros Institute of Mental Measurements.

Linehan, M.M., Armstrong, H.E., Suarez, A., Allmon, D. and Heard, H.L. (1991) Cognitive behavioral treatment of chronically parasuicidal borderline patients. *Archives of General Psychiatry*, 48, 1060–4.

Lipsey, M.W. and Wilson, D.B. (1993) The efficacy of psychological, educational, and behavioral treatment: confirmation from meta-analysis. *American Psychologist*, 48, 1181–209.

LoPiccolo, J. and Stock, W.E. (1986) Treatment of sexual dysfunction. *Journal of Consulting and Clinical Psychology*, 54, 158–67.

Luborsky L. (1984) *Principles of Psychoanalytic Psychotherapy: A Manual for Supportive-Expressive (SE) Treatment*. New York, NY: Basic Books.

Mattick, R.P., Andrews, G., Hadzi-Pavlovic, D. and Christensen, H. (1990) Treatment of panic and agoraphobia: an integrative review. *Journal of Nervous and Mental Disease*, 178, 567–76.

McNeilly, C.L. and Howard, K.I. (1991) The effects of psychotherapy: a re-evaluation based on dosage. *Psychotherapy Research*, 1, 74–8.

Meile, R.L., and Whitt, H.P. (1981) Cultural consensus and definition of mental illness. *Social Science and Medicine Part A: Medical Sociology*, 15, 231–42.

Miller, W.R. and Brown, S.A. (1997) Why psychologists should treat alcohol and drug problems. *American Psychologist*, 52, 1269–79.

Mintz, J., Mintz, L.I., Arruda, M.J. and Hwang, S.S. (1992) Treatments of depression and the functional capacity to work. *Archives of General Psychiatry*, 49, 761–8.

Newman, F.L. and Howard, K.I. (1991) Introduction to the special section on seeking new clinical research methods. *Journal of Consulting and Clinical Psychology*, 59, 8–11.

Regier, D.A., Boyd, J.H., Burke, J.D., Rae, D.S., Myers, J.K., Kramer, M., Robins, L.N., George, L.K., Karno, M., and Locke, B.Z. (1988) One-month prevalence of mental disorders in the United States. *Archives of General Psychiatry*, 45, 977–86.

Robinson, L.A., Berman, J.S. and Neimeyer, R.A., (1990) Psychotherapy for the treatment of depression: a comprehensive review of controlled outcome research. *Psychological Bulletin*, 108, 30–49.

Rollnick, S. and Miller, W.R. (1995) What is motivational interviewing? *Behavioural and Cognitive Psychotherapy*, 23, 325–34.

Rosenberg, H. (1993) Prediction of controlled drinking by alcoholics and problem drinkers. *Psychological Bulletin*, 113, 129–39.

Rosenthal, R. and Rubin, D.B. (1986) Meta-analytic procedures for combining studies with multiple effect sizes. *Psychological Bulletin*, 99, 400–6.

Saunders, S.M. (1993) Applicants' experience of the process of seeking psychotherapy. *Psychotherapy*, 30, 554–64.

Saunders, S.M. (2000) Examining the relationship between the therapeutic bond and the phases of treatment outcome. *Psychotherapy*, 37, 206–18.

Scogin, F. and McElreath, L. (1994) Efficacy of psychosocial treatments for geriatric depression: a quantitative review. *Journal of Consulting and Clinical Psychology*, 62, 69–73.

Seligman, M.E.P. (1995) The effectiveness of psychotherapy: the *Consumer Reports* study. *American Psychologist*, 50, 965–74.

Shadish, W.R. and Ragsdale, K. (1996) Random versus nonrandom assignment in controlled experiments: Do you get the same answer? *Journal of Consulting and Clinical Psychology*, 64, 1290–305.

Shadish, W.R., Matt, G.E., Navarro, A.M., Siegle, G. et al. (1997) Evidence that therapy works in clinically representative conditions. *Journal of Consulting and Clinical Psychology*, 65, 355–65.

Shapiro, D.A. (1995) Finding out how psychotherapies help people change. *Psychotherapy Research*, 5, 1–21.

Shapiro, D. and Firth, J. (1987) Prescriptive v. exploratory psychotherapy: outcomes of the Sheffield Psychotherapy Project. *British Journal of Psychiatry*, 151, 790–9.

Shapiro, D.A., Barkham, M., Rees, A., Hardy, G.E. et al. (1994) Effects of treatment duration and severity of depression on the effectiveness of cognitive-behavioral and psychodynamic-interpersonal psychotherapy. *Journal of Consulting and Clinical Psychology*, 62, 522–34.

Shapiro, S., Skinner, E.A., Kessler, L.G., Von Korff, M., German, P.S., Tischler, G.L., Leaf, P.J., Benham, L., Cottler, L. and Regier, D.A. (1984) Utilization of health and mental health services: three epidemiologic catchment area sites. *Archives of General Psychiatry*, 41, 971–8.

Sherman, J.J. (1998) Effects of psychotherapeutic treatments for PTSD: a meta-analysis of controlled clinical trials. *Journal of Traumatic Stress*, 11, 413–35.

Smith, M.L., Glass, G.V. and Miller, T.I. (1980) *The Benefits of Psychotherapy*. Baltimore, MD: Johns Hopkins University Press.

Spitzer, R.L., Williams, J.B., Gibbon, M. et al. (1992) The structured clinical interview for DSM-III-R (SCID): history, rationale and description. *Archives General Psychiatry*, 49, 624–30.

Steketee, G., Foa, E.B. and Grayson, J.B. (1982) Recent advances in the behavioral treatment of obsessive-compulsives. *Archives of General Psychiatry*, 39, 1365–71.

Svartberg, M. and Stiles, T. (1991) Comparative effect of short-term psychodynamic psychotherapy: a meta-analysis. *Journal of Consulting and Clinical Psychology*, 59, 704–14.

Taylor, S. (1996) Meta-analysis of cognitive-behavioral treatment for social phobia. *Journal of Behavior Therapy and Experimental Psychiatry*, 27, 1–9.

Thase, M.E., Greenhouse, J.B., Frank, E., Reynolds, C.F. III., Pilkonis, P.A., Hurley, K., Grochocinski, V. and Kupfer, D.J. (1997) Treatment of major depression with psychotherapy or psychotherapy-pharmacotherapy combinations. *Archives of General Psychiatry*, 54, 1009–15.

Tischler, G.L., Henisz, J.K., Myers, J.K. and Boswell, P.C. (1975) Utilization of mental health services: I. Patienthood and the prevalence of symptomology in the community. *Archives of General Psychiatry*, 32, 411–15.

Tsuang, M. (2000) Schizophrenia: genes and environment. *Biological Psychiatry*, 47, 210–20.

van Blakom, A.J.L.M., van Oppen, P., Vermeulen, A.W.A., van Dyck, R. et al. (1994) A meta-analysis on the treatment of obsessive compulsive disorder: a comparison of antidepressants, behavior, and cognitive therapy. *Clinical Psychology Review*, 14, 359–81.

van der Sande, R., Buskens, E., Allart, E., van der Graaf, Y. and van Engeland, H. (1997) Psychosocial intervention following suicide attempt: a systematic review of treatment interventions. *Acta Psychiatrica Scandinavica*, 96, 43–50.

Veroff, J., Douvan, E. and Kulka, R.A. (1981a) *The Inner-American: A Self-Portrait from 1957 to 1976*. New York, NY: Basic Books.

Veroff, J., Kulka, R.A. and Douvan, E. (1981b) *Mental Health in America: Patterns of Help-seeking from 1957 to 1976*. New York, NY: Basic Books.

Waring, M. and Ricks, D. (1965) Family patterns of children who become adult schizophrenics. *Journal of Nervous and Mental Disease*, 140, 351–64.

Weisz, J.R., Weiss, B., Alicke, M.D. and Klotz, M. (1987) Effectiveness of psychotherapy with children and adolescents: a meta-analysis for clinicians. *Journal of Consulting and Clinical Psychology*, 55, 542–9.

Weisz, J.R., Weiss, B. and Donenberg, G.R. (1992) The lab versus the clinic: effects of children and adolescent psychotherapy. *American Psychologist*, 47, 1578–85.

Weisz, J.R., Donenberg, G.R., Han, S.S. and Weiss, B. (1995) Bridging the gap between laboratory and clinic in child and adolescent psychotherapy. *Journal of Consulting and Clinical Psychology*, 63, 688–701.

Westerberg, V.S., Miller, W.R. and Tonigan, J.S. (2000) Comparison of outcomes for clients in randomized versus open trials of treatment for alcohol use disorders. *Journal of Studies on Alcohol*, 61, 720–7.

Whitt, H.P. and Meile, R.L. (1985) Alignment, magnification and snowballing processes in the definition of symptoms of mental illness. *Social Forces*, 63, 682–97.

Whittal, M.L., Agras, W.S. and Gould, R.A. (1999) Bulimia nervosa: a meta-analysis of psychosocial and pharmacological treatments. *Behavior Therapy*, 30, 117–35.

Wilkins, W. (1986) Placebo problems in psychotherapy research: social-psychological alternatives to chemotherapy concepts. *American Psychologist*, 41, 551–6.

Wing, J.K., Cooper, J.E. and Sartorius, N. (1974) *The Measurement and Classification of Psychiatric Symptoms*. Cambridge: Cambridge University Press.

Wilson, G.T. (1996a) Treatment of bulimia nervosa: when CBT fails. *Behavior Research and Therapy*, 34, 197–212.

Wilson, G.T. (1996b) Empirically validated treatments: reality and resistance. *Clinical Psychology: Science and Practice*, 3, 241–4.

Wilson, G.T. (1998) The clinical utility of randomized controlled trials. *International Journal of Eating Disorders*, 24, 13–29.

World Health Organisation (1977) *Manual of the International Statistical Classification of Diseases, Injuries, and Causes of Death (9th edn)*. Geneva: World Health Organisation.

16
THE PHILOSOPHICAL AND ETHICAL BASIS OF BENEFIT
Digby Tantam

In this chapter, I shall consider the benefits of counselling and psychotherapy from two points of view: what a person is entitled to, and what a person should be entitled to. Both these points of view command a landscape rather than a close-up. Other chapters in this book will have considered how the benefits of psychotherapy can be measured. This is often a quite pragmatic decision, say about which outcome questionnaires are suitable. In this chapter, I shall step back to ask what a benefit is, and how it might apply to psychotherapy.

It may be timely to do this because the benefits that psychotherapy has been expected to provide have not materialized. Or rather, the undoubted benefits of psychotherapy are also shown by drug therapy, and probably other interventions, too. Research, as opposed to anecdote or supposition, has not shown that particular modalities have particular benefits, either. If longer-term therapy or counselling, or exploratory therapy or counselling, have a particular virtue, our current range of measurable benefit has not unequivocally identified it. Either they do not have a particular virtue or, as seems more likely, we need to look again at what benefits we expect. This is what I attempt to do in this chapter.

Clearing the ground

The terms 'counselling' and 'psychotherapy' are often used interchangeably. Or rather, the same activity may be described as counselling or as psychotherapy depending on the audience. Many people find the term 'counselling' less stigmatising, less impregnated with the medical model of therapy. Psychotherapy may also seem to be claiming an inappropriate degree of expertise, as if psychotherapists want to put a barrier between themselves and their ... well here's another difficult point. Is the other person or the other people in psychotherapy – the ones who are not therapists – clients, patients, users, or what?

Very often we, like a growing number of our colleagues, side-step these issues. We are happy to describe ourselves as counsellors, and the people we counsel as clients. Life is too short to get caught up in battles over nomenclature. The range of activities that are legitimately termed counselling is so large that it can hold almost all of us in the talking professions. Why make unnecessary divisions? And the fact that lawyers, accountants and dentists have clients just as counsellors do seems, if anything, an advantage. We are providing a service to the public, just as they are.

If we do take the high street as our model of the counsellor/therapist–client relationship, there is little need to consider benefit. Clients employ the professionals whose help they seek. It is the client who determines whether or not they get value for money, and the client who determines whether or not contact with the professional has been of benefit. The range of possible benefits that might justify a person seeking advice from a solicitor or handing over their finances to an accountant is too great for anyone to want to itemise them. In a way, it does not matter. Suppose that someone goes to an accountant having already completed their self-assessment tax form and sent it to the appropriate authorities. And suppose that the accountant makes no suggestions about changing the way that the person keeps their accounts, saying that it is just fine as it is. We do not worry about whether or not the person has benefited from going to the accountant. We only say, if they were satisfied, they must have received some benefit.

Call this the *contractual model*. Contrast this with the situation when it is not the client, but a third person, who is paying. Then the third person needs to be convinced that money has been well spent on the professional intervention. This is true whether the third person is a family member, an insurance company, or a nationalised health service. A family member might make a subjective judgement about an individual, but an insurer or a government has to make decisions that are open to scrutiny about groups of clients. Benefit therefore tends to be put in terms of 'efficacy'.[1] What the third party considers efficacious may not be the most satisfactory outcome as far as the client is concerned, and what satisfies the client may not be considered efficacious by the third party.

An example of this difference is contained in the sixth report of the Select Committee on Science and Technology of the House of Lords (the upper house of the UK Parliament), which was on complementary and alternative medicine (CAM):

4.27 In conclusion, patient satisfaction has its place as part of the evidence base for CAM but its position is complicated, as Sir Michael Rawlins, explained: 'The difficulty, of course, is that very often the anecdotal evidence relates to conditions where there is fluctuation in the clinical course and people who start an intervention at a time when there is a natural resolution of the disease, very understandably, are likely to attribute cause and effect when it may not be. But, on the other hand, there are some anecdotes that are quite clearly important.' Therefore, ideally studies should include patient satisfaction as one of a number of measures in evaluating a treatment, but it alone cannot be taken as a proof or otherwise of a treatment's efficacy or as evidence to justify provision.

Determining therapeutic efficacy requires an agreement beforehand about what type of benefit is to be expected. This requires a therapeutic claim. It is the difference between the accountant who says, 'Become my client, and I will help you with your tax' and the one who says, 'Become my client, and I will save you thousands of pounds a year in overpaid tax'.

The ethos of counselling has often tended towards the contractual relationship, and is based only on a promise that the counsellor will be committed to helping the client. In this relationship, it is for the client to determine whether the counsellor has helped; there is no need to specify beforehand what kind of help is available since this can emerge during the course of the counselling, and there is no necessity to establish efficacy because no third party is involved.

The counsellor described in the previous paragraph makes no therapeutic claim. This is in contrast to the majority of psychotherapists and therapeutic counsellors who, it seems to me, do. They would claim that something more is being aimed for than just satisfying the client with the interaction. Or, if the aim might be to make the patient more satisfied, this aim is based on the expectation that if the client can have a more satisfactory relationship with their therapist they can also have more satisfactory relationships with other people who are of more emotional importance to them.

This claim to 'treatment efficacy', as it was termed in the passage quoted from the House of Lords' report, implies that there is an agreement, even if it is never explicitly stated, about what benefits might follow from the therapy. This claim is therefore similar to that of the accountant who promises to save thousands of pounds a year for his or her clients. Many consequences follow from this claim. It opens up the possibility of complaints about incompetence, for example. If my accountant simply claims to be helpful, and is so, then I could not complain about their incompetent advice. However, if my accountant claims to save me tax and, it turns out, has not done so, I can complain about their incompetence as an accountant.

More importantly, once treatment efficacy has been established, then it is a short step to there being a need for the treatment, and a right to receive it. This is why the UK government has created the National Institute for Clinical Excellence (NICE). NICE reviews the evidence base for new treatments. When a drug company introduces a new drug, and charges a premium to recoup its research and developments costs, there is usually an immediate demand. However, the health service will not pay for the drug even if it prescribed by a general practitioner unless NICE has reported that it is efficacious. The health service is under considerable ethical pressure not to refuse to pay if it is efficacious, because this would be counter to the rights of patients to receive the best possible care. So once the general right to health care has been conceded, the step that determines the right to any particular item of health care is the determination about the efficacy of that particular item.

The rights associated with contractual counselling are those that pertain to fundamental freedoms: for example, free speech, or the free pursuit of religion. If a putative European state decided to prohibit counselling for whatever reason, it would be this curtailment of non-specific freedoms which might form the basis of an appeal to the European Court of Human Rights.

If the counsellors concerned claimed a therapeutic benefit, it would be another matter. Consider a European state that banned radiotherapy. Radiotherapists would be able to point to the benefits of radiotherapy, and the consequences in increased pain and mortality for patients who were denied it.

The state would therefore be abrogating its citizens' human right to receive medical care that reduces suffering and prolongs life.

In the remainder of this chapter, I shall consider these two therapeutic claims in more detail:

1   that counselling and psychotherapy have characteristic benefits which can be specified before the therapy begins (the therapeutic efficacy claim); and
2   that there is right to these benefits.

The reader will note that they are closely related, and I shall not therefore attempt to deal with them sequentially, but will go back and forwards between them.

Therapeutic efficacy

As a client once told me, counsellors reflect, psychotherapists interfere. By interference I think she meant that change is intrinsic to the therapeutic process. Consider again the distinction between being helped and receiving some specified benefit.

Harriet, a college counsellor, was consulted by Debbie. Debbie had gone home in the last vacation to discover that her parents were on the brink of splitting up. She knew that they had been alienated for years, but not that they were waiting for her to leave home to separate. She felt more let down and abandoned than she could believe. Her parents told her that she was being selfish. After all, they had put up with each other for years so that she had a united home. That no longer mattered to her now she had left for University: why should she complain? Harriet explained to Debbie that it was a common misconception of parents that when their children left home, it no longer mattered to them what their parents did. In fact, said Harriet, this was one of the times when young people felt especially upset by change in what they still considered to be their homes. The stability of that home was very important, even if it was a background concern that was not often made explicit. Debbie was reassured. She felt her reaction was understandable, and that she was not being selfish. She felt that she had regained some emotional poise and could discuss the situation more effectively with her parents, either together or separately.

Harriet did not interfere with Debbie's thinking about her problem, but she did validate it. Debbie was very satisfied with her interview with Harriet, and Harriet felt that she had acted in the best traditions of counselling. She did not think that she had provided therapeutic counselling, but nor did she think this would have been appropriate. Harriet, like other college counsellors, did provide therapeutic counselling to other students who needed it. But Debbie did not.

Had the college authorities considered the matter, they would most likely say that although they did pay for the counselling session, they saw counselling as one of the services provided by the college. Having a good counselling service was one of the things that the college put into its brochures, and it attracted students. The fact that Debbie was satisfied was a good outcome, so far as they were concerned. This does not make counselling unimportant. The college may well have said the same thing about the library: that it was not necessary to show that students benefited from having access to library books, only that they were satisfied with the library service. (I am not considering the harmfulness of counselling or libraries. Colleges certainly do want to ensure that their libraries do not contain racist tracts, pornography, or other materials that might cause offence, if not harm. Similarly, counselling services have a duty not to cause harm.)

> Harriet saw Roger the same afternoon that she saw Debbie. She had first seen Roger about two months before. He had come at the prompting of his personal tutor who was concerned at a falling-off of Roger's academic work. Harriet thought that Roger was depressed and had asked him to see the college GP, but Roger had refused. He was a considerable worry for Harriet. He had cut himself quite severely on three occasions, one requiring a visit to the local casualty department. He often spoke of his hopelessness about his future. Harriet was using a cognitive approach to try to help Roger to become more aware of his negative automatic thoughts, and she was having a little success. Roger was more able to confront some of his assumptions about other people's condemnation of him.

Harriet's work with Roger was definitely therapeutic counselling. Harriet felt a responsibility to try to change Roger's mood. It would not have been enough for her that Roger was satisfied with her therapy if he continued as depressed as he had been when she first saw him. The college authorities would almost certainly have taken this view, too. What the college was providing to Roger was not comparable to other college services that made students feel more satisfied about their college life. It was a part of the health provision in the college.

Were the college to undertake a review of the counselling service, it would be necessary to separate these two aspects of the work. Working with people like Debbie could be evaluated simply on the basis of a satisfaction measure, but the University might consider that it was not the core business of the counselling centre or that counselling of this kind could be provided by postgraduates acting as personal tutors.

Working with people like Roger would have to be considered differently. Some traditionalists might argue that the college should not have a health service, but should avoid recruiting students who might have a liability to mental health problems and, if students developed these problems at the college, they should go to the mental health service locally. If that did not work, the college should give them a year off to 'get themselves sorted out'. These traditionalist views would be likely to be overwhelmed by college officers who wanted to widen recruitment, to reduce discrimination and social exclusion, and who felt that the college should seek to hold on to its students rather than suspending them.

The fact that the fee income of the college is proportional to recruitment and retention would reinforce this argument, but would probably not drive it. The driving force for many college officials, particular those whose attitudes were formed when students all came to college on leaving school, would be a sense that the college had a duty of care. It would be the nature of this duty that would determine how the college would evaluate the efficacy of the counselling service. If this duty was primarily to prevent adverse events such as suicide or break-down, then the efficacy of the counselling service would best be evaluated using ratings of symptoms scores and suicidality. If this duty was to enable students to study and to complete their courses, outcome measures like drop-out rates or examination failure rates might be appropriate. If the college conceived its duty of care to be to minimize the disruption to other students, then the counselling service's ability to reduce incidents might be an appropriate outcome.

Right to provision

I have argued in the previous section that the benefits of counselling or psychotherapy hardly need to be spelt out when a person is paying for the counselling themselves, and when the person paying wants a specified service rather than wanting the other person to take charge. I shall argue in this section that wanting someone else to take charge raises the immediate question of whether or not a person has a right to ask this.

Roger had run out of friends. Unbeknown to Roger, his friends had met in the Union bar one day to discuss what they were going to do about his constant demands. He would ring one of them in the early hours and say that he was suicidal. Usually Roger would expect the friend to come round but at the least he would want to talk on the phone for at least an hour. His friends were sympathetic. They could see he was suffering. But, as Alison said, all this stress wasn't doing them any good. They had examinations coming up. They owed it to themselves and their families to do well in them. They didn't owe Roger anything. They had fully discharged the obligations of friendship already. His friends decided they were going to have to draw a line. Whilst not wanting to be hostile, they were going to have to say that they could not take any more emergency phone calls. Roger would have to sort out his problems with his counsellor, and not with them.

If Roger does not have a right to ask his friends for help – and opinion might be divided about this – does he have a right to professional help?

In some cultures, Roger might have a right to call on his family for assistance. This right has become substantially attenuated in the West. College authorities no longer consider themselves to be *in loco parentis*, for example. In proportion to its attenuation, so the state itself has accepted an increased duty to its citizens.

Philosophers have disagreed on the basis of these duties. Hobbes argued for the provision of a police force on the basis of mutual self-interest. It is, he argued, more important for the average citizen that they receive the benefits of being protected from harm by their neighbours than that they lose the possibility of being able to harm their neighbours with impunity. An implicit covenant therefore exists to create and to obey a government. Protection also applies to the provision of health and social care. It is in my interest to provide that to my neighbour if, in the future, my neighbour will provide it to me. Mutual self-interest therefore also creates a duty of states to care for their citizens.

Hume's argument was also based on self-interest, but with the added element of sympathy. If someone else suffers, I too may be inclined to suffer, out of sympathy with them. It is therefore in my interests to minimise the suffering of others. Hume did not anticipate a national health service, but it is fully consistent with this principle. I give money through taxation to the health service and, in return, I expect to have less experience of suffering and death.

Perhaps the earliest example of the state formally accepting a duty of care to an individual is the statute introduced during the reign of Edward II in 1324 [De Prerogative Regis, 17 Edward II, Stat. 1, 1324] which authorised the King to take responsibility for the custody of lands belonging to 'idiots', 'natural fools' and children without guardians. Later, this jurisdiction was delegated by the King to the Lord Chancellor, and then to the Courts of Chancery. It is the basis for the parens patriae duties – the state as parent – of modern legislatures based on Anglo-Saxon traditions.

Counselling and psychotherapy are not, by their nature, provisions for people who cannot choose for themselves; rather the opposite, in fact. The parens patriae duties of the state do not therefore apply. However, there are other duties that states have accepted over subsequent centuries, and these duties have created reciprocal rights for their citizens. In Europe, these duties have been codified in the European Convention for the Protection of Human Rights and Fundamental Freedoms signed at Rome on 4 November 1950 and derived from the Universal Declaration of Human Rights signed two years before; the European Social Charter opened for signature in Turin on 18 October 1961; and subsequent Protocols. Many of these rights, and possibly some new ones, are likely to be included in the European Union's Charter of Fundamental Rights, a draft version of which was published in October 2000.

The EU draft charter is much more clearly based on the Napoleonic Code. It classifies rights under the three familiar headings of freedom, equality and solidarity, with additional headings of dignity, citizenship and justice. The draft charter has already stirred up a great deal of opposition, and will almost certainly be amended. However, two articles are notable for counsellors and psychotherapists. Article 23 (Protection of Children) states: 'Children shall have the right to such protection and care as is necessary for their well-being ...' and Article 33 (Health Care) that 'Everyone has the right of access to preventive health care and the right to benefit from medical treatment under the conditions established by national laws and practices'.

It reads a bit strangely in English that people have a right to benefit since benefit cannot be granted, only made possible. Nor do the drafters of the charter necessarily intend by medical the same as 'provided by doctors'. Probably what the drafters of the charter were intending is to establish a right to 'beneficial treatment of medically recognised disorders'.

Article 33 reflects current UK approaches to the state provision of counselling and psychotherapy. Psychotherapy has existed within the NHS since its inception, and counselling has been equally accepted in recent years, principally in primary care. Both psychotherapy and counselling are seen as treatments, and their provision is justified according to the same rights and duties that pertain to the provision of drugs or surgery for other disorders. As Article 33 indicates, the same justification for the treatment of disorder also applied to its prevention.

The right to treatment or prevention of medical conditions is not just to be found in the EU's draft charter. It exists already in the revised European social charter, which the UK signed on 7 November 1997, as a right to the protection of health. A right to the provision of psychotherapy and counselling has already been established so long as psychotherapy and counselling can be shown to be effective in the treatment or the prevention of medical conditions. But, let us flag up these possible benefits for consideration later in this chapter, for to restrict psychotherapy and counselling to being treatments or prophylactics for medical conditions strikes many psychotherapists and counsellors as falling short of what benefits psychotherapy and counselling can provide, and what benefits should be made available to people in need of them.

Some hint of these benefits can be found in Article 23 of the EU draft charter, where it states that 'children should have the right to such protection and care as is necessary for their well-being'. Well-being has figured in definitions of what has been called 'positive health', most famously the World Health Organisation's definition of health as 'a state of complete physical, mental, and social well-being and not merely the absence of disease or infirmity' (World Health Organisation, 1948).

There are dangers in seeming to assert that a person has a right to well-being. Well-being is closely linked with living well. A right to well-being may therefore imply a duty to live life according to another's prescription for well-being. If all of us experienced well-being all the time, there would be no criterion by which we could judge what is good or bad for us. Moreover, many of us would rather that people did not feel well about themselves if they have acted badly, or harmfully.

But this is suffering that people bring on themselves. What about involuntary suffering? It would be absurd to hope for a life in which there was no suffering. Without suffering there would be no resilience, nor courage, nor hope.

Nor would there be any possibility of rising beyond suffering into the bliss of nirvana or the certain hope of salvation. However, many people experience so much suffering that any resilience is crushed, and any hope defeated.

Well-being – or happiness – also figures prominently in the American Declaration of Independence, which begins 'We hold these truths to be self-evident, that all men ... are endowed by their Creator with certain unalienable Rights, that among these are Life, Liberty and the pursuit of Happiness ...' Jefferson, when he framed the Declaration, was canny enough not to make happiness itself a right. What men (and women) had a right to was the *pursuit* of happiness.

Pursuing happiness is a slightly old-fashioned idea. For one thing, it smacks of a hunting metaphor that is no longer so attractive. For another, many of us would think that pursuing happiness implies a kind of hedonism. It suggests that happiness is a goal to which we can direct ourselves. For me, this is not an attractive way of looking at the world. I would be inclined to think of happiness as a corollary of my actions rather than their goal. It is an indication that I am thriving. Inversely, suffering of all kinds is an indication that a person is not thriving.

However, 'the pursuit of happiness' remains a resonant phrase. It is an image that we can all conjure up. We all know what pursuing something successfully entails. We must have the capacity to do it, we must have the opportunity to do it, and we have to be able to overcome any obstacles placed in our path. The pursuit of happiness, in other words, implies that each of us should have the opportunity to pursue happiness, free of constraints or incapacities imposed by others.

If we express this in the inverse, individuals or groups that cause undeserved suffering in another or a group of others have a duty to remedy that suffering. 'Undeserved' has to be included because making someone suffer might be justified by the failings of the victim. This duty is a commonplace when it applies to physical suffering. If I fall over a badly laid paving stone, I can sue the council who was responsible for laying it. If I am hurt in a robbery, I can sue the robber or, if that is not possible, I can apply to the Criminal Injuries Board for compensation. What the Declaration of Independence implies is that we can expect to be spared emotional suffering, too, if that suffering is avoidable, if the actions of another or a group of others causes it, and if it is undeserved. For simplicity, I shall call this kind of suffering involuntary emotional suffering.

Emotional suffering: a spiritual dimension

Suffering is the enemy of content. All of us know what that means. But what is suffering? Ill-health, and its treatment or prevention, are specified in all of the modern European charters considered in this chapter. So it seems clear that a right to the relief of physical suffering is already established. What is missing from these charters is a recognition that much suffering is emotional in nature.

Emotional suffering is one of the main concerns of psychotherapists and counsellors. It is easy to think of instances of emotional suffering, from the child who lives in an atmosphere of fear to the man or woman who loses a long-term partner with whom he or she has grown old. However, for many people such experiences are a part of life, and not something to be problematised. Perhaps over the past twenty or thirty years there has been something of a shift in attitudes to children, and few people would now consider that it is 'part of life' for a child to live in fear. But grief? Without sadness, how would we know when we are happy?

There are those who would argue that emotional suffering is a spiritual and not a scientific or professional matter at all (House, 1999). In my view, it is not clear whether the issue of benefit applies if it is. House certainly seems to suggest that evaluating benefit might only support the 'officially sanctioned regime of truth'. However, religious thinkers do not always oppose spiritual to material benefit. Jenkins concludes from a detailed study of Buddhist scriptures that they show 'a distinction and relation between material and moral goods, where material goods have priority as a prerequisite for moral well-being' (Jenkins, 2000: 3).

Jenkins is writing about want, and the duty of the spiritually ambitious person, the *bodhisattva*, to relieve it. However, the argument would seem to apply equally to involuntary emotional suffering, particularly as many types of emotional suffering can be construed as a want – for affection, for support, for human contact and so on.

We think from conversations with professionals that many counsellors and psychotherapists do see their work as connected with spirituality in this way: that although counselling or psychotherapy may not be a spiritual activity itself, by relieving emotional suffering, counsellors and psychotherapists may enable their clients to be more aware of the spiritual in their lives.

Those holding this view would, we assume, consider that one benefit of counselling or psychotherapy is that it allows a person's spirituality to flourish. Note that this is not the same as saying that a person has a beneficial spiritual life, if such a term even applies, but that a person might have more spiritual life, for good or ill. The distinction is analogous to that between happiness and the pursuit of happiness. Having the opportunity and the hopefulness to pursue happiness does not guarantee happiness, but it is a prerequisite of it. Similarly, having enough peace of mind to become aware of the spiritual elements in life does not guarantee an active spiritual life, but it is a prerequisite of it.

So far as I know, no one has considered spirituality as a beneficial outcome of counselling or psychotherapy in any study. It is an area fraught with pitfalls. We would, for example, expect that scientology would be one of the more successful interventions if a concern about spiritual development was taken to be a good outcome, but it was precisely because the UK government of the day wanted to discourage scientology without discouraging psychotherapy that the UK psychotherapy registration process was begun.

Emotional suffering: the health dimension

Let's look at the other end of the range of possible benefits of counselling and psychotherapy, and to the most sharply defined criteria of 'emotional suffering'. At this medical end, the assumption is made that there are natural kinds of emotional suffering which correspond to brain states, and not mind states at all.

These brain states can be induced in animals other than humans (Stenzel-Poore et al., 1994), and can be created in people by using drugs that deplete neuro-transmitters (Ames, 1998).

The mental corollaries of these brain states are symptoms like depressed mood, sleep difficulties, or anxious feelings. Such symptoms are very common. In the late 1940s, there were a series of large-scale epidemiological studies carried out in North America which typically showed that about 70–80% of the populations surveyed had symptoms of emotional distress. There was a recognition that a person might be distressed after a row, or when there had been a serious problem at work or at home, but that this suffering is short-lived. So procedures were introduced to exclude transient distress, but even so about a quarter of the populations surveyed reported what the researchers thought was significant suffering.

Similar findings emerged about physical health when the National Morbidity Surveys began in this country. Only a minority of people described feeling healthy. The majority of people had something wrong with them, from backache to oesophageal reflux.

The findings of the community studies in North America were pilloried (Leighton, personal communication) and ignored. The findings of the National Morbidity Surveys have led to the bottomless pit hypothesis of health: that some sort of rationing of health care is always needed because people will simply consume more and more health care because no one ever feels satisfied with their health. The same bottomless pit hypothesis has been extended to the uptake of counselling and psychotherapy. It is assumed that the more that is provided, the more will be consumed.

Defining benefit as what is feasible

The sky's the limit, so far as happiness is concerned. No sooner am I happy that I have got a television set than I am unhappy because my neighbour has satellite. It is not surprising that emotional suffering seems like a bottomless pit to many planners, and to many beleaguered practitioners, too.

One way of dealing with this is to rule that emotional suffering is normal and inescapable, but that many people are just unwilling to accept this, just as many people show a reluctance to do the washing up or to work for a living. These people are the 'worried well', who think that they have a right to treatment but really do not. The fact that the worried well might benefit from psychotherapy and counselling and will often be highly satisfied with it does not constitute a right to receive these interventions. The right should be restricted to those who are really ill, or so the argument goes.

The existence of the 'worried well' helps insurance companies and health service managers out of a difficult place. The worried well have symptoms, but no right to third party payments or, in the UK, to free health care because they are not ill. The very weakness of the concept is its strength. There is no accepted criterion of what constitutes psychological illness, and no consensus about the demarcation between ill and well, psychologically. So the category of the 'worried well' can be expanded or contracted according to the provision available.

There *is* a kind of rationality in this process. In an analysis of the most recent British National Survey of Psychiatric Morbidity, in which one member of 10,108 households in the UK was interviewed during 1993, it was found that severity of symptoms was the best predictor of prescription of antidepressants and that severity of symptoms and a reduction in the activities of daily living were the best predictors of the provision of counselling or psychotherapy. This suggests that antidepressants and psychotherapy are going to the people who have most symptoms, in general – though there was still a quarter of the most severely symptomatic (a score of over 24 on the revised Clinical Interview Schedule) who were receiving no help at all.

Well-ness, or ill-ness, in this survey was a continuum. There was no clearly defined well group, or ill group, just a range of scores. But, more importantly, defining illness in terms of the number of symptoms (the type of symptoms seems to have been less important) is to define it using only one of a number of possible criteria. Another criterion, which was more influential in determining whether or not a person was referred by a GP for counselling, was an impairment of their activities of daily living: personal care, managing money, doing paperwork, and so on.

A quite different criterion of illness is whether or not a person can perform at their peak. This became apparent when surveys of physical health were first introduced in the UK in the late nineteenth century.

Widespread compulsory medical examination was introduced then as part of the selection of conscripts for the Boer War, between Britain and South Africa. The government of the day was shocked by the high proportion of the men examined who were found unfit for military service. As a consequence of this, the 15-year period between 1901 and 1916 saw the introduction of free school meals and health checks at school, the National Insurance Act to give sick pay and medical care in return for a subscription each week, an extension of the census to include questions on the number of rooms per household, and the Factory and Workshop Act which raised standards of safety and sanitation at work, and prohibited child labour.

This conception of illness, unfitness for some demanding service, could be applied to psychological fitness, too. How many men are emotionally unfit to partner women? How many women emotionally unfit to mother children? These are unpleasant questions, particularly if unfitness is something that needs to be corrected. The response to the unfitness of Victorian men was to prevent it by a series of sweeping reforms that removed many of the causes of unfitness: accidents, over-crowding and malnutrition.

Fitness implies that a person is thriving, a lack of fitness that their body is functioning below its capacity. I have already proposed that it is involuntary emotional suffering that a person has a right to be remedied; and I defined involuntary as meaning the imposition of some undeserved constraint on a person's ability to achieve what they need for emotional satisfaction in life. If we look at it this way, it does not seem to me to matter how many people there are who would benefit from psychotherapy or counselling because they are emotionally unfit, nor how many people there are who have a right to it. What matters is whether these constraints, these restrictions on a person's ability to pursue happiness, can be remedied.

Remedying involuntary emotional suffering

Jill had been having niggling abdominal pain for a few days, and then collapsed at work, quite suddenly. The occupational nurse was called and noticed that Jill was very pale, and her skin was clammy. An ambulance was called, and Jill was rushed into hospital where she was given three pints of blood and operated on the same day. She had an ectopic pregnancy which had ruptured causing bleeding. Jill was quite unwell after the operation but gradually improved and at 3 months was back at work, having made a full recovery.

This surgical example is one end of the spectrum of diseases. Jill has something wrong – an ectopic pregnancy – which is potentially life-threatening. However, once it is removed, she makes a full recovery. Moreover, there is no mistaking Jill's state for normal tiredness or faintness.

Joan had been pregnant for 20 weeks. The baby's father had turned out to be unreliable, and Joan had become increasingly worried that she would have to look after the baby on her own. Fortunately, she had a good job with good maternity leave arrangements and a crèche. She liked her work, and her colleagues, which encouraged her. She had been coming in late a few days because of severe morning sickness and when her boss called her in, she thought that it would be about this. However her boss told her that money had been siphoned out of one of her client's accounts, and the IT department had traced the transactions to her machine. She was suspended with immediate effect until the investigations could be completed. Joan was stunned, and got home in a daze. She felt that she had to lie down, but when she had it was as if all her energy drained away. She started to cry and cried for hours. Over the next few days, Joan did not feel that she could do anything. She hardly ate, could only doze fitfully, and cried most of the time.

When this had gone on for a few weeks, her mother insisted that she contact her GP. The GP did not want to prescribe antidepressants given Joan's pregnancy. The GP thought that even if there was likely to be little harm to the baby, it would be just another thing for Joan to blame herself for. The GP contacted her colleague, the practice counsellor, and arranged an appointment within a few days. The counsellor was able to allow Joan to ventilate her fears about the future, and her anger about being let down, as she felt that she had been. Jill began to plan how she could defend herself against the accusations at work, and rediscovered her hopefulness about the baby. Her depressive disorder remitted.

Jill's case and Joan's case are similar. Both had something clearly wrong with them, an episode of something, both had a treatment, and both got better. The disease model seems to apply to both.

However, clear-cut episodes of depression may be the exception rather than the norm in the work of counsellors and psychotherapists. If a disease model applies to this work, it is more the model of chronic than acute disease.

Robert had severe arthritis. It responded to high doses of non-steroidal anti-inflammatory drugs, but he had almost constant heartburn when he took these. He had to think the whole time about what he should and should not eat and drink. He did not want to start steroids, because he was sure that they would just make him frail before his time. What he hated about his condition was not so much the pain, as the feeling that it was always there, dominating his life. After trying out many alternative therapies, Robert found that regular visits to the acupuncturist seemed to make him less stiff. Although his doctors told him that this was an unproven treatment, and that he was conceivably worsening the long-term outcome of his arthritis by not taking NSAIDs, Robert was adamant. He did not feel a proper person unless he could move about, and feel independent. And when he was having acupuncture, there were hours when he forgot his arthritis.

Contrary to his doctors' prognostications, Robert's arthritis did not progress as rapidly as they expected. In fact, he seemed to stabilise and even, to a slight extent, improve.

There may be exacerbations of chronic disease producing episodes of symptomatic worsening – but there is no possibility of a return to health. In the face of this, a person may not simply want to get rid of symptoms as quickly as possible. Other values come into play. In Robert's case, he wanted to hang on to his perception of himself as independent for as long as possible, and the relief of pain was a subsidiary concern. Social and emotional factors, as well as purely organic ones, come into play.

The impact of these factors is still within the compass of the medical model, which has always given an important place to social and emotional factors. Research findings demonstrating their impact, including psychotherapy, on the outcome of somatic disorders, including cancer, have been generally accepted

(Spiegel, 1996). What is not conceded is that there is anything particularly human about this. Doctors are familiar with research showing that social factors ameliorate depression in animals too (Ruis et al., 1999). Or, to put it in a less inflammatory way, bodily change, society, emotions and thoughts are interlinked aspects of personal functioning. Doctors accept this interlinkage but concentrate on how it impacts on actual or putative bodily functioning. Within the medical model, there is no difference in principal between a drug treatment, and counselling or psychotherapy. Both act by having an effect on the brain. Both are therefore comparable, using the same outcome measures, an assumption that psychotherapy researchers have dubbed the drug metaphor (Stiles and Shapiro, 1994).

The drug metaphor and the benefits of psychotherapy

The approach has been very valuable. It has brought into psychotherapy research many of the benefits of research methods developed to measure medical or psychological outcomes in other fields. Standardised, well-validated outcome scales have been developed which will provide a reliable indication of whether or not a person has a range of psychological symptoms, and other standardised methods are available for aggregating these and determining whether someone has a disorder and what sort of disorder it is. The randomised controlled trial has set a new standard for the conduct of quantitative research.

The findings of drug metaphor research are usually taken to be the most reliable evidence basis for counselling or psychotherapy which is now being demanded by third party payers. In the narrative about psychotherapy as a drug, a person who controls decisions about whether or not to fund the counselling or psychotherapy of another person can consult a randomised controlled trial and see whether or not that method of counselling or psychotherapy has proven efficacious in treating the condition from which the client suffers. The trial might also provide evidence about efficiency: the costliness of the intervention for a particular increment of efficacy. Trials do not provide evidence about effectiveness, that is, the outcome of the intervention when used by ordinary practitioners in everyday clinical practice.

The drug metaphor of psychotherapy also has shortcomings. It has not shown the differential effects between methods, or between one type of outcome and another, that it should have if psychotherapy were truly like a drug. Nor has a completely effective method been devised to show whether or not the effects of psychotherapy or counselling are due to placebo (Klein, 1997).

This is a bigger problem than it seems. One of the great psychotherapy researchers, Jerome Frank, was convinced that the benefits of psychotherapy were placebo effects, and were no different from the effects of giving a person a pill of an inert substance which they expected to be therapeutic (Frank, 1961). Far from being shy about placebo effects, Frank pointed out that a placebo effect could be strengthened or weakened by manipulating a person's expectations, and that psychotherapists should seek to learn more about increasing its strength.

Counsellors and psychotherapists who want to compete on equal terms with their medical or psychological colleagues want to show that their interventions are not 'mere placebos' but that they have an effect above and beyond a placebo control, just like taking aspirin works better on headache than taking a pill composed only of chalk. There are good reasons for this concern. If the benefit of psychotherapy or counselling were purely that of a placebo, it would be hard to differentiate the practitioners of the craft from good salesmen who peddled snake-oil or any sort of psychological healing, however eccentric.

Two difficulties make this problem more acute. First, psychotherapy placebos, like relaxation training, are not really placebos. People already have clear expectations of the likely benefit of psychological treatments and often expect as little of placebo treatments as the researchers who provide them. Secondly, a *sine qua non* of a specific treatment effect is that a comparison of two supposedly active treatments should, at least sometimes, show that one is superior to the other. But over and over again, a comparison of two methods of psychotherapy shows that they are the same in the symptom relief that they provide. The suggestion that there might be nothing specific about the action of different psychotherapeutic approaches has been called the 'Dodo bird conjecture' (Howard et al., 1997) after the Lewis Carroll character who states, as quoted in an influential paper by Luborsky et al. (1975), that 'everyone has won, and all must have prizes'.

Establishing the medical benefits of psychotherapy or counselling may therefore turn out to be important for medicine more than it is important for psychotherapy or counselling. For it does not really establish anything in relation to our profession. It certainly does not give us an indication of how we should develop it, or what we should aim for.

Some of the most striking questions about psychotherapy are not touched by the medical approach. Why, for example, do so many people prefer counselling or psychotherapy to drugs for the relief of depression or anxiety? The medical benefits of drugs are well-established in these conditions and are as great, and sometimes greater, than any of the modalities of counselling or psychotherapy that have been tested against them. But the public continues to want counselling or psychotherapy (Priest et al., 1996). This may reflect a suspicion of drugs, since the public also prefers minerals and vitamins (Jorm and Duncan-Jones, 1990). But it may also reflect a view that the way to overcome emotional suffering is to understand what is causing it, not to suppress it. Severe anxiety or sadness may surpass a person's understanding and, anyway, relieving a person's distress and finding its cause are not incompatible. Counselling or psychotherapy may be combined with drug treatment, but if the public are right, there is some dimension of emotional suffering that drugs do not touch, but which counselling or psychotherapy does.

The preventative model

An extension of the drug metaphor might be an explanation for the difference in the application of drugs and counselling or psychotherapy. According to this preventative model, psychotherapy works both to alleviate distress and to prevent its recurrence. The superiority of psychotherapy over drugs, it has been claimed, was that psychotherapy was a preventative treatment. Cognitive therapy has, for example, been suggested to lead to more long-lasting and more sustained treatment for depression because it changes the schemata which make a person vulnerable to depression. The clearest evidence for this has been provided by the NIMH collaborative study of depression which showed that patients who received cognitive or interpersonal therapy were less likely to relapse than untreated controls (Shea et al., 1992). However, the preventative effects of psychotherapy disappeared once the psychotherapy ended. Not only that, but maintenance imipramine was as effective as psychotherapy.

Another explanation for these findings is that the follow-up period was too short to show the benefits of psychotherapy, or possibly that other psychotherapies, more dynamic in nature, might have prevented further depression by improving the quality of interpersonal relationships. However, a meta-analysis of carefully selected short-term dynamic interventions (Crits-Christoph, 1992) did not show a differential effect of dynamic psychotherapy on interpersonal relationships compared to symptomatic outcome.

One of the most commonly used measures of the quality of relationships is the Inventory of Interpersonal Problems (IIP). Psychotherapy researchers have in the past hoped that psychotherapy would have a particularly beneficial effect on interpersonal problems, and that scores on the IIP would show differential improvement. However, this hope, too, has not been fulfilled. IIP scores also improve after treatment with antidepressants (Markowitz et al., 1996).

It seems that the medical model applies to the symptomatic benefits of psychotherapy, which are undoubted, but does not give psychotherapy a place that is distinct from drug treatment and so does not explain why the public should value psychotherapy over drugs. Other alternative outcome measures, such as the IIP, which try to measure outcome in domains that are specific to psychotherapy, do not alter this situation. However, recent studies do suggest that, even using medically orientated measures of outcome, the addition of psychotherapy to antidepressant treatment has greater benefit than either intervention given alone (Thase et al., 1997).

There are two possible explanations for continuing ignorance about the benefits of psychotherapy. The first is that psychotherapy just benefits some people, whilst other interventions benefit others. In other words, studies need to be linked to selection criteria. This seems unlikely given the lack of evidence that selection for psychotherapy is linked to outcome. The second possible explanation is that the outcome measures that are currently being used do not adequately assess the benefits of psychotherapy or counselling: that there is some domain of benefit that is missing. What this missing domain might be is considered in the next section.

Emotional suffering and quality of life

Neither the spiritual nor the medical model seem to apply fully to counselling or psychotherapy. Is there an alternative?

It has already been noted that most mental health problems correspond more closely to chronic disease than to acute disorders. One similarity not previously mentioned is that survival is not the final, definitive benefit for either the person with depression, or the person with a mental health problem. Indeed, community studies regularly demonstrate that most people rate being dead preferable to being alive, but depressed (Bennett et al., 2000).

What matters in evaluating interventions in chronic disease is the quality of a person's life gain. One common way of combining these is to express the benefit of an intervention in terms of the 'Quality of Life Years' (QALYs) that are added by that intervention. Measuring quality of life is one of the major areas of growth in health economics, introducing into this subject a much broader range of economic outcomes than the monetary costs that have dominated it in the past. In order to estimate quality of life it is necessary to know the value that is put on particular outcomes, or benefits. Health economists interpret these as utilities. These are a measure, between 0 and 1, of a person's preference for a health outcome. Perfect health is defined to have a utility of 1. Utilities may be calculated using a visual analogue scale, by asking people how much they would be willing to risk to improve their health status, or by asking how many years of their life they would be prepared to give up to improve quality of life.

Utility scores can be used to ensure that a scarce resource can be used with the greatest benefit to quality of life. Take the example of senile dementia of Alzheimer type (SDAT). There are currently drugs which are apparently effective in slowing the rate of progression of the disease, but they are very expensive. Consequently, they are currently subject to 'postcode prescribing' in the UK, with only the richer health trusts able to afford to fund them. Consider one of these richer trusts, say Middlehamptom Community Trust. This trust has some funds for tacrine, one of the drugs shown to be effective in this way. However, there is not enough money to give tacrine to everyone with SDAT. The therapeutics committee comes across a study by Neumann et al. (1999) in which the Health Utilities Index mark II was given to 679 caregivers of people with SDAT in 13 US sites. Global utility scores were calculated for the quality of life at each of six stages of SDAT: these were 0.79 for 'questionable' diagnosis, 0.69 for mild, 0.53 for moderate, 0.38 for severe, 0.27 for profound and 0.14 for terminal (it is interesting to compare this figure with the utility of severe depression of 0.04; see Bennett et al., 2000).

The therapeutics committee has already concluded that tacrine can extend the life of someone with SDAT by two years. However, they now note that two years of someone with mild SDAT is equivalent to $0.73*2 = 1.5$ years of perfect health, that is one and a half QALYs. But two years of life with profound SDAT is only equivalent to a third of a QALY. They therefore decide to restrict the prescription of tacrine to people with mild SDAT.

Many readers will note oversimplifications in this approach. It assumes, for example, that the mean utility values of a population can be applied to an individual case. Moreover, the study by Neumann et al. used the utilities of carers, and not the patients themselves. Perhaps the latter would have differed. Utilities may also differ according to whether they are influenced by remembered past benefit, anticipated future benefit, or emotional satisfaction in the present (Frey and Stutzer, 2000).

What is important for the psychotherapist is that utilities bring together a range of benefits which are wider than symptomatic relief. For example, Hawthorne et al. (1999) have suggested that five independent dimensions contribute to individuals' judgement of utility: illness, independent living, social relationships, physical senses and psychological well-being. According to Hawthorne et al.'s analysis, if counselling or psychotherapy increased a person's well-being without affecting their 'illness', it would still contribute to their quality of life.

This can be clearly seen in studies of psychotherapy or counselling in patients with cancer, whose quality of life may be enhanced even if the progression of their illness is unaffected. However, psychotherapy often also slows the progression of cancer because well-being and illness are not independent. In one study of women with breast cancer given two types of counselling or psychotherapy, intervention increased quality of life and increased well-being, but also increased interferon production (Richardson et al., 1997).

Earlier on in this chapter, I noted that emotional suffering is the enemy of content. There are many economists and psychologists who would agree with this. Moreover, they suggest that happiness, content, or subjective well-being are defined states. Frey and Stutzer (2000) summarize the evidence as follows:

> The surveys on happiness have a high scientific standard. The measures of happiness have high consistency, reliability and validity. Happy people are e.g. more often smiling during social interactions (Fernández-Dols and Ruiz-Belda, 1995), are rated as happy by friends and family members (Sandvik, Diener and Seidlitz, 1993), as well as by spouses (Costa and McCrae, 1988). Furthermore, the measures of subjective well-being have a high degree of stability over time (Headey and Wearing, 1989). Happiness measures have also been shown to be reflected in behaviour, e.g. 'people who call themselves happy ... are more likely to initiate social contacts with friends; more likely to respond to requests for help; ... less likely to be absent from work; less likely to be involved in disputes at work ...' (Frank, 1997: 5); the text and references can also be found at http://www.iew.unizh.ch/wp/iewwp022.pdf, one of the web pages of the Institute for Empirical Research in Economics at the University of Zurich)

Frey and Stutzer suggest that the quality of life is entirely determined by subjective well-being – or perceived happiness – and that the effects of health or unemployment on the quality of life are indirect. Poor health reduces our life quality if, and only if, it reduces our well-being (Diener et al., 1998).

It is often assumed that the absence of emotional suffering is equivalent to happiness. Clearly it must be rare for a person who is depressed or anxious to experience well-being, although perhaps not so rare for someone who is normally happy to experience transient sadness or anxiety. However, it may be more common for someone not to suffer, and not to be happy either. There is some empirical evidence for this. Jorm and Duncan-Jones, for example, found in a community survey of emotional suffering (Jorm and Duncan-Jones, 1990) that a principal components analysis yielded correlated but independent factors of symptoms and well-being.

Leval (1995) has suggested that suffering and life quality might be based on two quite different judgements. Depression is, he suggests, caused by the passage from a healthy past to a painful present, suffering is a reaction to that painful present, but subjective well-being is determined by the extent to which the present is commensurate with a person's aspirations for their future.

Surprisingly little attention has been given to using utility scores as a measure of the benefits of psychotherapy and counselling (Frasch and Neumann, 1999). Perhaps one of the problems has been a lack of clarity about what well-being is. It is easily confounded with satisfaction, hopefulness, or compliance. The CORE outcome battery, widely used in the UK as a means of assessing benefit from psychotherapy or counselling, contains four items that purport to measure well-being. These are 'I have felt OK about myself', 'I have felt like crying', 'I have felt optimistic about my future', and 'I have felt overwhelmed by my problems' (CORE Group, 1998). However, these well-being questions are designed to tap into the immediate 'remoralising' effects of being offered an intervention, a kind of well-being that might be called 'state' in contrast to the trait 'well-being' which has been previously described.

The SF-36 has been widely used as a measure of the quality of life in medical populations . It contains the following items on 'emotional role functioning': during the last four weeks, Did you feel full of life?, Have you been very nervous? Have you felt so down in the dumps that nothing could cheer you up? Have you felt calm and peaceful? Did you have a lot of energy? Have you felt downhearted and depressed? Did you feel worn out? Have you been happy? Did you feel tired? In a recent study of home versus hospital care, one of the largest benefits to the home care group was the emotional role functioning of terminally ill patients, which was greater in those who were treated at home. But, as Bartlett points out, the validation of these questions as a measure of well-being still needs to be done and there is no currently available measure of quality of life that fully incorporates well-being (Bartlett and Coles, 1998).

Quality of life instruments are only just starting to be used in the evaluation of psychotherapy or counselling (Halperin, 2000), so there is considerable potential to further develop the measures of happiness or subjective well-being which currently used instruments have begun to incorporate. However, to really make these measures useful it is necessary for counsellors and psychotherapists to consider more carefully what does constitute subjective well-being.

Conclusions

The benefits of counselling and psychotherapy have to be related to the aims of the intervention. The benefits of the type of counselling or psychotherapy that is intended to provide relief of emotional suffering can be measured by the reduction of symptom scores on one or more of the widely used instruments currently available.

However, if counsellors or psychotherapists are aiming to achieve more than relief; if, in other words, they are aiming to be providing more than a drug-equivalent, they should specify what benefits they are aiming at. In this chapter, I have argued that one valid and achievable benefit is happiness, or subjective well-being. I have argued that, far from being a fanciful notion, happiness is a trait that can be measured and that, indeed, health economists are currently trying to estimate it. Paradoxically, happiness may be consistent with some kinds of emotional suffering. A happy person may be more compassionate, and so more open to vicarious suffering, for example. Happiness is incompatible with involuntary emotional suffering, however.

Counsellors or psychotherapists could individually increase the benefit of their work by understanding better how to increase the capacity of each of their clients for emotional well-being. Collectively, counsellors or psychotherapists could have most benefit on society by emphasising the relief of involuntary emotional suffering, which is a bar to emotional well-being in every group, and in every society. The best way of achieving this may be by the removal of factors that reduce emotional fitness.

Notes

1 Efficacy is a measure of the attainment of an objective. It is sometimes defined as the ratio of the benefits obtained to the benefits expected. In the psychotherapy literature its use is restricted to the benefits measured in highly standardised situations, for example in a controlled trial of a manualised treatment in a defined population. It is therefore often contrasted with 'effectiveness' which can be defined as the benefit that will be achieved in practice – for example, the benefit of cognitive-behavioural therapy when it is used by GP counsellors in all the clients referred to them for help with depression. It is also contrasted with efficiency, the amount of benefit produced by a unit of resource. Cost-efficiency is the amount of benefit produced by a unit of expenditure.

References

Ames, D. (1998) Reserpine exhumed [letter]. *British Journal of Psychiatry*, 173, 440.

Bartlett, C.J. and Coles, E.C. (1998) Psychological health and well-being: why and how should public health specialists measure it? Part 2: Stress, subjective well-being and overall conclusions. *Journal of Public Health Medicine*, 20, 288–94.

Bennett, K.J., Torrance, G.W., Boyle, M.H., Guscott, R. and Moran, L.A. (2000) Development and testing of a utility measure for major, unipolar depression (McSad). *Quality of Life Research*, 9, 109–20.

CORE Group (1998) *CORE System Information Management Handbook*, Leeds: Psychological Therapies Research Centre.

Crits-Christoph, P. (1992) The efficacy of brief dynamic psychotherapy: a meta-analysis. *American Journal of Psychiatry*, 149, 151–8.

Diener, E., Sapyta, J.J. and Suh, E. (1998) Subjective well-being is essential to well-being. *Psychological Inquiry*, 9, 33–7.

Frank, J. (1961) *Persuasion and Healing*, Baltimore, MD: Johns Hopkins University Press.

Frank, R. (1997) The frame of reference as a public good. *Economic Journal*, 107, 1832–47.

Frasch, K. and Neumann, N.U. (1999) Economic aspects of psychotherapy management in psychosomatics and psychiatry. A systematic survey of the literature. *Nervenarzt*, 70, 387–90.

Frey, B. and Stutzer, A. (2000) Maximizing happiness? *German Economic Review*, 1, 145–67.

Halperin, S. (2000) A cognitive-behavioural, group-based intervention for social anxiety in schizophrenia. *Australian and New Zealand Journal of Psychiatry*, 34, 809–13.

Hawthorne, G., Richardson, J. and Osborne, R. (1999) The Assessment of Quality of Life (AQoL) instrument: a psychometric measure of health-related quality of life. *Quality of Life Research*, 8, 209–24.

House, R. (1999) The place of psychotherapy and counselling in a healthy European social order: a commentary on Tantam and van Deurzen. *European Journal of Psychotherapy, Counselling and Health*, 2, 236–43.

Howard, K., Krause, M.S., Saunders, S.M. and Kopta, S.M. (1997) Trials and tribulations in the meta-analysis of treatment differences: comment on Wampold et al. (1997). *Psychological Bulletin*, 122, 221–5.

Jenkins, S. (2000) Do bodhisattvas relieve poverty? The distinction between economic and spiritual development and their interrelation in Indian Buddhist texts. *Journal of Buddhist Ethics On-line Conference*, 7, 2000.

Jorm, A. and Duncan-Jones, P. (1990) Neurotic symptoms and subjective well-being in a community sample: different sides of the same coin. *Psychological Medicine*, 20, 647–54.

Klein, D. (1997) Control groups in pharmacotherapy and psychotherapy evaluations. *Treatment*, 1, 1-e.

Leval, N. de (1995) Scales of depression, ill-being and the quality of life – is there any difference? An assay in taxonomy. *Quality of Life Research*, 4, 259–69.

Luborsky, L., Singer, B. and Luborsky, L. (1975) Comparative studies of psychotherapies. Is it true that 'everyone has won and all must have prizes'? *Archives of General Psychiatry*, 32 (8), 995–1008.

Markowitz, J.C., Friedman, R.A., Miller, N., Spielman, L.A., Moran, M.E. and Kocsis, J.H. (1996) Interpersonal improvement in chronically depressed patients treated with desipramine. *Journal of Affective Disorders*, 41, 59–62.

Neumann, P.J., Kuntz, K.M., Leon, J., Araki, S.S., Hermann, R.C., Hsu, M.A. and Weinstein, M.C. (1999) Health utilities in Alzheimer's disease: a cross-sectional study of patients and caregivers. *Medical Care*, 37, 27–32.

Priest, R.G., Vize, C., Roberts, A., Roberts, M. and Tylee, A. (1996) Lay people's attitudes to treatment of depression: results of opinion poll for Defeat Depression Campaign just before its launch. *British Medical Journal*, 313, 858–9.

Richardson, M.A., Post-White, J., Grimm, E.A., Moye, L.A., Singletary, S.E. and Justice, B. (1997) Coping, life attitudes, and immune responses to imagery and group support after breast cancer treatment. *Alternative Therapies in Health and Medicine*, 3, 62–70.

Ruis, M.A., te Brake, J.H., Buwalda, B., de Boer, S.F., Meerlo, P., Korte, S.M., Blokhuis, H.J. and Koolhaas, J.M. (1999) Housing familiar male wildtype rats together reduces the long-term adverse behavioural and physiological effects of social defeat. *Psychoneuroendocrinology*, 24, 285–300.

Shea, M.T., Elkin, I., Imber, S.D., Sotsky, S.M., Watkins, J.T., Collins, J.F., Pilkonis, P.A., Beckham, E., Glass, D.R., Dolan, R.T. et al. (1992) Course of depressive symptoms over follow-up. Findings from the National Institute of Mental Health Treatment of Depression Collaborative Research Program. *Archives of General Psychiatry*, 49 (10), 782–7.

Spiegel, D. (1996) Cancer and depression. [Review] [76 references] *British Journal of Psychiatry* (Supplement), 30, 109–16.

Stenzel-Poore, M.P., Heinrichs, S.C., Rivest, S., Koob, G.F. and Vale, W.W. (1994) Overproduction of corticotrophin-releasing factor in transgenic mice: a genetic model of anxiogenic behavior. *Journal of Neuroscience*, 14 (5), 2579–84.

Stiles, W.B. and Shapiro, D.A. (1994) Disabuse of the drug metaphor: psychotherapy process-outcome correlations. *Journal of Consulting and Clinical Psychology*, 62 (5), 942–8.

Thase, M.E., Greenhouse, J.B., Frank, E., Reynolds, C.F., III, Pilkonis, P.A., Hurley, K., Grochocinski, V. and Kupfer, D.J. (1997) Treatment of major depression with psychotherapy or psychotherapy-pharmacotherapy combinations [see comments]. *Archives of General Psychiatry*, 54, 1009–15.

World Health Organisation (1948) *Constitution in Basic Documents*. Geneva: World Health Organisation.

INDEX